A Most Magnificent Machine

A MOST MAGNIFICENT
MACHINE

America Adopts the Railroad, 1825–1862

CRAIG MINER

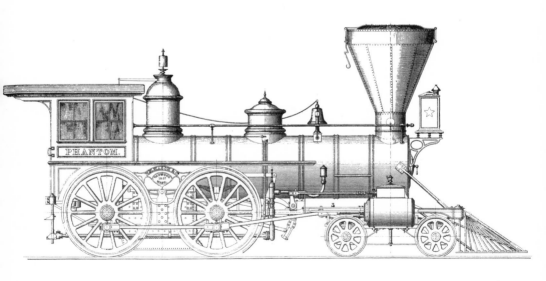

 University Press of Kansas

© 2010 by the University Press of Kansas
All rights reserved

Published by the University Press of Kansas (Lawrence, Kansas 66045), which was
organized by the Kansas Board of Regents and is operated and funded by Emporia
State University, Fort Hays State University, Kansas State University, Pittsburg State
University, the University of Kansas, and Wichita State University

Library of Congress Cataloging-in-Publication Data

Miner, H. Craig.
A most magnificent machine : America adopts the railroad, 1825–1862 / Craig Miner.
     p.   cm.
Includes bibliographical references and index.
ISBN 978-0-7006-1755-5 (cloth : acid-free paper)
1. Railroads—United States—History—19th century. 2. Railroads—Social aspects—
United States—History—19th century. I. Title.
HE2751.M56 2010
385.0973'09034—dc22
                                        2010026138

British Library Cataloguing-in-Publication Data is available.

Printed in the United States of America

10 9 8 7 6 5 4 3 2 1

The paper used in this publication is recycled and contains 30 percent postconsumer
waste. It is acid free and meets the minimum requirements of the American National
Standard for Permanence of Paper for Printed Library Materials Z39.48-1992.

CONTENTS

PREFACE

"he generation of 1830 to 1860," wrote historian Paul Gates in his 1934 study of the Illinois Central Railroad, "witnessed as new and startling changes in transportation methods in the United States as has the generation of 1900 to 1930." The introduction of the railroad network, he continued, "completely transformed the economic life of millions of Americans and vastly changed their social existence."[1] Paul Larson, writing in 1984 on rail entrepreneur John Murray Forbes, agreed:

> Originally an engineering problem alone, the steam railroad quickly became a business organization and a network of trade that profoundly affected the enterprise of other people. Questions of economic and social policy arose, and these found expression in politics at all levels. Fundamental assumptions about government and the economy were ultimately adjusted to suit the railway age. As the railroad accumulated real and symbolic influence, it changed the fabric of American society.[2]

Many writers in the early nineteenth century emphasized the wide influence of railroads. "We are accustomed," wrote George Peabody of Boston, "to regard the discovery of America and the Protestant Reformation as two great events which have contributed largely to advance the interests of the human race; so [future generations], with perhaps a more clear conception and a more evident deduction of consequences, will point to the American Revolution and the Era of Steam Travel."[3] A foreign visitor in 1851 observed, "It would seem as though . . . man himself were under the influence of the formidable power he has evoked. . . . The railroad, animated by its powerful locomotive, appears to be the characteristic personification of the American. The one seems to hear and understand the other—to have been made for the other—to be indispensable to the other."[4]

A writer for the *United States Magazine and Democratic Review* in the 1850s ruminated on a single aspect of the railroad revolution, its effect on urban places:

> In the last fifteen years this great leveler has sprung into existence, and produced immense changes in the condition of localities, called forth resources that otherwise would have lain dormant, and greatly enhanced the welfare of the people at large as well as of those in the particular sections through which they run. They are the means by which, in default of natural means of transportation, the interior of the country communicates with towns; and the growth of a city, which formerly depended upon its geographical situation, now depends upon the enterprise of its citizens in making a larger extent of the country, as it were, tributary to its growth, by means of connecting railroads. Before the era of railroads, cities were the result of slow and expensive transit, and beyond certain limits their growth became almost impossible. . . . With the advent of railways, this difficulty ceased, and cities and towns may now expand almost indefinitely.[5]

John Majewski's detailed study of the economic development of counties in Virginia and Pennsylvania noted that the main disadvantages of the slave system to rail development were that it prevented in Virginia both rural population density and the development of a large city of the wealth and political influence of Philadelphia.[6]

Although there have been many studies of railroad companies and railroad managers, there is room for further research addressing the interactions of railroads with the larger society. Such studies of rail's broad social impact as Bruce Mazlish's *The Railroad and the Space Program*, James Ward's *Railroads and the Character of America*, or Leo Marx's *The Machine in the Garden* are relatively scarce.[7] Langdon Winner's 1977 book, *Autonomous Technology*, made the point that "while technological developments are commonly cited as among the most important causes of the shape of modern society, the tendency is to see the matter solely in terms of economics and economic history, perspectives that due to their special mode of abstraction and selectivity give us a very limited vision of the role technics have played in modern history."[8]

Many recent economic historians have agreed with L. Ray Gunn in noticing a "dynamic relationship between social, economic, and political development."[9] In the 1950s and 1960s, however, there was a negative reaction among some influential economic historians to the idea that it was important to study the impacts of the railroad that were not strictly economic and measurable statistically. The "econometricians," or "cliometricians," eschewed "subjective" evaluations.

Albert Fishlow's *Railroads and the Transformation of the Ante Bellum Economy* showed the impact of the railroad on the economy but said little about society, politics, or literature. There was more mentioned in that book on the impact of alternative fuels on locomotive firebox design than on the impact of speed on Americans' idea of time and distance. "Spawned in response to interregional commercial competition," Fishlow wrote, "the railroad was soon adopted for other less far-reaching objectives."[10]

Robert Fogel had a similar pragmatic focus. In *Railroads and American Economic Growth: Essays in Econometric History*, Fogel argued that prevailing interpretations of the influence of railroads on American economic growth, not to mention American society and culture, were dominated by unscientific hypotheses generated in the rail-building era itself by promoters who had less interest in objectivity than in stock sales. He scoffed at the more extreme estimates of the importance of railroad building in the nineteenth century, dismissing them as newspaper fluff. Not all the important effects of railroads were unique, Fogel wrote, and not all its unique effects were important. Researchers could be easily taken in by rhetoric. Quantitative measurement was "an essential and unavoidable matter." Only a researcher using that approach knew "what is *unique, special* and *peculiar* about a given historical problem. . . . The casual interloper cannot possess this knowledge."[11]

This book adopts primarily the Gates/Larson rather than the Fishlow/Fogel approach and uses newspapers, printed pamphlets, books, and reports rather than corporate records or other manuscript materials as its major sources. I am cognizant of the dangers of accepting promotional rhetoric at face value. Newspaper owners and editors were often promoters and per-suaders, advancers of causes, and they were also businesspeople in their communities. Their personal economic futures depended upon the growth of these communities, which they often thought depended upon establish-ing the proper rail connections. Certain urban interests, such as themselves and merchants and manufacturers, benefited more from the railroads than did farmers, and some regions benefited more than others, yet all shared the enormous costs. Newspapers regularly emphasized, however, that the indirect and long-term benefits of railroads were more important than the direct and short-term ones. Should a state or region stagnate economically due to falling behind in the railroad competition, every business and every consumer there would suffer. The fact that state governments were much involved in rail investment and in creating an easy legal atmosphere for their growth is evidence of an early assumption that railroads were a kind of public utility, not just an ordinary business.[12]

Newspapers were far from being simply cheerleaders for rail corpora-tions. Pamphlet literature regarding railroads was as often critical as promo-tional. Their constituencies had political and social concerns, which were often at odds with the style of the new businesses, and it was dangerous for writers and speakers on railroads to forget that. Public meetings on rail-roads were contentious, and objections on legal, social, political, financial, environmental, engineering, health, safety, and even moral and religious grounds were advanced effectively. There was serious criticism in the news-papers, not so much of the need for railroads in general but of the form in which they advanced. Newspapers documented well not only the direct costs but also the indirect costs, as well as touting the direct and indirect benefits. Clearly, too, for every local editor pushing the dreams of a home-town or region, there was a rival newspaper elsewhere trying to deflate those ambitions and plans. The negative mood was especially prominent during the economic downturns, or "revulsions," as contemporaries called them. But these, though painful and clearly connected with mistakes in fi-nancing railroads, were brief, their lessons easily forgotten.

There is no question that the dissenting voices were in the end drowned out in the enthusiasm, and the dissenters were characterized as "old fogeys." There was every reason that they should have been. The majority mind-set in the United States when railroads appeared on the scene was already materialistic, optimistic, and "progressive." Railroads only intensified these preexisting characteristics of the culture. Henry Steele Commager in *The American Mind* wrote that to the early-nineteenth-century American "progress was not . . . a philosophical idea but a commonplace of experience: he saw it daily in the transformation of wilderness into farm land, in the growth of villages into cities, in the steady rise of community and nation to wealth and power." This made the American future oriented, seeing not the "dusty town but the shining city, not the shabby shop but the throbbing factory, not the rutted roads but gleaming rail." Nothing in history had ever succeeded like America, Commager concluded, and every American knew it.[13]

Given this atmosphere, and given that the behavior of human beings is not entirely rational, or their motivations strictly or totally economic, there is reason to document the details of what might be called "industrial mythology." Railroad rhetoric was sometimes unscientific, but all aspects of conveying public information served to build consensus on a certain oversimplified course of action. Whigs and radical Democrats continued to disagree on the proper balance between economic development and democracy in creating centers of authority for the distribution of the new economic gains. But those who advocated seriously throttling economic development were few. In the interest of more fully describing the medium in which the railroad transformation took place, I therefore risk being regarded in some circles as a casual interloper doing literary analysis masquerading as economic history.

Newspapers were major conduits for communicating vital economic and political information to citizens who were not naive and to whom railroad building was a vital, practical, and serious issue. Editors published scientific and engineering reports, surveys, economic analyses, legislative debates, details of financing, and topographical tables, as well as travelers' impressions and editorial analysis. Their role was to inform. "Every thing in, or relating to them [railroads], which is *useful* and *economical*, is now interesting to the public," wrote a Connecticut editor in 1832. "There is no danger of appreciating their utility higher than it ought to be done—the only danger there is, consists in people's remaining too much and too long in a state of ignorance, growing out of inattention to the subjects."[14]

But it was not only the science and the economic data that represented important information to a public making a major policy decision. People had to believe as well as to understand, and the instruments of compelling belief were persuasive language and memorable, attractive, and understandable communication of possible future scenarios. A study of America's adoption of the railway in the early nineteenth century provides a model for interpreting or predicting the starts and stops, the ups and downs, of the introduction of mind-boggling and culture-modifying technologies throughout American history.

Listening to a professor from Illinois speaking on the topic of railroads in 1850, a reporter was impressed by the imagery conveyed. The speaker, the reporter wrote, "has, in an eminent degree, that power of making pictures which clothes even a dead tree with buds and blossoms, and covers every object drawn by his verbal pencil with a new creation of conceptions; so that the frame-work is hardly recognized as the one with which we were before familiar." It was a skill of "wreathing around the dry skeleton of statistics" the "foliage of his fertile imagination." Images should not be off the mark, the writer thought, not "trifling, light, or gaudy," but there needed to be some translation of the ruminations of engineers, surveyors, and capitalists before the public got on board.[15]

I have long admired the work of Walter Lippmann, particularly his 1922 book, *Public Opinion*. It is the "pictures in our heads," Lippmann concluded, rather than some raw and unreachable reality, that motivates public action. The progressive scientist in him found that discouraging, but the keen observer found it true.[16] Perhaps newspaper readers were tired of the subject of railroads, an editor opined in 1849, but the topic was too vast to be left to politicians.[17] "The press not only records the history of passing events," stated a Louisville editorial in 1854, "but, as a creative power, it tends to make and form the destiny of future times."[18] There was no escaping the aesthetic appeal or psychological excitement of railway travel, whatever the science or economics might be. Frederick Marryat wrote in his diary during a rail journey in 1839 that the speed took away his enjoyment of the countryside, but the power of the train was thrilling. "As the evening closed in we actually were whirled along through a stream of fiery threads—a beautiful, although humble imitation of the tail of a comet."[19]

The railroad attracted writers, famous and obscure, specialists and generalists. Charles Dickens traveled by rail through the United States and wrote about the experience in *American Notes*. "There is a great deal of jolting," he wrote, "a great deal of noise, a great deal of wall, not much window, a locomotive engine, a shriek, and a bell. . . . It is insufferably close." He was impressed by rushing through ordinary life as though almost unobserved.

> There—with mechanics working at their trades, and people leaning from their doors and windows, and boys flying kites and playing marbles, and men smoking, and women talking, and children crawling, and pigs burrowing, and unaccustomed

horses plunging and rearing, close to the very rails—there—on, on, on—tears the mad dragon of an engine with its train of cars; scattering in all directions a shower of burning sparks from its wood fire; screeching, hissing, yelling, panting; until at last the thirsty monster stops beneath a covered way to drink, the people cluster around, and you have time to breathe again.[20]

Daniel Drake of Cincinnati, one of the great western promoters of business, analyzed in 1834 the relationship between the literary and the mechanical or economic. "Our literature," he wrote,

> will be tinctured with the thoughts and terms of business. The mechanic arts have become locomotive, both in temper and capacity—they travel abroad, and exhibit themselves in every department of society. To a certain degree, they modify the public mind; supply new topics for the tongue and pen; generate strange words and phrases, as if by machinery; suggest novel modes of illustration, and manufacture figures of speech by steam power. They afford canal transportation to the ponderous compiler of statistics; a turnpike to the historian; a tunnel to the metaphysician; a scale of definite proportions to the moral philosopher; a power loom and steam press to the novelist; fulminating powder to the orator; corrosive acids to the satirist . . . a railroad to the enthusiast, and nitrous oxide to the dunce.[21]

Drake in that statement not only described a trend but also illustrated it.

Science had escaped the cloister. Joseph Story, the distinguished jurist, said in 1835:

> We live in an age full of intellectual excitement. It is not with us, as it was in former times, when science belonged to solitary studies, or philosophical ease, or antiquarian curiosity. It has escaped from the closet, and become an habitual accompaniment of every department of life. . . . It seems a very spirit of all work, assuming all shapes, and figuring out all sorts of wonders, in that epitome of a world, a factory.[22]

Sometimes railroads seemed almost a new religion. The *Scientific American* contained a paean to the new god in 1860. Regarding the influence of steam, one writer stated that people felt "awe-stricken at times, in the presence of this awful force. . . . The fires of sacrifice that burned of old on altars and hill tops no longer gleam and startle the terrified people with the victims' shrieks and cries; but through all the night, and through the summer's heat and winter's cold, the genial furnace-fires flame and burn, and render good return to man."[23]

The majority of accounts, however, were strictly secular. The spirit of the age *was* the spirit of enterprise. "In our whole tone of temper and conduct," stated an 1849 treatise on the topic, "through all domestic and civil intercourse, we must take one side or the other, and become enlisted under the banner of fate or of freedom. We cannot buy stock in a rail-road . . . without helping or hindering the Social Transformation, through which the nations of Europe and the United States are destined to pass."[24]

Naturally the fact that the public gains much of its information on complex technological issues through the media has been discouraging to some scholars. Langdon Winner, for instance, was disturbed in the 1970s that the "ordinary citizen must rely on signals transmitted by the mass media." He made the point that the information thus conveyed about technology was highly simplified and regularly exaggerated. "Thus, the shape of history comes to be seen as a sequence of disconnected specials, which temporarily 'interrupt our regular scheduled programming.' . . . Human beings do make their own history. Yes, but they do so in the same way that they make a situation comedy or the TV Game of the Week."[25] Winner added that there was a "lag in public language" as these new machines appeared, which made the public understanding insufficient to the task of controlling the new industrial worlds.[26] No doubt that is true, and no doubt it has been ever thus. But to neglect the study of how the public gathers information and of the basis upon which it acts and reacts because one has some contempt for the intelligence of that public is to miss much of the point of studying history as it really was.

In using newspapers, I have taken advantage of a relatively new tool, namely digital databases, which allow a breadth and depth of national coverage formerly impractical. I have employed also magazine, pamphlet, and book collections in digital form. These allowed easier access to many thousands of railroad items, some of which are excessively rare in the original editions. For some single years in the 1850s, the databases turned up more than 30,000 articles for the search term "railroad" or its spelling variants. In total I examined about 400,000 articles from 185 distinct newspapers (not to mention many other papers cited in these). More than 3,000 books and pamphlets on railroads from the early nineteenth century became available to me by electronic means to add to the usual manuscript, government documents, and secondary sources. I took about two million words of notes.

The benefits of such research become immediately evident. Obviously, one avoids a good deal of travel time and expense, as well as interlibrary loan orders and the vagaries of imperfect microfilm readers. But there are more substantive advantages.

For example, one can balance sources geographically. This quickly revealed that it is a myth that the South in the antebellum period was a nonindustrial society with a backward attitude. The Charleston & Hamburg was one of the first railways in the country, and the Central of Georgia was one of the best managed and most profitable right up to the outbreak of the Civil War. Newspapers allow one to evaluate attitudes by region, by political persuasion, and even by economic interest.

One can get the perspective of rival cities—large, medium, and small—competing for the trade of the western interior or in their own immediate regions in an era when the old turnpike, coastal shipping, and canal trading patterns were destroyed by the new rail technology. Philadelphia, Boston, Baltimore, New York City, Charleston, and others were locked during the 1830s and 1840s in that struggle over trade, each with unique rail systems, challenges, and strategies. There is no better way to understand and describe these than to use the day-by-day newspapers printed in all these places.

Any group of sources can be faulted for representing only a sampling of what it might be possible to read and therefore to learn. Using the electronic databases, that sample can be so large, including subtle intracity as well as interregional variations, as to raise the question of what return could come from going farther. It is easy to point out that newspapers have inaccuracies and biases, as do all sources. However, the ability to get the quotidian outlook in great volume and from multiple perspectives adds depth and credibility to the traditional foundations of any written history.

I have not attempted in any sense to give a definitive account of every rail company in the United States during this period. The rail system, even in its relatively embryonic stage in the 1830s, was variegated and complex. And should an encyclopedic account be possible, there would be a question whether it would be desirable. It would be about as clear and appealing to a reader as plowing through a large and turgid shelf of reference works. Such detail would also detract from the themes related to public "adoption" of the railroad generally that is the core of this book. Therefore, I have truly "sampled" individual railroads, picking out significant companies or ones evocative of the character of the whole. This is not a book of details for the rail fan, devoted to rolling stock configurations and car numbers. There is material on technological innovation, as that was part of the larger story of impact and adaptation by corporations and society. But there is no attempt to be exacting on each company's inventory of locomotives and rolling stock.

There are advantages in the broad scope. It provides, for example, insights on regional and town strategies that do not come easily through the focus of a corporate history of a single company. I found this was true years ago when writing my book *The Corporation and the Indian* and looking at intertribal relations and strategy rather than writing the history of a single tribe. There are similar limits to writing a biography, even if one frames it as a "life and times." The "times" tend to get short shrift, or the "life" disappears in generalities. Here I attempt to combine some salient detail, particularly at critical points, of the corporate history of individual companies, with my central account of the impact of railroads in general on many aspects of American culture in the early nineteenth century.

This is an economic history, as well as a social history, and recognizes the genius of the United States speaking in its material creativity. A writer in Charleston stated in 1856 that the deeds of the warrior and the politician were regularly well recognized, the merchant and businessperson less so. Still, "the monuments of their intelligence and devotion to the material interests of their fellow men are no less enduring."[27]

As always, and more than ever, I am grateful to my wife, Susan, for a lifetime of love and support in all conditions. I am especially appreciative, too, to Wichita State University, particularly the library, for providing me with some unique materials, and to the Garvey family for support of my professorship.

Craig Miner
Wichita State University
April 2010

A Most Magnificent Machine

INTRODUCTION

Treading on Enchanted Ground

 young lady wrote to a Pennsylvania newspaper in the summer of 1827 about her journey along the state-operated system of internal improvements. Having left Reading at three in the afternoon, she arrived at Mount Carbon the next evening after a passage of 49 miles by canal, "a great journey for me to make in one day." The mountain scenery impressed her, as did the band on board the canal boat, but greater wonders awaited. From Mauch Chunk (population 1,300), she elected to ride to the nearby coal mines, 9 miles up a considerable slope, on the Mauch Chunk Railway. This line, built in September 1826, comprised, along with a shorter (3-mile) one from the Boston tidewater to a granite quarry at Quincy, Massachusetts, the first elements of the railway system in the United States.

There were three carriages that day, each loaded with six passengers. A horse drew the train up the 3-foot, 7-inch gauge track to the mine, 900 feet above the Lehigh River, in 1 hour and 25 minutes. Coming down, there was no horse, only a rope wound at the top around a wheel with a friction brake to control the descent. That ride reached speeds of 30 miles per hour—faster than the passengers had ever experienced. The cars seemed at times on the verge of shooting off a cliff before a curve came into view and took the gasping tourists around. Wrote the young lady, clinging to her seat: "It really appeared like flying."[1]

The Mauch Chunk and Quincy Railroads were in those years (the mid-1820s) a national phenomenon, a tourist attraction of a magnitude far beyond their limited economic function. Newspapers competed for details. Also, they collected news from British journals of the architecturally impressive railroad lines completed in 1826 between Stockton and Darlington and Liverpool and Manchester.[2]

At Quincy the attraction was the tremendous weights that could be moved with relatively little effort by means of rails. A load of 21 tons of stone made its way down a slight grade along the Quincy road in October 1826, pulled by a single horse. The horse easily pulled the empty cars back.[3] "It is a matter of astonishment," went a Massachusetts governmental report, "to consider how great an advantage is gained, by merely providing smooth iron tracks for the wheels of carriages to run on; and though, in every kind of machinery, simplicity tends to increase its value and beauty, yet in no instance, can we find, from so simple an arrangement, effects so striking, or which promise to be so extensively beneficial." An extension of a railroad system, the report concluded, would impart energy to all kinds of business and produce circumstances that would improve the reputation of the state and of society in general.[4] By the spring of 1827, people from around the nation were visiting the Quincy railroad, giving business to an inn and interfering substantially with the main business of the road in order to satisfy the demands of tourists.[5] The little Quincy Railroad became an object of study for civil engineers and legislative committees thinking of more ambitious rail projects.[6] The economic advantages were obvious. The railroad had made granite so inexpensive that in Boston a house could be built of that durable material more cheaply than with bricks, even when the bricks sold for as low as $4 per thousand.[7]

The Mauch Chunk line drew more attention still, so much that one editor commented it had become a "place of notoriety."[8] Pleasure cars made the round-trip once every day and were always booked in advance.[9] One passenger reported riding "in pleasure carriages, which have seats like sleighs, and precisely like the sleigh, but longer and without back and front, and have small iron wheels." It seemed a pleasant way to travel, "not a jolt, jar, or movement, to the right or left." Birds, cats, and cows flew for their lives before the train: "They must have thought the end of the world was at hand."[10] A correspondent noticed that the rails were of pitch pine, 6 by

4 feet, 18–20 feet long, laid on layers of stone and "sleepers" (ties) of rock oak and topped with iron strips 1 1/4 inches wide and 5/16 inches thick. The road cost $2,500 per mile to build and was completed in two months. It cost 3 cents per ton to transport coal from the mine to the river, and the company expected a dividend of 8 percent on invested capital. Achieving such results in such topography with a canal or regular wagon road was impossible. One engineer estimated that it would take twenty-four horses or mules to pull the load up the hill that three horses were able to accomplish with the railroad in place. "The success of this railway is complete, and exceeds the expectations of the company and all who have seen it."[11]

Robert Mills, an experienced civil engineer, wrote several enthusiastic letters from Mauch Chunk in the fall of 1827. The vision of it, he said, excited him about the prospects of railroads in general.

> When the powers of *steam* and its useful operations were foretold in days of prejudice and skepticism, that are past and gone forever, the announcement of the wonders in arts and science which it would produce were considered the idle dreams of a disturbed mind.... But when the fact was realized, and this secret agent was seen propelling the reluctant barge through the waters, unaided by sail or oar ... then did the unbelieving world become convinced.

Mills quoted many statistics. But he concluded that the railroad itself "has tended more to inform the public mind on this deeply interesting subject than volumes of theory."[12]

True, there was some danger.[13] Passengers on the downward careen worried that a small chip or stone on the rail, or the breaking of an axle, could lead to a catastrophic accident. One rider said he had kept his courage up "but with a sort of consciousness that the next moment might be my last."[14] There was a conflict between feelings of fear and excitement. One passenger noted that the Mauch Chunk trip awakened a "sensation in the mind of an indescribable nature."[15] Mules enjoyed it. A Savannah editor, visiting in 1828, reported that the mules had begun to refuse to walk back down the hill and were therefore loaded on the cars. "It is ludicrous to see the poor animals riding by at the rate of 15 miles an hour, unconcernedly munching their corn, and quite indifferent to their novel situation."[16]

The reason for the interest on the part of Americans with no direct economic stake in these small rail companies was a combination of amazed reflection on the progress of transportation innovation in the recent past and curiosity about what might happen in the future. It was clear that it might not be many years before railroads became a national phenomenon of significance to every American citizen.

An observer of steamboat traffic on the rivers, initiated as a practical commercial enterprise by Robert Fulton's voyage upstream on the Hudson in his boat *Clermont* in 1807, commented: "A vast field is opened for the arts! *Steam* and *Iron* are the great agents, which the Genius of the age directs."[17] Canals had indifferent success early, but the completion of the Erie Canal in 1825 demonstrated dramatically the potential profitability and usefulness of internal improvements connecting the eastern seaboard with the developing western farming region.

Railroads quickly became competitive. The route of one of the earliest steam railroads in the United States, the Mohawk & Hudson, followed that of the Erie Canal. It was only 16 miles long but took passengers in one hour past the twenty-seven locks and full day's travel needed to cover the distance by canal.[18]

Many states and numerous investors were badly fooled by this species of "Future Shock." Ironically, those who entered the internal improvements game earliest and enthusiastically during the mania immediately following the triumph of the Erie were the worst burned by the ensuing fundamental and rapid changes. These included Pennsylvania, with its primarily canal-dependent state-owned system, and Maryland, which committed heavily (along with the State of Virginia and the federal government) to the Chesapeake & Ohio Canal as an outlet to western trade, just at the moment when private investors organized the Baltimore & Ohio Railroad.[19]

Canals seemed already on the defensive in 1825. Wrote an observer in Louisville: "A very short time since, canals had the ascendancy in the public mind, and bade fair to carry all before them; at the present rail roads bid fair to *bear off* the palm."[20] A Washington, D.C., newspaper criticized the C&O canal just as initial plans were published while apologizing to the promoters for "having their day dreams disturbed." He thought a railroad would save two-thirds of the time and expense of a canal.[21]

A year later there was thought of a railroad from Pittsburgh to Philadelphia. Why, the projectors said, should a canal even be considered for this mountainous route? One hundred stationary engines, pulling cars over the higher elevations via inclined planes, could do as much as 600 or more locks, "without taking into calculation the army of attendants that such a number of locks would require, the immense expense of yearly repairs from breaches, freshest &c., the damage done to farms and mills, the total stoppage of trade in the winter," the limited capacity of the locks, and the slow speed of canal travel.[22] It became a standard part of any railroad promotional speech for years to remind of the agonies of travel by canal or by stagecoach and to point out how mild the inconveniences of the railroad were by comparison.

There had been talk of railways for a long time. Primitive lines had appeared at collieries around Newcastle, England, about 1680, and for a long time railways were connected in people's minds exclusively with mining—thus Quincy and Mauch Chunk.

A very early rail proposal came from a Virginian in 1808, suggesting a railroad of cast iron laid on a stone foundation. The line would consist "of two pair of parallel ways, one for going, the other for returning carriages." The railroad might carry "astonishing loads" due to the diminution of friction provided by the rails. Still, the proposer thought it likely that railroads would not be practical "excepting on a very small scale, and that chiefly in the coal country near Richmond." Other Virginia markets and sources of produce were too scattered for railroads to succeed as common carriers.[23] Virginians were more sanguine by 1817. There was then a proposal for a railroad as part of a system connecting the James and Kanawah Rivers.[24] Historian John Majewski characterized the slow progress of this project over the years as an "utter disaster," but it seemed promising initially.[25] Two years later the *Richmond Enquirer* published a piece suggesting that river improvement was not nearly as promising as railroad building but admitted there was "the greatest prejudice" against railroads.[26]

There was activity elsewhere. Robert Livingston of New York State wrote a widely circulated letter in 1811 in which he stated that railways would be liable to serious objection and would be more expensive than canals.[27] In 1812 a lecturer on chemistry and mineralogy opined that "the first step . . . in this country [America] toward such a labour-saving system, by which men may be spared, not for depopulating contests, but for populating our deserts—must begin . . . with the universal encouragements of Roads, Railways and Canals. . . . Rail-ways are roads of easy inclination, having cast iron rails upon which wagons with wheels adapted to those rails, move."[28]

In 1814 Oliver Evans proposed to drive carriages on a railroad from Philadelphia to New York by steam, but he was widely considered an impractical visionary.[29] Still, that year New Jersey issued a charter for the New Jersey Rail Road Company with a capitalization of 500 shares of stock at $100 each.[30]

In 1824 there was talk of steam power. Hitherto, wrote an editor in England, railroads worked by horses had little advantage over canals, "but rail roads worked by the locomotive steam engine, have so decided a superiority, both as regards time and expense, that there can be no question but they will be generally adopted wherever a new line of conveyance becomes necessary, either from an increase of trade, or from the exorbitant demands of canal proprietors." By locomotive, 50 tons of goods could be conveyed by a 10-horsepower engine at 6 miles per hour on the level. Surely the United States, as well as Great Britain, would pursue that technology. An editor in Vermont reprinted that English article.[31]

There was a serious railroad proposal in New York State in 1826, advanced by Stephen Van Renssalaer and G.W. Featherstonhaugh. There were objections in the legislature that there were no railroads in the United States of any extent and, therefore, the whole technology was an experiment. And there were fears of competition with the Erie Canal. But most seemed to think there was room for both.[32] The proposal resulted in the incorporation of the Mohawk & Hudson Railroad in March 1826.[33] New York representatives the next year visited both England and the Mauch Chunk Railroad to get ideas.[34]

There were similar discussions in the South. Railroads, a paper in North Carolina reported, were "well calculated to suit the local circumstances of the South."[35] Georgia, although it had a recent unsatisfactory experience with a corrupt Board of Public Works and felt hampered in laying out railroad routes by the presence of the Cherokee Indians, was eager to advance railroads, too.[36] By 1828, Georgia had a state chief engineer who was making specific estimates of rail cost.[37] The wide-awake at Louisville paid attention also. No aid could be expected from the federal government, businesspeople there said, but Kentucky, having no good sites or water supplies for canals of any length, should get busy building a railroad from Louisville to Lexington as a start.[38]

In South Carolina the city of Charleston was active early. There was an ad in a newspaper there in 1822 offering to build a railroad from that city to Hamburg for $800,000. Such a line, it claimed, would make its stockholders $50,000 a year by shipping cotton from western regions at $1 a bale and other goods at 50 cents a hundredweight. The engine pictured was a "circular wheelbarrow" pushed with a pole. The Charleston editor thought this "new species of Velocipede," however primitive, would be enough and that the railroad would enjoy strong patronage.[39] Late in 1827, Charleston advanced a bill in the state legislature to charter a road to Hamburg, Columbia, and Camden.[40] The next year a miniature "model railroad" 200 feet long demonstrated the new technology in the city. A car bearing thirty-six bales of cotton and weighing 36,000 pounds could be drawn by a single person.[41] Subscribers took 7,000 shares of $100 each with the understanding that passenger fares on the new line would not exceed 5 cents per mile.[42] Business in Charleston was stagnating.[43] Even though many in the South took the position that the federal government should have nothing to do with promoting enterprises in the states, it was the sense of a railroad meeting at Charleston that for the new railroad an exception might be made. It was not a "common speculation," after all, but "a work . . . which is worth encouraging on public grounds."[44]

Baltimore moved most vigorously of all. Reporting in 1827 on the idea of building a railroad from Baltimore all the way to the Ohio River, the local press believed that a canal would be impractical and a railroad efficacious. "It will certainly be an ample recompense for the anxiety with which, for some time past, we have seen the trade of the interior gradually diverted to other channels."[45] Maryland incorporated the Baltimore & Ohio Railroad in March with capital of $3 million.[46] Lobbyists reported a good welcome in Richmond, where they went to line up legislation authorizing the route through Virginia.[47] Pennsylvania, though more reluctant, was approached also.[48] The new company was often described as a *national* work supported by a state and a city.[49] According to an editorial in the *Baltimore American:* "Though it is far from our wish to contribute in the least to any false excitement, yet it is with great satisfaction that we perceive the promptness with which the present plan has been adopted by all classes, not only as evidence of the enterprise of the city, but as *prima facie* proof of the reasonableness of the scheme itself."[50]

In 1827, there circulated in Baltimore a pamphlet titled *Proceedings of Sundry Citizens of Baltimore; Convened for the Purpose of Devising the Most Efficient Means of Improving the Intercourse Between the City and the Western States.* It was typical of the careful planning, including science and trade statistics, that went into the preparation of seaboard cities to enter the railroad field. A group met on February 12 and again on February 19 to discuss railroads in general and Baltimore's prospects for one in particular. Charleston, Philadelphia, and New York seemed to be on the move, although New York to some degree was still resting on its laurels with the Erie Canal. A delegation from Baltimore had visited the Quincy Railroad, which had cost more than $11,000 per mile to construct, and thought it could built a railroad for one-third less. The success of the Stockton & Darlington road in England led a London paper to write that "the strides which steam is making in the economy of the country, are more gigantic and surprising than those who are domesticated at a distance from its immediate operation imagine."

But not for long, the Baltimore leaders thought. A western railroad could attract to Baltimore's port a large proportion of the $21 million in products that now followed the route by other means. A barrel of flour at Wheeling, the proposed terminus of the road, sold in 1827 for $1 a barrel but cost $4 to ship (very slowly in summer and even more slowly in winter), making the price at Baltimore $5. A railroad could ship the same barrel the same distance much more quickly for $1. Cotton could be hauled from the Ohio River to Baltimore at about 1/4 cent per pound and coal from the Allegheny Mountains to the city at 11 or 12 cents per bushel. Given the shortage of whale oil for domestic light and wood for heat, Allegheny coal might well revolutionize daily life in Baltimore and change its industry fundamentally.[51] There followed another pamphlet of 180 pages containing a survey, engineering details, and an estimate of resources along the route.[52] Phillip Thomas, Alexander Brown, and Thomas Elicott of the railroad company visited the Mauch Chunk and Quincy Railroads and gathered data. They reported they had not the slightest doubt "but that there is ample skill in our country for the execution . . . of the work."[53]

Gary Browne, historian of Baltimore, claimed, "An astonishing thing happened in Baltimore during the 1830s; all the historical forces that had been at work for more than a generation suddenly cohered." It changed its cultural ways as fast as it increased its population and changed in appearance. A laissez-faire attitude of risk capitalism displaced the old merchant economy, and a new business elite demanded moral behavior enforced by law. At the time the Baltimore businesspeople could look neither to the federal government nor to the State of Maryland for much support. They had to invent and institute their economic adventures on their own.[54]

Hezekiah Niles, publisher of Baltimore's own *Weekly Register*, one of the first journals devoted at least partly to business, was ecstatic at the prospect. "It is with no ordinary feelings," he announced in his March 17, 1827, issue, "that we announce the fact that a plan for making *a rail road from the city Baltimore to some point on the Ohio river*, has been considered and adopted by certain of our most intelligent, public spirited and wealthy citizens." Who could calculate its effects? Baltimore certainly would achieve by it a place in home trade that New York City occupied in foreign trade, "and while the Erie Canal pours its invaluable supplies into the latter, the railway will not be of less importance to us; and, happily, there 'is room enough for us all!'" Science, capital, and will would overcome the difficulties. Even the Allegheny Mountains would "sink, as it were, beneath the pressure of unconquered steam, nay, the laws of gravitation give way before the march of mind!" Niles as a little boy had heard Oliver Evans says that a man then living would see the Ohio and Mississippi Rivers covered with steamboats and that he could travel from Philadelphia to Boston in one day.[55] That storied future seemed suddenly to have arrived.

By April 1827, people at Baltimore had subscribed more than $4 million to the project. In addition, $1 million had come from the state and $200,000 from other places, making a total of more than $5 million in capital.[56] The Maryland legislature said that the area was "impoverished in the midst of untouched resources." While the railroad was in "embryo," it was true that "in all new enterprises, the first step taken dissolves half the difficulty."[57] It must be obvious, a report from a meeting in Frederick, Maryland, concluded, "that Maryland must either further works of internal improvement, or fall into insignificance."[58] In the spring of 1827, the new railroad company imported from England a section of rail and a railroad carriage as used on the Liverpool & Manchester line. These artifacts went on public exhibit.[59] In January 1828, the city sent a committee to England to inspect the main railroads there.[60]

Other places thought the thing might actually work. A letter that May reported the arrival of the steamboat *Tecumseh* at Louisville from New Orleans after a journey of nine days and four hours, having lost a whole night in fog. Just a few years earlier a captain had been honored at a public dinner for making the trip in twenty-five days. A letter from New Orleans, commenting on this and a dull local market, hoped that soon the Ohio Canal and the B&O Railroad would "receive our produce, and give us a fair stand 'among the people of the earth.'"[61] Louisville felt ashamed. Baltimore, a city with a smaller population than Louisville, had "set on foot an enterprise, which would be worthy of an Empire."[62] A public meeting at Wilmington, Delaware, concluded that in building a railroad Baltimore had "hit upon a mode of transportation that places us beyond all fear of competition." There would be "ten thousand ramifications of business."[63] Reporters in Ohio were suggesting ways of extending the railroad, already finished in imagination to Wheeling, on through their state.[64] It was even suggested that a St. Louis terminus was not out of the question.[65]

Among the major players in the early rail competition, Pennsylvania was more committed to canals than most, with a large amount of state funding invested in an extensive canal system. The state was a pioneer in promoting internal improvements generally, its legislature having strongly backed the

National Road in 1814.[66] Its "Main Line" system cost more than $10 million and extended eventually (in 1834) from Philadelphia to Pittsburgh, more than 350 miles.[67] Pennsylvania consequently got a late start in railroads and was initially known more for its opposition to allowing the B&O to build through its territory than for any rail activity of its own. By 1831, mass meetings there concluded that railroads would be desirable when it was not possible to command a supply of fresh water for canals. However, Pennsylvanians still felt that railroads were overrated. At the end of 1831, with only 39 miles of railroad under contract from Philadelphia, it was still the general consensus that canals were superior. Statistics should be presented "to counteract the wild speculations of visionary men, and to allay the honest fear and prejudices of many of our citizens, who have been induced to believe that rail roads are better than canals."[68]

Pennsylvania's vested interest prejudiced it against railroad building. "Those interested in the present dilatory and laborious methods of conveying our exports and imports," wrote one editor unkindly, "have raised a sort of opposition." These critics depended "upon the existing state of things, which are necessarily sacrificed by so great a revolution, which in its results changes the whole course of business."[69] Baltimore promoters, frustrated and angry about what they considered to be "dog in the manger" tactics by Pennsylvania regarding the ambitions of Maryland, thought Philadelphia was simply frightened that the interior trade would be diverted from that city to Baltimore.

> Is it not passing strange that the mode of transportation which, only 4 years ago [1825] was rejected as vastly inferior to canals and as utterly "inadequate," should now be acknowledged as in all respects so greatly superior, that the very canals with which it could *then* not bear comparison, are *now* confessedly unable on any terms to compete with it! Certainly there are strange changes in this whirligig world![70]

Still, Pennsylvanians understood that railroads of some kind would have to supplement canals over the mountains. At Philadelphia in 1823 a company formed for building a railroad to Columbia and sought subscriptions. The subscriber could pay in installments, so that he could see how the first section of the line worked before committing further.[71] The press at Pittsburgh in the spring of 1825 published a memorial to the Pennsylvania legislature "inquiring into the expediency of *Rail Roads*." Many citizens, newspaper reports said, had begun to consider railroads as superior to canals. They were cheaper in original construction, easier to keep in order, and easier to clear of accidents. "In dry seasons, there is no danger of failure, in wet seasons of injury, or in seasons of frost of total stoppage." And they could cross mountains.[72]

Philadelphians began to wonder why farmers should lie idle all winter before seeking a distant market by water in the spring. It proposed in 1828 a railroad to Pottsville. "Let the railway be made, and it is inevitable, as that mankind seek their own interest, and water its own level, that during the winter season, when rivers and canals are locked up in ice, our farmers will empty their crops into the lap of Pottsville, there to embark at the opening of navigation for the great emporium." That crop movement would be but "one *sleighing frolic* upon the railroad."[73]

Nor was New England remiss. Daniel Webster, speaking in 1826, said that few people could believe how much weight a railroad could carry with modest power, especially when it used a steam engine.

> How much more may be gained in this way, time, alone, can determine, but it does not require an extraordinary degree of sagacity in any one (acquainted with *Yankee* ingenuity and enterprise) to prophesy, that, in less than five years, we shall see a complete line of intercourse over these hills, from Albany to Boston, with merchandize and passengers, travelling each way at the rate of ten miles an hour.[74]

Massachusetts appointed engineers late in 1826 to survey a possible rail route between Boston and Albany.[75] It also published an extensive scientific report on the economic advantages of railroads. There was, the author of that report wrote, no end to detail, but it should be obvious that the railroad was a "powerful spring of action" that would impart energy to all kinds of business. It would also improve "the reputation of our State, which is now stigmatized as destitute of enterprise."[76]

There was a mass meeting at the state supreme court in Boston in mid-January 1827. It was difficult, the reporting committee stated, to get sufficient detail. Therefore they could offer only "general views and speculative opinions" designed to call the attention of capital to railroads. But it needed doing. "Shall Massachusetts, whose Revolutionary luster is equal to that of the brightest star in the constellation of liberty, be exceeded in the race of public utility?" Every farmer should think of the time and expense it now took to get his goods to market. It was hardly a matter of profit to a few stockholders but rather a benefit to the entire community and "a positive addition to the public wealth." There were challenges. "Your committee are aware that some difficulties are presented in the lofty mountains and deep vallies intervening between Boston and the Hudson River. But most of these can probably be avoided, and those which cannot, may be surmounted with greater facility than superficial observers would suppose."[77] In June 1827, 200 members of the state legislature visited Quincy to examine the practicalities of railroading in operation.[78]

Towns across the state organized public meetings to discuss railroads. Despite bad weather and bad roads, there was a good turnout at Pittsfield on December 12, where R.P. Morgan of the town exhibited sections of rail from England. "The Rail Road system is a novelty in this country," wrote a local participant, "and the people of Massachusetts will not adopt it, till they understand it."[79]

There was an extensive debate in the Massachusetts legislature in August 1827 about the possibility of state aid for a western railroad. There was a question of the "propriety" of building such a line at this point, but the legislature thought it wise to set some policy about state involvement. "When we see what is going on in the world, and especially in our neighboring states, this is a question which we shall be compelled to look in the face." Public opinion would force it. One of the debaters thought it was a disaster to allow "the great channels of commerce to pass into the hands of private persons. . . . All great public improvements if they can be rendered profitable to companies, may be so to the state, and should belong to the whole people." One should not judge future possibilities by past accomplishments or "previous habits and associations." All would be changed. There was a dense population in Massachusetts, and though "it would be premature to say absolutely what we can and what we cannot do," it seemed to many that the railroad was a creator and equalizer of wealth.[80]

One citizen from Dedham advised electing businesspeople to the legislature who would study the details of railroads and who would be able to communicate a good plan. Otherwise "their imbecility may turn away from us in disgust, the favorable opinion of the engineers and directors." The great question before Massachusetts, he wrote, was whether the capital available could be profitably employed in making railroads. That could not be settled by "vague conjecture" but only by evidence "derived from a rigid and severe examination under the direction of responsible agents of the government." Otherwise there would only be talk—surveys and speeches.[81]

Such thinking represented a sea change, as Oscar and Mary Handlin demonstrated in their masterful book *Commonwealth: A Study of the Role*

of Government in the American Economy: Massachusetts, 1774–1861. Social changes modified traditional modes of action and thought, leading to
what the Handlins characterize as a jettisoning of the old mode of class
and privilege in favor of an "optimistic and rational humanism." There was
a "community of interest" that could best be represented by the state. Perhaps railroads were too important to be left entirely to private initiative and
investment.[82]

Early in 1828, New Jersey incorporated the Camden & Amboy Railroad
to connect New York City with Philadelphia.[83] Even frontier Ohio and Indiana were thinking of railroads. It was known that New Orleans was a sickly
place and many died there. Perhaps, therefore, Ohio ought to develop some
other means than the passage down the Mississippi River and across the
Gulf and up the Atlantic for reaching the New York City market.[84] At the
opening of 1828, there circulated a pamphlet titled *A Sinoptical List of the
Principal Canals and Rail Roads Completed, in progress, or of which a reasonable probability exists that they will shortly be commenced in the United
States.*[85] Only 23 miles of railroad were then actually completed, but 544
were projected.[86]

After that, the deluge.

The new United States between 1825 and the outbreak of the Civil War in
1861 experienced bewildering, one might say awesome, even miraculous,
changes. They came one after another in rapid succession, hardly allowing
the population to appreciate fully, much less adapt adequately, to each in
turn, not to mention the cumulative impact.

In the long run and from the perspective of hindsight, the most significant of these changes were economic. But they had long tentacles, deep
implications, affecting society and culture at their cores. There were great
shifts in social and individual psychology; in the influence of geography;
in the nature of financing and financial instruments; in ideas about the environment; in urban politics and economics; in labor policy; in the use of
fuels; in the profession and practice of engineering; in the fate of alternate
technologies; in the destinies of towns, cities, and regions; in the situation
of public health; in the pricing system for agricultural and manufactured
products; in legal and constitutional theory and practice; in the tenor and
method of politics; and even in such areas as architecture and historic
preservation. Railroads created the American engineering profession, the
American iron industry, the American locomotive- and car-building industry, the American coal industry, and to some extent the American oil

industry. They made commuting to suburbs possible. They influenced business cycles. They modified city, township, county, state, national, and international finance. In short, the entire society and culture were affected, more or less deeply. People were carried along through these changes with a feeling of excitement but also one of vague fear, equivalent to the experience of many passengers upon first traveling by railroad.

"Railroads have become the great leading fact of the age," claimed a Louisville writer, "a vast machinery that has more than any one thing stamped on the times the impress of progress."[87] Progress, before it became rhetorical, consisted of dramatic, rapid changes in the landscape; in real estate values; in products, mixes, and markets; and in the manner and pace of doing things.

A visitor to Philadelphia in 1853 passed down Market Street and saw "tier upon tier of boxes, crates, and bales of goods" in front of jobbing houses, with hundreds of men coopering, marking, and lifting them, forming a continuous line from Third Street to the Pennsylvania Railroad depot. There were some who talked about "keeping the spirit of improvement within safe bounds, and restricting all movements for facilitating the growth of the town to the point of present necessity." Sometimes they complained, as "when it was proposed to pull down a row of miserable old sheds that obstruct and virtually destroy for all legitimate uses, the most valuable business avenue in our metropolis." But these people were deluded and impractical, the writer thought.

> They imagine that the world has been standing still for a quarter or a half a century, and consequently form their views of the policy and need of any proposed undertaking for affording commerce ampler space to move in, or opening channels for its passage to a market, and the like, with reference to the state of things that has long given way before a silent, but positive advancement, of which they have seen little and suspected less.[88]

Railroads, Edmund Gaines wrote to the Georgia governor in 1834, would be constructed "mainly by calling into action that class of native American genius, which would otherwise languish and waste itself away, for want of judicious direction and profitable employment."[89] It seemed an unmixed blessing.

"Magnificent Enterprise!" wrote an observer of the first locomotive to reach Raleigh, North Carolina, over the Raleigh & Gaston Railroad in 1840. "We have now ocular demonstration of that which no man would have believed, thirty years ago, to be within the compass of human power. Truly has it been said that the last few years have unfolded more that is novel, vast, and wonderful than the whole eighteen centuries of the Christian era."[90] The boldest minds, wrote a New York City journalist in 1831, could scarcely keep pace with the wonderful phenomenon of steam. "Whilst we are pursuing a train of experiments, founded on the strictest principles of philosophy and mechanics, so forcibly is the imagination impressed by their novelty and brilliancy, that we seem to be treading on enchanted ground, and participating in the wonders of romance."[91]

No one, of course, could have predicted or perfectly understood a future arriving at "railroad speed." The changes were well beyond the capacity of a sluggish and heavy world, which had been working in the deep tracks of agricultural and rural ways for millennia. But in the seventeenth and eighteenth centuries there had arrived the Industrial Revolution, heralded by the giant strides of steam and credit, which between them revolutionized technology and the methods of doing business, cross-fertilizing and influencing each other in complex ways all the while.

The fact that there was a dark side to such progress was not completely unrecognized at the time but has become in hindsight more obvious. Massachusetts railroad commissioners warned in 1828 that the modern steam railroad might not "comport with the common habits and opinions of the people."[92] Horrific accidents, often caused by imperfect technology combined with irresponsible management, did get the attention of contemporaries. There were those in New Hampshire who worried about the power of corporations with their limited liability and capacity for taking lands through eminent domain laws with government cooperation. They could "swindle according to law."[93] Some sympathized with the displaced Native American tribes, first in the Southeast and later beyond the Mississippi. Others sympathized with freed African Americans who sometimes were segregated in special cars. A few were concerned about the environment. Railroads were bringing noise, sparks, and devil-may-care speed to former sylvan groves, not to mention burning holes in ladies' dresses and making their eyes water.

A writer in Boston in the early 1850s saw too much "effervescence" in American society, with many forced into positions for which their nature did not fit them. There was too much lust for power and pride in wealth. "The merchant lives in his counting room, his Bible is his ledger, and his adventures are his gods." His life was synonymous with enterprises, which fluctuated and consequently were generators of "nervousness and irritability." He read his newspaper and took part in the "commotions of the civilized world." Even the farmer was affected, now located as he was near a railroad. "He dares not sell a bushel of potatoes or a stack of hay, without consulting first, his newspaper, and then the telegraphic wires, to learn whether some event has occurred which may enhance the price of his product."

It was a life of "external forms."[94] There was so much to read that people often read nothing, so much to think of that they need not think at all. "There is a steam power acting physically, so there is a steam power acting morally—intellectually—to which is given the name of EXCITEMENT. The creature, PUBLIC, is fed on this, and over fed. . . . The public, like some great beast, roars for food, reckless of what food may be, provided it is a highly seasoned dish." Railroads encouraged irresponsible speculation, the stress of the life engendered by new urban wealth, and the financial "defalcations" to which the morally weak were tempted. A new and debased railroad version of the American language emerged, consisting of acronyms and crude slang. Everywhere there was hurry. Wall Street was "full of little steam locomotives, chattering of stocks, news, etc., whizzing and buzzing like the pipe of a Mississippi steamboat."[95] "Nothing appalls us. . . . Everybody is awake and wide-awake. Society seems to be in a whirl. There is, as it were an atmospheric maelstrom about us. Talk in a hurry. Walk in a hurry. Make love in a hurry. . . . Eat, sleep and die in a hurry."[96] America, a New York editor wrote in 1837, was "overbanking, overtrading, overspending, overliving, overdashing, overdriving, overreaching, overcheating, overpraying, oversinning, overthinking, overplaying, overriding, overtippling, overfiddling, and overacting of every kind and description except overploughing."[97]

Credit and its use could be marvelous, but there was increasing recognition, especially during two major panics, or "revulsions," in 1837 and 1857 that it was much subject to abuse with debilitating consequences for the masses as well as for the plungers (reckless speculators in today's parlance). States, which were major providers of railroad credit before the 1850s, regularly defaulted on the bond interest obligations, often owed to English banks. The fact that lessons are contained in studying such "delusive seasons" of the past, which help in understanding the workings of American capitalism at other times, is near axiomatic, however often it is ignored.

Some felt the trend was natural. Edward Everett, speaking at a Boston railroad convention in 1835, stated that it was folly to hear that artificial works could not or should not conquer nature or the natural channels of trade. "It is as natural," he said, "for a civilized man to make a railway or canal, as for a savage to descend a river in a bark or canoe."[98]

Others doubted that. A Frenchman wrote: "Sometimes the American pays the price for his temerity. His machine explodes, and an eternal repose punishes his unlimited and unbridled activity."[99] An engineer in Russia in 1839 manufactured a steam man, a reflection perhaps of the changes he saw in real men around him. The feet were mounted on wheels "and as he goes thundering over the course the steam comes puffing out of his nostrils in a manner to give the appearance of Satan."[100] A New York writer made the direct connection. He said that the men on Broadway were "the two-legged locomotives of these steam-going United States of America. Broadway is their railroad track."[101]

And just as the anthropomorphic became mechanical, so the mechanical became animate in the mind's eye. "He neighs aloud as he dashes by" went an 1840 example of industrial poetry referring to the locomotive as an Iron Horse, "And the fire-spars flash from his gleaming eye / And vales resound, and the hills reply, / To the rapid rush of the flashing wheels."[102] An 1851 article in *Scientific American* called the locomotive the most perfect machine. "It approaches nearer to the spiritual and physical combination of the human machine, than any other." To "stand at night by the side of a railroad, when a large train is rushing at a rate of 30 miles per hour, affords a sight both sublime and terrific. It was, a backwoodsman said, 'pandemonium in harness.'"[103] That the machine could be so benign, so friendly, and that the human being could be so clockwork, so regular, so predictable, was disturbing.

Still, for the most part the future looked bright to the first railroad builders, investors, and riders. In 1832 a writer imagined he was 80 years old and railroads were everywhere "so that a man requiring locomotion, kept a little steam sulk-buggy of his own, which could be lighted with a cigar, and set in motion with the flame of a single newspaper. . . . Every railroad route had six or eight tracks." People in the future would ride around on their own railroad cars. They would have no vocation and would wander about the country, deserting cities altogether.[104] How would one keep them down on the farm, asked another in 1835? The apprentice boy would want to make a trip from New England to Ohio every Saturday evening to be with his sweetheart. "Grave, plodding citizens will be flying about like comets." The writer thought on the whole it was a "pestilential, topsy-turvy, harum-scarum whirligig."[105] Some imagined "velocipede trains" and others steam-powered flying machines.[106] A visionary writing in 1830 imagined a Grand Union Railroad Hotel in the future where "it was steam, steam, nothing but steam!" The rooms would be heated by steam, the beds made by steam robots, and the meals cooked by steam. The slow trains would run faster than 100 miles per hour.[107]

Perhaps the remains of railroads would interest future archaeologists even as Roman ruins did those of the nineteenth century. They might serve as the most appropriate monuments of American civilization. "'Creatures of a day,' the contemplation of perpetuity, even of that which is inanimate, cannot but excite an interest, and we cannot but ask what changes it will witness." If moral and intellectual progress in the United States equaled its technological strides, it would be "a beacon . . . [to] guide the nations to a rational freedom and universal peace."[108] Ralph Waldo Emerson, lecturing in 1850, regretted that he had not lived later in order to see the new steam tools in full play.[109]

Mind and matter seemed to have been comfortably joined in the railroad enterprise. The Yankee was ubiquitous worldwide, and "if you take the wings of the morning for the uttermost parts of the earth, you may expect that they have got there long before you to carry off the best bargains, and set up a newspaper." Whatever they were doing, from contriving a new kind of pocket comb to building a railroad, Americans were always on their feet, "if not the broadest and most comprehensive of thinkers, at least the most resolute and persistent of doers."[110] A writer in 1850 predicted that soon "the world will be encircled by a common medium of instant intercourse." It was true, a Baltimore journalist warned in 1850, that people must cultivate the social and moral elements of their being in order to be worthy of such a fine future, and this could happen only with the "proper cultivation of the common man." But, that done, "Who shall declare the extremity of human attainment—who will venture to set up the standard of perfection?"[111] A nonplussed British traveler in the United States mused in 1844, "I verily believe the Americans would, if Canada belonged to them, run a railroad to the North Pole."[112]

In 1973, the poet Elizabeth Bishop wrote her friend, the poet Robert Lowell, about a condominium she had purchased in a Boston building called the "Granite Warehouse." It was built in 1838 and the stone quarried at Quincy. "I fell in love with the building," she said, and Bishop did great creative work there.[113] It was an example of how far the unintended, unimagined influences of the construction of the Quincy mining railroad went in 1826. It clearly influenced the nature and cost of buildings constructed in Boston over the ensuing decades ("once put up it endures forever," wrote a reporter in 1831), but who knew what else?[114]

CHAPTER 1

Baltimore Looks West

asil Hall, traveling in the United States in 1828, was able to meet at Baltimore a signer of the Declaration of Independence, Charles Carroll of Carrolltown, and at the same time to hear about the city's plans for a railroad to the Ohio River. Hall thought the effort on the railroad would be wasted because the natural obstacles in the West were too great. Americans exaggerated. They talked of railroads hardly begun as if they were finished. Still, he had to admit that Baltimore had "projects afloat."[1]

For some time, the Baltimore & Ohio Railroad was indeed mostly talk. But it was serious talk and glorious talk. If the railroad were a kind of new religion, then the civic railroad celebration was its liturgy. Great energy went into these, and the organizers were convinced that they mattered. An example was the July 4, 1828, groundbreaking ceremony for the B&O. It was more than a railroad event; it involved the whole city in an enormous parade of its trades- and craftspeople—hatters, coopers, cabinetmakers, booksellers—forty-seven categories in all.[2] The stonecutters donated a white marble cornerstone for placing at the spot where railroad construction would begin.[3] Citizens could view "transparencies" showing the imagined railroad on exhibit at Peale's museum.[4]

The actual day was the fifty-second anniversary of the Declaration of Independence, and Baltimore thought its celebration was the best ever. The weather was mild, about 70 degrees, and by midmorning every house window and niche filled with spectators. The whole Frederick Turnpike out to the point west of the city where the cornerstone was to be laid was lined with spectators. The crowd was about 70,000 and, people said, was exceeded locally only when Lafayette had entered the city years earlier. About 8:30 A.M. the parade began to move, with floats and banners for every craft. The printers had a car 16 feet long drawn by four bay horses and displaying a banner reading "Truth is a victor without violence."[5] It could have been a motto for the whole new business enterprise in transportation.

The field selected for the main ceremony was a high ridge with a pavilion erected at its top. The railroad was to proceed along the rugged valley of the Patapsco River toward a ridge about 40 miles west near a place called Parr's Spring.[6] John B. Morris in the main address stated that the enterprise would "raise our native city to that rank which the advantages of her situation, and the enterprise of her citizens entitle her to hold. The result of our labours will be felt, not only by ourselves, but by posterity— not only by Baltimore, but also by Maryland and by the United States." In a cavity of the cornerstone, the participants placed a copy of the railroad charter, Virginia and Maryland newspapers of the day, and a bound copy of the B&O engineering report done up by the bookbinders.[7] Old Charles Carroll was the star of the show, drawn there in a barouche pulled by four horses.[8] Niles quoted with approval the local press: "It is not in mortals to command success, but if a determination to yield to no obstacle which human exertion can overcome; an enthusiastic devotion to the cause; a firm belief that the completion of the magnificent work will confer the most important benefits upon our country; and a thorough conviction that it is practicable—if all these, urging to action, can ensure success—success shall be ours."[9]

"An Old Citizen" wrote to the *Baltimore Patriot* in January 1829 on the prospects for the city in a new age. "The current of human events may be compared to a mighty river, on whose bosom floats various products; sometimes gliding onward in an even course, and occasionally tossed by the waves of hidden tempests. . . . The Genius of Liberty has opened a new era, and causes, unknown to the old world, have operated like the certainty of destiny, to usher into being astonishing events!"[10] In 1830 a Kentucky article suggested a railroad to the Pacific . . . or farther. "We are almost out of the notion of these Rail Roads, Canals & c. They are too old fashioned.

We are up for BALLOONING. What think you of a line of Balloons from Batavia [to] . . . the Moon, Pleiades, and Great Bear?"[11]

That was a high point; then came the challenges. There were three major ones right away: competition from the Chesapeake & Ohio canal, the intransigence of the State of Pennsylvania in giving right-of-way permission across its territory, and the construction challenges of the scenic but topographically challenging Patapsco River valley.

The C&O fight broke out immediately and lasted long. The groundbreaking for the canal took place on the same day as the Baltimore celebration, July 4, at Washington, D.C. The president of the United States, John Q. Adams, turned the first shovel of earth. Adams, in typical fashion for him, emphasized the power of mind and learning over nature. George Washington had been interested in a canal connected with the Potomac River, and Adams said in his speech, "The Empire which his great mind, piercing into the darkness of futurity, foretold in America, was the Empire of Learning and Arts—the domination of man over himself, and over physical nature—acquired by the inspirations of genius, and the toils of industry." What an alternative a canal was to wars and widows' tears![12]

It might seem that the C&O canal and the B&O Railroad were two arrows in a common quiver, but a battle was raging over which mode of transport was best, and there were places near Harper's Ferry, toward which both railroad and canal were building, where the river was too close to the cliffs easily to accommodate both. Baltimore tried to be tolerant. "The coincidence in the time of commencement is remarkable," went a piece in the *Baltimore Patriot*. "We wish that in the prosecution of the two designs, one or both, may not be found vain or impracticable." Washington, D.C., which would benefit most from the canal, and Baltimore, which would benefit most from the railroad, were fewer than 40 miles apart, and each planned to spend $10 million or more on its outreach to the western trade. However, the Baltimore writer suspected coexistence would not be easy. "Both cannot succeed—and we hope rather than believe, that both will not fall through." Therefore, there had to be a winner and a loser.[13]

A Philadelphia writer that summer of 1828 described the stakes clearly. The canal and the railroad were "in some ways rival works, at least each are [*sic*] candidates for public favor. The lines of the respective improvements will run parallel to each other for a considerable part of the route; at other places they will be brought forcibly into contact, and with a predisposition . . . on the part of the managers and directors to jostle each other as much as possible." Should both works be completed, it would be an acid test of the comparative value of railroads and canals generally. But, however desirable such a test might be, "we regret the magnitude of the experiment." The loss on account of the competition would be enormous, not only to individuals and companies "but [also] to the cause of improvement generally." Would it not be wisdom now for one or the other to give way?[14]

That was not to be. Bitterness only increased. The *New York Spectator* reported early in 1829 that the B&O had "called upon Hercules" by asking for federal aid, but it was "in bad odor" generally among the public because many thought the only goal of the railroad was to discourage the C&O canal "of which the Baltimoreans are so unreasonably jealous."[15] There was a proposal to introduce slaves from Virginia to work on the canal, which increased prejudice against it by some.[16] But advocates thought the crowing of the railroad advocates was premature. "A Rail-Road for distant transportation is an *experiment*, wholly untried in any country."[17] A letter to the editor in Washington, D.C., expressed the belief that the farmer, having plenty of leisure and often no use for his horses, would not care about a savings of a few days getting his goods to market. "It will be no object to him to fly over the road driven by steam." A large proportion of U.S. citizens, this writer thought, "may have cause to regret it for generations to come . . . should the Rail Road Company, in the present contest with the Canal Company, do the enterprise of the latter a serious injury."[18] Railways, another canal advocate wrote in a letter to the paper, were artificial things, whereas canals, once fed with waters, were part of the landscape, a "natural agent, on which your boat is floated, as on a river." A farmer could build a boat and put it on a canal. Could he build a locomotive, and, if he could, would he be allowed to run it on a railway?[19]

The Baltimore press emphasized damage to adjacent lands from canal leakage and the "noxious miasma" from stagnant water, which endangered health.[20] A ride on any railroad by the "canalites" would "uproot" their obsolete faith.[21] Baltimore was not alone. A Bostonian suggested that railroads used a third of the land canals occupied and did not require ponds, reservoirs, and feeders. They were not interrupted by winter, except in snow, which could be easily removed. They could carry freight right to the doors of warehouses and could be built for half the cost per mile.[22] In regard to railroads, Niles commented in 1831: "The spirit is moving, and it cannot be arrested."[23] Suggestions that the C&O canal and the B&O Railroad unite, or that they compromise on their routes, fell on deaf ears.[24]

Litigation seemed inevitable. The C&O directors told their stockholders in 1831 that they came to it reluctantly, but negotiation seemed not to have worked. "We have tried to accommodate as best we can." However, "the repeated occasions on which the subject of this controversy has been brought before the public; the disingenuous statements which have been made in relation to it; the imposing manner in which these misrepresentations have been promulgated" led the committee to court. Legal arguments took place over two weeks in October 1831, with Daniel Webster representing the railroad. The canal was the nominal victor there and also in appeals court on rights-of-way and other questions. That forced the railroad into a more awkward routing than originally intended, and there was a real crunch with railroad and canal running close beside each other at several places.[25] A commentator in Washington thought mutual concessions were appropriate: "Both are equally *dependent* upon legislative favor and public patronage, and both equally bound to conciliate." Even if the canal had a legal right to shut off the railroad, would it be politic, or in the public interest?[26] Many came to the conclusion that Maryland, despite its earlier commitment to a canal, could hardly fail to promote a railroad also in the railroad age. It was unfortunate that geography at points did not cooperate with the dual initiative and that "irritated feelings" had arisen.[27] Maryland as a state was naturally interested in a compromise, but it was not easy to arrange.[28] As a final fillip, the canal company offered to permit the railroad company to apply its funds to the completion of the canal and abandon its own ambition to build a line to the Ohio River in favor of constructing a lateral canal from the narrow place at Point of Rocks, which it was temporarily enjoined from passing to Baltimore, in order that that city might enjoy the benefit of the C&O canal in reaching the West.[29]

Legal niceties ultimately, however, could not hide the fact that the future belonged to the railway. Eventually the canal and the railroad agreed to some joint construction that allowed both to proceed, even in tight quarters with each other in places.[30] The B&O started planning in the spring of 1829 for a railroad from Baltimore to Washington, noting that there were ten four-horse stages a day plying that route.[31] "A few hundred thousand dollars brings Washington practically at our doors."[32] Chartered by the Maryland legislature and begun in 1833, the Washington Branch took four years to build, costing eight lives and nearly $1.5 million.[33] But it did provide an all-rail alternative to the C&O canal.

The editorial stance of the *Baltimore Patriot* in 1830 was that the canal age was over. It quoted an Englishman writing to a Baltimorean, who claimed, "Canal or river navigation, excepting under particular circumstances, such as . . . in rivers like the Hudson, requiring no outlays to make them navigable . . . must be abandoned. Your country ought to witness the construction of no more Canals, and your best way will be to convert those which you have into Rail Ways."[34] A writer noticed: "It is by comparison that benefits are measured."[35]

Edward Hungerford, writing his history of the B&O in 1928, commented, after describing the Railroad vs. Canal legal battles: "To the passenger who rides along the line of the Baltimore and Ohio today between Harper's Ferry and the Point of Rocks and who observes the ancient and grass-grown canal that so closely parallels the tracks for almost every mile of the distance, it seems unbelievable that it could ever have been so real an antagonist of the railroad—and for so long a time."[36]

A second major challenge to the B&O at its outset, this time political as much as strictly economic, was a controversy with Pennsylvania. Pennsylvania built several railroads early, including the pioneering Mauch Chunk. However, none of these was more than 10 miles long, and all served coal mines with the express purpose of getting the coal to the state-owned Main Line Canal and river improvement system. Pennsylvania seemingly did not want to build an extensive cross-country rail system of its own or allow the Baltimore company to penetrate its territory. As early as the spring of 1827, there was notice that Pennsylvania was "evidencing hostility" toward the B&O Railroad.[37]

That opposition reflected in many ways an early emergence of the urban rivalries among eastern cities for western trade. Just as the C&O issue was in many ways part of the urban war between Baltimore and Washington, this one was between Baltimore and Philadelphia. The strategy of each place in regard to the railroad and canal network was critical to its future prosperity. All eastern opponents agreed that in the future, given that rivers were not the only way to carry weight, some city would take the place of New Orleans as the entrepôt of western trade. New Orleans, a Baltimore booster wrote, was "a sepulcher festooned with gold" whose "scorching climate and pestilential miasmas" would no longer be tolerated in the railroad age.[38]

Some in Pennsylvania disliked its intransigence about railroads, native or not. The proprietors of a new ironworks at Shamokin, 120 miles from Philadelphia, needed coal and could not get it from the mines or ship the iron efficiently to market by canal. "If the *Hercules* of Philadelphia, or the *Jupiter* of Harrisburg, would inspire us with the *pecuniary* power, we would most willingly whip the horses and put our shoulders to the wheels, but, without such interposition, our coal must sleep until wealth and capital awake." To drag coal to the river, "racking wagons . . . and wrenching horses' legs," was impractical and to ship it on the state canal was a "project too desperate, as we are now situated, to be tried more than once." The works needed a railroad or a connection with Baltimore via its railroad.[39] Why should western Pennsylvania have to market to an inconvenient and expensive point (Philadelphia) simply because it was located in the same state?[40] Maybe the B&O should be allowed into Pennsylvania with some condition, such as that it build a branch to Pittsburgh.[41]

Feelings were exacerbated when Baltimore began promoting a railroad direct to the Susquehanna River (it was as close to that river as was Philadelphia), specifically to tap the Pennsylvania coal mines.[42] The Maryland charter came in 1827.[43] The first stone of the Baltimore & Susquehanna was laid in the summer of 1829, although of course a charter from the Pennsylvania legislature was much delayed.[44] The full line did not open until 1837.[45]

That was a frustration to many in Pennsylvania, causing a political split there. As one western Pennsylvanian put it: "The people of this section are as patriotic as any in the state, but they do not like to be forced into acts of patriotism. They wish to be left to regulate that according to their *free will*."[46] Other middle-states locations, like Wilmington, Delaware, asked in public meetings for a railroad connection.[47] In deference to this trend in public opinion, a Philadelphia newspaper advised, "Whatever may be thought of its feasibility or expediency," no "sentiment of jealousy, or selfish apprehension," should be allowed toward the B&O.[48]

Even that paper, however, thought it odd that Baltimore should be surprised at opposition in the Pennsylvania legislature to its attempts to intercept with its railroad the trade of the Pennsylvania canal system, built mostly with Philadelphia capital. "If the Legislature thinks proper that the trade of west Pennsylvania should go to Baltimore, so be it. Thither then will also go the surplus capital of Philadelphia."[49] Was it not ludicrous to think that trade would overload the capacity of the Pennsylvania canal system? And when it did, would there not be time enough for the state to consider railroads of its own? Baltimore was being so kind, a Philadelphia editor wrote, "they desire to go with us to the main sources of our inland commerce, and there relieve us of all they possibly can."[50] Baltimore was, wrote another, welcome to prosperity drawn from its own resources and enterprise, "but they cannot expect us to be so totally lost and insensible to our own rights and interests as to desire their elevation by our depression."[51] Pennsylvania eventually largely acceded, with restrictions, to the B&O's desire to build through the state to Ohio. Did it have to throw away the rest of its trade? It was the constant business of Baltimore, the Philadel-phia press claimed, "to misrepresent the policy, views and feelings of this metropolis to excite hostility and ill-will towards her in the minds of the inhabitants of the interior." The cry from Baltimore residents always was to give and give "and if aught be withheld, they can scarcely set bounds to the measure of their revilings."[52] Perhaps Baltimore should be honest, declare war, and mark its route through Pennsylvania with the point of a bayonet. "It is a very bad thing to have bad neighbors."[53]

The response out of Baltimore was caustic. Why did Philadelphia not call a town meeting to petition the state legislature to erect a wall at the Maryland line and thus stop the attempt of Baltimore and parts of Pennsyl-vania from seeking the best market?[54]

Philadelphia had nine fine hotels to welcome western merchants, splen-did walks and streets, and 30,000 houses.[55] But that prosperity was vulner-able to change. By 1829, Pennsylvania was having some trouble attracting financing for its mixed canal/rail system and admitted that its public works had been badly managed. But having invested so much, it could hardly abandon them now.[56] Rail projects, such as the attempt in 1831, based in Carlisle, to build a Pennsylvania-owned railway to the Susquehanna coal mines, called the Columbian Valley Railroad, failed to raise enough sub-scriptions to get started. The Carlisle promoters were as hard on the Penn-sylvania legislature as were the Baltimore people. It was not the want of means, they said, but the want of spirit, "the absence of soul and energy in the body politic." This was not appropriate, they thought, "in a country of adventure and industry."[57] Still, it was 1846 before Pennsylvania chartered the Pennsylvania Railroad to replace its unusual mixed system.[58]

The third of the B&O's initial challenges was the landscape itself and the challenge of building through the terrain using technology that was still largely experimental. In hindsight, the company overdid it. In contradis-tinction to later American practices, it followed the English model and laid the iron-stripped wood rails on a granite base. Its bridges were marvels of masonry and architecture, and the price was very high. Unfortunately, the population was not as dense as in England, and, consequently, the revenue was not nearly so great. It took the B&O until 1853 to reach Wheeling and the Ohio River. Nevertheless, the line did proceed at a steady pace, to the amazement of all who visited it—and of all who carped at it from afar.

Early in December 1829 the famous locomotive trials took place in En-gland, dominated by Robert Stephenson's engine, the *Rocket*.[59] The reporter from the *Liverpool Times* was ecstatic. "Whether the caricatures which represent a steam engine as flying like a balloon through the air, shall ever become anything more than a caricature may be doubted; but such have been the achievements of science and art within the last three quarters of a century, that it is really difficult to fix any limit to their future conquests." To place a steam engine on wheels and make it move by itself was remarkable enough, but to make it move at considerable speed pulling considerable weight was a revelation. "You may glide along with this bird-like speed [30 miles per hour] with as little discomfort as if you were sitting in your arm chair, reading a volume of the diamond poets."[60]

The steam engine impressed the whole world. It never tired or slept. "It appears," wrote an American journalist,

> a thing almost endowed with intelligence. . . . It opens and shuts its valves with absolute precision as to time and manner; it oils its joints . . . and, when any thing goes wrong which it cannot of itself rectify, it warns its attendant by ringing a bell. . . . It is the kind of machine, and permanent realization of the genii of eastern fable, whose supernatural powers were occasionally at the command of men.[61]

Things were more modest, but equally fascinating, in Baltimore. For nearly a year visitors had been riding horses along the route. In other countries, one noticed, such projects went through populated areas, but here there was a "wilderness of wood." It was striking to emerge from the forest and see hundreds of workmen with their tools.[62] At the end of December 1830, the directors and officers of the B&O held a quiet test of some of the first trackage running west up the Patapsco Valley. A horse at a trot (9–10 miles per hour) pulled first two cars loaded with 15 tons of freight, then twenty-five passengers, then eighty-four passengers, the 1.5 miles from the Pratt Street Depot in Baltimore to Carrollton Viaduct.[63] There followed several days of trials, attracting growing crowds.[64] An installment of $5 a share fell due on B&O stock, and not a single stockholder gave up his stock. And why should he?

On January 4, 1830, a new car of "singular appearance" went onto the road with two floors, the upper for men and the lower for women. Forty people packed it for every trip, and the railroad, modest as it was, had to organize the trade and sell tickets.[65] The railroad had become "a fashionable resort for parties of pleasure." It had been designed for merchants and farmers but had found a new audience who wanted to plunk down 9 cents for a ride.[66]

Masonry viaduct over Patapsco River. It was built by the B&O for the ages. Library of Congress

Tourists were even more attracted when the railroad reached Ellicott's Mills in May 1830, charging a fare of 75 cents for the 26-mile journey.[67] The president of the Camden & Amboy Railroad took that ride, as did the president of the projected Lexington & Ohio and numerous members of Congress. The viaducts were impressive, the scenery spectacular. The railroad at times ran 60 feet above the river valley and the landscape. It was "picturesque, wild and romantic scenery." The granite crossties gave way in the newer section to wood as the line snaked past Buzzard Rock in a cut 58 feet deep. The experimental stage ended and the line opened for regular scheduled travel.[68] Neither cold nor rain slowed the interest. "The desire to ride on the Rail Road is so general, that it is not found practicable to gratify one fifth part of the applicants for want of a greater number of cars."[69]

Riders outdid themselves writing memoirs or letters to the editor about their experience riding along the First Division of the Baltimore & Ohio Railroad. A Philadelphian reached Baltimore by steamboat and canals, marveling at the dinner on the steamboat and at a canal boat that gave "the security and comfort like those of a spacious and solid mansion." Still, the ride on the new railroad was the highlight of his trip. Railroads had been written about extensively, but one could not get an adequate idea without inspection. The scenery on the railroad was "diversified in its grace and dignity," and the "gothic cast" of the bridges was "well adapted to the massive and lofty character of the rocky pass." More marvelous still was "the spectacle and feeling of the cars, while they rapidly and surely glide along the rail." But they were "vulgar and insignificant" compared to what the rider could imagine in the future when he could foresee a locomotive engine "with fire and smoke, whirling at a rate of thirty miles per hour over the mountains, and the three hundred miles of similar road, by which the western region is to be connected with the Atlantic border." He wished that President Andrew Jackson could be with him in the car, as it would surely mollify his tendency to veto internal improvement bills. On the bell of a barge, he read the lines: "Now Fulton is gone, and he is no more,/ But he left us his genius to carry us from shore to shore."[70] Another passenger believed, "Such great progress in so short a time has never before been made in any undertaking in America."[71]

A visitor in June said that the new railroad was an "all engrossing topic" with the people at Baltimore, as well it should be. The line was often elevated above the tops of trees,

> at one time riving hills and rocks, and holding converse with the spirits of the earth,—at another mounting, as it would appear, into the ethereal regions—Here wending their way along the base of a wall of solid granite, with its beetling top frowning on, and [rather] threatening the pigmy pageant below,—and there, on the other side, skimming along within a few feet of a precipitous height—Then they will be borne *over* roads and *under* roads; over rivulets, and ravines, until they fall in company with the gentle Patapsco.[72]

Former president J.Q. Adams rode, and so did DeWitt Clinton, the canal promoter. Gross income from passenger traffic was $1,000 per week by summer. Clinton wrote: "I know of no manner of travelling more pleasant than on the rail road, as you escape the smoke, noise and jar of the steamboat, the dust and jots of our common stages, and the snail pace of the canal boat; nor do you suffer apprehension from the common casualties of travelling, as you are in great personal security, and proceed along equally swift and sure." It took three hours to make the round-trip, with horses changed four times. "It is truly an interesting sight," Clinton wrote, "to see a long line of carriages following in procession, covered outside and inside with a dense mass of passengers, enlivened with gay plumes, dresses, and smiling faces, the carriages darting swiftly along."[73]

Property values along the line did increase, but there was some concern about the cost of the line. All respected the chief engineer, the former West Pointer and explorer Stephen Long, but wondered whether he had not erred in building the line as a monument for the ages. The Carollton Viaduct was supposed to cost $54,000 but cost $76,000 in the end. The Deep Cut was $129,000, not $88,000 as planned, and the passage across the ravine at Gadsby's Run cost more than $91,000, not the $15,000 that a good wooden bridge would have cost.[74] The directors promised that the route would level out, that new techniques would lower costs, and that the Third Division, from the forks of the Patapsco to the planned inclined plane passage over Parr's Ridge, would cost no more than $7,000 per mile.[75] They reassured stockholders that banks were willing to loan the company money and that the project was sound. A few among the original group were selling their stock, but it was a small fraction compared to the total number of shares. There was a perpetual charter, which protected the stock from taxation. Also the amount of dividends was not limited, so the entire profit, when it came, could be divided among the stockholders. B&O stock sold often through 1830 at par.[76]

Late in August 1830 there appeared a new phenomenon on the B&O line to Ellicott's Mills: the steam locomotive. Peter Cooper of New York had manufactured a little upright boiler engine making only 2 horsepower and named appropriately *Tom Thumb*. It conveyed fourteen people riding on the engine itself to the halfway house 7 miles from the city at a speed of 14 miles per hour. Early in September, the *Tom Thumb* went all the way to Ellicott's Mills, negotiating the sharp 400-foot-radius curves in the Patapsco Gorge perfectly. It proved, observers said, that it was not necessary to look to England for perfectly adequate locomotives.[77] Among the passengers riding behind the new locomotive on its early runs was Charles Carroll of Carrollton, who had recently celebrated his ninety-fourth birthday.[78]

It was not all glory. There was, for example, considerable fussing among Baltimore merchants about the plan to bring the railroad right to the wharves. The smoke of the engines and the din of their running would be an abomination in town. Carts could not back up to the curbstone anymore. "It will be unsafe to trust horses in any carriage, or to ride or hitch them any where in Pratt Street, where cars and steam engines are passing along. No lady will ever come into Pratt Street in her carriage and shop across a railway." Parents would be apprehensive about sending children on errands or to school.[79] Most cities in the early years of railroads banned steam, forcing the lines to switch to horses at the city limits. But that restriction soon gave way to the pure force of economics. A report in September 1831 had the railroad running happily, albeit with cars drawn by horses, down Pratt Street to the docks, with other vehicles passing over the track easily at all angles.[80]

Other cities, of course, thought less well of the B&O than did Baltimore. A New York City paper wrote that Maryland was "a clamorous, selfish sister," where everyone fed upon speculation and greed and railroad building.

> They launched forth in these measures, beyond their ways—in the face of reason and experience.... Every public man . . . that could be caught on his way to Washington, was huddled into a rail road car—rode up and down—through the deep cut, the great cut, and the long cut, as we do rickety babies on the Battery. His pulse was felt, his heart touched, and his pocket . . . picked. He was questioned and teased, and perplexed with their rail roads.[81]

There was some room for reflection upon steam power when a member of Parliament misjudged the distance at the opening celebration for the Liverpool & Manchester line and was run over and killed by a speeding locomotive.[82] But the excitement and the financial promise remained greater than the danger in most people's minds.

The wilderness was tamed, and that was attractive. "Here in the very heart of the lonely and unexplored forest, amid the forbidding solitudes of the mountain wilderness, still the home of the bear, the wolf, and the eagle, where the mossy rocks [are] yet in their rest of ages beneath the shadows of the eternal forests—even here, the hand of improvement has been laid, and the repose of nature is broken forever."[83] The "March of Mind" transformed everything—maybe at the expense of peace and quiet, yet to the diminishment of boredom and poverty. One could not walk the streets of cities and towns, wrote a visitor in 1829, without noticing improvements in houses and in markets and in mode of dress. "Ask any man whose recollection extends back forty or fifty years, to draw for you a contrast between the state of things at that period, and that which exists in our day." Steam was the great delight of the philanthropist because, more than any sermon, it was improving the condition of everyone. The writer was proud that "God made us Americans."[84]

In 1856, reminiscing about these early days of railroads, Horatio Allen, an engineer for the New York & Erie Railroad, talked about his experience in August 1829 running the first steam locomotive in the United States along a tiny rail line connecting the canal of the Delaware & Hudson Canal Company in Pennsylvania with some of the company's anthracite coal mines. The railroad was built of hemlock timber, which had cracked and warped some in the sun, but Allen drove along 300 feet of straight track where the line crossed a creek on a 30-foot-high trestle.[85] On that, at least, he was sure he could operate the locomotive *Stourbridge Lion*, which he had acquired on a trip to England. And so he proceeded with a coal-fired machine of about 9 horsepower, with a boiler mounted on four wheels, and on either side "an engine the pistons of which work on rods extending to one pair of wheels, and thus by a crank motion, the whole is made to move."[86]

"The impression was very general that this iron monster would either break down the road or it would leave the track and plunge into the creek." But the risk was only to one person. "As I placed my hand on the throttle valve handle, I was undecided whether I would move slowly or with a fair degree of speed, but believing that the road would prove safe, and preferring, if we did go down, to go handsomely and without any evidence of timidity, I started with considerable velocity, passed the curve over the creek safely, and was soon out of hearing of the cheers of the vast assemblage." He ran the engine 3 miles, the whole length of the line, reversed the valve, and returned.[87] It was a modest thing, but the crowd was overcome with the thrill and the promise of it. There was no going back to things as they had been.

CHAPTER 2

———◦◦◦———

The Vast Machinery

n June 1830 a thin octavo book appeared titled *A Treatise on Rail Roads and Internal Communications, Compiled from the Best and Latest Authorities: With Original Suggestions and Remarks.* It was written by Thomas Earle of Philadelphia. Naturally, given its date, it concerned mostly canals. There were only 41 miles of railroad in operation in the United States. But the projections indicated that the rail system would expand quickly outside the little mining railroad experiments and beyond the Baltimore initiative. The B&O had 13 miles of track at that time, and there were several mining railroads in Pennsylvania beyond the Mauch Chunk, including the 8-mile Mount Carbon Railway and the 10-mile Schuylkill Valley Railroad. Planned were lines from Boston to Lowell, Providence, and Albany; the Camden & Amboy in New Jersey; the Newcastle & Frenchtown in Pennsylvania; the Mohawk & Hudson in New York; the Charleston & Hamburg in South Carolina; and a line from Lexington to Louisville, among others.[1] It was a little less than impressive, but a little more than idle talk.

If Baltimore was active, so must be Boston. Massachusetts, often criticized by others for being true heirs of the Puritans in morality, was never considered less than enterprising. Bostonians, therefore, were shocked at being characterized by others as timid participants in the new age. A New Hampshire editor, noting that "the cradle of Liberty was rocked by no wearied hand," thought now that a "demon of terror" had gotten possession of Boston. "The idea of a railroad costing $50,000 freezes her blood; and rather than unclench the fist of avarice, and with a trifling sum to secure an immense future income, she will squander her advantages to be secured by the enterprise of her neighbors. The axioms of Poor Richard teach a different economy. Massachusetts should lead, not follow."[2]

Stephen Salsbury, in his study of the Boston & Albany project, confirmed that between 1790 and 1820, Massachusetts grew by 30 percent, compared to 150 percent for the United States as a whole. The response of cities to the stimulus of both the success of the Erie Canal and the promise of rail technology was quite different. Boston, Salsbury says, was conservative, Baltimore daring, and Philadelphia panic-stricken and imitative. In Boston a "railroad clique" sold the idea of building railroads, then took responsibility for operating them.[3]

Railroad building to Massachusetts was a challenge to history. The "Yankee" was considered to be the typical innovative American, especially native to New England.[4] The first person to propose a railroad in Massachusetts, and later president of the Boston & Worcester, was Nathan Hale, descendant of the Revolutionary War patriot of that name.[5] It reminds one of Charles Francis Adams of the famous Adamses later taking the reigns of the Union Pacific. As a colony Massachusetts had spent $2 million on the Revolutionary War at a time when it had much less wealth than in the 1820s. A man at Salem, writing under the pseudonym "Old Farmer," thought that a railroad would be so beneficial that no one would complain of "private sufferings." He reminded his brother farmers that it was the age of improvement and that Maryland had more railroad mileage than Massachusetts. "Shall old Massachusetts, the old Bay State, the cradle of liberty, of arts and religion, now become mean and niggard? God forbid."[6]

Nor did "Old Farmer" stop there, writing a series of letters to his local paper. In one, he expressed a belief that a railroad to Albany would be a good state-owned enterprise that could bring prestige and ensure that the state's reputation could "forever be guarded against vexatious monopolies, from the proprietors and their speculating agents."[7] In another, he touted the practicality of a western railroad. The West was the best market for Boston cod. Fish coming by way of New Orleans had to be stored in a hot and damp place before going upriver, whereas by rail they could avoid that terminal and slow transport altogether. Woolen and cotton goods from the textile mills of Massachusetts would benefit also.[8] Another letter pointed out the benefits to the state of getting the sections in touch with one another. People on the coast were better acquainted with Liverpool and Manchester than with the trading community to their west. They knew nothing beyond "what they discover in a barrel of Genesee flour." In his opinion, many state legislators thought more of the pudding made from that flour than they did of railroad building. As long as they could feed on puddings made of flour coming by canal, why should they trouble themselves on the topic of railroads?[9]

Other elements of public opinion seemed to agree. A public meeting at Windsor, Vermont, during the winter pointed out that the New England climate was not well adapted to canals. If regional legislatures did not understand the need for railroad building, they should be flooded with petitions from town meetings.[10] Windsor people went farther, suggesting that the Erie Canal be filled in and two railroads, one for passengers and one for produce, laid on top of it.[11]

The Massachusetts governor spoke in favor of railroads in the spring of 1829. The "convictions of experience," he said, had been added to knowledge of the laws of nature and mechanical power in their favor. And internal communication needed help. "If there is any thing sound in the maxims of political economy, if the counsels of the wise and the conduct of the prudent can avail anything, they teach the importance of facilitating intercourse, reducing the cost of transportation, saving manual labour, opening new avenues to trade, and new markets to produce." Massachusetts must not fall behind New York and Pennsylvania in this.[12] He recommended a road to Albany and the Hudson River as the most advantageous, having the unique advantage perhaps of diverting some New York State trade from New York City to Boston. It was inevitable that this should be done, if not by this generation, then by the next. "Inquiry and investigation will remove obstacles, which prejudice, from the novelty of this species of improvement, has hitherto opposed, and give that confidence in its success which will ultimately either impel by a sense of public duty, or influence by motives of private interest to its execution."

First, however, two questions had to be answered: What is the most practical form for a railroad? And by what agency will it be built? Some in the state opposed all railroads, arguing that they would benefit only Boston. The governor thought that argument should not prevail with the more enlightened. "If there be a place in the Commonwealth so situate[d] that it will feel no direct beneficial influence from the occupation of this new highway, neither is there a place which will be prejudiced, *in its essential interests,* by its construction." Boston, as it grew richer by the railroad, would add more tax revenue to state coffers.[13]

In January 1830 Edward Robbins and James Hayward, appointed by the legislature of Massachusetts to study railroads, visited rail lines in Pennsylvania and Maryland. They noticed that already there was a striking impact on real estate prices in areas that had railroads. They felt that engineers had good data to suggest that railroading was viable technically, and capitalists whom they interviewed were sanguine about the economic stability of the new companies.[14] By March there were four bills before the Massachusetts legislature with the thought of building railroads from Boston to the textile town of Lowell; from Boston to Providence, Rhode Island (maybe with a branch to Taunton, New Jersey); and eventually from Boston to Albany. Although the legislature on that occasion rejected the idea of the state's taking shares (shortly changing its mind), it was not averse to encouraging private enterprise in railroads.[15]

There was immediate debate in the press on the question of state aid, with proposals emerging for the state to loan the railroads money or to take one-third of the stock.[16] A leading light, Theodore Sedgwick Jr., wrote that many felt that internal improvements were not a proper enterprise for the state. Why not? Railroads were "the great Machinery, the greatest by far, in an age in which Machinery has produced changes, with which, in the same time, nothing in former periods, bears any comparison." Maybe the state should not be involved in every little branch, but it should influence and control the main highways as trustee and manager for the people. A railroad to Albany would reduce the fare to that city from $9 to $4.50 and save a day's travel. Some 29,000 people used the route each year, and that could easily triple with the new facility. Was it possible that the citizens of Massachusetts "whose glory is their mechanical talent, who live by manufactures, by the arts of machinery, should deliberately with their eyes open, in the face of public opinion, in the face of satisfactory experiments in Europe . . . shut their eyes to such palpable advantages?" Physical and moral changes went in parallel, and Massachusetts could not limp along in the rear of either.[17]

Humorists loved the legislative debate. A poem in the *Boston Daily Advertiser* went: "We are told, Mr. Speaker, that we'll travel this road / Twenty miles in an hour, with twenty tons load; / And all this to be done, sir, with a gallon of steam; / By jinks, Mr. Speaker, 'tis a pretty smart team." Apologizing for wasting time with members eager to go home, the speaker concluded: "Sir, I'm not flat, and I knows what I knows, / And I shan't give my vote, till I know *where* it goes."[18]

State ownership was not to be, but state stock subscriptions were forthcoming, as were appropriations for surveys. The governor lobbied to change the state constitution to allow railroad corporations to have limited liability for stockholders, unlike Massachusetts manufacturing corporations at the time, in which stockholders were individually liable for corporate debts.[19] By the time the line to Albany was finished in 1842, it had a capital investment of $9 million, only one-third of which was from private sources. It was clear, however, that without private initiative it would not have started when it did.[20]

The first charters in Massachusetts were those of the Boston & Lowell, Boston & Worcester, and Boston & Providence. The charter for the Boston-to-Albany project, known as the Western Railroad, came in 1833 and eventually incorporated the trackage of the Boston & Worcester. These lines were true "common carriers" from the start and almost immediately profitable.[21]

A survey of the Boston & Lowell, 23 miles, was made early in 1830. The cost estimate was approximately $7,000 per mile for a single track and $13,500 for a double track.[22] There was talk of extending this northern route one day through Nashua and Amherst, Massachusetts; Rutland and Burlington, Vermont; and on to Ogdensburg, New York.[23] Even though one bill after another was "decapitated" in the state legislature, even though sectional jealousies were rampant, even though the initial attempt at getting a stock subscription to the Boston & Lowell failed miserably, and even though there were still complaints that Massachusetts was "slow to believe," it was a start.[24]

There was a large rail meeting at Faneuil Hall, Boston, on June 3, 1830, to consider "the means by which the trade and prosperity of the city of Boston may be most effectively promoted and secured." The sense of the meeting was that the railroad was able "to overcome time, weight and distance, to an extent far beyond what the powers of any thing else can accomplish." Prevailing opinion in the state was that a railroad would be a safe investment for capital and that the city of Boston, which would benefit most, should not be a passive spectator but instead place representatives on the rail's board of directors. The railroad was not a temporary palliative but a benefit for all future time.

As usual with these meetings, there was, in addition to the presentation of statistics, an emotional appeal:

Let our time and attention and our means be devoted to the accomplishing of this most important work; let the minds and energies of our most enlightened and patriotic citizens be consecrated to this object, lest our widened and spacious streets, our markets, our city wharves and other splendid improvements should testify to posterity, not the wisdom and public spirit, but the short-sightedness and ill directed efforts of the present generation.

The city should not build the railroad itself, but it should not sit idly by either.[25]

Deep doubts, however, remained. Laying aside constitutional objections to state aid, a Boston editor asked, was it expedient that the city corporation of Boston subscribe $1 million to the railroad as was being proposed (and eventually accomplished)? Things were too "vague and abstract" for that, he thought. Would the railroad cure Boston's ills? Would it really draw trade away from New York City? Or would merchants who now went on buying trips to New York by steamboat simply find easier access by rail? Would New York City not get the main advantage of a railroad from Boston to Albany?[26]

A letter to the editor of the same paper expressed similar doubts. The railroad, that writer said, was just a "wishing cap" in the interest of speculators and not for cool, reflecting people. "Rash and miscalculating men" had already expanded the number of houses, stores, and wharves in Boston in the recent past far beyond the probable needs of the city, and rents consequently had fallen. Would a large city debt for the payment of rail bonds not make the current "enfeebled state" worse? Estimates were that a railroad could be built for $7,000 per mile, but the ones in England were costing $100,000 per mile. Yes, Baltimore was moving. But would it not be wise for Boston to "see the result of *her* game, before we throw the dice"? A few hoped to win a prize in a lottery in which others would buy the tickets.[27] Another correspondent thought the city was already misusing credit and that people were living beyond their means. All those people had to do was raise the specter of impending ruin and public bodies would come forth with money and trample the rights of the minority. Was not government framed to regulate rule by a few?[28] Poor people would see their taxes triple. Was Boston ready to assume such an "appalling" responsibility?[29]

Apparently, it was. When the Boston & Worcester began full operations in 1834, it had two 6-ton Stephenson engines from England, the *Meteor* and the *Comet*, as well as an American-built engine called *Yankee*. After 1836, it used all American locomotives, mostly supplied by the William Norris Company in Philadelphia. "What an object of wonder!" wrote one B&W passenger. "How marvelous it is in every particular! It appears like a thing of life. . . . I cannot describe the strange sensations produced on seeing the train of cars come up. And when I started for Boston it seemed like a dream."[30]

There was some delay before anything concrete could be reported in Massachusetts in the way of construction. Late in 1832, two steam engines for the Boston & Lowell arrived from Liverpool.[31] That line was completed in the spring of 1835.[32] The Boston & Worcester and Boston & Providence opened for business that summer.[33]

Early negative opinions in hindsight must have seemed remarkable, with Boston & Lowell, Boston & Worcester, and Boston & Providence stock selling in 1835 at 20 percent above par.[34] The Boston & Providence cost $1 million, right on estimate. Based on already existing stage and packet traffic, which the railroad would attract, it was not unreasonable to expect a gross income for the railroad of $200,000 per year, even assuming there was not an increase in trade.[35] Elkanah Watson, an elderly gentleman from New York writing in 1830, could not imagine why people would oppose the Lowell railroad. Future ages, he wrote, would seek in the "scattered archives of the present committees" a history of important progress, not "sneering ridicule."[36] Adjoining states agreed. An editor in Portsmouth, New Hampshire, noticed in 1835 that the state had expended about as many dollars as New York and Pennsylvania had millions. But it still needed to be involved in railroads, maybe by connecting Portsmouth with the Boston & Lowell. It was time to stop "groping in darkness" and make a beginning. "A Rail-Road in New Hampshire! In this little State! Indeed, this would be something new!"[37]

The effect on Boston was obvious. The Boston & Providence Railroad had invested $250,000 in Boston real estate by mid-1835.[38] Brick buildings rapidly replaced wood ones.[39] There were plans in 1835 to level the heights at Green's Garden in order to use the earth to fill up water lots at the termination of the Lowell road. A company had purchased the estate of William Pratt at the intersection of Pearl and Milk and planned a line of warehouses at a cost of $47,000. Elegant dwelling houses were going up everywhere in new railroad subdivisions.[40] The Boston & Worcester depot was to be built on land owned by South Cove Corporation, and streets were to be extended to connect the new lands with the city proper. The Boston & Lowell depot went up on a large tract near the Canal Bridge, which had been artificially raised above tidewater and opened for development.[41]

Such impacts on Boston were written about well into the future, both in imaginative literature and in scientific sociology. William Dean Howells, in his delightful book of essays *Suburban Sketches*, classically chronicled the life of railroad commuters in Boston in the 1870s, and Sam Bass Warner's *Streetcar Suburbs*, published in 1962, shows in detail how the "weave of small patterns" in late-nineteenth-century Boston was heavily influenced by its rail system.[42]

There was no question that the threat to drive into the state of New York by Massachusetts aroused New York City and led to the development of its own New York & Erie route. "Cities as well established as ours have fallen before the efforts of rivals in commerce," according to an article in the *New York Spectator*. Commerce in all history had "changed the face of countries." It had caused Tyre and Alexandria and Venice to fail, and that could happen to New York City also.[43] New Yorkers, someone wrote, were "in a state of extreme trepidation and alarm. If there was an irruption of Tartars, or the Goths were descending in hordes upon the city from the north, there could be no more visible consternation" than when the Yankees pushed their Western Railroad toward Albany.[44]

In some ways, the South, particularly South Carolina and Georgia, was more prescient in seeing and reacting to the industrial changes than were some areas in the North. New York City and Philadelphia were for different reasons originally complacent in the rail age during a period when Charleston was quite active.

There was a proposal in late 1827 to construct a railroad from Charleston to Hamburg (a town now defunct but located across the Savannah River from Augusta, Georgia).[45] The South Carolina legislature chartered such a route in January 1828. At around 170 miles, the distance was ambitious for the time, about equal to that between Boston and Albany.[46] Several parishes sponsored a meeting that month in the U.S. Court House at Charleston to request from the legislature funds for a survey of the Charleston & Hamburg and to complain about the restrictions in the charter. "If the contemplated Railway did not more interest the community than a common speculation a disposition to grant as few privileges as possible to the Company might be expected," spokesman Timothy Ford wrote. However, it was a work worth encouraging on public grounds, as it would affect Charleston's status as a major seaboard trade center in a future of technological change.[47] Also in January, visitors could see a miniature railroad laid down on one of Charleston's wharves. It illustrated that one man with his little finger and without much effort could move three bags of cotton weighing 1,000 pounds by this method.[48]

Merchants in Charleston, however, were worried. "The contemplated Rail Road hence to Augusta," one wrote, "is much spoken of, but very few with whom I have spoken seem to be at all sanguine of its completion."[49] However, subscriptions to the new line went better than expected, with $100,000 being subscribed by the spring of 1828, mostly by people of small means but strong local patriotism.[50]

West Point–trained U.S. engineers visited the city in January 1829 to talk about a railroad running to the west, but many in the city thought river improvements would be better. Henry Shultz, the indefatigable promoter of the town of Hamburg and also of the railroad, made strong arguments but did not succeed well. Wrote an editor in Augusta, Georgia: "His services and claims were . . . coldly disregarded and neglected by the people of Charleston, who fancied themselves secure in the trade they had obtained." Shultz, thought the writer, would get no credit if he succeeded in the railroad and would be blamed if he failed. "His active and persevering spirit will be clogged and controlled by numerous others of a less penetrating and decisive nature."[51] Early in 1829 the South Carolina legislature chartered three railroads, from Augusta (Hamburg) to Charleston, from Columbia to Charleston, and from Orangeburg to Charleston. They were to be of wood, topped with strips of iron, the iron to come from England at $62.50 per ton.[52]

In this southern project, as in all projects in the South, there was a philosophical aversion to applying for government aid, particularly federal aid. But that did not stop the Charleston & Hamburg line (officially the South Carolina Canal & Rail Road Company) from sending William Aiken and Alexander Black to Congress in February 1829 to ask for a $250,000 stock subscription.[53] Perhaps the company felt this was a modest request, as the federal government was not being asked to build the road. However, a writer at the *Charleston Mercury* opposed any involvement by Congress, even if it were technically legal and beneficial to the city and state. Such a request was against the "political creed of South Carolina" and would hurt the state in its fight against the assumed powers of the federal government in general. The request put South Carolina's senators and House members in a difficult position.

> Respect for the Company, and a patriotic desire to aid in the accomplishment of their great undertaking, will of course impel them, on the one side, to exert all their influence in support of the memorial, whilst they will find themselves positively inhibited from doing so, on the other, not only by their own avowed

and well known principles, but by the solemn protests of the State against the right of Congress to grant the application.[54]

The company kept up the requests to Washington for a year. "We don't want to offend your principles," rail president William Aiken wrote the South Carolina representatives in 1830. "This is different than other internal improvement plans." The federal government would be "joint proprietors" with individuals under a state charter.[55]

Nothing more came of the South Carolina applications any more than a similar approach to Congress by the B&O.[56] Partly it was the times. The great age of federal largesse to American railroads was well in the future. And South Carolina's representatives in Washington refused to push it personally.[57] One wrote that he hoped for the success of the railroad "but we do not wish to see it done by an open and barefaced bribe from the General Government. . . . Other States may be willing to be bribed and bought by a mercenary system of Internal Improvement, but we hope South Carolina will not."[58] The company itself rejected the offer of a $100,000 state loan on the grounds that it contained too many restrictions.[59] Many around the state approved rejection of all aid, wishing that the proceedings of the company asking for aid could be blotted from memory. A company "led by foreigners," wrote the Columbia *Southern Times*, would be a disaster. Was Charleston to be given up, "is South Carolina to be looked upon as swerving from her principles, because a few money-mongers and haranguers are able to stir up a meeting . . . when many of the leading citizens were out of Town?"[60]

Still, there was frustration evidenced by rail promoters about the governmental philosophy in the South. A local newspaper editorial put it bluntly: "We look upon it as certain, that the day is near at hand when the silly dogmas incorporated in what is termed the Southern policy will give way to the plainest dictates of common sense and political wisdom."[61]

Sectional differences can be exaggerated. It has been common in historical literature to suggest that the South fell behind industrially in the early nineteenth century and did so because of a stubborn adherence to a Jeffersonian agrarian philosophy.[62] In 1908 Ulrich Phillips, in his pioneering study *A History of Transportation in the Eastern Cotton Belt to 1869*, saw this as a distortion of the record. "Railroads with steam locomotives, when once invented," he wrote, "were speedily recognized as dwarfing in importance all that had gone before; and nowhere was their acceptance more eager than in the staple regions of the South." Phillips noted that southern planners realized that the railroad was not an end in itself but a means of developing resources and strengthening society.[63]

A recent student of the topic of southern rail development, Aaron Marrs, has taken a similar tack: "Railroads never lacked for advocates in the antebellum South. Southerners quickly grasped the utility of this new mode of transportation. Boosters employed a three-pronged attack when urging construction, pointing to the railroad's technological advantages over other forms of transportation, the economic benefits the South would receive, and the fact that railroads would bind the country together, preserving both the union and slavery." Where historians have gone wrong in analyzing the prewar South as industrially backward both technologically and ideologically is their narrow focus on raw economic statistics, particularly in the era before the great southern rail expansion of the 1850s, as well as a failure to look beyond economics to the social atmosphere surrounding railroads. Marrs argues that the social result of railroads was not perceived as necessarily limited to the northern model. The South thought it could have both an efficient rail system and an efficient slave economy. The contemporary northern and subsequent academic interpretations that the two were incompatible, and that the railroads would automatically bring the end of slavery, were far from the thinking of progressive southerners in the 1830s. The South, Marrs claims, "pursued modernity in service to its own demands."[64] The region was determined to adapt only to a point, beyond which more traditional economic and cultural considerations would prevail.

The impression that the South was lukewarm to railroads emerges strongly from reading the political and philosophical speeches and letters of the southern political leadership of the time, but it becomes less evident when assessing public attitudes through the reading of newspapers and the tracing of actual railroad building progress in the South. It is clear that there was a philosophical split in the South over the inroads of corporations and the appropriateness of government aid and that the same philosophical divisions existed in the North. No stronger anticorporate, antirailroad, antigovernment stance can be found anywhere during this period than New Hampshire.[65] The debate on state aid from Massachusetts had not been too different, in tenor or outcome, than in South Carolina. There was tremendous suspicion of the doings of the state legislature in New York, not to mention disrespect there for Congress and fear of congressional power. President Andrew Jackson's Maysville Road veto of 1830 and the war over the chartering of the U.S. Bank suggest that the federal government did not desire such authority very much either.[66] Research in day-to-day sources appealing to the public rather than the intellectual or political elite leads one to the conclusion that the Civil War was fought between two advanced industrial societies, not one industrial and one agrarian.[67] It is significant that Charleston was not only not remiss in joining the railroad age; it was as early and as vigorous in doing so as was Baltimore. Kentucky, Georgia, North Carolina, and Virginia were not far behind in starting; nor were they necessarily inferior in building and operating new railroads.

One could argue that the South goaded the North into building the kind of railroads that went beyond mere service lines running from mines to canals and rivers. And South Carolina's efforts encouraged other southern states to enter the rail field. In May 1830, when visitors could ride 4 miles on the railroad at Charleston, a letter from Fayetteville, North Carolina, said the progress in South Carolina showed the difference between enterprise and inactivity in internal improvements. Fayetteville's own trade would get away from it soon enough unless the activity of its neighbor drove it from "*our* inertness."[68]

Considerable detailed analysis made its way into the press. Charleston, according to an article in *The Southern Review*, was situated well to make a commercial emporium, but nature had so far done more for it than art. Rich inhabitants of the backcountries of South Carolina, North Carolina, and Georgia, who traded with Charleston, had to transport their produce at great expense and often wait weeks or months to receive their supplies. The freight ate up profits, and merchants could not control inventory. Capital that would otherwise be active was dormant much of the time due to such inefficiencies. The climate was a problem for three months every year. Rivers were unhealthy and often low. The roads were "sandy, heavy, and hot," and animals suffered. The railroad would help all that. Studying the history of other successful rail projects, it was no trick "to trace these effects to rational causes, and apply them to our own situation."[69]

The same kind of comment was heard elsewhere in the South. At Richmond an article commented: "If we had slept on, we were lost. . . . In an age, when the spirit of Internal Improvements is abroad; when turnpikes, and rail-roads, and locomotive engines . . . are the order of the day, can we expect that the citizens of the Western part of Virginia will submit to our apathy?"[70] The spirit of improvement was abroad, and Virginians "must be blinder than bats at mid-day, not to see our own true Interests—and weaker than children, not to act upon them."[71] Some good blow must be struck at Richmond, an editor thought, "which will arrest the attention of the inconsiderate, dispel the fears of the timid, animate the luke-warm, and cheer the enterprising and persevering."

Perhaps the little Lynchburg & New River road, organized in the fall of 1831, would not quite do that, but it was a start.[72] It was the same with the Winchester & Potomac. "Shall *Ruin* drive its ploughshare through our streets, and no effort be made to stay its progress?" asked a small-town sub-scriber in Virginia.[73] Another Virginian proposed:

> Let us picture ourselves a train coming rapidly down to James river, across which is a rail-road viaduct; on this an elegant lo-comotive engine is in waiting, which, in one day will carry the whole train to Baltimore, without delay, without unloading; on the other side are negroes, resting on their long poles, inviting the produce to the safe conveyance of their boat . . . down to Richmond at the rate of 1½ miles an hour. . . . Which of these, I ask, will tempt the trade?[74]

In Huntsville, Alabama, people talked about a possible railroad connecting the Tennessee River valley with the Mississippi.[75] In Raleigh, North Caro-lina, people discussed altering the state constitution to accommodate rail-roads. "The welfare of the State," a writer from Fayetteville, North Carolina, thought, "requires that Raleigh should remain the Seat of Government, that a mammoth rail road, to build up a large commercial town in the East should be constructed."[76] The superintendent of public works in North Carolina visited Charleston to study its railroad.[77] A paper in Milledgeville, Georgia, predicted that fifty years hence all markets would be served by steam.[78]

Things on the ground in South Carolina moved quickly. In June 1829 iron for the new railroad arrived via the ship *Hogarth* from Liverpool.[79] In January 1830 rails went down in Line Street at the upper extremity of Charleston.[80] In the spring of 1831 there were 6 miles in operation, built on piles. The company owned two wood-burning steam engines (including the iconic *Best Friend of Charleston*), which were "carrying materials for the continuation of the road, and passengers for amusement."[81] This was a time when the B&O was testing a new engine, named *York*, made in Penn-sylvania, which was to institute regular steam service on its line.[82] Similar experiments were proceeding on the Mohawk & Hudson in New York with a temperamental engine with a modern-looking horizontal boiler from the West Point Foundry, named *DeWitt Clinton*. That line had ordered a sec-ond, *Robert Fulton*, from England.[83] However, on both the B&O and M&H, regular service was still mostly horse-drawn.

The locomotive Atlantic, *built at York, Pennsylvania, for the Baltimore & Ohio Railroad. Train pictured in 1832 was typical of the look of earliest railroading. Bettmann/Corbis*

In October 1831 a delegation from Charleston visited Baltimore and studied its railroad for a week. They were impressed: "You scarcely turn a corner without seeing the mechanic employed in erecting some new edifice." The B&O seemed to have energized the local population in a way that the Charleston & Hamburg project had not. "Could the people of our State see the manner in which the city road is built, the money expended on the same, and the advantages already derived from it by this, they would certainly rise *en masse* and render all the aid in their power to the enterprising company of our Charleston Rail Road, who are now contending, with all their might, against the unfortunate prejudices of a large number of unenterprising people."

The B&O was, at the time the Charleston people visited, only 26 miles long, but by the end of the season it would run to Frederick, 60 miles, making it the longest railroad in the United States.[84] It had by then a "locomotive steam machine" running at 13 miles per hour. A passenger commented on that: "For our part, we have no desire to be carried, by any mode of conveyance, more rapidly than at the rate of thirteen miles per hour." And even that was too much at night.[85]

But it universally fascinated.

> No traveller passes through Baltimore without stopping to look
> at the solid far stretching construction destined in the minds of
> its projectors to divert the commerce in the productions of the
> fertile valley of the Ohio from its natural channel the Mississippi,
> and bring it to the port of Baltimore. No one who has a few hours
> to spare, would be able to frame a decent excuse, if he could
> not say on his return to his wife and children and wondering
> neighbors, that he had taken an airing on the great rail road.[86]

Baltimoreans calmly said that their railroad would be a ten-year project.
Tell that to a Charleston resident about the South Carolina railroad, the
committee thought, and he would "die of despair."[87]

As with Baltimore, there was controversy at Charleston about how the
railroad would interact with city streets. There was concern, too, about accidents.[88] There were some broken axles, and the boiler on *Best Friend* exploded. But in the spring of 1832, with the railroad extending 15 miles and
enjoying the first contract in America for carrying mail, its managers were
happy with it. "It was not to be imagined that in the bustle and confusion
of construction, arrangement, conveyance of materials, and travelling upon
an *unfinished* road with engines of great weight and power, and complicated
structure, agents somewhat new and inexperienced in the management of
them, and laborers of well known thoughtlessness and inattention to their
own safety, accidents of various nature would not occur."[89]

There were 1,300 hands engaged in building the railroad. Due, the directors said, "to the extreme difficulty and expensiveness of occasional hiring,"
the railroad purchased sixteen slaves.[90] This policy continued. Contracting
for the Second Division in 1838, the railroad again used slaves, both its own
and others loaned by planters along the line. "It is found," wrote a reporter
at that time, "that the slaves, under proper direction and superintendence,
are doing the work in the very best manner." It considered the question
settled whether a railroad could be built by slave labor "on terms mutually
advantageous to the Company and to the Planters."[91]

In the fall of 1832 the Charleston road was 73 miles long and had four
new locomotives on order.[92] It had passed through the troublesome Cy-
press and Four Hole Swamp and constructed the difficult bridge over the
Edisto River as well as the inclined planes at Horse-pen Ponds.

Cost was running about $5,000 per mile, and hope for profit was great.
Augusta and Hamburg collected about one-fourth of the cotton crop

B&O depot at Frederick, Maryland. Construction is typical of early solid style. Library of Congress

grown in the United States. Revenue from cotton alone could be $100,000 per year, and as many as 40,000 passengers might ride annually. Property rose in value. "It is like opening a river navigable by steam, through a country without even the advantages of a water communication, or even good roads."[93]

At the annual meeting of the South Carolina Canal & Rail Road Company in the spring of 1833, the company operating the Charleston & Hamburg made the claim that its locomotives traveled over more miles of railroad daily than any other system in the world and that it had successfully used its pioneering steam power profitably for 18 months.[94] There was a celebration of its completion to Hamburg in October 1833, at which time one wag said: "It is cheaper to owners of negroes to pay their passage on the Rail Road than to make them walk on the common road free of expense."[95] A Charleston paper commented:

> Taking into view the unpopularity of this undertaking, when first commenced; —the many difficulties which were encountered in its progress, arising from the inexperience of those who had the management of it—the prejudices which it was necessary to overcome—the little assistance which was received from the State or corporate bodies, and the almost inexcusable

supineness of our capitalists, it is somewhat surprising that it has been so nearly completed in so short a time.

The company president, William Aiken, was, the editor thought, "a hero."[96]

There were detractors. The new railroad was 5-foot gauge. Although there was no fixed gauge in the United States at that time, it would not be long before 4 feet, 8 and ½ inches became the standard and the wider-gauge lines were an anachronism.[97] The writer "Smeaton" from Richmond noticed that the complete road had cost more than $1 million for 135 miles, whereas the early estimates were for a cost of no more than $400,000. It had eventually agreed to a state loan of $100,000, and for that pittance it was mortgaged to the state. It was hard to find workers willing to risk their lives in the swamps, and thus came the necessity to use slave labor. There had been an incident in New Orleans, as that city started to build a railroad across swampy ground to Lake Ponchartrain, when a "gang" of fifteen African-American workers had tried to board a railroad car reserved for whites. A battle ensued with pistols drawn.[98] And locomotives were impressive, but expensive. Those on the Charleston line had so far cost more than $100,000.[99]

But to the majority the Charleston railroad was an impressive success. The final estimate of the cost per mile of the South Carolina road was $6,500. This compared to $18,366 for the Camden & Amboy, $25,000 for the Newcastle & Frenchtown, $50,000 for the Mohawk & Hudson, and $30,000 for the Baltimore & Ohio.[100] Landowners along the way had contributed slave labor and given right-of-way for free.[101] Most thought that revenues would quickly pay the $150,000 debt of the company.[102]

When a passenger locomotive arrived downtown, station agents hoisted a red flag in celebration. Freight was plentiful. The locomotive *Hamburg* arrived one day in May 1834 hauling twenty-six freight cars loaded with cotton.[103] Already in the summer of 1834 Colonel Stephen Long went west to survey for something called the Mississippi & Atlantic Railroad, which might someday run from Charleston to Memphis.[104] In 1835 the Charleston line made an 8.5 percent return on its capital.[105] Any reflecting mind, a writer in *The Southern Patriot* thought, would understand "that brighter auspices are now shedding their influence over the city." Even if the railroad should never extend beyond the boundaries of South Carolina, there would never again be talk of grass growing on the streets of Charleston.[106]

A Washington paper, surveying the rail activity in the South at the end of 1833, expressed amazement: "A new start will be given to the whole country South of the Potomac, in the career of prosperity, when zeal in the advancement of State welfare, and enterprise in developing State resources, shall have occupied the minds of the leading politicians of the country, instead of metaphysical studies how to contrive causes of reproach and pretences of jealousy against the federal government."[107] The Charleston & Hamburg by the summer of 1836 carried fifty passengers every day each way, up 2,300 percent from the number that had once gone by stage. The Pennsylvania system carried more than 300 per day, three times that of one year earlier. These were facts to make people think, "if they are capable of thinking."[108]

An 1833 pamphlet titled *Friends of Internal Improvement in the Southern States* and published in Augusta, Georgia, made strong arguments highlighting the advantages of the South. These included saving labor expenses through the use of slaves (the financial advantage said to be about 50 percent). Values of land through which the South Carolina Railroad ran were up 1,000 percent, and its running expenses were one-fourth those of railroads in the North.[109]

The benefit could not, however, be estimated solely by looking at income and expense. There were the obvious increases in land prices, the obvious decreases in freight costs for farmers and merchants, but also less quantifiable yet real advantages to society at large. David Swain of Raleigh, North Carolina, estimated that the greatest gain the railroad brought was knowledge. Local people, not only direct investors but also those who might be taxed for rail support, had to study the question of the new technology and become informed about regional trade. There was no more accurate criterion by which to judge the advance of a country in intellectual improvement, he thought, than the scale upon which physical improvements were constructed. "The existence of one gives rise to the other," and a good common school education presaged both.[110]

There was comment on a more illuminating scale as well. A man addressing a rail convention at Oswego, New York, in the fall of 1835 said that nature had "cut out the mighty garment, and left man nought to do but sew it up and fit it to use." The world had exhausted resources throughout history in war and architecture; railroads were better. Greece and Rome wasted their energies on monuments without significance to commerce. "Look at modern Europe, covered with abbeys, castles, and the nonsense of Kings." It was time to stop crying about monopoly. And if a railroad *were* a monopoly, then it was a fine one "in which the rich man's money is expended making the poor man's road."[111]

The real honor, however, was not so much in philosophy as in imitation. As soon as the Charleston & Hamburg started running, a new railroad was proposed to connect Columbia with Charleston. There were "suspicions and fears and forebodings" of the type that "can be conjured up against the most rational and best-conceived attempts," but the counterargument was to simply look at the regional railroad already operating. The "fever and chill of public cupidity," the new promoters hoped, would yield to persons judging a project from "a thorough knowledge of its merits, and a high stake in its success."[112] Natchez, Mississippi, began promoting a railroad to the interior, again with the thought that "the objections of the prudent and timid were capable of being dispersed by demonstrations founded on the deductions of reason and experience."[113] Richmond shortly projected and began work on the Richmond, Fredericksburg & Potomac Railroad.[114]

John Bruce, president of the Winchester & Potomac, wrote that despite some temporary "derangement of private property," everything about railroads was coming up roses. Farmers were delighted. "To some plantations, but little known, it will give a local habitation and a name." The railroad would transport grain easily accumulated along the line by threshing machines, plaster ready for immediate use, and bulky produce. "Connected, through the Baltimore and Ohio rail-road, with such a stream of trade and travel, can any one doubt that vast benefit to Western Virginia will flow from the completion of the Winchester branch of that improvement?"[115] A Richmond man thought, "If our men of capital prefer to invest all their money in brick houses in town, in bank stock, or to lend it out to individuals, they probably err." If southern farmers insisted on continuing eking out a scanty living by traditional methods, then "other men will come from other quarters and buy up their lands and make them what a kind Providence intended them to be."[116] The South had its advantages for railroad building. The climate was mild, slave labor was available, there was plenty of wood, and the topography was advantageous.[117]

Perhaps Baltimore, Boston, and Charleston were in the first tier in the advancement of local fortunes by proprietary railroads, but New York, New Jersey, Pennsylvania, and Georgia were in the next tier chronologically— and no less ambitious or successful. By the late 1830s many smaller places— Wilmington, Richmond, Raleigh, Petersburg—were into the fray, as were the more western states of Ohio, Illinois, and Indiana.

Typical of the assessment of the stakes was the speech titled "Address to the Citizens of North Carolina," given to a railroad convention assembled in

Salisbury, North Carolina, on October 17, 1833. "We forbear," Thomas Polk began, "to press upon public consideration the melancholy and destitute condition of our state, because we think late circumstances . . . have awakened the public mind to a full sense of our humiliation." It was time to abandon nostalgia for old times and old forms. The true wealth of a country depended upon its capacity for production and industry and upon the wealth of its citizens. Too many prosperous people were moving out of North Carolina. Railroads would bind the sections together economically and the classes as well by providing a common project for intellectuals and common laborers. Few abstractly contemplated the resources of a "sovereignty" like the state of North Carolina, but they were numerous and included the right to borrow money to finance railroads. "We can get any sum we wish on 100 year terms." North Carolina had been burned by internal improvements before, as early as 1818. So had other states. But the dead hand of the past must not constrain the possibilities of the future. This time, however, it should be in the control of businesspeople and not politicians.[118]

The hope to be free of political interference was a chimera, but the rest of it was somethng that could and would come true.

CHAPTER 3

Network

he state of New York illustrates the way in which a history such as this must be selective. In the spring of 1832 the state legislature granted thirty-two charters for internal improvements projects with aggregate capital topping $24 million. A list of the railroads incorporated at that session includes New York & Erie ($10 million capital), Lake Champlain & Ogdensburg, Watertown & Rome, Utica & Susquehanna, Ithaca & Geneva, Duchess Railroad, Buffalo & Erie, Towanda Railroad (Rochester to Attica), Hudson & Berkshire, Schoharie & Otsego, Danesville & Rochester, Aurora & Buffalo, Rensselaer & Saratoga, Brooklyn & Jamaica, Saratoga & Fort Edward, Otsego Railroad (Cooperstown to Collierville), and others.[1] What had been isolated lines, ribbons of hope into the wilderness ending nowhere in particular, was by the mid-1830s a rail network generating traffic and profits and increasingly connecting major producers and markets. "These modern improvements are gaining every day upon public confidence and approbation," wrote a New Yorker in 1834. "In every part of the United States we observe notices of their present or prospective construction. The whole surface of our country seems destined to be decked at no distant day, with these striped ribbons."[2]

The system grew in impressiveness as well as extent. Most attractive to writers and tourists, the equivalent in pull to what the Mauch Chunk Railroad had been ten years earlier, was the Portage Railroad finished late in 1833 and connecting the eastern and western sections of Pennsylvania's canal system.[3] The line, running 31 miles from Hollidaysburg on the east to Johnstown on the west, cost $3.5 million and reached an elevation of 1,400 feet. It was the prime example of the early rail practice of overcoming mountains through the use of inclined planes and stationery steam engines pulling passenger cars up considerable grades with ropes or cables.[4] One traveler, reporting that he was raised 1,172 feet and lowered again 1,400 feet in six hours "by complicated, powerful and *frangible* machinery," concluded that "the idea of rising so rapidly in the world, particularly by steam or a *rope*, is very agitating to the simple minds of those who have always walked in humble paths." He added, "The sense-absorbing power of the Mountain Rail-Road entirely deprived us of eyes and ears for external objects for a time."[5]

Solomon Roberts, one of the engineers on the Portage Railroad, gave a vivid description of its building in an 1878 address. His pay was $2 a day, and in April 1831, his team began a survey of the mountain route. They slept in tents covered by buffalo robes, and ate venison and turkey, an adventure more than a hardship for a 28-year-old.[6]

A description by a traveler from Massachusetts in October 1834 was typical of the awed reaction generated by this particular section. After passing through fifty-two locks on the canal branch from Juniata to Hollidaysburg, he reached the Portage Railroad. There were ten inclined planes separated by flatter sections negotiated by ordinary locomotives yet passing over a "stupendous viaduct" and through an impressive tunnel. It then took nine to ten hours to make the passage across the mountains, but the man thought that with the planned installation of a double track along most of the route the time might be no more than five hours. Sylvester Welch was the chief engineer on the project and had, in this observer's estimate, "raised a monument to the intelligence, enterprise, and public spirit of Pennsylvania, more honorable than the temples and pyramids of Egypt, or the triumphal arches and columns of Rome."[7]

Such enthusiasm was typical. Wrote a passenger in 1835:

> The sensation whilst rising by this process, cannot be described. It is fearful, yet exhilarating. You shrink from it, yet you love it. There is something unspeakably grand in the operation. Awaiting our arrival at the top stood the locomotive, spitting off its

The first locomotive to cross the Allegheny Mountains. Bettmann/Corbis

steam spitefully, as if vexed by our long delay. It was like a spirited steed champing the bit and impatient to be gone. We were soon under its control; and giving a few rapid puffs, it bore us onward in a majestic line with accelerated velocity, until our speed was absolutely bedizening.[8]

The Portage Railroad was even more dramatic at night. "As we neared the mountains," wrote a night visitor, "their lofty precipices were dimly visible and terrifically grand. It was a moment of intense interest to us all; the scene was new; the ascent by night formidable." The cars seemed to that passenger to hang on the steep plane, and the single rope seemed hardly thick enough as "every heart seemed to tremble at the possibility of its rupture." But it was a unique experience, one that seemed "like Jacob's labor to be carrying us to the very heavens." It was a tribute to an age of enterprise. "These Pennsylvanians think the region of Time is over; they are building for eternity."[9]

Until the charter of the Pennsylvania Railroad in 1846 started that state on its path to rail dominance, it did not boast the most extensive rail system, but it certainly could boast of the most prominent rail feature in the United States. A man who saw one of the ropes for the Portage Railroad coiled on the docks at Philadelphia described it as something that would make an "excellent line to fish for Leviathans and Sea Serpents." Manufactured at Poughkeepsie, New York, the coil was 6 feet in diameter, 7 and ½ feet high, and weighed 3,500 pounds.[10] Crossing the Allegheny Mountains was no longer done "with the lumbering coach and sweat of tugging horses; with sleepless eye and wearied frame for three or four long nights of dog-watches; but with a single stage, seated at your ease in the steam-drawn car." It was triumph over nature:

> The high places have been leveled for the thoroughfare of the nation's commerce, her secluded fastnesses have been opened to the "garish blaze of day," and the tall tops of the ancient trees stir with the breath of an age, the going forth of whose spirit is like a whirlwind. Here, where but yesterday, the foot of the wandering hunter had been, is seen the long train of heavy cars hurrying onward, laden with the merchandise of the east and west, and making the slumbering echoes of the old woods roar with the noise of their coming. Truly this road may be regarded as a beacon of improvement, exalted upon the mountain top for the admiration of the world. What American can stand and cast his eyes over the wide spread country below him, the happy view of whose beauty and resources greet him on the right hand and on the left, and not feel proud of his nation and its growing fame? God grant that we may not forfeit our high privileges by lapsing into sins that shall call down upon us a doom more dreadful than that of Sodom!

The descent might remind one of the trip of Aeneas to Hades, and the ultimate goal—Pittsburgh—might seem like "the city of smoke and din," but the dominant reaction, whether looking at the "pontic architecture" of bridges or the cleverness of the tunnels, was to be awestruck.[11] The Portage Railroad, wrote one author in 1838, "exhibits in a surprising manner the amazing power of mind, and its vast superiority over the corporeal world." Wild and beautiful scenery, he thought, gave way, while proceeding at 8 miles per hour on the five inclined planes of the Portage Railroad, to "awful and stupendous."[12] Statistics demonstrated usefulness amid all the romance. In 1835 the Portage Railroad carried 50,000 tons of freight and 20,000 passengers.[13]

Of course, the impressiveness of the journey over the Portage Railroad tended to mask the fact that the Main Line system of Pennsylvania, of which it was a part, was largely a failure. A Philadelphia man said his state's system was "an ambitious connection of land and water, consisting of two railways separated by a canal, and of two canals separated by a railway—happily elucidating the defects peculiar to both methods of transit, with the advantages of neither."[14]

Philadelphia did strike out in a modest yet interesting way on rail development independent of its canal system. In 1835 a sort of commuter railroad, the Philadelphia, Germantown & Norristown, was finished to the Philadelphia suburb of Germantown.[15] Late in 1832 it tried out a new locomotive built by Philadelphian M.W. Baldwin.[16] There was some talk of an all-rail route from Philadelphia to Baltimore. "Such a road would make a vast change in the existing condition of things—and especially in the winter season; when passengers and mails have to be dragged through the mud—hub deep in many places."[17] The Germantown railroad had elegant passenger cars, named *William Penn, Thomas Jefferson, Benjamin Franklin, James Madison,* and *Robert Morris.* People in the early days of the line flocked to the depot to cheer when the train came in.[18] When 20,000 people attended the funeral of the great Philadelphia entrepreneur Stephen Girard in 1832, there were, no doubt, some thoughts about what his ilk could accomplish for the city in the future.[19]

There was a modest start, too, in Delaware, when the Newcastle & Frenchtown Railroad connected the Delaware River to the headwaters of Chesapeake Bay, a distance of 17 miles. At Frenchtown passengers could board steamboats for Baltimore.[20] The line got its charter from the State of Delaware in 1829 and was completed in February 1832.[21] In the spring of 1832 there was a trial on the Newcastle & Frenchtown of a "Locomotor" steam engine designed by Stephen Long. It covered 27 miles, the last 3 miles in a little more than seven minutes, "the steam blowing off the safety valve, under a pressure of seventy-five pounds to the square inch."[22] That year a reporter noted that the cars on that railroad were free of dust and concussion and perfectly safe—"the passengers may read or converse as if they were in a hotel or in a steam boat."[23] By the summer of 1833 the line had four locomotives, and one of them had been used seventy consecutive days, 66 miles per day, without repairs or delays.[24]

New York State was understandably complacent about railroads at first. The Erie Canal began operations in 1825, at the very beginning of the era of America rail. It was a model for a state-owned and -operated canal system. Should there not be some interim simply to enjoy this triumph, as well as New York City's increasing foreign and coastal trade? But it was not to be, particularly given the activities of Baltimore and Boston and given the rapid growth of New York City's outlying suburbs, leading to a plethora of omnibuses and the threat of an urban landscape knee-deep in manure. Many ancillary rail lines, which soon developed, like the Delaware & Hudson, the Stonington Railroad, and the Camden & Amboy, though not located in or chartered by the State of New York, were to be also part of its domain. Baltimore and Philadelphia might battle one with the other, but either might well outdistance New York City in the process.

Early discussions in New York were grandiose and vague. There was in 1830 some discussion, for example, of a railroad from New York City to St. Louis.[25] The *New York Spectator*, however, thought that the mania following the steam trials of locomotives in England was premature. Some of the canal enthusiasm had been overdrawn: "A canal to the moon, to be filled with nectar, was spoken of, and we don't know but an aqueduct from New York to Liverpool might have been in contemplation." Now the rage was for railroads, and the papers were so filled with the subject that "we have become wearied with the very looks of the letters which form the words." Baltimore was completely carried away, and someone in New York had even published a pamphlet in 1830 suggesting a railroad from New York City to Lake Erie and then "to the remote West as far as the country is settled." Another pamphlet proposed a railroad from New York to New Orleans, a project in which DeWitt Clinton was interested. A writer in Buffalo thought the New York–to–Mississippi River idea was simply too big and that skepticism had gone out of favor to the point that he who doubted was damned. Ambitious projects were well and good, but a New York City editor despaired that "we shall one day see some rail-roads other than printed ones."[26]

Intra-urban commuter railroads, beyond those simply for the purpose of bringing a trunk line to dockside, seemed more practical and eminently applicable to large cities. A Philadelphia writer speculated in 1830 about the advantages of such lines in spreading out the population of cities and allowing development far from the port itself and on higher and healthier ground, where people could have large lots and be separated from smoky industrial areas.[27] A New York City writer in 1833 enumerated the advantages of connecting the "cultivated garden" on the east and west ends of Long Island with New York City, which exceeded 100,000 in population. Thence an easy connection could be made across Long Island Sound with Stonington, Connecticut. "Why Sir, while penning this," the planner said, "I almost imagine myself flying with inconceivable rapidity."[28]

New York City certainly could use some change. In May 1831 a reporter decided the streets there were in the worst condition ever with "piles of manure—the mountains and pyramids of earth" lying "in huge cones and heaps" on every street in the city. There was no hope for removal anytime soon. Broadway was the most beautiful street in America, the reporter thought, and the worst to pass through. If it did not get better, then people would stop riding in carriages, as at present there was a "jolting of our bodies into a jelly, and the danger of dislocating our bones."[29] Apropos of that, the Harlem Railroad opened its subscription books in the spring of 1831 with the goal of taking rail passengers north up Manhattan Island into still rather rural Harlem.[30] Ground was broken for this line in March 1832.[31]

Perhaps the earliest specific action directly affecting New York was the incorporation by New Jersey in 1830 of the Camden & Amboy, connecting indirectly as it did New York City and Philadelphia.[32] The claims of the railroad, said the governor of New Jersey at that time, were "full of interest," and connecting canal and river systems by rail made sense.[33] A railroad across New Jersey, one New York paper wrote, would make New York City and Philadelphia "like two neighboring towns, where they could go and pay morning visits summer and winter."[34] Some complained that such a railroad would interfere with the Morris Canal, but such people, wrote a correspondent to the New York Herald, did not "keep pace with the progress of information and liberality."[35] When the subscription books of the Camden & Amboy opened in March 1830, stockholders took $1 million worth in ten minutes, and many interested persons had to be turned away.[36]

New York State also launched operations. One of the earliest successes was the Mohawk & Hudson Railroad connecting Albany with Schenectady.[37] That road, the first of the components of what was to become the New York Central system, bragged in 1831 that it was built on rock and used only steam power.[38] Its engine, named DeWitt Clinton and built at the West Point Foundry, became, like so many of the earliest steam locomotives, subsequently famous in rail fans' pictorial lore.[39] It shortly added an engine from England, dubbed Robert Fulton.[40] "To the superficial observer of a rail road . . . it may appear slight and incapable of continued use," a contemporary commented. But in the fall of 1831 it carried 900 passengers per day.[41] Regional feeders, like the Troy & Vermont, the Catskill & Canajoharie, the Patterson & Hoboken, and other modest lines were planning and building, too.[42]

New York's very success engendered competition. The "natural jealousy" of Pennsylvania and Maryland led those states to construct railroads instead of canals and connect with Great Lakes ports that opened earlier in the spring. DeWitt Clinton himself, the promoter of the Erie Canal, proposed in 1831 that New York build a railroad along roughly the same route

A later copy of the DeWitt Clinton *on the New York & Erie with a string of cars.*
Bettmann/Corbis

as taken by the canal. He and others urged that New Yorkers should not pay
attention to the argument that it would interfere with the existing improvements. These had been of value, wrote a merchant, "but if, in consequence
of some recent discoveries and improvements, we may anticipate that they
cannot compete with the projects of our neighbors, the part of wisdom,
certainly is, to avail ourselves at once of these improvements, and rely, as we
have hitherto done . . . on our enterprise for remuneration."[43]

The railroad thus projected was to become the New York & Erie, the
state's major pride and frustration. Chartered in the spring of 1832, it did
not reach its goal of Dunkirk on Lake Erie until 1851 after several years–
long interruptions, threats of bankruptcy, and legislative wrangling.[44] The
New York Herald once claimed that the "most prodigious speculations" and
"amusing money-making intrigues" in the world were connected with the
Erie Railroad, including arguments over its terminus. "There is as much
diplomatic talent now extended on the Erie Railroad location," an article
in 1836 stated, "as would preserve the balance of Europe for twenty years—
make peace between Mexico and Texas."[45] There were regular charges that
the Erie Railroad was intended to make fortunes for a few on Wall Street at

the expense of the broader community.[46] In its slow progress west, however, the Erie was not much more dilatory than the B&O, which reached Wheeling on the Ohio only in 1852, or the much shorter Western of Massachusetts, which took until 1841 to reach Albany.[47] These were more ambitious projects than the first short lines, and they ran through territories where there was little traffic and where financing was a continuing difficulty.

The beginnings of the Erie road seemed auspicious. In the autumn of 1831 Eleazar Lord, who was as much the strong personality behind the Erie Railroad as DeWitt Clinton had been the one behind the canal of the same name, proposed that the state legislature charter a railroad running from New York City to Lake Erie. At the time, according to Lord's 1855 reminiscence, legislators thought the idea of incorporating such a gigantic line under one corporation and one charter "presumptuous and hopeless."[48]

In January 1832, New York City citizens met at the Bank Coffee House to consider what they then called the "Hudson River Rail Road Company," a different line proposed to be constructed to Albany with capital of $3 million. There was concern about competition with river and canal traffic but no question that such a line would be useful after the close of steamboat navigation at least.[49] At the same time, there was discussion of a rail line from Brooklyn to the eastern end of Long Island. If that could be accomplished, it would be a short journey to Boston.[50] Mrs. Francis Trollope, visiting America in 1832, wrote that Americans, "could they once be persuaded that any point of the ocean had a hoard of dollars beneath it, I have no doubt that in about eighteen months we should see a snug covered railroad leading direct to the spot."[51]

The charter passed that year. The Erie road had capital of $10 million. It was to begin within four years and reach Lake Erie within twenty. It used, strangely, a 6-foot gauge, perhaps the widest in the United States.[52] There was a section in the charter prohibiting the Erie from connecting with any railroad leading into Pennsylvania or New Jersey. Eight persons in widely separated counties became commissioners and received subscriptions, with Lord as chairman of the board. Lord applied to Congress to fund a survey but failed to get any money from that source. But pressure from Congress members representing western states convinced the federal government to lend members of the U.S. Army Corps of Engineers to do the survey as volunteers. In 1833 the company reached the $1 million in subscriptions required by the charter to permit formal organization. Therefore, the New York & Erie officially organized on August 9, 1833, with Lord as president. In 1835 Lord resigned as a condition of the railroad's being taken over by the bankers and merchants of New York City, who, it was hoped, could infuse desperately needed capital.[53]

Directors broke ground for the Erie on November 7, 1835, when 40 miles were put under contract in forty-four sections taken by twenty-six different contractors from among seventy bidding.[54] At first the charter allowed only extension to Albany, but an amendment in the spring of 1836 provided for it to run to Lake Erie.[55] The Erie's chief engineer, Benjamin Wright, had consulted with other eminent U.S. civil engineers on exactly how to proceed.[56] It was hard to see far ahead, but the goal at that time was to build a railroad nearly 500 miles long, estimated to cost more than $6 million, and terminating at Dunkirk on Lake Erie.[57] That town did not amount to much then, but the Erie promoters said it would be a "place of consequence" when the railroad reached it.[58]

Eventually Dunkirk would join such places at Cairo, Illinois, and Port Beaufort, North Carolina, as railroad might-have-beens. But there was no foretelling that. There was a proposed tunnel under the Hudson River to communicate with the new railroad.[59] Buffalo underwent a boom on the very prospect of a new connection.[60] One journal there doubted the substance of the promises, however, claiming that the Erie was a stock speculation and "one of the merest bubbles on the street."[61] Yet whatever the road's faults, it seemed necessary to try. After all, railroad stocks were better than insurance stocks, as no one could burn up a railroad; something would always be there.[62] The first annual report of the company, issued in 1835, noted that "nothing short of a connection between the Hudson and the Allegheny can save to the city of New York the early trade of the upper lakes."[63] In 1836 the State of New York loaned its credit of $3 million to the railroad and began a series of remarkable debates in the state legislature lasting for years. Pennsylvania was ahead with its completed canal system in the competition for western trade, but Maryland and New York were also active. "The prize for which these sister States are contending is a magnificent one, and is richly worth all the exertions making to secure it."[64]

Americans, historian L. Ray Gunn has noted, until the Panic of 1837 accepted intervention in the economy as a "legitimate, indeed essential, function of [state] government." The justification was the public interest in stimulating economic growth through positive governmental action. It was a part of modernization, defined as the "enshrinement of the productive ideal," and there was at first little thought of any conflict between the goals of government and private industry. A modern and "restless" personality type appeared along with structural changes like differentiation, rationalization, and integration of social and political structure, as well as specialization of economic functions, the creation of centralized bureaucracies, and the expansion of markets. Localism and the dominance of community at the village level declined, partly due to the requirements of the new physical and organizational machinery. The United States during this period of its history was moving from a primarily agricultural, rural, and commercial society to an industrial and urban one.[65]

As with every other growing railroad, the Erie enriched and enlivened cities. Poughkeepsie opened new streets and underwent a building boom from 1833 to 1836, changing from a country village to a manufacturing city. There was a new sash and blind factory, a screw-manufacturing company, and a gun and rifle company, and carpet and chair factories were planned.[66]

But the going was not smooth. The state legislature authorized $3 million in aid in 1836, but not without considerable controversy.[67] A commentator defended the aid on the grounds that helping an ambitious trunk line was better than responding to every local request for a line to build up a particular town.[68] Other places tended to agree. "It is not for the legislature," wrote an editor in Virginia, "to build up or pull down towns."[69]

Still, the investment was heavy and the progress slow. The company suspended active operations entirely for a time at the end of 1836. "The concern was virtually broken down," Lord remembered. "The condition and prospects of the Company were utterly discouraging and deeply mortifying; the fanciful and improvident plans which had been pursued, and the overweening and boastful confidence which had been expressed. . . . now forced themselves in their true light upon the attention of all." The reports, he thought, were filled with "puerile, superficial, and visionary" notions, even with "hallucinations." When the Panic of 1837 struck, repeal of the charter was a definite possibility.

Somehow the line came to vacillating life again, though it received little support from either the press or politicians. The legislature investigated Erie operations, and although the 700-page report it produced mostly vindicated management, the line suspended operations in 1842, this time for three years.

Lord blamed petty New York politics and a speculative turn on Wall Street for the difficulties of a railroad that was a long-term and developmental proposition. "No public work involving the expenditure of millions, and affecting the interests of half a continent, was ever, after being persevered in during eight or ten years, through successive periods of calamity, and against the increasing opposition of rival interests, and political management, subjected to so relentless and so searching an ordeal."[70]

By the time the Erie suspended operations for three years in 1842, it had cost already more than $12 million, and there was despair that it would ever reopen, much less reach Lake Erie.[71] The estimate was that it would require an investment of at least $6 million more, and the directors, disrespected as they were in the state, had little hope of getting it.

As Lord remembered:

> The whole question of railway property, management, policy, morals, and legislation, has ... been brought into doubt, disrepute, and danger. There are on the outskirts of every profession some practitioners of insinuating and plausible exterior, who, lacking other intellectual gifts, and having, by means of a facile memory, picked upon some theory of their destined subject and some formulas of practice, fancy themselves qualified to perform the duties of their vocation. Being constitutionally deficient of understanding, discrimination, judgment—the faculty of analyzing, comparing, reasoning—the power of discerning and comprehending the relations of different facts of propositions to one another; of perceiving the force of evidence and argument—forming opinions of their own, and determining whether any fact of proposition is or is not proved by the evidence adduced, or whether one result or another will ensue from a given state of things or course of measures—they fearlessly go forward, trusting to their theory and their formulas, and justifying themselves by what they have read in some book, or quoting men who, for the same reasons, hold the same opinions.

Around these vacant managers gathered "sychophants ... and hangers-on."[72] Something better would be required.

Massachusetts was not standing idly while New York moved; it was advancing the Western Railroad all the while. There was a mass meeting at Faneuil Hall, Boston, in October 1835 to encourage more rapid progress on this road.[73] There was a subscription, with $1.2 million of stock taken that month, to extend the line of the Boston & Worcester west toward Albany, perhaps to meet with lines extending from there to the Massachusetts line at West Stockbridge, and perhaps extending on its own into New York State.[74]

New Hampshire people were impressed. Bostonians, an editor there said, "are certainly the strangest '*critters*' for '*going-a-head*' in the world. They have extended their internal trade to all parts of the country by rail roads, canals, &c. and already contemplate by means of a rail-road to Albany, to cut off a large portion of the internal trade of New York. They do every thing by steam."[75]

The Western Railroad was a more difficult project than those former ones in the state running through river valleys between industrial towns. This project involved "breaking a mountain asunder." However, it would be an avenue to the west by which many towns would connect. Boston pork and Boston beef would gain "elbow room" for sales in the larger market.[76] Consequently before 1838, the State of Massachusetts provided more than $2 million in aid to the Western road, with more to come.[77]

Irish laborers, using steam-powered construction equipment and working for 85 cents per day, made good progress. One particularly noticed machine was a sheet-iron scoop swinging by chains in a crane struck into hills and filled with dirt. It then swung around over a cart and dumped. The Irish called it "digging by stame," and local reporters said that "thus the hills are laid low and the valleys made high."[78]

Completion of the Western, however, was far off. More encouraging was the continued successful operations of the short lines: the Boston & Worcester, the Boston & Providence, the Boston & Lowell, and the Eastern Railroad (this last running from East Boston to Salem).

Perhaps foremost among the second tier of states that caught the railroad spirit was Georgia. A regional newspaper was, as early as the summer of 1829, "mortified at our apathy" in the internal improvements area.[79] It had been unfortunate for that state, wrote an observer in Macon late in 1834, "that public attention has been so entirely absorbed in the struggles of rival parties for power, and the schemes of ambitious politicians for personal aggrandizement, that but little thought has been bestowed on those works of permanent utility, which add to the wealth and resources of the state."[80] That had to change.

Georgia displayed a longtime inclination to use state power for economic improvements. The historian Milton Heath has called its stance "constructive liberalism" and traces it to a philosophy of society dating to the philanthropic purposes and planning tendencies of Georgia as a royal colony. The state took stock in canals and turnpike companies in the 1820s and undertook careful planning for a rail system to connect at Augusta with the Charleston & Hamburg.[81] Rail conventions in Macon and in Knoxville, Tennessee, in 1836 drew large numbers of delegates and came to a certain consensus.

There was, however, some caution, learned from difficult experience. The *Augusta Chronicle* in 1825 expressed fear that Georgia might be caught in the future, like South Carolina, "without a *source* to account for the internal destruction of the finances of the State." Boards of public works, as canal building had shown, could be dangerous, especially when dominated by northern and eastern "schemers." So often these people had a "butterfly" kind of talent, and their activities led to bankruptcy and the confiscation of the money of the state and the people. "No one can *then* be found to bear the useless blame; they have taken *early* care to screen themselves behind some clause in the charter, of which the people are ignorant—have fattened upon the big salaries, stockjobbing, and speculation."[82] With that caveat, things went forward.

After some local starts, three companies came to dominate: the Monroe Railroad Company, the Central of Georgia, and the Western & Atlantic (which was owned and operated by the state itself). The first received its charter late in 1833 and then, after a lapse, a renewed charter in 1835. The original route was from Macon to nearby Forsythe, Georgia, but things became more ambitious soon.[83] Grading started in 1836, and eventually the line (as the Macon & Western) extended from Macon to the new rail hub of Atlanta. The second, related to the Georgia Banking & Railroad Company chartered in 1833, received a charter in 1835, with Macon taking 2,400 shares. In 1836 it took the name Central of Georgia Railroad & Banking Company, with William Gordon, former mayor of Savannah, as president. The Western & Atlantic had its origins in a state action of 1836. John Calhoun had proposed in 1835 that the federal surplus, to be transferred to South Carolina and Georgia, be used to build a railroad through Georgia to Memphis on the Mississippi. The Western & Atlantic became that western outlet, completing its 190 miles from Atlanta to the Tennessee River in 1843 at a cost of $2.5 million.

Its developmental aspects made it appropriate as a state-controlled project. "The Western and Atlantic," historian Ulrich Phillips wrote, "is of large historical concern in two regards: it was the perfecting member in the well-devised railway system which made Georgia the keystone state of the South, and Atlanta the gate city from the northwest to the eastern cotton belt; and it furnished the most important example in American history . . . of the state ownership and operation of railroads."[84]

These three Georgia railroads were to operate as a "functionally integrated whole." They arose, Heath claims, out of "necessity, tradition, and established principles of social policy."[85]

Governor Lumpkin, speaking to the legislature in Milledgeville, the capital in 1835, noticed that there were no foreign wars or domestic panics. Crops were good, and there was an opportunity for the American character to accomplish the best things of which it was capable. Georgia should build a central railroad from the seaboard to the center of the state and eventually to its northwest boundary. It would serve as a key link in the "gigantic conception" of a line eventually connecting the Mississippi River with the Atlantic Ocean. "There will then be but little reason to inquire whether Savannah or Charleston will afford the best market, both being brought so nearly to the same standard."[86] A Savannah paper expressed the same feeling when analyzing a report on a rail line from there to Macon and approving the city council's subscription of 5,000 shares of stock. State pride required action, especially as other states built railroads.[87]

The Western & Atlantic originated as a reaction to plans that were promulgated at two rail conventions in 1836, one in Macon and the other in Knoxville, to discuss a huge and windy project called the Louisville, Cincinnati & Charleston Railroad.[88] The Central of Georgia (Savannah to Macon, 160 miles) was, like the other lines, slow to reach completion, and being confined to Georgia it did not figure centrally in the great strategies of settling America's so-called Near West.

Such a railroad as the Central had been discussed by the Georgia legislature since the end of 1829. Construction got under way in the fall of 1835 under the superintendence of J. Edgar Thomson.[89] In 1836 the railroad sent an agent to Europe to enlist 1,000 German workers, whose addition, some thought, would improve society in Georgia.[90]

One innovation with the Central of Georgia, which became common elsewhere, was to join railroad and bank, a method to finance the former and secure the issues of the latter. Such a bank "of large proportions and wide privileges" was also associated with the Louisville, Cincinnati & Charleston project, which was undergoing planning in 1836.[91] The idea of such banks was, "to ensure the construction of the Road, the *Means*, are to give the Stockholders of the Road the privilege of Banking, to such an extent as will yield interest on their investments from the beginning, and which will hold out a temptation to extend the Road as far as possible, by expanding the capital of the Bank with the extension of the Road."[92] Because it was thought that the hazards of banking were slight and the returns liberal by comparison with railroad building, the establishment of a bank would be a means to attract capital to a region and then attach its growth and the investment of its surplus to the progress of a railroad.[93] So popular was the device, at least until the Panic of 1837 put a damper on the economy, that Texas in 1837 granted a charter to the Texas Railroad and Banking Company to connect the Sabine and Rio Grand Rivers.[94]

Construction progress was steady and powered, it was said, by "a phalanx of Georgian hearts, panting in the race for state supremacy." In the spring of 1838, locomotives ran on 23 miles, and 65 miles more were graded.[95] The press reported that all three major Georgia railroads were going "swimmingly" and that the Monroe road would be in operation in six months.[96]

However, as with the Erie, the Panic of 1837 and its repercussions took their toll on Georgia railroads. The legislature rejected a bill increasing the capital stock of the Central Railroad & Banking Company that year and balked at appropriating another $3 million to continue the Western & Atlantic.[97] Recovery, however, was rapid. An analysis in 1839 found the Georgia Railroad & Banking Company a success unexampled in the history of railroads. It had then within the past three years completed 80 miles of railroad and graded 50 more. It earned annual dividends of 8 percent on the whole capital of the railroad and bank. Receipts were averaging $16,000 per month, and when completed to Greensboro and in a position to attract "the whole southern travel," it would earn $26,000 per month.[98] This contrasted with an average return on Virginia's railroads of less than 1 percent, and it highlights the dangers of generalizing about geographic regions.[99]

Although Georgia's effort was particularly notable, many other southern states became active in railroads in the 1830s and developed the entrepreneurial attitude to go with it. A paper in Washington, D.C., commented in 1833 that the constitutional scruples expressed by the *Richmond Enquirer* were out of date and out of style. "With the *Enquirer* . . . it is 'unconstitutional' to do *good*—it is 'unconstitutional' to have roads in Virginia. . . . But it *is* 'constitutional' to *do evil*" (for example by waging war).[100]

The Richmond *Whig* caught the spirit. Documenting the good success of the Richmond, Fredericksburg & Potomac Railroad in 1837, the editor admitted that

> it is . . . manifest that let the times fluctuate as they may, or be as bad as they may, this improvement, resting on the broad basis of public utility, will not fail to sustain itself, indemnify the stockholders, or justify the calculations of its projectors. And in contemplating its results, one cannot help regretting that more of the capital of the country which has been irretrievably sunk

in frantic speculations upon cotton and tobacco continuing to maintain a certain price, or in shaving and gambling operations, had not been invested in needful and judicious improvements, which, while they will always repay to the adventurer the legitimated yearly value of his money, at the same time promote public convenience, and adorn and strengthen the country. He who thus invests is a practical patriot, and will find his reward in the security and improving value of his investment, when the grasping speculator, who considered nothing but making millions in the short period, is dashed into pieces, by the retributive revolutions of trade.[101]

The overall impression of the works was enormously positive. "The Southern editors are all in raptures with their new railroads," wrote a reporter in New York City in 1838, and the editor of the *Savannah Georgian* had described with "infinite gusto" a flying trip on the Central of Georgia.[102]

One typical early southern effort of limited scope but great regional interest was the Petersburg & Roanoke, designed to connect the James and Roanoke Rivers. In October 1832 it ran an excursion with the locomotive *Roanoke* and 130 feet of passenger cars carrying forty people from Petersburg, Virginia, to a temporary depot at North Spring and returning, a round-trip of 60 miles. The freight rate was 15 cents per hundred pounds.[103] Although then only half its projected route was complete, it had constructed several substantial bridges.[104] There was a good harvest in 1832, and Petersburg, with its own railroad, prospered more than ever before—to a degree "not anticipated by even the most sanguine."[105] It was impossible, wrote an observer, "to convey to those who have not witnessed a similar scene, an adequate conception of the pride and pleasure which beamed from every countenance, when the Engine was first seen descending the plain from North Spring, wending her way, with sylph like beauty, into the bosom of the town; and, like conquerors of old, proudly bearing in her train, the evidence of the victory of Art over the obstructions of Nature."[106] With the completion of the railroad the next year, Petersburg was able to report a 35 percent increase in property sales and a great building boom. Perhaps, wrote an editor in Lynchburg, his town might expect the same if it could get a rail branch. "May she not hope that her untenanted store-houses will be filled up—the rents will advance—that the value of real estate and, with it, the value of produce, will be increased—and that all classes of the community will feel its beneficial influences."[107]

A regional paper hoped that this progress would quiet the criticism that "the *people* of Virginia are incapable of appreciating or acquiring the blessings of public improvements."[108] "Henry," writing to the *Richmond Enquirer* in the spring of 1833, said there were too many plodding wagons in Virginia yet making their slow way to market and that the business of farmers and farm towns was too much "liable to sudden and vexatious fluctuations." Virginia needed more canals and railroads and needed them right away, and it needed legislators who would cooperate.[109] A convention in North Carolina concluded that when people understood the truth about their situation, they would take their destiny in their own hands. "If there ever was a time for a people to rouse, and put forth a united, vigorous, and continued effort, it is the present." The "inert, dormant" condition of the South, the "benumbing incubus" that northern writers thought slavery represented, were partly mythological characterizations. Yet insofar as they were true, they required a practical and obvious response.[110]

The bridge on the wide James River, completed in 1838, was a particular pride. "There are longer bridges of less altitude and higher bridges of shorter span," wrote a Richmond observer, "but when the altitude and length of span of this bridge [are] taken collectively, there is perhaps not its equal in the world." Moncure Robinson, the chief engineer, had integrated courses of strong masonry with a wooden superstructure, complete with galleries and walks below the main floor. The bridge took two years to construct and cost $100,000 and was, most thought, worth every penny. "The work itself stands, like a mighty Colossus, bestriding the ancient Powhatan, destined to hand down to posterity both itself and its authors; and whose piers of imperishable granite will remain as proud monuments to remote generations of the present State of Virginia and her sons, as connected with the sciences and the mechanic arts."[111] There was plenty of capital available in the United States and in Europe, and there was "no reservoir of water so deep, but that it may be reached by a long rope and a good bucket."[112]

The Petersburg & Roanoke was mature enough to have an accident. In October 1833, passengers on that line noticed that the speed of their train had diminished, and finally the cars came to a standstill. They then realized that the locomotive had disappeared. The engineer jumped off when the engine detached from the train, and the locomotive ran on 8 miles by itself until the fire died. "As may be supposed the natives were not a little surprised at the strange apparition of this flaming monster rushing over the road unattended by any human being—some thought it was the tariff—some nullification—some said it was one of Gen. Jackson's Expresses, and

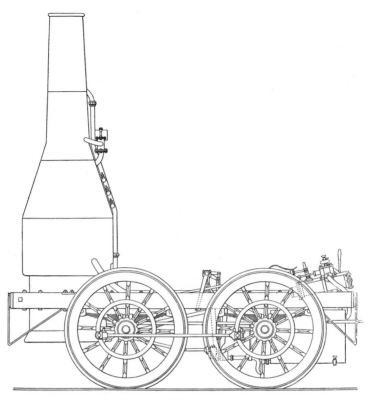

The Best Friend of Charleston, *1830.*

some thought it was Lucifer himself in the shape of a steam engine taking a little brush against time."[113]

Apropos of the escalation of activity, the North Carolina legislature, at its session in January 1834, declined to take any railroad stock itself but authorized the incorporation of the following: North Carolina Centre & Seaport Railroad Company; Wilmington & Raleigh Railroad; Greenville & Roanoke Railroad; Halifax, Roanoke & Yadkin Railroad; Lumber River & Cape Fear Railroad; Cape Fear, Yadkin & Pedee Railroad, and the Roanoke & Raleigh Railroad.[114] A toast given that month was to "THE PRESENT AGE: On the railroad of mental improvement, propelled by the steam power of Public Opinion."[115]

But it was not so much the myriad railroads filling in the eastern network that began to fascinate the nation in the latter part of the 1830s and the early 1840s as much as it was those roads in the Near West region of America. Baltimore continued to push for the Great Lakes, as did New York City.

The Georgia system had the Mississippi River in its sights, and along that river towns like Vicksburg and Natchez were connecting the hinterlands to the city centers by rail.[116] Suddenly there was talk of bypassing the Great Lakes altogether and building across Michigan to Chicago. That new and surprising entrepôt, along with Detroit, Cincinnati, and Cleveland, began to compete to see which city would benefit from the rail network that could be foreseen in the West just as vividly as had New York, Boston, Baltimore, and Charleston before them. There began to be talk about connecting New York or Washington with New Orleans and some about connecting the Crescent City with the Pacific coast.[117] Announcing the opening of the subscription books of the Lake Erie & Mad River Railroad in the fall of 1836, a New York newspaper concluded that "Cincinnati is already the New York of the West—the great commercial trans-Alleghanean depot."[118]

The social approach to that new rail territory, however, was more than a little different from the relatively unalloyed enthusiasm, combined with amazement, when the pioneer lines using novel rail technology were accomplished. In the first fifteen years of America's experience with railroads, there were many expected and unexpected adjustments to be made. It might have been hoped that the machine would comport itself politely and fit seamlessly into the Edenic garden that the United States imagined itself to be. But it did not happen that way. The robotic monster revealed a dark side. It was, it turned out, not the obedient beast of burden that was supposed. Its impact on towns was more complex than simply booming real estate. It not only passed through the landscape; it altered landscapes in irreversible ways. And the people who rode the rails had to consider not only the thrill of newfound speed, comfort, and convenience but also the danger to life and limb, the specter of stressful time schedules, the spread of cholera and other diseases, more frequent panics and depressions, peculation, the threat of monopoly, the bribing of legislators, random fires, annoying noise, increased racial and ethnic tensions, lost baggage, temperance and Sunday travel difficulties, the destruction of historic buildings and neighborhoods, labor riots, and surely conductors. Ralph Waldo Emerson and Henry David Thoreau could wax about the little railroad that wended its way through the quiet town of Concord and past Walden Pond. But their neighbor, Nathaniel Hawthorne, would live to wonder, in his 1843 short story "The Celestial Railroad," whether, despite all the positive rhetoric about the Iron Horse, it was not often the participants in Vanity Fair who rode and the devil who drove.

CHAPTER 4

Default

here was a terribly difficult thing about railroads, as difficult as figuring out how to build them and how to operate them safely. They had to be paid for. Because the cost was so enormous, new lines could hardly be paid for with a single cash payment, leading to the extensive use of a dangerous (though popular) instrument: credit. Credit had built the railroads, one writer noted, and there was no use in recrimination when the financing bills came due. Properly guarded credit could return beneficent results again after a crash, and borrowers could surely learn through experience.[1] But in the meantime, banks had been tempted to use depositors' funds to invest in risky stocks. "I am aware of the very great difficulty that exists at the present time in employing our bank capital," wrote a burned depositor, "and willingly excite the desire to increase the demand for it; and, for that reason, do not object to temporary loans of unquestionably sound stocks, such as Government Loans, New York City, or State Stocks; but I do object . . . if my hard earnings are jeopardized by loans on such trash as Long Island Railroad, Harlem Railroad, &c." He would rather have a 2.5 percent return in a safe investment than the promise of more in such enterprises.[2]

The financing for American railroads was formidable and almost as experimental as the steam engines and cars. There were choices between public, private, and mixed financing—choices that contained elements beyond the purely economic and with implications well beyond the present. There was no predicting how long-term financing would work out amid the business cycles suffered by American rail companies and the states through which they traveled.

In the antebellum railroad era there were two major financial events, which we might call recessions, but which at the time were called "panics" or "revulsions"—one in 1837 and the other in 1857. However, there were constant smaller booms and dips and therefore alternations between enthusiasm and despair as stockholders either collected handsome dividends or faced a sheriff's sale. Complicating the whole matter were the facts that state governments were much involved in extending credit to early American railroads and that those state bonds often sold in Europe, particularly in England, which almost exclusively provided rails on credit during the first period. British citizens in 1837 held about $165 million in American securities. The defaults, which inevitably came, affected international relations as well as the strict matter of extending credit.

The credit crisis went so far as to endanger the republican experiment in America. Europeans during and after the Panic of 1837 came to question the strength and integrity of the U.S. system of government and even ridiculed it at times. By 1842, Florida, Mississippi, Arkansas, Indiana, Illinois, Maryland, Michigan, Maryland, and Louisiana had defaulted on interest payments on their state railroad debt. Arkansas, Michigan, and Mississippi entirely repudiated debts amounting to about $10 million. The upshot was serious. Samuel Young in his "Lecture on Civilization," given in 1841, said that America might not survive its misuse of credit. The states, he said, "had attempted to hypothecate the earnings of after times in order to satiate the vulture rapacity of the present . . . and to bind the limbs of the men of future days with the iron chains of public debt." New York, among other states, reacted with a move to direct taxation and a "stop and pay" policy for railroad construction.[3]

Washington Irving wrote an insightful piece following the Panic of 1837 about the "delusive seasons" when "the 'credit system,' as it is called, expands to full luxuriance: everybody trusts everybody; a bad debt is a thing unheard of; the broad way to certain and sudden wealth lies plain and open." Speculation grew by what it fed on and "bubble rises on bubble; every one helps with his breath to swell the windy superstructure, and admires and wonders at the magnitude of the inflation he has contributed to produce."[4]

It was as though a "short railroad cut to wealth had been invented . . . a road which was entirely to supersede the old beaten track of industry and frugality along which our fathers used to toil their slow but steady way." Now was the time, Irving said, for speculators, as well as for banks that could "coin words into cash." Speculation was the "romance of trade" and

> casts contempt upon all its sober realities. It renders the stock-jobber a magician, and the exchange a region of enchantment.— It elevates the merchant into a kind of knight-errant, or rather a commercial Quixote. The slow but sure gain of snug per centage becomes despicable in his eyes; no "operation" is thought worthy of attention that does not double or treble the investment. No business is worth following that does not promise an immediate fortune. As he sits musing over his ledger, with pen behind his ear, he is like La Mancha's hero in his study dreaming over his books of chivalry.[5]

Benjamin Curtis, writing in 1844 and looking back on the debts of states in the hard times of the 1830s, commented: "The ease with which money was obtained, and the apparent profit from its use, led to the multiplication of engagements of all kinds and to every form of speculation, to an amount, which, if it could be correctly ascertained, would, even now fill us with astonishment." Former times "may have exhibited as great madness, but it reached fewer persons." There was a "morbid tendency to excess." Confidence was such that lenders asked for little security. To obtain money, nothing more was necessary than to show the lender that the funds were to be employed in some magnificent scheme.[6]

What we would now call consumer confidence shifted with the financial winds, and therefore the investment scenario for railroad securities peaked and troughed. Always there was the underlying suspicion of big companies, potential monopolies, exploiters of the people, a suspicion that was almost as endemic to early Americans as fear of monarchy. There was no substitute for big in the case of railroads, but Wall Street never had a heroic reputation. Scandal-mongering was as popular with newspaper readers then as now, and there were plenty of individual peccadilloes and defalcations to feed the worst of the public's fears about the morality of the new age. All in all, watching the railroads grow, exciting as it was, was a pressure cooker too, not only for those who invested directly but also for those who simply wondered what effect the doings of the big capitalists would have upon the rest of the population and on its everyday concerns.

The Panic of 1837 was the first major shock involving railroads and, indeed, involving industry generally. The Panic of 1819–1820 was tied to misuse of credit, but as it applied mostly to land sales in the public domain. The 1837 Panic represented more ambitious speculation and was a deeper reverse.

"The causes of the present distress," wrote an always skeptical New Hampshire man in the spring of 1837, "are attributed to the rage for speculation, in land, eastern and western; city lots, 'water lots,' and all sorts of lots (which have obtained a fictitious value); the immense sums used for railroads."[7] Another New Hampshire observer thought, "Confidence in all personal securities has almost vanished." The country would have to suspend public works like railroad and canals altogether for a time.[8] A reporter in Richmond thought executive salaries were too high at the railroad and that the "great retinue" of salary grabbers were hurting profits and ordinary investors.[9]

All seemed to agree that credit was vital and that it had been badly abused.[10] The country had progressed well for half a century "under a system as favorable to its prosperity, as any perhaps that can be devised," preserving its faith and credit all the while. But recent events threatened that reputation. Abundant means to wealth had attracted immigrants, and the government had tried to give these and the domestic poor a stake in society by making western lands available on easy terms. But this rapid increase in population and easy credit had been observed "by people shrewdly active to their own interests." The rage of speculation that ensued affected all classes. Merchants of the South made enormous advances to the cotton planters in anticipation of their crops. The capitalists of the large towns engaged all their surplus funds in speculation or in loans for speculation, and banks were called upon to provide more leverage. Creditors all over the world withdrew money from more conservative enterprises to put it into ventures, which they valued "not upon their intrinsic worth, but upon the probable price which they might accidentally obtain in an excited market." A U.S. Treasury Department order of July 1836 requiring payment for public lands in cash, the failure of the southern cotton crop that year, and the maturation of a large amount of foreign railroad debt were perhaps the immediate causes of the Panic of 1837, but the underlying cause was the building of a speculative bubble that had to burst.[11]

The *New York Herald* was quick to get on board when there was a scandal or a chance to call for reform. In reporting on a meeting of laborers in New York City, the *Herald* expressed the hope it would not get out of hand, particularly as the present evils were the joint responsibility of all classes. A passion had arisen among all ranks to become rich, not by work or frugality but by operating in stocks and buying and selling real estate. All were licentious and living beyond their means.[12] The *Herald* view was that morals and integrity, honor and principle, were missing. The financial classes were "thoroughly rotten, insolvent, corrupt, and demoralizing," and the only hope was with farmers.[13]

New York was an easy target, and Wall Street came to represent America in a negative way when the riches ceased to flow from there. In the city could be observed

> the two-legged locomotives of the steam-going United States of America. Broadway is their railroad track. They whiz and buzz by each other with a puff, puff, puff, and woe to the luckless wight that falls in their way. . . . Never, never, never were there such as people as we Yankee people for doing business, no matter what it be. If he has goods to sell, he bustles about like a sky-rocket until all are sold. . . . A wife, it may be, cannot see a husband often enough to remember how he looks. . . . Every thing is thus done on the high-pressure principle in this great Babylon of America. Men eat, drink, sleep, and dream in a hurry. . . . They live, die, and are buried too, in a hurry. . . . Everything stalks in superlatives, and adjectives are all "the go."[14]

Banks had been famously controversial during the Jackson administration, and now the worst fears of the radical Democrats seemed to have come to fruition. It had been thought that the hazards of banking were slight and the returns were liberal, but it turned out it was not always so.[15] The impressive building and the conservatively dressed officers behind their desks could conceal speculation that would put a gambler to shame.

There had been an impassioned defense of Americans as plungers. People often bragged that the cultural tolerance of risk was something that differentiated Americans from Europeans and that would ensure the economic dominance of the United States in the long run despite temporary reverses. It was no accident that such risks were encouraged by newspapers and that there were so many newspapers in the United States. In 1835 some 1,265 U.S. newspapers sold 90 million copies per year, compared to only 360 newspapers in Great Britain. There were those who criticized a newspaper-reading public. "But," wrote a New England editor, "we regard every scheme that is calculated to make mankind *think*—every thing that, by detaching the mind from the present moment, and leading it to reflect on the past or future, rescues it from the domination of mere sense—as calculated to exalt us in the scale of being; and whether it be a newspaper or a volume that serves this end, the instrument is worthy of honor at the hands of enlightened philanthropists."[16] The enemy was not credit, not risk, some thought, but stagnation. Those long accustomed to the dreary round of village and agricultural life yearned for the visceral excitement that change brought and preferred uncertainty with hope to the certainties of poverty, despair, and tradition.

There was admonition during the 1837 Panic that lessons needed to be learned, but there was warning also about killing the goose that laid the golden egg. It was a particular theme of the Whig Party that there was illegitimate speculation, but there was also legitimate, although risky, investment. Without the latter, the future would be bleak. Commenting on the Richmond & Fredericksburg rail project, a letter writer using the pseudonym "Whig" concluded:

> It is therefore manifest that let the times fluctuate as they may, or be as bad as they may, this improvement, resting on the broad basis of public utility, will not fail to sustain itself, indemnify the stockholders, or justify the calculations of its projectors. And in contemplating its results, one cannot help regretting that more of the capital of the country which has been irretrievably sunk in frantic speculations upon cotton and tobacco continuing to maintain a certain price, or in shaving and gambling operations, had not been invested in needful and judicious improvements, which, while they will always repay to the adventurer the legitimated yearly value of his money, at the same time promote public convenience, and adorn and strengthen the country. He who thus invests is a practical patriot, and will find his reward in the security and improving value of his investment, when the grasping speculator, who considered nothing but making millions in the short period, is dashed into pieces, by the retributive revolutions of trade.[17]

Analysts farther to the political left also hoped that the system would survive and that reforms could be instituted that would prevent another panic. There was the conventional wisdom that reverses were healthy just as purges of the digestive system or therapeutic bleeding of a fever victim might be. It was common to note that the Panic of 1837 was caused by certain classes and did not indicate terrible general weakness. "And on mature consideration it cannot be considered as dearly purchased by the overthrow and destruction of the Wall-street brokers and gamblers in New-York, and the monopolizing cotton-factors of Canal-Street, New Orleans. Their failure, (disconnected from the working classes), excites no emotion of pity with us, because they were swallowing up rapidly the fruits of other people's industry." If the pain got rid of some "claptrap" railroads run in the interests of stock gamblers, so much the better.[18] In other companies the crisis might serve to cap executive salaries and lead to healthy efficiencies.[19]

Nicholas Biddle, the prominent Philadelphia banker, commented at the opening of the Baltimore & Philadelphia Railroad in August 1837 that hard times, as well as the troubles of his own Bank of the United States, indicated a tension between democracy and economic growth, between a yearning for decentralized institutions and the need to tie together an expanding country. Banks and railroads were not really engines to benefit a few but the means of enriching "every man in the country." No imagination could yet foresee all the advantages the railroad would bring, not only commercial but social and political. "The irrepressible energy, the restless activity of our citizens, carry them to the utmost limits of our country. There they might become insulated. Education could not penetrate their retreats. They would gradually be alienated from their homes, and might regard with indifference, perhaps with hostility, their distant brethren with whom all communion had ceased. Not so now." Railroads led to measuring by space, not time.

> They make him feel that if he has left his home he has not abandoned his country. . . . These seem small things, sir, but they are the minute fibres which make up the living mass of the best domestic sympathies and the purest patriotism. These improvements thus counteract the hazards of our expanding population. They solve the great problem of free institutions—how to create a central power at once not too strong for freedom, yet strong enough to radiate vigorously to the extremities.[20]

To a greater extent than ever before, one recent scholar has pointed out, "businessmen of all kinds found themselves enmeshed in a regional, national, and even international system of commerce and exchange and subject to economic conditions beyond their immediate control." Banks, corporations, and insurance companies were necessary in the accumulation of risk capital and in managing the flow of goods and services through a market economy, their flaws notwithstanding.[21]

The progress of the years preceding the 1837 Panic surely would resume, many wrote. Apparently insurmountable obstacles had been overcome.

The "howling wilderness" was disappearing. "McAdamized highways, railroads and canals, have pervaded the country in every direction, giving free circulation to the products of mechanical skill, of art, and of labor, and animating the whole, immense, diversified country, with every sort of active business and intelligent enterprise." That was no mean feat. No wonder, however, that types arose who tended to abuse the opportunity—people all too "shrewdly alive to their own interest." There came a "universal mania" for wealth. "The old beaten track of plodding for our gains, was forsaken and contemned by the restless anxiety for change, and all seemed to engage in the alluring game of running hazards." A long period of peace and prosperity emboldened them, as though the boom would never end.[22] Yet there was wide consensus that the achievement was impressive. "We take the ground," wrote a Baltimore man, "that the laborer who turns up a spadeful of earth in excavating a canal, or strikes a blow in constructing a railroad, becomes, by so doing, one of the builders up of a system, the benefits of which will endure so long as the continent on which we live shall endure."[23]

In the wake of the panic came a long and related crisis over state debts, a large proportion of which had been contracted in order to build railroads. The national debt was nonexistent; in fact there was often a surplus, but it was different with the states, which had borne the brunt of subsidizing rail finance. An Ohio editor estimated in 1839 that eighteen states had authorized public stock for canals and railroads amounting to $170 million, "which is as much a mortgage on our farms as was the national debt." Interest ran about $12 million per year.[24] It was ridiculous, the regional press thought, that Ohio had an agent in Europe to try to arrange more debt. The Ohio state legislature at its last session had, according to one critic, done more to "degrade the State abroad, and beggar its people at home, than the accumulated energy and labor of years can undo."[25]

Maybe it was not all bad, a New Yorker commented. Speculation had created 3,000 miles of railroad. "The parent may die, but the offspring will live to enlighten and bless."[26] A Massachusetts man argued that the Western Railroad there would be completed eventually and would be a good thing. Delays required credit, and credit required the payment of interest and the raising of taxes, but this was not "inconsistent with the business-like character of a business people." The states received many indirect benefits from the railroads that did not show on their balance sheets proper.[27]

To some that seemed cold comfort. People had been too extravagant in generally prosperous times, importing, for example, $41 million per year in foreign wines—half as much as was spent for railroad iron. Depressions came from overtrading. People seemed to have commenced business on too large a scale.[28] There was a penchant for outright gambling. "Confidence has been destroyed; public and private faith and credit have been grossly abused, and foul deeds of iniquity have been committed."[29] Public business seemed to be influenced primarily by private business lobbies, and no producers appeared in proportion to the growth in borrowing.[30] The credit of the states had been all too good. New York owed $23 million in 1839, Louisiana $23 million, Pennsylvania $27 million, Maryland $11 million, Massachusetts $4 million, Alabama $10 million, and Tennessee $7 million. And states were adding debt all the time. "Our credit is so good that it will ruin us, if we do not stop and think of the consequences of so severely testing it. . . . Are we not getting in jeopardy the dearest interests, the honor and independence of our country, and selling our glorious national birthright for a mess of pottage?"[31]

There was continued danger that the pendulum would swing too far, as was often the case in a crisis. An address to the Convention of Young Men in New York City in the fall of 1838 emphasized that danger:

> What do we hear from the Fanny Wrights and the Silas Wrights at home? "Down with all Banks, they are the contrivances of fraud and corruption" "Cripple, if not destroy credit, for it is the engine of an Aristocracy to oppress the Poor" "Collect the Revenue of New York (at times $22,000,000) in Gold and silver!" and in this steamship age, with the Great Western departing at one door and the Erie Rail Road about to stretch to Canada from the other, deposit it with Sub-Treasurers, who with Locomotive speed, can fly with the taxes of the People beyond the jurisdiction of our laws, and thus become public plunderers with impunity.

Credit, the speaker emphasized, along with the "faculty of associated action in Corporate Powers," was "the Engine of the New World." The United States was rich in land and resources yet poor in money.

> What can we do better, than pledge in associations our Faith and our Credit for that capital with which Europe abounds, to clear the Wilderness, to create Towns and Villages, to build Railroads and Canals, thus furnishing the industrious Immigrant labor, thus laying European Capitalists under tribute to our greatness, by using others' money to develop our latent power, and thus

too aggrandizing the American character, and adding to the honors of an American citizen?

Credit was the "fulcrum" to lift the American laborer and to make real the American dream of rising in the world through enterprise.[32] A report from Baring Brothers in London early in 1840 expressed confidence that no American state would "so entirely lose her self-respect and forget her duty as to violate the faith solemnly pledged for her pecuniary engagements."[33]

What did all the whining about credit and debt accomplish, one writer thought, other than to "alarm the timid and nervous."[34] Surely no one was suggesting cutting back on foreign wines, or going back to dressing in animal skins. Was the panic such a big thing? Was it not just a little overtrading by people who "have modeled their operations on too large a scale?"[35] Seid Hamed Ben Hamed from Arabia seemed impressed enough with his tour of the United States. He was presented with a small model railroad to show in his own country.[36]

Was it state debt that was the major problem? Or the inefficiencies of private corporations? Maybe if the states were to do so much of the funding of railroads, they should own and operate them directly. That was the view of a New York newspaper looking at the record of the New York & Erie Railroad. That corporation, the writer said, was

> crippled in its resources, and shorn of its strength. . . . Nothing short of some miraculous power, which could impart to the limbs of the cripple strength and activity, will enable this prostrated corporation to go on with the enterprise. If it be done, it must be done by the state. The great proprietor—the one entrusted with the sovereign authority, the power of eminent domain—is alone competent to this great work. . . . By coming forward in a moment of general depression to construct this and other great public works, the state best fulfills the duties devolving upon it as the great capitalists, and exemplifies the true advantages of credit founded upon substantial wealth. Employment is given to labor in a season of idleness; industry no longer languishes for want of motive; private enterprise is again awakened to exertion, by the impulse given by the state.[37]

Why not run up as much debt as possible? a New York writer asked. His piece was tongue-in-cheek, but it contained a kernel of truth. Nothing would teach economy but the lessons of too much debt. In the general scramble some would be ruined, but many would prosper.

Let us build, construct, erect, every kind of thing, no matter if we break, for the works themselves will remain—prices will rise during the process of building and expending—the rail roads won't melt—canals won't fly away, nor the docks run away— wages will rise—every one will be prosperous—the women will be more beautiful—and all a scene of delight, till the bubble burst—but who cares for that? It's all a spice of variety.[38]

Still, the concerns were real. The national debt was miniscule, but the state debts were huge and were as much a mortgage on American business as was any federal debt. Much of the interest went to foreigners "who are at least aliens to our country, if not secretly hostile to its institutions and prosperity." No individual could be free when deeply in debt.

He has not always the power willing and determining according to the dictates of his conscience, or his sense of right. He is, though sometimes unconscious of it, more or less subservient to the will of his creditor; because he feels conscious that the creditor can harass and harm him.—Hence a man with limited means, who is under no pecuniary obligations, is more independent, if not more honest in his intercourse with society, than he who nomi- nally possesses great wealth on the sufferance of others.

Should not the states and the nation act as prudently as a family should? Should it not be recognized that there were ten blanks to a prize in any lot- tery?[39] "We must pause," wrote a man in Ohio,"—retrench,—contract no more debts except such as are necessary to finish the works of improvement already begun;—and we must utterly reject the suicidal policy of *mortgag- ing* not only the property and resources of the present generation, but of those to come after them."[40]

Corporations themselves were suspect, and hard times brought the sus- picions to the fore. A Virginian composed a long letter in 1839 concern- ing the rapacity of the Baltimore & Ohio Railroad. It seemed beyond the jurisdiction of the State of Virginia and was a "close monopoly." The letter writer said he was no foe of corporations in their proper places but had no faith in their patriotism. "They are without souls, and consequently without sympathies. They are to be known only by their charters—to be governed only by their bond. If they intend to do that which is morally obligatory on them, they will not object to legal obligation; if they intend to prove slip- pery, they ought to be bound."[41]

When state aid was most needed—that is, during the developmental stage of railroad building—the ultimate profits of the companies and the value of the lands they might open and pledge for loans were most in doubt. It was then that those concerned about tax and debt were most loud and most influential. A Locofoco senator from New York spoke in 1839 about the "bloody and tyrannical system of internal improvements," which, he claimed, was "grinding the people with eternal taxation" and "murdering with hunger whole generations of infants yet unborn."[42]

People in Illinois were embarrassed by their state's debt. A reporter from the *Chicago Democrat* wrote in 1839, "It is no longer to be disguised that we have undertaken too much. We are like the foolish man who began to build, but was not able to finish."[43] An Illinois man wrote from Alton in 1840 about the large expenditures of his state to promote railroads and the pitiful results thus far. Deficit spending and massive borrowing surely could not continue, no matter what the hopes for the future. "I hope and trust that the finances of no other State in the Union have been so wretchedly managed as ours." With great natural resources, but a small population, frontier Illinois was weighed down by debt.[44] Every resident of Illinois, one man estimated, would be charged a dollar per year to support "pauper canals and rickety rail roads. Our stock in banks is in jeopardy. The improvements consist of mounds, ditches, and embankments checkering the State in graceless variety—monuments of our folly and sepulchers of five million of our wealth and industry." Illinois had "commenced many things and executed nothing."[45] The state was further embarrassed in 1841 when its bond agent in London, Wright & Company, failed.[46]

Maryland was in deep trouble also. The governor's message there in January 1840 noted that the "first, great, and absorbing" topic was the internal improvements in which the state held stock. The interest fell heavily on the state, particularly as the works themselves were not complete enough to provide offsetting revenues. Recent fluctuations in the money and stock markets in the United States and Europe had added pain. The legislature must guard "against existing evils" and provide for redemption of debt. Public expenditure must be cut and taxes increased. A reporter commenting on the speech thought that the debt would never be paid because the people would not consent to be taxed.[47]

Maryland complained of "stagnation of trade, scarcity of money, oppressive taxation, and abundance and cheapness of produce." People blamed corporations and the "reckless spirit of the age," which had yoked them with debt. "Lordly" capitalists, partly from Europe, escaped tax while the poor sweated under it. Could someone not relieve Maryland from "the boa constrictor folds of the numerous corporations that wind around her, and stifle her energies?" The picture of Laocoön hemmed in by snakes was "a striking emblem of those States whose finances are deranged by their connection with corporations."[48]

Pennsylvanians were surprised at their sudden postpanic troubles. A reporter looking over a report on state finances issued early in 1840 found it merely sad: "Dry as it looks in its array of figures, to a heart warm with considerations of the best interests of the millions of human beings, who make up *our country*, and whose destiny is suspended on the result of public legislation, its cold numerical calculations quicken into an intensity of meaning, which slang and cant, and humbug shall in vain endeavor to stifle or conceal." Pennsylvania had great resources, it had $50 million in bank capital, yet it was on the verge of bankruptcy. The state was $34 million in debt, and the repairs alone on its internal improvements system were running $350,000 annually. Corrupt banks, newspapers claimed, had suspended cash payments "under circumstances that not only disgraced Pennsylvania before the Union, but dishonored the Union before the world."[49] The state levied a personal property tax on property valued at more than $300, as well as levying a tax on brokers. The annual budget deficit in 1840 was $1 million and rising.[50] The state was in danger of not being able to pay workers on public works, and its credit was about to sink "to the lowest point of degradation."[51] The Pennsylvania state works remained for sale for years with no takers.[52] Sidney Smith, a famous minister in England and an investor in Pennsylvania railroad bonds, complained in 1843 that "no conduct was ever more profligate than the State of Pennsylvania. History cannot pattern it; and let no deluded being imagine that they will ever re-pay a single farthing—their people have [trusted] the dangerous rule of dishonesty, and they will never be brought to the homely rule of right."[53]

There were defenders of debt in Pennsylvania. The attacks on it, some said, were mounted by poverty-stricken states and the press in the interest of brokers. Pennsylvania had great resources and could and would pay its debt. Meanwhile, it was wise to recognize that the public debt had not been contracted for nothing. Pennsylvania would never have been able to work its mines without internal improvements, and these improvements were returning more than $1 million in tolls per year. Pennsylvania produced $160 million worth of goods every year and had "all the resources of a great nation within herself."[54] There was nothing to fear in the long run.

The antitax and antidebt movement was strong in Massachusetts in the early 1840s. The governor objected to the further use of public credit until the railroads were in successful operation.[55] However, there was strong hope in Massachusetts that the crisis was temporary and that entrepreneurs there, "gaining experience from witnessing the follies of others . . . will be enabled to carry on their projects at the least expense practicable, and in the most direct manner."[56] Massachusetts was thankful to Baring Brothers, in London, for extending the state a low interest rate and allowing it to continue its payments through the panic. At a time when money was loaned at 3 percent monthly in the United States, Baring kept the Massachusetts obligation at 5 percent annually.[57]

Florida was worried about $1 million in unsold bonds of $3.9 million issued. "What have we got for all this? Not an inch of rail road." It was the doing of gamblers and "loafers," even now asking Congress for a new bankruptcy law to release them from their obligations. Who was left to pay for this folly? The hardworking and frugal people who paid taxes "while the gamblers are released from all their obligations by act of Congress, and sent at large to act the fool again."[58]

The South took some pride in not having gotten itself into such a fix as some of its northern neighbors and pilloried the Whig policy that had led in that direction. On repudiation, a North Carolina editor wrote there was no chance of "this abominable doctrine" getting a foothold in his state, where "our whole people without distinction of party, esteem a good name for honesty, justice, and strict regard to the obligations of morality."[59] Whig leaders in the North, wrote a journalist in Jackson, Mississippi, in 1840, had "a low selfish ambition," which would allow them to plunge the country into ruin "in order to secure their own promotion." Politics had been thoroughly infiltrated by business interests and power. The stock gamblers of England and the banks of America were contributing large sums to presidential elections, so much so that "politics is now the proper business of business men." That was dangerous on a level far deeper than a temporary credit reverse might suggest.

> If the destinies of this country shall now fall into the hands of this band of public robbers, the "credit system," as the whigs call the "Alladin lamp," credit, will march with gigantic strides. More bonds will be created, more debts contracted, more hypothecations of State and corporation stocks in Europe. No producers will, of course, increase in proportion as the credit system ex-

tends, until finally, we are unable to export sufficient to pay the interest on the enormous debts in Europe. Our condition will become as pitiable as that of Great Britain, where nine-tenths of the people are reduced to pauperism, and compelled to labor sixteen hours in the day for the smallest quantity of food which can support human nature.[60]

The North, especially New York City, was regarded by southern newspapers as a place where "all sorts of Political and Religious chicanery grow and flourish like the rank weeds of the dunghill."[61]

Perhaps railroads had expanded too quickly and with too little planning and prudence. "By endeavoring in the short space of eight or ten years," a North Carolina writer stated, "to push a Railroad to every point in the land, which is ever likely to become important, we have scattered our means, weakened our energies, and retarded our progress."[62]

Georgia, where the state government had been especially active in advancing and controlling railroads, thought that more intervention and regulation was the answer to the questions the 1837 Panic had raised. State loans should be sustained by pledges of revenue such "as will put the punctual payment of interest and principal beyond the possibility of failure or doubt." That would require taxation—not onerous taxation, but enough to ensure disposal of state bonds at a decent price.[63]

The greatest fears surrounded the repudiation of debt by states, combined with decline of companies into bankruptcy and the effects on the future ability to expand the economy at a reasonable pace. Maryland missed some interest payments in 1842 but responded with a tax and sinking fund.[64] Michigan that year repudiated a portion of its bonds and offered to give its ownership interest in state railroads to irate bondholders.[65] "The inability to pay," wrote a Washington editor, "if frankly avowed, would at least not forfeit the character, though it might bring into question the prudence of a State; but to borrow money, and then refuse to acknowledge the debt, is sheer robbery."[66]

The situation was serious. Some suggested that no more rail charters should be issued until the money market was better. It was a shame that those who had watched the management of railroads more closely had not warned of the abuses and of the industry's vulnerability in a downturn.[67] Some suggested the assumption of state debts by the federal government, but that would punish states like New Hampshire, which had contracted no debt.[68] There were suggestions to subsidize the American iron industry in order to avoid purchasing iron from Britain.[69] In 1844 it was said that American credit in Europe was gone, no matter what the security offered.[70] "No subject lies nearer to the heart of every true patriot," wrote an editor in Washington, "than the rescue of the reputation of our country from the reproach cast upon it from abroad, and keenly felt at home, of unwillingness or inability to pay its just debts."[71]

The Panic of 1837 was a watershed indeed, at least the "end of the beginning" for railroad enterprise, and the first great crisis in its progress. The reaction was probably overdone for political purposes. "One would suppose," one writer commented, "that the Whigs were the most profligate, extravagant dogs in the whole world, while the Locofocos were the most wise, scrupulous, economical, and trust-worthy gentlemen imaginable."[72] That was hardly the case. Certainly, also, like so many lessons, the impact of the instruction those hard times might have given was diminished by rapid recovery and subsequent prosperity. Surely, also, our view is affected by hindsight. Howard Bloom, in his recent book *The Genius of the Beast: A Radical Re-vision of Capitalism*, competes with any booster mentality of the early nineteenth century. The Panic of 1837, Bloom argues, was a mere blip in the long upward tour of American capitalism. Out of a "manic-depressive" state cycling from "frenzied belief to doubt, panic and blame" came the effect of giving the United States a different kind of creativity. The country at the time blamed railroads for the economic panic, but railroad growth had only begun. After the railroad bubble was declared to be an "insane fantasy," rail mileage in the ensuing sixty years went from about 200 miles to 200,000 miles and made big money for investors.[73] The country had taken "physic," and it was now expected to be restored to health.

> There is no good thing under the sun but what may be put to bad purposes, and yet, on the whole may have rendered infinite service to the community. Steamboat boilers sometimes explode with horrible effects, and railroad cars are occasionally thrown off their track, and even the Christian religion is every day run mad by fools and fanatics and knaves, but no sane and honest man would dispense with either of them.[74]

The power of intellect and execution was important, but without money and credit that potential did not amount to much.[75]

CHAPTER 5

Riding the Rails

ailroad travel, management, and finance had a dark side. However, the predominant impression of early railroad travelers was of a thrilling novelty—aggravating sometimes, but worth it. They flocked from all over the world to experience the railroad. Even the rankest amateur writer tried his hand at composing an article, a book, or at least a letter to the editor about the experience. To ignore these, repetitive as they can be, sentimental as they can be, awkward as they can be, but expressing in the writers' own style when the experiences were fresh, is to miss a vital part of the contemporary experience of the new railroad world.

As passengers struggled to describe what they saw and how they felt, they communicated to others the elements of what would eventually become a social adaptation of considerable magnitude. Foreigners, in describing their experiences on American railroads, were also describing the emerging culture of the industrializing United States. Native passengers documented the changes within themselves and to their environs. And all was accomplished at a speed just as remarkable in the annals of social and political change as was the pace of the new steam locomotives relative to the straining horse car.

A visitor from England noticed in 1820 that in the United States, access to the reading public was easy, and material changes had an outsized effect: "Any person for a small sum may obtain from certain editors as much renown as his vanity or his necessities require. As the newspapers are the standard of literature as well as of politics, this arrangement is found very convenient."[1] And so, with the impact of technology on newspapers in addition to travel came the popular genre of the railroad travelogue.

The first accounts were of almost unmixed enthusiasm. The Mauch Chunk and the Quincy short lines fascinated, as did the Mohawk & Hudson, the Charleston & Hamburg, the New Castle & Frenchtown, and the Baltimore & Ohio.

A newspaper editor from Washington, D.C., rode the Baltimore & Ohio in the fall of 1831. He had never ridden a railroad before and had much to learn, he said, about the nature and capacities of this new improvement. "We found it in some respects considerably to exceed our anticipations, and in none to fall short of them." There was some jarring, and he was alarmed at cows along and crossing the road, but in general it was great.[2]

An excursion on the New Castle & Frenchtown in October 1832, accompanied by "rather too good" wines, led to a journalist's enthusiasm about a 16-mile trip made in one hour, nine minutes. "Not an incident happened to break the spell of the enchantment which we all felt in cutting the air at this rate—the houses and trees all seemed to be rapidly passing us, and sometimes a bird would, when we were descending, look to the eye as if its wings were of no use to it." The passenger felt so secure that he took a nap along the way. He reflected on recent times, when the stage trip over the same distance took five hours, and he dreamed of a future when things would be even more comfortable.[3]

Another Pennsylvania traveler on the Columbia Railroad a month later loved the inclined plane west of the Schuylkill River. The thirty passengers "seemed to be sailing on land with a steady breeze."[4]

Pennsylvania travelers were especially sanguine about the prospects for marketing coal and the usefulness of short lines for opening the coal resources in their state. Wood for fuel was running short all over the United States. Cheap anthracite coal could revolutionize the way urban residents heated their homes, not to mention the way locomotives were powered. Consequently, things could change greatly for the mining economy of Pennsylvania. Starting with the Mauch Chunk and Schuylkill Valley Railroads in the late 1820s, Pennsylvania created a web of short lines to the coalfields integrated with the canal system that was still thought best for carrying such heavy, low-value loads.[5]

Located, as they often were, in previously inaccessible terrain, the coal mines illustrated strongly the revolutionary status of the railroad. The 120-mile route from the mines at Carbondale, Pennsylvania, to New York City was mountainous.

> Could any one before the invention of rail-roads and the steam engine, have stood on the summit of this mountain . . . and looked down into the deep, dark, and almost impenetrable forest and swamp below, and have been told that from that spot, five hundred tons of coal would each day be brought to the height where he stood . . . he would reasonably have been staggered in his belief of so marvelous a tale.[6]

In 1820, mines exported 365 tons of Pennsylvania anthracite. In 1833 that figure was 123,000 tons per year.[7] Farmers loved the promise of coal for a more diversified income and the promise of railroads to improve their markets. A traveler reported in 1835 that "absolute dreariness now reigns on the turnpike between Philadelphia and Harrisburg. . . . *Stare super vias antiquas* is an abandoned maxim, which will certainly become obsolete in due season."[8]

Rail travel was a delight for Pennsylvania passengers. At the opening excursion for the Philadelphia, Germantown & Norristown in the summer of 1835, one passenger wrote that the excursion was of the "gayest" style imaginable. "It was a noble triumph of art, to see the iron fire-horses, belching volumes of smoke, speeding their airy-like things to life, through the mazes of the country. . . . It was a break upon their long reign of seclusion and stillness, which will make a record upon the table of their memories as long as they live."

Pennsylvania had much of which to be proud, but none more than the infant railroads.

> Our rail roads, canals, and rising towns and improvements, inland, are the proper glory of our country. These are the things, which foreign journalists and carping strangers should be taught to consider and respect. If we have not all the minutiae of courtly luxury for ornament, and the artificial refinements of creative fancy . . . we have all the substantials of happiness and comfort, better adapted to our notions of republican simplicity.[9]

Railroad depots came to dominate urban architecture, and their size brought much comment. The Boston & Maine depot in Boston, constructed in 1846, was 200 feet long and 80 feet wide. It had Corinthian columns, and on its upper story was the largest meeting hall in the city. Behind it was a freight depot 500 feet long and 50 feet wide.[10] The Union depot at Troy, New York, constructed in 1853, was 400 feet long and 150 feet wide. The distance from the top of the roof arch to the floor was 65 feet. The roof was made entirely of iron supported by twenty trusses.[11]

Time only increased the impressiveness of these structures. A reporter for the *Chicago Daily Tribune* visited the new buildings constructed by the Illinois Central Railroad along the lakeshore in 1854. The passenger depot at the foot of Water Street was all of stone. It was 500 feet long, 166 feet wide, and 60 feet high to the top of its towers. Its windows were 16 feet high. The walls looked like they would "remain in all their strength when the final 'wreck of matter and the crash of worlds' shall come." The turntable there would hold eighteen locomotives.[12]

The depots were the entry to a new world of travel, every aspect of which became a subject for travelogue comments. John Daggett, riding the B&O in 1834, thought the beginning of his rail journey was its highlight:

> One of the happiest effects of traveling on railroads is the freedom it gives you from the impertinence and impositions of porters, cartmen, *et omne id genus*, who infest common steamboat landings. A long and solitary row of carriages was standing on the shore awaiting our arrival; not a shout was heard, scarcely any thing was seen to move except the locomotive, and the arms of the man who caught the rope from our boat. The passengers were filed off along a planked walk to the carriages through one gangway, while their luggage, which had already been stowed safely away, was rolled on shore by another, in two light wagons; and almost without speaking a word, the seats were occupied, the wagons attached behind, the half-locomotive began to snort, and the whole retinue was on the way with as little ado and as little loss of time as I have been guilty of in telling the story.[13]

Others, however, were not so impressed with the stressful experience of boarding a train. A Frenchman, Michel Chevalier, thought that the pandemonium at the railroad station reflected the nervousness and disorder of American society itself. The American, he wrote, was "devoured with a passion for locomotion" and could not stay still. His competitive nature

Depot of Baltimore & Washington Railroad at Washington, D.C., 1853. Bettmann/Corbis

gave an exaggerated estimate of the value of time, and that kept his nervous system agitated.

> He always has something to be done, he is always in a terrible hurry. He is fit for all sorts of work, except those which require slow and minute processes. The idea of these fills him with horror; it is his hell. "We are born in haste," says an American writer, "Our body is a locomotive, going at the rate of twenty five miles an hour; our soul a high-pressure engine; our life is like a shooting star, and death overtakes us at last like a flash of lightning."

The American penchant for competition was so strong, the Frenchman thought, that if a hundred Americans were going to be shot, they would contend for priority.[14]

Eliza Steele, riding from Boston to Albany in 1840, got on the railroad at "an ugly building at the head of State Street where we alighted and stood in a large barn-like apartment among men and trunks and boys—the latter screaming, '*Albany Argus*'—'*Evening Journal*!'—and among all sorts of confusion, until we were seated in the cars." Her train was hauled by horses to the edge of town, where "the snort of a steampipe and perfume of grease and smoke, announced the vicinity of our locomotive; and, as if to show off its paces, the engineer whirled the hideous thing back and forth before our—at least my—*nil admirari* eyes." Then away they rushed, "leaving our fine steeds gazing after us with tears in their eyes, to see themselves outdone by a great tea-kettle."[15]

Alexander Mackay visited from England in 1846–1847. He rode the Boston & Worcester, and upon arriving at the depot at Worchester he noted that there was an insane asylum in that town. That seemed appropriate to him, and he was ready to assign to that institution as inmates many of the people he observed on the platform at the depot.

> For some minutes it appeared to me as if the Bedlam hard by had been let loose upon the station, or depot, as it is universally called in America. To give a true picture of the confusion—the rushing to and fro—and the noise, with which all this was accompanied, is impossible. Some pounced upon the refreshment room, as if they fancied it the up-train, and in danger of an immediate start; others flew about, frantically giving orders, which there was no one to obey; whilst by far the greater number were assuring themselves of the safety of their baggage.[16]

The handling of that baggage drew mixed reviews. The signs that were common on rail property that the company was not responsible for baggage were not as bad as the implicit policy that railroad companies were not responsible for the lives of passengers either, but baggage handling was a cause for complaint nevertheless.[17] It resulted regularly in lawsuits for damages, and plaintiffs were often successful. The duties of common carriers in this regard were clear: "As quiet or ignorant people may perhaps be induced to submit to the imposition of a loss of their freight or baggage rather than litigate with a great monopoly, especially when the above notices are thrust in their faces, and they are told *they were bound to take notice of them*," they still had a right to compensation for lost baggage.[18]

Luggage was often carried on a car directly behind the engine, partly for safety in providing a buffer for the following passenger cars in the case of an accident. This meant that the sparks produced by engines were a hazard. In 1835 in New York the baggage car caught fire some distance from water. The crew looked for an axe to cut away the sides of the car but could not find one. So they turned it over. It came to rest bottom-up, preventing access to the trunks. The passengers, 200 in all, stood by and sometimes snatched an article or two, but most of the possessions went up in the fire, including the mail bag and the cargo of newspapers. The $3,000 in diamonds in one trunk survived, but the $15,000 in cash one man had entrusted to his luggage did not.[19] In 1836, newspapers began advertising a fireproof trunk made of iron plates covered with leather.[20]

Foreigners commented favorably on the system for checking baggage and getting a brass chit for it.[21] This could be handed to the conductor before one came to the station, and presumably one's bags would be waiting on the landing when the passenger alighted. Officials on many lines, however, one observer said, "evidently regard a passenger's trunk as a nuisance, and handle it as if they intended to destroy it before it had reached its destination."[22] It was common for railroads to limit strictly the amount of baggage it would carry for the cost of the ticket and to charge high fees for any extras. Baggage could include a trunk, a valise, a carpetbag, a small bundle, or a bandbox. Anything else was freight and was often sent to the freight house, causing considerable delay and vexation to passengers. Rail officials tended to be arrogant, leading to the conclusion that "no private enterprise can succeed for any length of time, where the rule is to vex and annoy customers."[23]

The arrival at a destination tended to be as chaotic as the departure. "A passenger landing at the Walnut street wharf, Philadelphia, from New York, after fighting and scratching, and shouting, amongst porters, negroes, &c. on board the boat, to get his baggage, finds that he has to travel half over the city before he can reach the depot of the cars which take him to Baltimore." Pickpockets and sharpers (the nineteenth-century term for swindlers) abounded at depots to prey on confused and dazed travelers.[24] Within the station, the "hurry-scurry" was worse than outside, men "jostling each other, and rushing in at every available aperture into the cars, like so many maniacs."[25]

The accoutrements of the railroad itself, particularly the locomotive engine, were admired in and of themselves as aesthetic objects and impressive engineering feats, independent of any actual economic utility they might possess. At the opening of the Danville & Pottsville in Pennsylvania late in 1834, an excursionist was overawed by the sight of the engine house on Broad Street and the 90-horsepower coal-fired stationary steam engine there. "Far from 'grating harsh thunder,' like Milton's gate of Erebus, its finely polished joints and tubes and wheels . . . hardly hummed as loud as a farmer's spinning wheel. No jarring nor creaking, nor clattering; yet its tremendous power reminded one of the Yankee's exclamation, 'Here's all hell in harness!'"[26] Dickens, in his *American Notes,* described an engine "buzzing along, like a great insect, its back of green and gold so shining in the sun, that if it had spread a pair of wings and soared away, no one would have had occasion . . . for the least surprise."[27] Frederika Bremer looked at some schoolchildren drawing in a courtyard and found that nearly every slate contained drawings of "moving machines," mostly locomotives or steamboats, and all in motion.[28]

Freeman Hunt, a well-known economic commentator at the time, took the railroad out of Boston in 1835 and was impressed with the car in which he rode. It was 24 feet long and 8 feet wide, divided into three compartments. The seat cushions were crimson morocco trimmed with lace. The outside paint was a "fawn" color with buff shading, decorated with picture panels and pink and gold borders with stripes of vermillion and black. Within the panels were reproduced masterpieces of European art, maybe 200 paintings on the twenty-four cars. The cars had been made in Troy, New York.[29] Another passenger, riding on a car made by the American firm Davenport & Bridges, said that it was painted in a plain olive color with landscape views of the town and neighborhood through which the railroad ran. There were armchairs of cast iron painted to mimic mahogany and upholstered with silk plush. "They are not quite as luxurious as some of the first class cars on the English railroads, but they are good enough for us plain republicans."[30]

Others were less impressed. A passenger on the Charleston & Hamburg in the 1850s reported disappointment in his car: "The ceiling was as black as the back of a kitchen chimney, the glasses of the windows so foul we could not see through them, and the only covering to the naked floor was . . . shells, orange peel, apple skins, interspersed here and there with generous puddles of tobacco spit, with hung quids moored in them, like islands in the ocean." The first chair he sat in collapsed under him. "Thump, thump, thump, jerk, jerk, creak, creak, rattle, rattle, went our wretched carriage, which seemed to get worse every mile. But we were moving, and felt so grateful for that much that we had no heart to complain of our abominable accommodations." At the end of the trip he was glad to escape alive and to get to his hotel "sleepy, tired, cold, and thoroughly disgusted."[31]

The railroad car was a home for travelers for lengthy journeys in the antebellum period, so it was no surprise that travelers often commented upon its layout and function. Europeans were first struck by the fact that American cars were generally larger than European cars, were not divided into compartments, and welcomed all classes of riders, with the exception of free blacks. This, they thought, was part of the egalitarian American way, and they found it attractive—at least in theory. Englishman Alexander Mackay wrote:

> In a land of social equality every one except the negro travels in the first class. The servant and the mistress, the navvie, the pedlar, the farmer, the merchant, the general, the lawyer, the senator, the judge, the governor of the State, with their wives, theirs sons, and their daughters, and even the Irish bogtrotter. . . . all mingle together in one long car, by no means so comfortable as a second-class carriage on any of the principal lines in Great Britain.[32]

Matilda Houston saw within the car on which she rode a "human menagerie" of about sixty people seated on small horsehair seats with wooden backs.

> These seats were placed, to use a nautical expression, *athwart ships*, instead of *fore* and *aft*, and every two people turned their backs on the two behind, and so on to the end of the carriage. Through the middle (for the seats extend along each of the bare wooden walls of the caravan) is a narrow pathway, through which every newcomer walks to his seat, by this means (and it is no trifling advantage) avoiding the foot-treading, gown-crushing, and begging-pardon process, to which, under different arrangements, unfortunate travellers are exposed. At the *door end* of the carriage a small placard was pasted on to the woodwork, and on it was a notice to the following effect—"Gentlemen are requested neither to smoke or spit in the carriages." Below this was a piece of advice, still more characteristic of the habits and manners of the country—"Gentlemen are likewise recommended not to hang their legs or heads out of the windows while the cars are in motion."

Once in motion, a "spare New-Englander," much in contrast in appearance to European rail officials, walked up and down taking tickets.[33]

Another universal presence was newsboys selling snacks and reading matter, both of questionable quality.[34] These boys jumped onto the train as it slowed for a station and jumped off again, just in time, as it speeded up along its ongoing journey.[35] Hugo Reid, riding an "alarming looking" American railroad in 1859, liked the convivial atmosphere in the railcar: "The passengers can rise, walk to the doors, and get the benefit now and then of a change of posture and a little motion; while persons selling newspapers, magazines, books, or refreshments for the body, are frequently passing through the carriages." He did find the conductors "cold, disobliging, and repulsive," and the printed schedules seemed to be for amusement only, as they were seldom met.[36]

Etiquette was slow in becoming established. For example, conceding a seat to a lady who had to stand was not often done, as every ticket holder was equal in the sight of the law.[37] All were treated poorly. Conductors in the United States seemed to "consider themselves exclusively in positions of command; and they too commonly seem to regard questions as personal insults."[38] Tickets were "a strip of paper about a half a year in length," and there were many confusing transfers, not only from railroad to railroad but also from railroads to canals and steamboats and back again. Rates seemed high, often much higher for passengers than for freight. Why should "self-loading and self-unloading bipeds" be charged more for transportation than a bale of cotton, especially when they were not treated any better?[39]

American rudeness was a subject of much comment. "Because we are the freest people on the face of the globe," wrote a reporter in 1857, "is it therefore necessary that we should be the worst-mannered?" On railroads they demonstrated that they were, proving intolerant of strangers with whom they came in contact. They refused to compromise their individual peculiarities and wants in the interest of the rest of the passengers. "Delicacy is wounded, decency offended, and good morals violated with impunity by crowds of well-dressed people."[40]

But how could one be expected to be polite aboard such conveyances, given the provocations? There were the surly conductors, a Boston reporter wrote, the tobacco chewers, a married woman, with her first baby, staring daggers at you because you did not notice the baby, an old man explaining a book at length, a disappointed office seeker, an old maid with a large bandbox and a parasol constantly asking the conductor where we were, an invalid with a graveyard cough, and a host of other undesirables.[41]

Dining cars and sleeping cars were not generally present until the late 1850s.[42] One woman spoke of living on green apples for most of her lengthy journey.[43] All commented that irregular and poor food and erratic sleep were among the discomforts of early rail travel. Often, bleary-eyed in the middle of the night, the passenger had to transfer. "Gathering up your cloak, umbrella, and scattered senses, you grope your way to the other train," reaching again for the extensive ticket to show the new conductor.[44]

Food was eaten as snacks or at stops, and often there was less than enough water aboard the trains for passengers' drinking needs.[45] The crowding and stress were extreme and the food poor, leading often to indigestion or "sea-sickness," as one man called it, when reboarding the jostling cars.[46]

William Chambers, visiting from England, took the train from Boston to Albany in about 1854, paying $5. The train stopped midroute with no explanation until the door of the car opened and a man in a rough cap announced: "You have an hour to wait, and there's good eating round the corner." Chambers, with the other passengers, crossed a complication of rails and ascended an outdoor wooden staircase to a room "which united the character of bar-room, shop, and kitchen." It was efficient. "At one side, a man behind a counter had charge of the liquoring department; in another quarter, a lad dispensed ham and pumpkin pie; and at the further end of the room, two women were assiduously engaged in dressing oysters in frying-pans. The scene was strange, and the place not exactly such as I should have selected for supper, had there been a choice."[47] A traveler from France estimated that the average time taken for a railroad meal was ten minutes, and in that time 300 people could be fed at one of these slapdash establishments.[48] Another English traveler commented: "The refreshment rooms at the different stations along the whole line of the railroad afford an animated spectacle; where, during the short period the cars halt, you observe two or three hundred people lining the tables, the national rapidity of mastication being here fourfold. All of a sudden they are seen flying, helter-skelter, at the tingling of a bell."[49]

The situation did not seem to improve. An 1857 article in the *New York Daily Times* expressed the continued outrage of rail passengers:

> If there is any word in the English language more shamefully misused than another, it is the word refreshment, as applied to the hurry-scurry of eating and drinking at railroad stations. The dreary places in which the painful and unhealthy performances take place are called "Refreshment Saloons"; but there could not be a more inappropriate designation for such abominations of desolation. Directors of railroads appear to have an idea that travelers are destitute of stomach; that eating and drinking are not at all necessary to human beings bound on long journeys, and that nothing more is required than to put them through their misery in as brief a time as possible.

Rail managers seemed to expect that women and children

accustomed to orderly homes can be whirled half a day over a dusty road, with hot cinders flying in their faces; and then, when they approach a station and are dying with weariness, hunger, and thirst, longing for an opportunity to bathe their faces at least before partaking of their much-needed refreshments, that they shall rush out helter-skelter into a dismal long room and dispatch a supper, breakfast, or dinner in fifteen minutes.

The consequences were not reported as railroad disasters, but in actuality they were.

> The traveler who has been riding all night in a dusty and crowded car, unable to sleep, and half suffocated with smoke and foul air, will be suddenly roused from his half lethargic condition by hearing the scream of the steam-whistle, which tells of the near approach to a station; but, before the train stops, the door of the car opens, and the conductor shouts at the top of his voice: "Pogramville—fifteen minutes for breakfast."[50]

Every ticket holder had to put up with the classless mingling aboard the cars and inside the eating houses of railways. Wrote a reporter for the *New York Sun* in 1844: "You cannot now tell the millionaire *en route* from the barber who takes him by the nose. The Southern chivalry, who used to visit our high northern latitudes with four in hand, now sit side by side with the Yankee pedlar. . . . They now rush out like everybody else, at the eating houses along the line, and demolish a six penny pie without self reproach, and swallow a glass of root beer without commiseration."[51]

Sleep was harder to come by than food. A rider in South Carolina in 1849 said that some attempt was made to accommodate passengers wishing to sleep, but it was a failure. Comfortable berths would occupy no more space than the other arrangements, and those berths might give the passenger at least the chance of a nap. This passenger crawled into one of the "miserable dormitories" provided at three in the morning and was exhausted enough to sleep a little, only to wake up with an aching head and nearly dislocated neck.[52] Wrote an English visitor at about the same time:

> Without a proper place to stow away one's hat; with no convenience even to repose the head or back, except to the ordinary height of a chair; with a current of cold outer air, continually streaming in, and rendered necessary by the . . . furnace; and with the constant slamming of the doors at either end of the

car, as the conductor goes in and out, or some weary passenger steps on to the platform to have a smoke, the passenger must, indeed, be "dead beat" who can sleep or even doze in a railway car in America.[53]

An English sportsman, traveling in 1860, agreed: "The boasted convenience for sleeping through the night in the railway cars was about the greatest mistake that it was possible to imagine."[54]

Then there were the smoking habits and the chewing. Mackay regarded chewing tobacco as representing "depravity" of taste and thought its aficionados were like animals chewing their cud. The floor was moist in minutes, few taking time to aim for the cuspidors. The floor was encrusted with deposits of tobacco spit. A fellow passenger had the courtesy to ask Mackay if he would object to his spitting. The Englishman could only reply that he supposed it was all right, as long as the chewer did not spit on him.[55]

Another foreign traveler put it succinctly:

> Oh! After I had experienced the travel of these boasted trains, how I longed for the cleanliness and privacy, and civility and choice of society, on the railways of Old England. The American trains are filthy, their floors not only always in a most disgusting condition, but the door at either end permits such a thorough draught right through, and the citizens of the United States have such a perpetual desire to open and shut them, that any man used to comfort is sure to catch the ear-ache.[56]

Fire was a hazard in many ways. The early wood-fired engines threw off sparks and cinders, which burned holes in women's dresses, made everyone's eyes water, and regularly burned down improvements along the right-of-way. Towns and buildings were flammable, leading to locomotives' being pulled into and out of urban areas by horses. Nor was the countryside safe from the steam engine. "Like a horse," wrote a traveler, "kept exclusively upon oats [they] are difficult to manage, from the nature of their diet. They are constantly attended by a formidable train of obdurate sparks, and sometimes amuse themselves by setting fire to a barn, a hayrick, and the like, and, when they have nothing else to do, burning down a fence."[57]

Passengers were aware of fire danger. Frederick Marryat, visiting from England in the late 1830s, rode an American train in weather too hot for the windows to be closed. Through his journey "the ladies, assisted by the gentlemen, were constantly employed in putting out the sparks, which settled on their clothes."[58] Harriet Martineau rode the Charleston & Hamburg, and at the end of her trip she counted thirteen holes burned in her gown.[59]

The most constant fire-related hazard was the ubiquitous and much-maligned heating stove. It could overturn and set the wooden car on fire in an accident, but it was an annoyance even when things were proceeding normally. Mackay averred that anthracite coal stoves were the greatest affliction on railroads, overheating the car and burning out the elasticity and moisture in the atmosphere. They quickened the pulse, inflamed the skin, and parched the tongue with a "sulphury and palpitating hotness."

Smoking a cigar on the platform to escape the heat of a stove, Mackay asked a fellow passenger whether there was any danger. The man told him it would be safer inside the car. Did accidents frequently happen? Yes, trains did sometimes run off the rail. This was disturbing. "There was but a pitiful choice, certainly, between an instantaneous crush to death, and a slow broil by the stove; but preferring the latter, I repaired to my place, and submitted to it until the train reached Worcester."[60]

Sir Charles Lyell, the famous British geologist, was reading a speech by the U.S. president while speeding through the countryside on a train. But "while I was indulging my thoughts on the rapid communication of intelligence by newspapers and the speed and safety of railway traveling, a fellow-passenger interrupted my pleasing reveries by telling me I was standing too near the iron stove, which had scorched my clothes and burned a hole in my great coat."[61]

Newspapers did not write about toilet facilities: that was doubtless taboo. But, no question, facilities were as primitive as those aboard railway trains well into the twentieth century.

There was also little writing about disease, other than the cholera that regularly affected rail workers, and a fear of "miasma," which, it was thought, might be contracted by traveling through swamps, particularly at night.[62] But in later years the medical profession became much concerned about the transmission of infectious diseases, particularly tuberculosis, both by the mixture of people from all origins in the cars and by the use of common drinking cups.[63]

There was some generalized complaint about something called "rail car poison," contracted from the generally horrible conditions aboard. One breathed the "hateful thing" and it shortened life by a minute, one observer said, for every mile of railroad you traveled.

> Imagine a rail car in the depot at night. This beautifully painted and well-cushioned vehicle has been in and out over the track

most of the day; but as well in as out of the depot, its doors and windows have been kept persistently shut, and the inside smells like the hold of an emigrant ship. The passengers come pouring in, and the seats are soon filled; and now we have sixty pairs of lungs rendering fouler and fouler the already vitiated atmosphere of this pest-box, which contains about twenty-four thousand cubic feet of air, or four hundred cubic feet of breathing material to each passenger, when every adult requires ten cubic feet of pure air per minute to sustain him in perfect health. No wonder, then, that, whereas you entered the car feeling like a lark, you in fifteen minutes find yourself as dull as a clod—that you feel uneasy and nervous, and wonder what you have eaten or drank that gives you this "sudden headache."

Better ventilation, spark arrestors, and some form of dust control might help, but these were no cure.[64]

Once aboard, the rail traveler proceeded into the countryside and was able to comment on the scenery, the motion, and the engineering. Most found the experience fatiguing and boring. Frederika Bremer liked the low fares but wrote, "After the first two hours, there is an end of all pleasure in traveling, and one sinks into a suffering and stupid state; one feels one's self not a human being, but a portmanteau."[65] Many observed that the speed of the train interfered with enjoyment of the landscape. The scenery, wrote one woman, was "all blurred, like a bad lithograph."[66]

Francis Lieber found the railroad journey tedious also, partly due to the speed, partly due to the discomfort.

The traveller, whose train of ideas is always influenced by the manner in which he proceeds, thinks in a steam car of nothing else but the place of his destination, for the very reason that he is moving so quickly. Pent up in a narrow space, rolling along on an even plain which seldom offers any objects of curiosity, and which, when it does, you pass with such rapidity, that your attention is never fixed; together with a number of people who have all the same object in view, and think like you of nothing else, but when they shall arrive at their journey's end.[67]

Harriet Martineau, however, thought that the railroad from Charleston fitted well into the natural scene of forest, with the straightness and regularity of the railroad contrasting pleasingly with the chaotic tangle of the forest. "I never saw an economical work of art harmonize so well with the

The wonderful railroad retinue passes. Bettmann/Corbis

vastness of the natural scene." When a train appeared in the distance, it was a "black dot, marked by its wreath of smoke," and it was impossible to stop watching it, "growing and self-moving, till it stops before the door."[68]

People seemed overawed by the rugged route of the Baltimore & Ohio. One frightened passenger wrote in 1852: "So we were in mid-air, as it were, without a plank under us; the body of the coach, of course, shelving over the track, and 300 feet from terra firma. The sight is appalling." In a tunnel, riders could touch wet and dripping sides of slate rock, could see the live spark from the locomotive, and hear the noise of wheels "like pulling a heavy chain over sheet iron."[69]

Many commented that the American wilderness was too wild, and the lack of towns and traffic was much in contrast to railroad routes in Europe, where enough trade and dense populations had to exist before a railroad was ever built. Alexander Majoribanks traveled on some of the more westerly U.S. railroads around 1852 and commented that American railroads were made in "the most rude and simple plan imaginable." They would be thought unfinished and dangerous in Europe. They were not "fenced in, nor banked in from the fields on each side, and running straight across lanes, streets and roads, without any other notice to those who may happen to be riding, or driving on them, than the following intimation, painted every where on boards elevated on high poles:—'When the bell rings, look out for the engine.'" Running right through the domains of livestock and wild animals, the Americans had invented something called a "pilot" or, more descriptively, a "cowcatcher." It was a kind of plough in front of the engine that "prepares as it were the way before them, lifting up bullocks, swine, sheep, or whatever other obstruction may be in the way, and throwing them gently, and to their astonishment, into the adjacent fields, or occasionally cutting them to pieces."[70]

There were no cross-country roads. American railroads seemed to English visitors to be a means of conveyance from one large town to another with "no omnibuses and private carriages waiting at the intermediate stations, as with us, to carry passengers in every direction into the interior." An Englishman named John Godley, visiting in 1843, was impressed with American rail building but doubtful of its success. "There is something imposing in the idea of 1,300 miles of continuous railroad such as extends (with the exception of a few steamboat 'trajets') from Portland in Maine to Savannah in Georgia; and I give the Americans full credit for the energy and enterprise to which the fact bears witness; but the question recurs, are they ripe for it?"[71]

Americans had an answer to that. German Johann Kohl quoted a fellow passenger as saying the railroad would create towns. "Railroads with us are magic wands, horns of plenty, from which we scatter the seeds of population, and they spring up and fill the place we have made for them as water does when you dig a canal in a moist country."[72]

Animals were astonished at the passage of the train. "The horses in the fields," wrote one passenger, "generally ran away, carrying their heads erect, and their ears bent downwards and backwards; and they turned their head alternately to one side and the other to catch a glimpse of the dreaded enemy behind." One hen flew straight into the air in fright.[73] The steam whistle seemed to some singularly inappropriate, however necessary, in rural climes. "No words can describe the shrill, wild and unearthly sound," one man said, that frightened livestock and wild animals.[74]

The standard for speed in early railroads seemed to be the pigeon. Passengers often pointed out that their train was keeping up with a flock of these heavy and slow-flying birds. It was an item of news in 1835 when an engine on the Camden & Amboy, running at speed with no cars attached, overtook a flock of pigeons flying along the right-of-way and killed two of them.[75]

Given all the discomforts of early rail travel, why did so many patronize the lines? Part of it may have been boredom. "This is truly an age of motion," wrote a journalist in 1855.

Everybody is in motion—rushing east and rushing west.—Railroads, steamboats, canals, stages and every kind of conveyance are crowded to their utmost capacity. Miss Romance delights in travel, she sees so many persons and places, and acquires such a find of wonders to her quiet, stay-at-home villagers. . . . Mr. Matter-of-fact travels because he makes money by it. He travels to select real estate, to learn the solvency of some new firm.—Young Rattlebrain travels because he has nothing to do and wants to do something fashionable, and it is fashionable to travel and so he travels.[76]

Certainly, people did not travel for comfort. "Men leave roomy houses and all modern improvements for cramped lodgings, little to eat, and that shamefully spoiled in the cooking." The conveyance there was the worst of it. "On board the railroad cars, cramped with long sitting in one position, eyes full of cinders, lungs full of dust, dirty, sleepy, stupid, annoyed about baggage, insulted by conductors, shaved by runners and agents? In hotels shunned by unfed waiters, swindled by landlords, tossing on sleepless beds?"[77] One offering hints for railroad travelers in 1840 suggested that, "as soon as you have taken your seat in the car, forget that you are on a railroad—go to thinking as hard as you can, about Gen. Harrison, the Northeastern Boundary, the bombardment of Beyrout, the last shot fired at Louis Phillippe, the long-tailed Celestials, Ali Pashan, Lord Byron . . . or anything else except your existing situation—keep cool and trust in Providence."[78] The explanation for going at all could only be psychological. We were "ruminating animals" and could not be at rest.[79]

Maybe it was partly, too, the sheer drama and adventure, the visceral excitement of riding the rails. There was the "luxury of a new sensation" that it provided, apparently worth considerable discomfort and intriguing the observer as well as the traveler. Wrote a commentator in 1853:

Take your stand six feet from a railroad track in the night, and await the passage of the express train. There is a wind stirring; clouds close in the light of the stars; the hum of light has ceased, blackness and silence brood together upon the face of the earth. Afar off, the listening ear catches the dawning roar. Half heard and half felt, it grows into more distinctness—partly revealed in the trembling earth, and partly felt as a shapeless horror filling the air. Every second swells its awful volume, and deepens its terror. The earth now quakes under its tread—a glaring fire flashes living horror into the surrounding air—and you see it, crawling along its shaky track, with fiery head crouched to the ground, and its long train sweeping from side to side with a wavy motion, a gigantic and terror breathing monster, instinct with life and power, crushing the earth with its tread, and creating a whirlwind with its blasting breath as it sweeps along. Is there anything in the world that impresses the mind with a more profound sense of resistless power than that enormous mass, with its blazing eyes and smoking breath, rushing with the speed of a cannon ball, and startling the air with the overwhelming horror of its flight? What could the savage think, seeing it for the first time?[80]

Regardless of one's station in life, rail travel in the early nineteenth century was one of the great novelties a person could experience. Few early travelers neglected to talk about the conveyance as well as the scenery or their destination. Many experienced railroads just for the thrill despite the inconveniences and absent any particular place to go or reason to arrive. As with users of any novel technology, it was not so much that the new technology was useful but that it was fascinating—a game, a marvelous toy for grown-ups. But in the long run it had to prove more than that—and it did.

CHAPTER 6

The Soulless Corporation

ne fine day in the spring of 1835, a bull grazing in a field along the Columbia Railroad in Georgia noticed a fire-breathing mechanical device pulling a train of cars through his domain. The bull did what he always did with intruders. He put his tail in the air and charged the locomotive at top speed. The engineer stopped the train and caught the blow on the front wheel. Dazed but undeterred, and angered by the hissing of the steam, the animal backed up and came forward again with a bellow. The engineer started to move and the beast struck short of his aim, missed his footing, and rolled down a high embankment "to the infinite gratification of those who had watched his behavior."[1] Apparently, this bull had not gotten the message that the world had changed.

That was true of some people, too. In 1833, Black Hawk, chief of the Sac and Fox tribe (and famous in newspapers because of the Black Hawk War a year earlier in which a young Abraham Lincoln participated), arrived with a delegation of warriors at Albany. He created a sensation and attracted a crowd of thousands. Because of the danger of hysteria, the men were secreted onto railroad cars under cover of darkness for the first leg of the journey back to their western homes.[2] It seemed that a year should be enough for Native Americans to transition from war with whites to giving newspaper interviews aboard a railroad car.

In Hartford, Connecticut, there was an old and, by 1836, neglected cemetery. All the talk was of millions for railroads, yet the cemetery's caretakers could not get a pittance to plant shade trees and to restore graves. In that ground rested the "founders of our civil and ecclesiastical institutions—men whose memories will be dear so long as liberty and religion have an advocate in New England." Yet their graves were being "trodden by the thoughtless" and ignored by the futurists. Money, enterprise, and skill could build railroads. Could it not prevent these graves from being defaced?[3]

Nor were bulls, Native Americans, and historic preservationists alone in being thrown off balance by the railroad. The regular citizenry seemed to have no more choice about the rapid coming of the future, and there was a significant minority who objected to being carried along pell-mell by that particular technological stream and the public mania that went along with it. Most, however, accepted the railroad as generally desirable and certainly inevitable and tried to adapt their lives and habits accordingly. However, it was not always easy.

There is some truth in the cliché that the winners write the history. There is, therefore, a tendency to see railroad development in hindsight as inevitable and to see it from the perspective of a place like Chicago, which the railroad truly made. The picture of universal acclaim, however, was much modified when drawn from the viewpoint of a town like the ancient village of Salem, Massachusetts, which in the 1830s felt it was being bypassed by the railroad and was not entirely sure it cared.

Clifford Pyncheon, a character in Nathaniel Hawthorne's 1851 novel *House of Seven Gables*, set in Salem, is described as the "most inveterate of conservatives," a man who loved the "antique fashions of the street" and the colorful history of his town. But that had changed as he sat ensconced in his seventeenth-century mansion.

> Clifford could hear the obstreperous howl of the steam-devil, and, by leaning a little way from the arched window, could catch a glimpse of the trains of cars, flashing a brief transit across the extremity of the street. The idea of terrible energy, thus forced upon him, was new at every recurrence, and seemed to affect him as disagreeably, and with almost as much surprise, the hundredth time as the first.

Hawthorne's authorial comment was rueful: "Nothing gives a sadder sense of decay than the loss or suspension of the power to deal with unaccustomed things, and to keep up with the swiftness of the passing moment."[4]

That was not atypical of early-nineteenth-century Salem opinion. A correspondent from Salem to the *Lowell Courier*, using the pseudonym "F," complained in 1835 that a railroad from Boston to the old seaport was not desirable. A legislative report two years earlier had shown that such a railroad could not be profitable to stockholders. Those who backed it, the critic claimed, did so because they were interested in the prosperity of Boston, not in that of Salem or other towns along the line. Some said transportation would become so cheap that people would live in Salem and commute to Boston. So what? What benefit would it be to Salem to attract these members of the wealthy and leisure class who would not bring business to the town or employ anyone there? And wouldn't people pay the 50-cent fare and go to Boston to shop, thus destroying the local retail trade?[5]

Another townsman disagreed—but in a frightening way. It was a free world, wasn't it? Whence came this idea that towns could make their own destinies independent of the rest of the world? Trade would seek its level. "It is behind the age to think of barring trade; we might as well attempt to compress the ocean in a thimble, or chain the mind of man." Why worry about the "birthright" of Salem, or even about its continued distinct identity? Might it not be as well-off as a suburb of Boston? "We must look at the project as it is; it is a part of the great chain of improvements which have commenced in Massachusetts; and wherever existing, designed by the Providence of God to harmonize communities rather than to make them jealous of each other."[6]

But the debate in Salem continued.[7] "F" responded that it had been argued that Salem had depended on commerce in the past and must depend on it in the future; that the contemplated railroad would have a tendency to withdraw commerce now carried on by Salem merchants in other markets from those markets and restore them to Salem; that whatever manufactures Salem had would be benefited in the transportation of materials and inventory; that the railroad between Salem and Boston would give Salem tradesmen advantages over those in the metropolis due to their lower overhead; and, last, that a railroad must be beneficial to all the places that it may connect, without reference to the particular or general interests of such places.

The writer disagreed with these arguments one by one. Salem had resources other than commerce. It could change its pattern. Would the railroad get rid of the difficulties that had made Salem merchants seek other markets? Why should a small town try to act like an inferior big city rather than to advertise the advantages it truly had? If the railroad did not induce Salem merchants to trade there, then why would it attract others to do so? Perhaps it would benefit Salem manufactures, but which manufactures did the promoters favor? There were hardly any. The railroad might benefit some people, but most Salem residents would be at a disadvantage.[8]

Some in town were shocked at the opposition and at the call for a town meeting to discuss whether to back a railroad when, to the promoters, the answer was obvious.[9] "Are our men of business, our proprietors of land, our house holders, aware of what is going on around them?" Neighboring Danvers was promoting a railroad; so should not Salem do the same or risk being "more secluded than now"? Who could be against growth? "Are we to be left on the rocks to perish, while a prosperous internal commerce carries Danvers, Andover, and all our satellites and neighbors onward? Are frothy arguments to prevail over the general sense of this community?—are a few old men and a fewer old women to rule in this matter?" Wouldn't all the young people leave Salem for the West if it did not keep up with the times? "Build your rail road so that the main and direct route from Boston to Bangor and Quebec will be through Salem, but do it soon, even now, or it will be too late for Salem."[10]

It was a classic bandwagon argument combined with intimidation, which in places like Salem had to be advanced with special vigor against the resistance of a substantial "old guard." Reporting on a meeting of potential subscribers to a Boston-to-Salem railroad, the *Newburyport Herald* concluded: "Every town between Boston and Newburyport is interested in a railroad, and if the Salem people do not choose to go *with us*, we must choose to go *without them*."[11]

Salem was not, however, the only town to resist. "A Man of Gray Hairs" living in Portsmouth, New Hampshire, wrote: "Ours is an *old* town, and of course has none of that excitement common to those cities which sprung up yesterday, where everything is to be done in one year." There was fishing and farming, and people could make good fortunes in Portsmouth, although some would complain about the "dull times" that would remain if the railroad did not come. So be it, said the elderly man. "It is true, should rail-roads *surround* us without *touching* us, we might, as a town, become isolated, as to inland communication, and so thrive less rapidly, in proportion, than our neighbors who live on the track." But thrive they would anyway, and they would do so while retaining the quality of life that made Portsmouth a worthwhile, even unique, place to reside.[12]

Newington, Connecticut, folks felt the same way. In 1836 they protested a proposed railroad from Hartford to New Haven running through their town, "representing that they were a peaceable, orderly people . . . and begged that their quiet might not be interrupted by steam cars and an influx of strangers."[13]

Salem residents advanced ever more subtle arguments against the seemingly inevitable triumph of railroads and railroad culture. "The people of Salem," stated a letter to the editor there, "cannot do a more stupid thing regarding their own real interests than to promote the building of a Railroad from this place to Boston. . . . Those places, which are so anxious to have rail roads pass through their territories, are most deeply in delusion. What are they to gain from them?" The staging inns and all their charm would disappear, and with it the harness making, carriage making, horseshoeing, and stabling that went with stagecoaches. Why was one form of business so much better than another? Because it was new? "Knock your horses in the head, and what becomes of the hay-growers in your vicinity—your coasting trade now employed in bringing grain?" Perhaps the railroad and its attendant stress would create more business for undertakers, but who cared for that? The railroad would go right through Salem and on to Portland, Maine, and no one would stop in the old village to buy anything.[14] Meanwhile farming was neglected in New England and wheat was imported from Canada "in the race of speculation" in which people preferred to live by their wits or the labor of others than to push a plow.[15] Writers from Salem documented corporate abuse, particularly that by the Boston & Lowell Railroad, in newspapers.[16] The town never comfortably adjusted or managed to go along well with the railroad program.

But, of course, the rest of the country ignored such places and swept on. The local newspaper pointed out in 1836 that protest was useless. Americans may prefer the stagecoach to the railroad, as they might once have preferred their fingers to a hoe, or their own backs to a horse, or a canoe to a ship. But progress was progress. "This is a point which the rest of the world have settled for us." If it used the railroad, "we shall be compelled to do the same; although we may succeed in keeping off the Railroad long enough to materially diminish its usefulness."[17]

By 1837, laborers on the Eastern Railroad, which was to serve Salem, were busy "evacuating hills, exalting the valleys, and making the rough places plain."[18] The company directors in 1838, the year the line was complete and a dinner for 600 put on in Salem, demolished an old wooden store at the bottom of Norman Street and purchased a Spanish convent bell to place at their spanking-new depot at Salem to give an aura of history and continuity to the place.[19] A toast at the opening celebration went: "The Loco Motive: May this modern chariot of Fire, never be under the guidance of Phaeton, to mar its beauty or impair its speed."[20]

The next year, however, another historic preservation issue arose when the Eastern Railroad proposed to pull down a "handsome and convenient" courthouse in Salem. If such buildings were to be pulled down and built all over again whenever a corporation wished, "we see no end or limit to the expense." Where did the corporation get such powers?

> If the Engineers of the Eastern rail road had not skill or ingenuity enough to go under the court house they should not have been permitted to go near it. As a matter of taste, as to the appearance of the city, we think it is decidedly bad. Clearing away is not always improvement, and when Salem is cut clean apart, and the Northeaster whistles through the market unchecked, we believe the Salem people will think it so.[21]

Soon after its completion to Salem, however, the Eastern was averaging 1,100 passengers per day and took in $2,000 in five days.[22] Who could longer resist? "All doubts are now vanished," said George Peabody of the company, "all serious obstacles are overcome." This latest achievement, he went on, showed the wisdom of the Commonwealth of Massachusetts in pursuing "a steady course of beneficent acts for the interests of her citizens" by commingling the capital of small places into one centralized corporate initiative. "The last twelve hours," Peabody said, "have produced an important change in the relations of Salem to her flourishing neighbor the Metropolis. Her condition to day is very much the same as if some invisible power during the night had removed the town with its unconscious inhabitants about ten miles to the South West."

The United States had an important role to play in the "great theater" of human affairs, and the Eastern Railroad was part of it. "The reasonable fears of the friends of mankind and the hopes of its worst enemies will alike be disappointed." Steam travel was a new age, a remarkable pageant:

> When the curtain is raised upon us, the scene presents none of those splendid pageants, which have for centuries dazzled the old world, where Kings, Princes, and Knights are drawn up on one side, and the multitude on the other; but the more interesting exhibition, of the whole people moving onward together

in a career of unexampled prosperity, bearing in their front the standard of Equal Rights, and placing their hopes of greatness in the general diffusion of "knowledge, industry, and humanity."

It was the perfect capstone to a long campaign to bring Salem and everyone else to the great industrial banquet.[23] "The Salem folks," wrote the *Boston Post*, "are in high spirits."[24]

Even Hawthorne's fictional Salem conservative, Clifford Pyncheon, eventually became infected with railroad mania. Leaving town on a railroad car, he opined that railroads were to make populations nomadic again and would "do away with those stale ideas of home and fireside." They gave people wings, so that no longer would anyone live over generations in a house like his, or in a town like Salem. With tongue in cheek, Hawthorne has Pyncheon mouth the standard rhetoric: "Why should he make himself a prisoner for life in brick and stone, an old worm-eaten timber, when he may just as easily dwell, in one sense nowhere,—in a better sense, wherever the fit and beautiful shall offer him a home."[25] And so Pyncheon whirls away from a Salem that is hardly Salem anymore.

What Salem was to cities in its stance toward railroads, New Hampshire was to states. It seemed at first that the state would be as enthusiastic as others. "Thirty-two miles an hour!" wrote a man at Concord in 1830. "What do you think of that dear readers. . . . Don't smile at this and say it is all a hoax."[26] Reporting on a railroad meeting in Windsor, Vermont, that same year, a newspaper in Amherst, New Hampshire, wrote that there could be no question about the importance of railroads, especially in New England with its winters.[27] But the native caution emerged soon enough. Reporting in the spring of 1831 on the demand for rail stocks in New York City, a paper at Concord advised, "This may all be well, but we must confess, to us, it looks too much like fever, to have a happy result. Projects that have been cautiously engaged in have frequently been the most successful."[28] The presence of pickpockets at the depots in Boston suggested that railroads would not exactly encourage the best social tendencies of mankind.[29]

It had been years, wrote an editor at Portsmouth in 1835, since New Hampshire had discussed internal improvements, and he had concluded that the subject might never come up again. However, it was no longer impossible to ignore the activities of other states. Railroads might be good for New Hampshire "if public spirit and persevering enterprise could only be enlisted in carrying forward some feasible plan."[30] A compatriot at Concord thought the spirit of speculation was all too rife, and he could not see why. Effects were too sudden and insubstantial. "The most sanguine and adventurous get up in the morning, rub their eyes, and look down the street to see if the railroad has got along!—and finding it is not yet in sight, set out in search of new speculations."[31] A "looker on" at Keene thought that the great mass of society was ignorant and was misinformed by party newspapers. Not one person in twenty ever read a twentieth part of arguments on great questions, and promises from politicians were easy to get. "In one part of the country, they or their agents go among the people and learn their wishes. If they want a rail road or a canal near them, they are assured that if they will vote for a certain party, they shall have a grant of the road or canal." Much of it was just pride and swagger. "The people . . . the majestic people are as noisy as so many schoolboys."[32] Riding the railroad from Boston to Lowell, a New Hampshire man felt spun like a top. "The sensation at first is like being hurried out of the world before your time or like being run away with." He found it "strangely unnatural."[33]

Soon debate began on a more fundamental level, namely the appropriateness of the corporate device through which railroads largely operated. By the mid-1830s some of the shine was off the miracle of the original rail lines, and there was considerable complaint against the abuses of monopoly, particularly directed at the Boston & Lowell. Why had that corporation's powers not been limited to a certain period of years, as was typical for bridge corporations? Did the Boston & Lowell not have a public responsibility, affecting, as it did, the interests of the community as well as the stockholders?[34]

Railroad officers felt obliged to respond to such charges. The president of the Winchester & Potomac, praising the progress of the B&O, said that subduing the wilderness was a way of advancing liberty, not imposing a new form of slavery. The railroad was a tool, and "who would refuse the aid of a skillful friend?" It was an abuse of language to call railroads monopolies and to criticize corporations. "Corporations, in modern times, have uniformly been associated with free institutions, and have been found the best auxiliaries of liberty, in promoting the civilization of mankind." Corporations laid out Jamestown and Plymouth and formed the Massachusetts Bay Colony. "It is under the protection of corporate powers that the friends of American improvement have moved in steady and irresistible phalanx, and have accomplished what scattered individual effort, unprotected, could never have achieved." But for the corporate influence "this fair valley would have been wrapped in the gloom of the forest, and the stark Indian might still have reveled in the wild confusion of the war-dance on the spot where we are now celebrating the peaceful triumphs of combined enterprise directed by enlightened legislation."[35]

New Hampshire, however, experiencing railroads up close rather late in the game, had mixed feelings. The Nashua & Lowell began operations in 1838, and one observer thought that had enlivened New Hampshire: "The people there are as busy as bees—every man steps quicker, and life seems almost to infuse itself in things inanimate." There was the usual rise in real estate in Nashua, and farmers seemed happy, as all they had to do was carry their produce to the depot in the evening or early in the morning and in three hours it was at market in Boston. But the regional press admitted that there had been some reservations, even among those who now seemed happy with the result. The state legislature had limited rail profits to 10 percent, and there had been rhetoric "against rich capitalists, overgrown corporations, monopolies, and all that sort of cant."[36] Even the most sanguine were uncertain about an 1839 proposal to invest the state's surplus revenue in extending the Eastern Railroad to Portsmouth. It might be better to invest it in an insane asylum. Even private investment was suspect, as it might detract from investment in local manufacturing. But maybe it was a fait accompli. "It might have been a matter of question whether on the whole our town would not be as well off were there no rail-road to pass from the Massachusetts line into our State—but that point once decided, we are left in the position of a sailor when the ship springs a leak—*pump or sink!*"[37]

The question broadened to whether the state had any right to extend credit to a railroad. Perhaps such power was reserved to the states rather than to Congress, but did it not ultimately rest with the people? "We hold," stated a newspaper article from Portsmouth, "that a man may be a very good democrat and yet hold to the opinion that neither the United States nor State governments possess the power to build Rail Roads or canals at the people's expense." Could or should the state back corporate debts, which the Panic of 1837 had shown often to be irresponsibly contracted?[38] Portsmouth debated the desirability of extending city aid to the railroad.[39] "These Railroad and Steamboat corporations have bodies," the newspaper concluded, "but emphatically, no souls."[40]

The town of Concord, New Hampshire, felt negative, too, about city aid. The friends of the railroad, the editor there wrote, would have to look elsewhere than to the public for funding. "The question is, cannot an interest be brought into service sufficient to carry on the enterprise?"[41]

As the Eastern Railroad proceeded into New Hampshire and attempted to purchase land, the issues of a corporation's right to the power of eminent domain and its liability for damages arose. Although the official press might more or less reflect the standard booster mentality, letters to the editor showed that members of the public thought otherwise. The corporation argued, a New Hampshire letter writer claimed, that its charter gave it the right to "enter any man's premises against his will, throw down his fences, dig up his grounds, and remove his buildings, and leave him to recover his damages hereafter in the way provided by the charter and statute upon that subject." It was true that the corporation had tendered a bond for damages, but that did not amount to payment. It was, the newspaper said, a "natural right" of every individual to hold and protect property, and this right had existed before governments. Even a legislature could not take land for public use without compensation.[42]

Of course, the writer was exaggerating the power of eminent domain, which did not grant a corporation the power to take property without compensation. However, delayed compensation, and the corporate power to take property without the consent of the owner, even if it paid an amount determined by arbitration, were offensive to many in New Hampshire. Did the Eastern Railroad have any right to place its depot at Portsmouth so near the Universalist Church? Did it have to cross twelve streets? Did these matters not involve "some of the most sacred rights of citizens"? The assumption of power by the railroad corporation should be resisted, and the company should be required to obtain the consent of the individual before entering his property.[43]

Other states were contemptuous of this stance. A New York newspaper called New Hampshire's restriction on land taken by railroads a "barbarian act," one that would "knock in the head" plans for expansion of New York railroads into New Hampshire. And was it a proper principle? "One million people," wrote the *New York Tribune,* "may earnestly desire the construction of a public work most vital to the interests of all, yet *one* rapacious knave or obstinate dunce, who owns fifty acres of good for nothing ravine in some mountain gorge, has the power to say to the whole state, 'you shall not cross my land unless you pay me five million dollars for it,' and the work is paralyzed."[44]

But New Hampshire was not finished. People there began questioning the terms of state rail charters.[45] A Concord writer thought that rail charters had been forced through in a "premature" manner and their conditions not fully digested. "Arbitrary and despotic principles have been incorporated into their charters in direct violation of the principles of a free government." There was an erroneous opinion, this analyst wrote, that railroads were for the public good and therefore had unusual rights to property taking. Not so!

Railroads are not indispensible to our necessities—they are a luxury for the rich—a convenience to the man of business, but the poor man buys his bushel of corn or his gallon of molasses no cheaper than before they were used. The manufacture of cotton cloth has advanced the good of the whole people more than all the Rail Roads in Christendom, and the greatest part of this is done by chartered companies, yet, they have no exclusive rights, arbitrary or despotic rules granted them.[46]

New Hampshire people also worried about state debts and about the reputation of states that defaulted on their bond obligations. States sold bonds in Europe for what they would bring, often only 65 cents on the dollar, and then spent the proceeds for railroads, which often were more expensive to build and less remunerative to operate than predicted. In 1840 the total debt held by U.S. states was upward of $300 million, but New Hampshire prided itself that it had no debt at all. There was a proposal that the federal government should absorb state debts. That would mean that New Hampshire would have to pay its share of the overreaching on railroads by Pennsylvania and Illinois. Go to the ballot box on this issue, a Concord newspaper advised, to save republican institutions.[47]

The Eastern Railroad arrived at Portsmouth, New Hampshire, in November 1840.[48] At that point there was some frustration at the obvious continued resistance to the corporation and its practices. Why was the New Hampshire state legislature so strict in issuing charters? Would this not cripple the state relative to others? A state law then set aside the usual procedures for eminent domain and required railroads to bargain with individuals for their land before building across it and to come to a free agreement on price before proceeding. Thus any individual possessed the power to stop the progress of a road. "It, indeed, amounts to a total prohibition of all future enterprises of the kind." People were well paid for their land along the Eastern road, a local editor thought, usually more than it was worth. There should be commissioners to fix the compensation and force landowners to take it, as was usual in other states. The paper admired the legislature's "disposition to protect the rights of individuals from grasping corporations, but in this case, it seems to us, the law operates as a bar to all projected Rail Roads, and is of questionable policy as it respects the rights of individuals."[49]

But New Hampshire had yet another arrow in its quiver. Many there, including a majority in the state legislature for a time, objected to the fundamental corporate characteristic of limited liability. The *New Hampshire Patriot and State Gazette* in Concord ran an editorial in the fall of 1840 entitled "Shall People or Corporations Rule?" The anticorporate rhetoric was extreme. "This class of intangible existences, of bodies without souls, is multiplying like the frogs of Egypt, and becoming more and more formidable." Railroad corporations never had enough and were daily "stealing and clutching" the political and social power from the people. "Seemingly banded together against the general interests of humanity by a common thirst for power and plunder, they are pervading and monopolizing every department of business and every source of influence, unless they threaten, if not seasonably and effectually checked, to swallow up alike the rights of individuals and the prerogatives of government."

The key to power was that stockholders of corporations did not, like the individual businessperson, do business on their own capital and responsibility. An individual was responsible personally, to the limit of his property, for any debt he contracted. Not so with corporations. They were reckless in the debt they contracted because they were structured so that individual losses were minor no matter what. "Like the horse leech they still cry *give, give.*"[50]

Why were railroads so great? Who had benefited? When the Eastern was proposed, stated one letter to the editor, people along the projected route in Massachusetts and New Hampshire were "lunatic" on the subject. "One would suppose that there was no other road in existence, that indeed to them belonged the discovery of the power of steam, engines, Railroads, &c, and that their fame exceeded the fame of any and all ancient and modern cities. It was said that the old men of the city assembled at the depot in the morning, and really forgot to go to their meals." Yet by 1841 most of the towns that had been courted had become minor way stations, hearing only the buzz of the engine on the way to Boston.[51] It seemed a bad bargain altogether.

New Hampshire debated the right-of-way issue into the mid-1840s. Enterprise should have full scope, wrote the paper in Concord, but the point in dispute was the right of the legislature to empower a private corporation for private gain to take from a man his land against his will. In that regard the New Hampshire debate was much like the modern controversy over the proper uses of the eminent domain power, and here the state did not regard railroads as a true public use. The chief purpose of a railroad, the legislators thought, was to make money, not to serve the public.[52] "If the constitution must be violated and the rights of individuals molested, it seems no good citizen can favor any project, which shall encroach upon the rights of freemen."[53] This led one commentator to write in dismay that he was certain that in the state's "lamentable" stance toward railroads, it had "shut itself out from one of the most beneficial improvements of modern times."[54]

Inevitably, the state eventually had more or less its share of railroads, and it learned to do what was necessary to accommodate them politically and socially.[55] But New Hampshire remained proud that it had not swallowed the whole package. An editor in Portsmouth noted that credit could not be separated from character: "Integrity, industry, virtue, and character it is that commands the capital which changes the sailor boy in his tarpaulin to the captain of the beautiful packet ship."[56] So at least it should be. New Hampshire retained its strict laws about individual liability and its narrow interpretation of eminent domain for some years.[57]

The *Albany Argus* wrote in 1841, in the wake of the Panic of 1837, that "New Hampshire may well congratulate herself, that she has never embarked in any of the wild and visionary schemes of internal improvements, which have plunged other states into such an embarrassing and wretched state of want and indebtedness. She has escaped the bitterness of learning by experience the folly of a large community attempting to carry on public works with prudence, economy or even honesty." Would that Pennsylvania and Indiana, burdened with state works not paying even their current expenses and repairs on state railroad systems, not to mention the debt service, had done the same.[58] The manic policy of the rest of the country was, according to some in New Hampshire, the "high road to beggary."[59]

The determination in New Hampshire was long-lived. A general rail bill in 1845 provided that the property of no individual should be taken by a private corporation for a private use without the owner's consent. It could be taken only by the state and only after the state declared the use to be for the public good. Stockholders in corporations were to be liable individually and without limit for all debts of the corporation. The corporate charter was subject to amendment or repeal by the state legislature at any time. In short, "the company and all its officers are held entirely and forever within the control of the legislature." This, an editor thought, was "calculated to promote the best interests of such railroad corporations as are willing to manage their affairs uprightly, with a view to the public good as well as their own emolument. Those who are not willing to proceed in this way ought not to go at all." New Hampshire would have railroads, but only when they were built and conducted "upon constitutional and equitable principles."[60]

Boston thought such a policy was a "dreaded obstruction" to its enterprise.[61] It was suspicious of presidential candidate Franklin Pierce just because he was from New Hampshire. What would the world be if it were all

New Hampshire? "The Bostonian would not invest the fruits of his industry and enterprise where the Legislature, at the instance of any influential demagogue, could step in at any moment, take away his corporative power, and leave him without protection." The idea that no land should be taken without the owner's consent was the view of "the old lady who pulled up the stakes as fast as the engineer put them down." Such people could not be allowed to prevail. What was wrong if New Hampshire preferred its traditions to the railroad, which would "start up villages on every waterfall in the State? It would startle the bears among the mountains with the whiz of machinery. White spires would point toward heaven, and troops of children would fill every schoolroom."[62]

New Hampshire did not seem to care about such criticism. If its restrictions were to be overturned, as so many wished, a regional paper stated, "the corporations would again rule by the sort of divine right, which they claim and again have the liberty to inflict upon the community the consequences of reckless speculations." Who cared what Boston thought? "Are we to render our legislation subordinate to the decrees of bankers and brokers? Are the people of New Hampshire to submit to the most humiliating degradation for the privilege of affording to capitalists the opportunity of making money in this State?" New Hampshire would be content with the teachings of the past: "Of all curses, spare us from the unbridled domination and will of the money power, and particularly when wielded in the form of corporations."[63]

The stubbornness in New Hampshire softened eventually, but even in 1847, progressives there complained about the radical dog-in-the-manger policy that remained and, in their view, restricted economic development in the state. "It cherishes the same hatred towards manufactures, rail-roads, the Protective policy, and progress in general, it then manifested; and the same desire to bar out capital; the same croaking spirit against all public improvements; the same desire to *level down* rather than *level up* the people; the same narrow mindedness in every matter which concerns the moral and physical condition of man."[64] When Asa Whitney proposed a Pacific railroad, New Hampshire, for a time almost alone, opposed it.[65] In 1850 the state was still "overdoing" railroad regulation, according to many. They seemed "to look upon Railroad Corporations as associations to be suspected, and against which the public must be protected."[66]

Certainly, New Hampshire's was no majority view. "Nobody out of New Hampshire and Arkansas doubts in these days the value of public improvements," wrote the *New York Daily Times* in 1857.[67] But it was a legitimate minority view, and it was strongly present amid all the railroad hoopla of the age. And as time passed, and the promotional stage of railroading gave way to the regulatory phase of the late nineteenth century, the early concerns of New Hampshire began more and more to have a national resonance.

Even in the 1840s there were other places that had a similar negative tone toward corporations. The situation in New Jersey, for example, created much comment. "New Jersey," went an 1848 polemic, "is the favoured land of monopolies, and the favoured residence of monopolists, the class of men who live by taxes imposed upon the labour of others, and thus compel their neighbors to plough their way through mud or sand, and to live in half-built houses, that they may ride in coaches and live in palaces." The farmer in New Jersey paid more for what he consumed and got less for what he produced. "If the railroad is attacked, it can rely on the assistance from the lottery and ferry monopolies. . . . It is one great league for the purpose of taxing you." Legislative votes in New Jersey were, it was said, bought

> at the low price of free tickets, oysters and champagne, while the outside support of lawyers, doctors, editors, and politicians, is secured by the aid of fees so moderate as to afford a strik- ing proof of the effect of the monopoly system, in crippling the growth of a State that should be one of the richest in the Union. Bribery and corruption prevail throughout to a degree unparal- leled, as I believe in the world.[68]

A Boston paper wrote in 1850 that anyone familiar with the history of rail corporations would know they had been guilty of "a multitude of great and little meannesses, which the persons composing them would have scorned, or not dared to do, in their individual capacity." That was in the nature of the corporation.[69] No one in New Hampshire could have put it more plainly.

Naturally, the vast majority of the population did not concern them- selves with abstract arguments about the politics of corporate rights. How- ever, there was a visceral reaction to the horrendous, graphic stories in local newspapers reporting on railroad accidents. It might be that statistically railroads were as safe or safer than stagecoaches, but steam, and the fire that went with it, added a particular horror to steamboat explosions and rail- road wrecks. Every passenger ran a considerable risk of sudden mangling injury or of becoming an unrecognizable corpse that relatives could not piece together well enough to give proper burial.

CHAPTER 7

---◦◦◦---

Scalded by the Steam

Boston paper ran a piece in 1836 documenting ways of dying by various means of transport. Railroads seemed the worse. Railroad promotion was in a way, the writer thought, as bad as encouraging the growth of mad dogs. "Time was when people were content with dying in their beds, requiring no other assistance than the aid of a physician. . . . The good things of life were leisurely enjoyed—journeys were made with caution, and with some attention to comfort and safety as well as expedition. A man's life was counted something worth, and he who accidentally lost his hold on it was reckoned unfortunate." Not so in modern times.

At first the accidents were shocking, then people seemed to get used to them. "Hecatombs" of passengers were sacrificed to the "Genius of Steam," even while the railroads disclaimed responsibility for the safety of their charges. More and more people were crowded upon more and more cars. Trains ran faster and faster on ever more exact schedules and often along single tracks with poor signaling and vague operating rules. When two trains going 20 miles per hour hit head-on, there was a pop like a lightning strike. "Disjecta membra—legs—arms—ribs—widows and orphans of the passengers dispatched in the cars—what matter these, while the stock is at ten percent advance, and New York papers are read in Boston the same day as published." The stagecoach martyr had "no chance for variety in the mode of immolation," but on the railroad death offered many choices.[1]

Even the most enthusiastic accounts of the new experience of riding the railroad contained an element of fear. A man riding from Boston to Lowell in the summer of 1835 felt shut up in the car and admitted that while waiting for the steam engine up ahead to start the train, "the boldest holds his breath for a time." At the start when the steam steed "coughs and then pants like a lolling dog," things "begin to spin like a top." The sensation, he wrote, was like "being hurried out of the world before your time or like being run away with." He found it "strangely unnatural."[2] Truly, there were some real disadvantages in the ride. And the press felt it was its duty to document these. Wrote a New England editor, describing a snow delay: "All the defects, as well as the advantages of Railroads should be known to the public."[3]

Probably the most newspaper ink on early railroads was not devoted to promoting the sale of stocks and bonds but instead described accidents, often in graphic detail. There was considerable parallel coverage concerning the responsibility of management for such accidents and documenting the lawsuits that were brought against the companies by victims. As with modern airline travel, it could be shown that statistically railroads were relatively safe. The annual report of the Philadelphia and Baltimore line in 1841 was typical in noting that of 600,000 passengers carried that year, only one died.[4] But, as with modern air travel, or evaluating whether to build a nuclear plant, the horror of the worst-case scenario description can cause all statistics to become irrelevant.

Eyewitness accounts were often reproduced. As is typical with people who have been through traumatic experiences, the emotion made vivid writers out of those most inexperienced in the craft. There is nothing in journalism, even of the modern sensationalist variety, to compare with a description such as that given by John Dougherty to the *Baltimore American* in 1841 about what it felt like to be crushed between a railroad car and a side wall at Lancaster, Pennsylvania. He sensed his ribs giving way "and to this succeeded the terrible sensation connected with the violent injection of the blood from the body to the head," which felt to him "like a flame passing from the latter to the former." He passed out, the train stopped and backed up, and Dougherty's body fell to the ground as though dead. He survived but perhaps at times wished he had not. Newspaper readers had no trouble imagining themselves in his place and calculating what would be the likelihood of that on their next journey by rail.[5]

Sometimes a professional was aboard when there was an accident. A collision on the Schenectady & Saratoga in September 1836 involved a correspondent of the New York *Journal of Commerce*. There was a signaling mistake. The agent insisted on starting the train down a single track, though the engineer warned against it and the passengers remonstrated with the agent. "All was done with such nonchalance on the part of the agent that we could not realize the danger . . . was serious." Two minutes of delay at the station would have avoided the accident. Passing around a curve, suddenly another train hove into view. "I thrust my head out of the window, and you may imagine my sensations on seeing, within a few rods, this huge machine, dragon-like, spouting fire, bearing down upon us with frightful rapidity!" The reporter's train, being drawn by a horse, was going slowly enough that he was able to jump off and witness the collision from a bank. The bodies of the cars were crushed "like an egg shell" and the passengers were thrown about, bloodied and bruised. It was not much of an accident, as those things went, but it made a considerable impression on the journalist and his readers.[6]

More serious, and evoking a similarly vivid description, was the wreck at the bridge over the Gasconade River in Missouri in 1855. The first excursion train on the new Pacific Railroad of Missouri had gone out from St. Louis and, on crossing a temporary timber bridge, plunged with all its distinguished guests down into the stream. Twenty-eight passengers on the eleven cars died and fifty were badly wounded.[7] But the raw numbers were nothing compared to what the reading public was forced to consider in sharing the experience of one who escaped. He wrote his account for the *St. Louis News*:

> It is before us now—that terrible scene. The moment before the long train with its load of life approached the fatal spot, many were intently observing from the windows the well marked line which separated the thick, turbid waves of the Missouri from the pellucid waters of the Gasconade; others looked out on the long bridge we were approaching, and remarked on its strength or its frailty; an old gentleman, whom we thought unduly cautious and nervous, wished he was out, "for," said he, "I believe that bridge will break down." We glanced out the window near us in a careless way, to see the structure, and turned round again

without the shadow of a fear that we were doomed not to cross it. At that moment came the destruction. We could see nothing, but we heard everything. A sharp, piercing sound, as of shattered timbers, came from the front. We knew its meaning. The bridge had broken down. Then followed four separate, well-defined crashes, and our car took the inevitable plunge. At the first sound, we sprang to our feet, and started to run backward. It seemed as though the ruin was approaching us, instead of our nearing it.

Every man in the crowded car in which we were, jumped up, as the shiver in front told of the coming danger. During these few terrible moments in which we approached the precipice, the intensest silence prevailed. Not a word was spoken. We had given two steps backward in an involuntary effort to avoid danger, when our time came to follow those who had gone before. Down, down, down, endlessly we seemed to go. We were not long falling, yet it seemed ages.

There was a loud noise, then silence, while the survivors crawled out and sat on rocks. The account continued:

Men were creeping, crawling, and hobbling from the shattered cars, some holding a leg, some pressing an arm, and some clasping the head. Several sat down near us, and breathed heavily, but spoke not. . . . A wooden shanty was standing a short distance off, and we got up and walked to it. Mayor King, with the blood streaming over his face, from a gash on his forehead, was trying to tear down the door. He finally succeeded, and we then, assisted by others, who had come up, tore off the sides, so as easily to admit the wounded being brought in. The floor was soon covered with the prostrate forms of men marked by every description of injury.—One had a leg lying unnaturally bent, or an arm doubled backward; here was one bending his head forward to let the blood drip from a gaping gash in his face, and there another with his bowels protruding from a hideous wound in his body. . . . Even through their agony shone the traits of a generous manhood. . . . A small boy was delirious with a wound on the head. A while he would lie moaning in the shanty, then jump up, run into the rain with shrieks that would have made the hardest heart shudder. A considerable time elapsed after the accident before men spoke about it. They were stunned, shocked, bewildered and unstrung by the overwhelming consciousness of the destruction they looked upon. As they recovered their senses, they began to talk. One knew that the man who sat next to him was killed, for a wheel had fallen upon him; another saw the man before him pierced by a huge splinter, and another still saw the roof of a car as it crushed the life out of this citizen, or that one.

At one part of the wreck, several wounded persons could be seen, directing the labors of those engaged in extricating them. One by one, as the timbers which pressed them were cut away, they were dragged out and borne away. Under the roof of one car could be seen the protruding limbs of seven lifeless bodies, crushed to instant death as they fell. . . . It was a terrible picture of blood and tears, of woe and sorrow, of suffering and fortitude, of silent agony and speechless grief, of life and death, which, we pray heaven, we may never look on again.[8]

There were numerous other opportunities for vivid description. A man from St. Louis described an accident on the Pittsburgh, Ft. Wayne & Chicago in the winter of 1860. A passenger car went off the track. "With its load of human life it is hurled over and over down a steep embankment on an adjacent fence. Its inmates scramble out, the fallen stoves set it on fire, and, abandoned to its fate, it is a beacon-light to what follows. Its flames throw over the ice and snow a lurid glare." A sleeping car detached itself from the passenger cars and rolled down an incline. "Down the precipice it turned; leap after leap it took; crash after crash came broken glass, falling like rain among its occupants." There were cries of help, but no one to help.

Picture to your mind's eye that sleeping car—fallen on its side at that moment—all prostrate! The lamps extinguished; the smoke of the overthrown stoves filling and stifling the car, adding to its gloom distraction and danger. The cry of fire was raised, and followed by the most terrible confusion, in the midst of which a lady was heard to cry, "Help!, my mother will be burned." The car was now filled with smoke, while all around was so dark that nothing whatever could be distinguished. The passengers knew not where they were, or the extent of their danger. At length the door was found, and a general rush for the open air was made.[9]

There were a few signature accidents during the pre–Civil War period that gained such wide publicity and attention that they reactivated the national debate. Among these were the accident on the Camden & Amboy in November 1833; on the Western of Massachusetts in October 1841; on the Boston & Maine in 1853, where the son of the president-elect, Franklin Pierce, died; at the Norwalk drawbridge on the New York & New Haven in 1853; on the Camden & Amboy and at the Gasconade Bridge on the Pacific of Missouri, both in 1855; and on the Michigan Southern in 1859. The fact that subsequent advances in safety did not prevent even more grim disasters was illustrated by the bridge collapse at Ashtabula, Ohio, in 1876, where ninety-two people died.

The first Camden & Amboy accident was by later standards not so horrible, but it was early and shocking. An axle gave way, perhaps from the heat of motion when the train was going 20 miles per hour. Twelve people were injured seriously, and one died.[10] This led to the publication of an "Address of the Camden and Amboy Rail Road and Transportation Company to the Public." The corporation claimed that the security of the passengers had always been its first concern. It had delayed using steam locomotives, despite complaints of passengers chafing at the slowness of horses, until the safety of the engines could be tested. There were strict speed limits. There was careful supervision by agents and timekeepers. The axle had been checked recently, and the accident was "produced by a combination of circumstances that have never before occurred, and in all human probability will never again occur."[11]

The 1841 accident on the Western was investigated by committees at the state and local levels and, at the time, was the worst ever in New England. Trains collided head-on at a joint speed of 60 miles per hour in a deep cut in a new section of the road where the rules were not perfectly established. The cars "were thrown into a total mass of ruins." Of the car behind the engine of the westbound train "not a vestige was left upon the wheels but the heavy timbered frame work, the whole body being shattered into atoms leaving nothing except the tin roof and the window frames of the sides." Forty of the 100 passengers, a few minutes before reading and writing comfortably and unaware of any danger, were injured, many badly mutilated.[12] A minister aboard described the scene as "awful, beyond the power of description."[13]

The Boston & Maine accident at Andover, Massachusetts, in January 1853 was the result of a broken axle precipitating cars over a 20-foot embankment. It received particular attention because among those killed was

Benjamin Pierce, the 11-year-old son of Franklin Pierce. The president-elect and his wife were both themselves injured and had to survey the horrible scene.[14] Probably a rock came through the window and hit young Pierce in the head. A fellow passenger saw Mrs. Pierce sitting without tears, and near her "in that ruin of shivering wood and iron, lay a more terrible ruin, her only son, one minute before so beautiful, so full of life and hope." Pierce and his wife took their son to a nearby house and laid him on a bed. He was bathed in blood, and the upper part of his head had been blown off, leaving the skull exposed.[15]

The Norwalk accident in May 1853 drew considerable nationwide attention, partly because it caused enormous damage, and partly because it seemed so obviously the result of carelessness and incompetence. Fifty people died when an express train, run by an engineer with little training who had been employed by the railroad only five weeks, ran through a primitive signal and drove his train into the water of a river where a drawbridge had opened for a passing boat.[16] The engine buried itself in the opposite bank, such was its speed and momentum. At the railroad station in Norwalk corpses littered the floor ready for identification by loved ones.[17]

After noting the "heart-sickening" particulars, a Washington, D.C., writer called it "wholesale murder." But it was only "the climax of similar sacrifices of life, less in extent, not in culpability, which are constantly occurring."[18] We are a thinking people, wrote one man commenting on the Norwalk accident. Why did we think so fast and dismiss the library of rail accident accounts that appeared every year? Railroads did not pay conductors, engineers, and switch tenders enough, and they did not employ enough of them. They were people looking for temporary employment, not those making railroading a profession. The public seemed to want speed, too, and was impatient with rules. Double track and signals were expensive.[19]

But the "blood-freezing" details of the Norwalk accident seemed to indicate that efforts thus far to improve things were in vain. They demonstrated, an editor wrote, "the utter uselessness of trying to enforce prudence, or carefulness, or common sense—no, not even common humanity—by example." Calling for bringing those at fault to justice was not enough. There had to be prevention in advance.

> For what boots it all? The forms of an investigation are always gone through with; a verdict of some sort is always rendered, (it matters not much whether it be guilty or not guilty); then a little public indignation always follows; but when that is spent, the ex-

citement is by common consent hushed up; nobody in particular is punished, and off we go again in a short while into rivers and creeks, drowning, as we have already drowned, men, women, and children by the score, else sending them headlong into eternity, quite as likely, by a collision at some cross road that might have been avoided, had there been less hurry to get ahead.

Something more should happen.

> The hecatomb of men, women, and children in Norwalk creek so ruthlessly robbed of life, as they were robbed, cry aloud for retribution. The wounded, who still survive in their agony, cry aloud too, for justice, if not for vengeance; while the hundreds of hearthstones made desolate all over the land send forth a mute but solemn appeal, which it will not do for Justice to sheath her sword unheeded.[20]

One report was that a director of the railroad was upset about the Norwalk accident primarily because the stock in his company had fallen by $25 a share.[21]

The second serious accident on the Camden & Amboy, which happened in August 1855, was not as costly in lives as that at the Norwalk Bridge, but it was costly enough. Twenty-five died and fifty were badly injured.[22] It was, again, a case of lack of double track and lack of adequate signaling. An engine, tender, and four passenger cars, with 180 people aboard, left Philadelphia at the usual time of 10:20 A.M. It ran 21 miles and was 2 miles beyond Burlington, New Jersey, when the engineer spotted the New York morning train. He reversed his engine and backed toward Burlington to let the oncoming train pass. The train was backing at about 25 miles per hour when it hit a carriage with a physician and five women on board. "There followed," a witness wrote, "a scene which those who beheld it represent as truly appalling—one that would shake the strongest nerves and sicken the stoutest heart. The cries of the mangled human beings who were buried beneath that chaotic wreck of material almost palsied the senses and disabled the arms of the few who were so fortunate as to be able to render assistance." A train from Burlington arrived to be piled with bodies.[23] But not all were removed before a man robbed several of the corpses.[24]

The national reaction was, again, deep shock. The whole thing was caused by one of the trains being behind schedule and trying to gain the next turn before the opposite train came up. The Camden & Amboy was

Accident on the New York Central, May 11, 1858. Bettmann/Corbis

one of the oldest and most profitable companies in the United States. "Yet we find," wrote a reporter at Charleston, "that, at the end of twenty years of profitable monopoly, it has adopted not a solitary improvement tending to the preservation of the mighty current of human life constantly sweeping through its channel."[25]

The C&A had recently lobbied to kill a liability law in the New Jersey state legislature.[26] The *New York Tribune* advised how to sue the company but did not give much hope for results. "The miasma of monopoly vitiates everything, even the jury-box."[27]

It was all too common and accepted. "This is truly an age of motion," a newspaper reporter in Wisconsin wrote. "You may be gliding along in the railcars at forty miles an hour, half asleep, dreaming possibly of her you are going to meet, when you wake up suddenly, and find yourself going down an embankment, making forty revolutions a minute, and land at the bottom [amid] broken cars, broken men, women and children, life and death. This is rather an unpleasant interruption."[28]

Then came the Gasconade wreck, just months later. Perhaps, wrote one, it deserved a separate chapter in the "gloomy history of railroad disasters which will some day be written." But in another sense it was all too familiar and could not really be called an accident. "It was the result of the most criminal ignorance on the part of the engineer who constructed the fatal bridge."[29] Thirty died there.[30]

The Michigan Southern accident of 1859 completed the horrible ante-bellum litany. At least forty died in that wreck, when a culvert over a stream between Chicago and Toledo gave way during a heavy rain with the train running at more than 40 miles per hour.[31]

"I felt myself violently thrown forward," wrote passenger W. J. Hawks, "and rolled up like a ball. I could feel the pressure of passengers piled upon me, and I felt the water gathering around me. I made a mighty effort to free myself, and succeeded." Hawks was a good swimmer and surfaced despite being hit by a crosstie. Trying to help, he found himself among piles of bodies.

> Some were just in the pangs of death. Others, caught and crushed by the falling timbers, begged me to kill them and put them out of misery. . . . The ground was strewed with heads, arms, legs, and dead bodies. I saw several with their backs broken and their lower limbs paralyzed, writhing in the sand. Some of them would clutch me as I passed with a grasp from which it was almost impossible to free myself.[32]

The tiny filler items were as horrifying as the full-blown accounts. On a Sunday, stated an 1840 short piece, a young man named Yerkes, 19 or 20 years old, had his head cut off by being run over by two railroad cars in Philadelphia. "The amputation was effected so completely, that the part severed from the main body was actually taken up on a shovel."[33] A peddler on the Columbia Railroad was looking out the window of his car when his hat blew off. He stepped out, lost his balance, and the train ran over him. It cut off both legs and an arm: the man lived only a few minutes.[34]

Often it seemed as though the slightest inattention, the least carelessness, a little of the slowness of age, even, could be fatal in the new fast and unforgiving world. An elderly woman coming into Newark by train was slow debarking from a train stopped at a bridge short of town. She stepped off just as it started again and caught one foot under a wheel. Her clothes were entangled in the journal of the wheel and stripped off, her life saved only by the train's slow speed.[35] A boy died on the Germantown railroad when he used the "perilous pillow" of the tracks to take a nap.[36] A deaf man failed to hear a bell.[37] A woman who had never seen a train and had visited Harper's Ferry just to see one, while standing with her husband misjudged the speed and the way the train would pass through the switches; she died under its wheels.[38]

There was a constant drumbeat of such news, so much so that some complained it seemed the press and public had become almost accustomed to a high level of risk in rail travel. "Mr. Miller, an agent on the railroad, was shockingly mutilated at Columbia, Pa., on Saturday, by the cars running over him. He died shortly afterwards, leaving a wife and four children."[39] The son of the Reverend David Kimball of Concord, aged 8, jumped onto the cars for a ride "as boys like to do." His legs caught between the cars and the flooring as the train advanced into the depot. He was carried along 100 feet, his flesh ground off to the bone. His brother saved him from certain death by catching him by the shoulder and holding his body up as his thigh dragged.[40] A man, his wife and three children, and a friend, trying to cross the railroad in a wagon in 1852, were hit by the express from Fitchburg running at 40 miles per hour near West Cambridge, Massachusetts. "Mr. Sawyer and Mr. Ames were torn to pieces, and their dismembered bodies scattered along the track. Miss Sawyer, a beautiful girl of 15 years, was also instantly killed. Mrs. Sawyer was thrown onto the engine and held her place there for a distance of half a mile. When taken up, her skull was found to be fractured." A 2-year-old child, held in her arms, was unharmed.[41] And so on and on, day after day, month after month, year after year.

There were little things, common things, part of the background of modern life. A Newark paper commented that accidents were lamentable but were often not the responsibility of the corporations. "If men will throw themselves in the way of danger, contrary to the dictates of prudence, and the warnings of experience, they must be prepared to reap the consequences of the temerity."[42]

Many disagreed with that assessment. Should not more liability and responsibility be assigned? And should that liability rest almost exclusively with the railroads, even if they could show they were operating as best they could, or that some passenger was not following the rules? Too often, newspaper writers thought, the official explanation was that no one was to blame; the accidents were simply a hazard of doing business, a reasonable risk for the new convenience.

With a deep sense of irony, a Boston writer commenting on the Western Railroad accident of 1841 and the outrage of many papers that this was due to the irresponsibility of men, not an act of God, wrote that these reformers did not understand the times. Such outrage, wrote the Boston man, was "an illustration of old-fashioned morbid feelings, that were fashionable and perhaps natural when steamboats and locomotives were unknown. In those dark and barbarous times, human life was thought to be of some value, but now a man who can entertain such expanded notions must be at least fifty years 'behind the age.'"[43] Making similar use of the ludicrousness of the situation, a Connecticut editor in 1850 wrote that government seemed to have given up on the idea of protecting the lives of its subjects. There was "a sort of modern Magna Charta, by virtue of which an American may with perfect impunity be blown up, scalded, or burnt to death on board a steamer, or run over by a Railway train, with the extreme satisfaction of knowing beforehand, that the coroners inquest will bring in a verdict of no blame to any one but the unfortunate subject of its deliberations."[44]

Maybe the *Book of Common Prayer* needed to include new petitions for the "exigencies of the age" and its perils. "The current history of the times is rapidly presenting railroad riding as among the most formidable foes of human life."[45] The Decalogue's warning about killing apparently did not apply to corporations. "Death inflicted by the individual is murder; death inflicted by society is eternal justice; death inflicted by corporations is by visitation of God. . . . The moralist must conform to the times by stretching his code to meet the exigencies of steam." Railroads picked unqualified employees because they were cheap, and the same was true of the selection of axles and wheels. Inquiries into railroad accidents, a reporter for the *New York Daily Times* commented in 1852, were the "merest pretense."[46]

The rhetoric only escalated as the problem continued. "To tell a man some hundreds of miles from home, who has been flung at a rate of forty miles an hour against the pier of a bridge, or crushed like an opera-hat, his cheek stove in, or a hole drilled in his skull, that he has his remedy by commencing an action against the Company, in which he may get a judgment in two years, is so ludicrous as to border closely on the sublime."[47] What good did constant headlines do when there was still such ennui? "Nobody to blame! Would it be possible to persuade the man who has been stricken down in the flower of his manhood, and rendered a hopeless and unsightly cripple, that nobody is to blame? Would it be possible to make that mother, who is wailing to loss of her loved child, believe that nobody is to blame?" Sidney Smith once said there was no security against the aggression of the Church hierarchy until a bishop was hanged. A writer at the *Chicago Daily Tribune* in 1858 thought the same was true of railway superintendents.[48]

Increasingly, nonchalance about accidents or blaming the victims did not seem acceptable. "The catalog of crimes—for crimes they are—committed on railroads, is daily increasing in magnitude," wrote a journalist at the *New York Herald* in 1843, "and yet they are passively observed and soon forgotten from the public mind, and the companies are permitted to sport with human destiny."[49] The *Herald* concluded that there was all too much of such news. There needed to be rigid inspection and more regulation.[50]

The rail president is quoted as saying the company will make some cosmetic changes and come out ahead by the next dividend. Bettmann/Corbis

It seemed to a writer in Connecticut in 1843 that every few days, there was a serious rail accident "by opposing trains, running from the track dashing through the car houses." The result was a dangerous complacency.

> There is blame, grievous blame, attachable to some who have the control and management of Railroads. . . . Is it to be winked at, or set down as a light thing, that some such accident should instantly kill several passengers, or send a score to their homes, to drag out months of distress with broken shoulders and limbs, and the public to be turned aside from these sickening results, by the *criminal* excuse, that the *up* train did not expect the *down* train to reach that place so soon?[51]

Why was the Harlem Railroad, along the streets of New York City, so dangerous? What authority did this "rickety railroad have" for mangling so many? Why did the City Council tolerate it? "Have the Wall Street brokers not sufficient worthless stocks to gamble without blowing up this bubble, and spreading another net to catch the unwary?"[52]

There was great hurry. "Talk not to us about physical suffering or mental anguish," wrote a journalist in a travel book published in 1855. "What are they to us? We have no time to listen. The bell rings, the steam whistle shrieks, 'All aboard!' cries the conductor, and we are off on the train that never returns."[53]

The call for reform became more strident as the years passed and accidents accumulated. "If railway people will persist in playing games of life and death with their passengers," a reporter concluded in 1852, "they may expect the public to watch them and their affairs with growing attention. . . . We make the bargain daily with a thriftless recklessness about the sum we bleed for. . . . Railways were invented for the people, and not for the corporation."[54] People actually enjoyed reading the titillating news of rail accidents. "Headlong we rush, some to fortune, some to greatness, and many to destruction. . . . We scarcely have time to stop and view the bodies which fall dead on the way."[55]

The Norwalk wreck did lead to some reaction in Connecticut, where it was said that the New York & New Haven Railroad must be made to understand that a road that is unsafe to the public is not profitable to the stockholders. "When the market price of the shares varies with the prudence of management on the road, then safety will become a part of the regular business of the company." Connecticut passed a bill providing for high compensation to victims if carelessness could be proved.[56]

Some of the press thought that was not enough. The railroad should pay for every life lost regardless of the cause and should make the road safe no matter what. "If we would secure the dog, let us fasten him with something better than a rope of sand; let us put a chain of iron around his neck."[57] The estimate was that the company's liability under New York statutes could be $250,000 and under Connecticut statutes $500,000.[58] Dr. Rufus Griswold received $10,000 from the New York & New Haven in compensation for injuries to his wife and daughter at Norwalk Bridge. Pal Newel of Newport received $3,000 for the death of his son. "Passengers are so completely helpless for their own safety in travelling on railroads," a reporter wrote then, "that the managers ought to be held to the strictest accountability for the prevention of disasters as far as lies in their power."[59] On State Street in Boston in June, various people suffering from railway injuries created a living exhibit, each with a sign on how they were hurt.[60]

Statistics came to the fore, indicating that American railroads were more dangerous than in Great Britain. One in 43,000 rail passengers was a casualty in New York, whereas it was one in 412,000 in England. In England there were gates at each crossing attended by a keeper, porters at every door when people boarded. "How different . . . from the hurly-burly that marks the departure of one of our Railroad trains."[61] Before mid-August 1853, there had been sixty-five U.S. rail accidents that year, with 176 killed and 333 injured. "There is a total which should put our civilization to the blush, and almost make men foreswear the progress of the age."[62] Yet when the New York & New Haven instituted a rule that trains must stop at drawbridges until safe conditions were confirmed, passengers complained that it added twelve minutes to the trip between New York and New Haven.[63] Double track was too expensive.[64]

An article in 1860 in *Frank Leslie's Illustrated Magazine* titled "The Public Verdict" made the judgment that man was inhumane to man. The public was shocked for a time at the news of each accident, yet it soon forgot due to a kind of "indifference to human misery." The public could not help itself. "They are at the mercy of Juggernauts, who care nothing for collisions until they find they are expensive. How is it that men, who would recoil from being personally concerned in a murder, should so readily lend themselves collectively to the slaughter of hundreds for a mere beggarly dividend?"[65]

The same magazine stated that "crime has always an excuse, and wealthy culprits always escape punishment." Railroads made "idiotic" arrangements. "In ordinary business transactions men making such manifest blunders would be called asses, but in these instances the mistake assumes a graver character, and the makers must be characterized as reckless, inhuman, incompetent men, unfit to hold positions which place in their hands the custody of millions of lives."[66]

There was certainly also a psychological factor independent of the actual risk. People would journey by stage without a tremor but "will scarcely breathe from fright while rushing along behind a snorting locomotive." This was true even though statistics showed one was seven times as likely to be injured on a stage. The trouble was that on the railroads, deaths were grouped together "and the mutilation of passengers and the accumulated horrors of the event are seen at a glance of the eye, and produce a tremendous effect on the imaginations." In 1858, there was the calculation that the chances of dying by traveling 1 mile on a railroad were 65 million to one.[67] But that did not quell the fear.

A Kentucky man during a legislative debate in 1838 denounced all railroads "as vile and modern innovations on the settled and professed habits and customs of our ancestors." He said he never wished to see a railroad.

> If you traveled in a car, and look out of a window to spit, you spit in your own face. If the children wished to stop for any purpose, you could not get them out; and if you wished to call and see an old friend, and talk over the politics of the day with him, you could not do it. You could see nothing, hear nothing, and know nothing.[68]

Dorothy Ramsbottom, a dialect humorist, agreed:

> We mean to go by railroad, which is the only way of traveling now; if it was not for not being able to stop if you want, and the being locked in, and the noise of the hinges, and the smell of the smoke from the chimney, and the ... rattlin, and the not being able to see nothing of the country, and the danger of being blowed up or nocked off the rales I do think hit wud be purfict.[69]

CHAPTER 8

The Near West

"he mass of the American people have heard of the 'great West,' the 'enterprising West,' the 'spiritually destitute West,'" wrote the *Home Missionary* magazine in 1841. "But the reality they have never seen, nor conceived of, even in mental vision. They have seen the faint resemblance on the map, not the out-spread empire itself. They have looked upon the ingenious drawings of the painter, not upon the living, growing reality." The State of Illinois spanned 16,000 square miles, larger than all of New England excepting Maine. At the turn of the nineteenth century, Illinois had 215 people and Massachusetts more than 420,000. By 1841, Illinois had a population of 475,000, Massachusetts 737,786. Eastern sentiment could not stop inevitable emigration toward the West. The only question was, "Who will direct this mighty influence?"[1]

In the fall of 1835 the citizens of Cincinnati, Ohio, had a mass meeting on the subject of railroads. Dr. Daniel Drake, an activist there, pointed out in the resulting report that Ohio was isolated, at least by the standards of the emerging age of rail. He thought it remarkable that the South and West, except through the medium of the Mississippi and Ohio river systems, knew little of each other, compared with the acquaintance of Ohio with the eastern states. The solution was a railroad, and Cincinnati proposed an ambitious one from that city to Charleston.[2] Drake was of the "build it and they shall come" persuasion. One should not wait for the development of the region "before resorting to the only cause that can produce it."[3]

The fledgling city of Chicago, perched at the southern edge of Lake Michigan and until recently considered a "remote Indian wilderness," had proposed two years earlier at a public meeting there a railroad connecting the Illinois River with Lake Michigan.[4] The Illinois state legislature reported in 1835 that the sentiment of the community favored railroads over any other form of transport. With "suitable restrictions" on their charters, railroads were the "most ready and effectual method" to promote prosperity, advance wealth, and populate the West.[5] The state sought federal land grants in 1836 for a line it was already planning as the Illinois Central.[6] Indiana was doing rail surveys that year as well and was courting foreign investors.[7] Promoters first proposed a railroad from New Orleans to Nashville in 1834, potentially reducing the 1,300-mile journey along the windings of the Cumberland, Ohio, and Mississippi Rivers to a pleasant two-day journey of about 500 miles.[8] There was a railroad talked about in 1835 from Wheeling, West Virginia, to St. Louis, long before the B&O came anywhere near Wheeling from the east.[9] A few papers in the mid-1830s were talking about a railroad to the Pacific Ocean. Although some thought that was "more desirable than practicable," others said that it could be constructed in the not too distant future.[10]

Charleston entrepreneurs pointed out that the states "engaged in the Cotton cultivation by slave labour" must improve their communications with each other "to present an undivided front to those who would assail their common interests and institutions." Railroads were but the "instruments of a political combination, having its source in affinities and sympathies that cannot be dissolved, but may be invigorated by improving these channels."[11] If the czar of Russia could institute a railroad from St. Petersburg to Moscow nearly 500 miles long and costing $30 million, invite an American to superintend it, and buy American-built locomotives for it (all of which the czar did in the early 1840s), then there should be no limits to the ambitions of American rail corporations in integrating far-flung regions.[12] New railroads, easily imaginable in the mind's eye, would form a "stupendous chain . . . which will cast into the shade all that is now the theme of our boasting." It was the era of the railroad. "If we were desired to designate the present age by a hieroglyphic," wrote a southern paper, "we could not think of a more expressive emblem than a well defined locomotive engine."[13]

There was no end to imagining. Cincinnati luxuriated in 1835 in obtaining fresh fish from the New York markets by special express and was delighted to think what would happen when the whole distance was covered by rail.[14] And the New Orleans & Nashville, with a 5-foot, 5-inch gauge for carrying cotton, might itself extend to the Pacific by connecting New Orleans with the Gulf of California and thus establishing a direct trade route with China![15]

The hope was to borrow largely and use the time thus gained to harvest revenue from the new towns and the new businesses they sowed. A report of the Maryland legislature on internal improvements in 1835 advised looking to the activity of states elsewhere and to the "rich fruits" for the taking available in the West for those willing to invest considerable capital. Public works, owned by or aided by states, had, the Maryland people wrote, "almost creative power, calling forth and disenthralling the hidden wealth and slumbering resources of whatever wilderness they penetrate."[16] The New Orleans & Nashville, one editor thought, would double the population of New Orleans ten years after completion. Every clerk in town should subscribe to the stock, which cost only $1 a share: "It will make us all rich."[17] It was not an age to tolerate inaction, a Richmond man wrote.[18]

Distances traveled came to be evaluated by the time it took, and therefore the distances separating one place from another shrank in people's minds when they thought of railroads. The 1836 publication "Circular to the Citizens of the State of Mississippi" made the point well:

> Already were the cars whirling thousands and tens of thousands of men, women, and children, at the rate of twenty miles per hour, from one state of the Union to another, with as much ease, and in the same time, as they could formerly have paid a visit, through the mud to their nearest neighbors; and all this, performed, too, by an agent which acts without toil or pain, and never tires as long as its iron harness lasts, and our coal mines and forests are able to supply it with food.[19]

Iowa was equally sanguine. A rail engineer, writing to the *Iowa News* in 1839, commented on the prospects of a rail line connecting Dubuque with Lake Michigan. This would avoid the problems associated with low water in the Mississippi.

> Suppose the rail road to the lake in operation, how different would be our situation! Instead of being confined to the St. Louis

market for our supplies, and excluded from that even, during at least six months in the year, by ice and low water together, we should have here open to us *daily* access, throughout the *entire* year to the *seaports* of Lake Michigan, and a much more direct and far less interrupted communication with New York, Philadelphia, Boston, &c. than we can *ever* have via the Mississippi and Ohio rivers.[20]

Perhaps the centralization of newspaper publishing, into media centers in modern parlance, would be one result of extending railroads to those centers, not to mention the easy and quick distribution of newspapers. James Gordon Bennett, editor of the *New York Herald*, thought it was a law of God that both the intellectual and material had a tendency toward centralization. "In the newspaper press," he wrote,

it begins already to indicate its powerful operation in this country, facilitated, as it is, by rail roads and steam power—for it is probable that, as the large cities of England are principally supplied with the London newspapers, so will the large cities of the United States be supplied with those of New York. The listless and unenergetic condition of the press in our provincial cities—their lazy pride and want of independence—particularly in Philadelphia—facilitate this revolution now in progress, giving to the energy and independence of the metropolitan press an ascendancy that cannot be assailed or weakened.[21]

In the United States, filled as it was by practical idealists, results would follow quickly in the train of information and ambitious analysis. Railroad investment was, wrote one man in the middle of the Panic of 1837, simply "practical patriotism."[22]

No matter how overblown such rhetoric was, it spawned more of its kind and found ready readers. It is impossible to tell how many were influenced by it and in exactly what way, but then as now, newspapers doubtless tried to increase their circulation by appealing to the prejudices or gullibility of readers. Rail promotion was a cash business for newspapers that fell on fertile ground.

Nearly every substantial city was in the 1840s thinking about western expansion. Charleston reached toward Nashville; Philadelphia backed the construction of the Pennsylvania Railroad over the old Main Line Canal system and toward Pittsburgh; and Louisville pointed rail lines toward

Memphis. New Orleans, Richmond, and Savannah at least talked a good fight. But there were four thrusts to America's Near West: the Western of Massachusetts, the New York & Erie, the Baltimore & Ohio, and the Western & Atlantic of Georgia—that definitely matured during the 1840s into major completed or nearly completed lines.

All got under way early but took some time to build. Their fortunes were closely watched by those who were backing projects still in the talking stage as tests of the "developmental" aspects that were typical of so many American railroads. Wrote a Memphis man: "It is an antiquated error to suppose that the building of roads should be postponed until the necessities of population demand them. Make the roads, and the population will go there along with the road."[23]

The Western of Massachusetts, which extended to Albany from the termination of the successful Boston & Worcester, was the first of these to reach its goal, partly because that goal was more modest than some. It opened its subscription books in the fall of 1835, and subscribers took immediately $1.2 million of the $2 million required. It seemed to promise to "bring the whole commerce of the [Erie] Canal as near to Boston, in point of time (though not as to the convenience of transporting heavy freight), as it is to New York."[24]

The topography was promising also. The route ran at right angles to the chains of mountains and large watercourses traversing Massachusetts. When it was finished, the railroads north and south of it and its eastern extension, the Boston & Worcester, would be finished easily through river valleys, thus interconnecting the whole state.[25] A local network developed rapidly. By the fall of 1840, lines east of the Hudson included the Boston & Portsmouth (Eastern), the Boston & Lowell, the Boston & Worcester, the Western of Massachusetts, the Boston & Providence, the Taunton Branch, the Providence & Stonington, the Worcester & Norwich, the Housatonic, the Long Island Railroad, the Harlem Railroad, and the New York & Albany (Erie).[26] The Western, although less than 150 miles long, was, a correspondent wrote, "the avenue to the whole of the great west."[27]

Enthusiasm overflowed when the line reached Springfield in October 1839. It was to be of incalculable advantage to Massachusetts in linking the eastern and western parts of the state and bringing the valley of the Connecticut River into contact with the seacoast. When it reached its final goal, Albany would be as near in point of travel to Boston as it was to New York in summer, and in winter it would be in effect half nearer. The fare from Boston to Springfield was $3.75, shared by the two companies constituting the through line. Freight was $6.50 per ton for this distance. These were advertised as some of the lowest rates in the nation.[28]

Consequently, there was quite a celebration at Springfield. Excursionists could pick one of two trains each day and make the journey (which formerly took two days) "in half a day with perfect ease and little fatigue." Prices on merchandise were down three-quarters from the former rates, and the views of the fall color were spectacular.[29] The company built a splendid depot at Springfield and stationed six locomotives there. James Gordon Bennett of the *New York Herald* rode the line and declared it the best he had ever experienced: "If the Boston capitalists carry through their road to Albany in the same style . . . they will do themselves great credit, and increase the travel through New England to a larger extent than we can yet form a conception of."[30]

Governor Edward Everett pointed all this out to the gathered crowd of 700.[31] He said he had no set speech but rather "feelings, emotions . . . anticipations, if you please, visions." He had been an original subscriber to the Western Railroad, which was now reducing the rivers to feeders at best. "Let us contemplate the entire railroad, with its cars and engines, as one vast machine! What a portent of art! Its fixed portion a hundred miles long; its moveable portion flying across the state line like a weaver's shuttle; by the sea side in the morning, here at noon, and back in the compass of an autumnal day! And the power which pulls all in movement—most wondrous." Providence had committed Massachusetts and the whole nation to the task of building railroads. "It is the law of our moral natures, that the great boons of life are to be obtained by a strenuous contest with natural difficulties." If it were a more poetic age, the governor thought the genius of steam communication might be personified and embodied as a "Colossus of iron and brass, instinct with elemental life and power." With one hand he would collect the furs of the Arctic Circle and with the other "smite the forests of the Western Peninsula."[32]

H.A. Dearborn passed over the line to Springfield in November 1840, described it in detail, and declared it good. He wrote that it appealed to the geologist, the scientific artist, and the promoter of internal improvements. It rivaled the works of the ancients, who only put up monuments to despotic power, but these advanced the human race.[33] By then there were 2,000 men at work on the line.[34]

Reaching the western boundary of Massachusetts, construction slowed. Once into the State of New York, there would be a question of building a bridge at Albany over the Hudson River. That would be an expense and might interfere with navigation. The solution adopted was to stop on the near side at a place called Greenbush, then use the ferry to cross the river. Troy, New York, already had a railroad bridge but was a bitter rival of Albany and competed for the terminus. It had not been the plan to build to Troy.[35]

The company seemed strong enough to do as it would. Stock sold at $80 per share, dividends were yielding 11 percent on investment, and the required $4.5 million in capital had been provided.[36] Yet there was a political hazard. The governor, Marcus Morton, in his annual message that year objected to the use of public credit for railroads, worrying how the state would pay the annual interest, not to mention the principal, if it loaned more resources to the Western and others. The Whigs in the state immediately responded that the governor was only reflecting the Locofoco side of politics. He was against internal improvements on principle and was not reasoning well about the actual risk. Most of the railroads to which the state had given aid were generating considerable profits, and mortgages on them provided adequate security for any risk the state might take. The state had not risked more than $500,000 on the Western, and even if it lost that, was it much to bear "compared with the opening of a rapid and constant line of communication between the Capital of the State and the great Western waters"? Massachusetts credit was strong in England, and the total debt of the state was modest.[37]

Other railroads were doing well with earnings. The Utica & Schenectady, only about 80 miles long, earned 13.5 percent on its capital in 1840.[38] There seemed no reason why the Western should not match them. There were 60,000 hogs brought from Albany and Troy, most of which would be loaded on the railroad rather than have them lose weight while being driven more than 100 miles.[39] The same would apply to sheep and cattle also. Cropland had sold for $20 an acre a few years before but had increased to $70 with news of the coming railroad. New York produced more flour and swine than Massachusetts, but Massachusetts topped New York in cottons, woolens, furniture, boots, shoes, hardware, oil, fish, and wheat. "Although the mountain defiles threaded by the road still shelter the virgin forests, on the outskirts lie rich pastures, mowing fields and tillage land, yielding to none in the State, and villages tenanted by an active and intelligent population. . . . Can a line of Railroads uniting two such States, leading through the centre of each to its most remote borders, fail to create a profitable commerce?"[40] Revenues of the Western during its first year of operation were $512,000, expenses $266,000.[41]

With the completion of the Western of Massachusetts in the fall of 1841, it became a kind of cottage industry among newspapers to write up articles comparing the current prosperity and growth of Boston with that of New York, usually to the advantage of Boston and causing trepidation in Gotham.[42] The Hudson River, wrote a New York paper in the summer of 1841, "may be considered, for all the purposes of trade and travel, as blotted from the map of the State—the beginning of a *half year* of prostration of N. York interests in favor of Boston interests, and yet the capitalists of the city of New York are as blind as beetles and cold as tortoises on the subject. . . . We may talk as we please of our geographical position, if we let Boston give a new confirmation to the earth's surface."[43] There was no use to disguise it, a New Yorker wrote early in 1842, "Boston has beat New York. . . . We are on the verge of a revolution, and unless something be done, the rents and real estate of New York will fall 30 per cent in three years."[44] A New York traveler in the spring of that year said that if any doubted that Boston was making inroads on the trade of New York City, then let him make a trip on the Western Railroad and see trains with thirty or forty cars "heavily laden with the products of almost every climate and nation, destined for the interior and purchased in Boston." There were also trains filled with western New York flour and staples. When one saw this, he would not doubt that Boston "by the exercise of an industry and enterprise which are worthy of all possible commendation, is drawing within her own magic circle with perfect impunity, the vast depositories of internal wealth which legitimately belong to the city of New York."[45] The Western was planning to put on refrigerator cars in which fresh pork, poultry, and venison, as well as eggs, fresh fish, and fruits, could be transported safely on ice.[46] An observer watching the Western depot at Greenbush, New York, late in 1845 saw the floors of the merchandise houses piled with flour, hides, beef, pork, salt, stoves, lumber, cotton, "and in truth everything that is bought and sold in this country."[47]

Boston boomed. In the three years after the completion of the Western, it "almost burst with its swelling greatness."[48] The new merchandise depot for the Western Railroad was said to be one of the largest in the world, exceeding 450 feet.[49] Railroad buildings, by 1845, covered 100 acres.[50] Old mansions were torn down in favor of blocks of "swelled front modern dwelling houses." The harbor was filled in to create more real estate.[51] "Who that walks the streets, morning, noon, or night, does not find himself in the midst of a moving mass of living beings?" Visiting the railroad depot, one saw a multitude of strangers disembark and head for the new hotels.[52] Bostonians seemed "to be stretching their arms all over the country," buying up other railroads (the Reading in Pennsylvania, for example) as well as developing their own.[53]

By 1845 it could be reported that real estate assessment in Boston since the completion of its railroad to Albany had increased $200 million, whereas that in New York City for the same period went up only $15 million.[54]

No one could fail to notice the change in the appearance of Boston. "Instead of the quiet literary emporium, accessible only by long bridges, and mostly covered with retired residences, its business being confined to the vicinity of Faneuil Hall and Long wharf, the visitor now finds a busy metropolis." Locomotives and trains were in evidence everywhere, seemingly headed for everywhere. There were rail depots in every sector, and there were plans to build a circle railroad around the city to connect these. Citizens moved to the suburbs and commuted from there—Roxbury, Dorchester, Cambridge. There was talk of annexing these former independent towns to the metropolitan area.[55] The stores of dry goods jobbers were "built like palaces, with an exuberance of cost which is almost in bad taste." Men worth $100,000 were common, and there were millionaires here and there. "They could do it," wrote a New Yorker, "for in Boston there is a concentration of the public mind, which brings out and directs its mighty force to great achievements."[56]

The only danger, Bostonians themselves thought, was if the new liberality of business was quashed by the old Puritan conservatism of the city. Why should someone in Boston be fined for smoking a cigar or for riding a railroad on Sunday? Ultra-orthodox reformers and "senseless bigots" could paralyze trade and must be guarded against.[57] This was a new Boston, and many liked it that way.

In the autumn of 1851, Boston celebrated with a jubilee—a spectacle, one reporter said, "such as modern times only have afforded." A spectator from the ancient world might have imagined there was a triumphal entry of some military general returning from a successful war, but this was a triumph of peace. "There is a city," wrote a reporter from New Orleans attending the festival,

> not of very large population, with no advantage but a good harbor, having no internal channels of communication with the interior of the continent, situated in a cold and inhospitable climate, and in the midst of a country comparatively sterile, which has nevertheless succeeded in concentrating more wealth, proportionately, than any city in the country, and by the exercise of well directed energy and enterprise, has drawn to itself the trade of an immense and productive region.[58]

Naturally, New York City and the State of New York reacted. And, logically, they reacted by pushing the New York & Erie broad-gauge railroad project. However, it seemed there was more factionalism, more of a speculative tenor, and consequently less drive on the ground in New York than in Boston.

"The miserable, rotten, rickety press of Wall Street," said the *New York Herald*, "is very busy endeavoring to prove the wholesomeness of a public debt of fifty millions," and some wanted more. All wanted debt and more debt, "more expenditures—more profusion," none of which was getting any railroad built.[59] At a party celebrating the railroad's progress in the fall of 1841, one analyst thought there was complacency also. New York City was proud that the Astor House could, thanks to the Erie road, serve fresh butter from farms at Goshen, 85 miles from the city.[60] But it was an "evil incident to great prosperity" that it begat false security, as the healthy man laughs at the chance of disease, the rich one at the possibility of adversity. New York was healthy, fat, and not very hungry. It had forgotten that "many of our advantages are artificial, and that others as well as we can construct channels of communication with distant States."[61]

The Erie, projected at 450 miles, would extend much farther into the West than did the Western of Massachusetts and eventually, perhaps, would have only the Baltimore & Ohio as a serious rival in the long-distance Near West trade.[62] At a meeting at Niblo's Musical Salon late in 1841, a speaker noted that it used to take fifteen days to get from Lake Erie to New York City. But when the railroad ran over the route, a drove of cattle could be put on the cars at Dunkirk on Lake Erie one morning and be sold in the New York City market the next morning. It would be the same with the flour and grain from Michigan, Indiana, Ohio, and Illinois, which were building local feeder lines. The "bright, sharp-witted Yankees" were to be feared, but New York could learn and react effectively to the activities of this "shrewd, calculating, cunning, far-seeing race."[63] The *Albany Journal* thought the rally was a good start: "The citizens of New York, on learning that the Bostonians, after digging through half a dozen Mountains, had found themselves at Albany upon a Rail Road, rubbed open their eyes, pulled off their night caps, met together at Niblo's Saloon and resolved that they would go to work. This was a very sensible determination."[64]

However worthy its goals, the corporate instrument—the New York & Erie Railroad—was flawed. There should be an investigation, several writers advised. "Let the public know how much money has been paid by the speculators in proportion to the sums they have received; who has purchased property in the neighborhood of the road; at what period the route will probably be completed, and whether, under the most favorable circumstances, it will ever pay interest on the money expended."[65]

A report by a special committee in New York City in January 1842 said that residents of the city had never before felt reason to unite their energies to accomplish some great local object, as their "intercourse with the whole country, and with the world at large," had always engrossed them, and the "great variety of material and diversity of interest, which compose our body politic, have always presented obstacles to a harmonious union of action, which other communities do not encounter." But this Boston rail initiative might change that. Flour was being transported from Albany to Boston at 50 cents per barrel, something that would have been considered an "idle phantom" five years earlier. The Erie Canal was no longer unassailable.[66] But New York City and Brooklyn, with a combined population of 400,000, could surely compete with Boston, which had 100,000.[67]

Still, New York "trembled as if shaken by an earthquake." There were restrictions, such as the legislature's forbidding the new railroad from carrying freight west of Albany or in winter, in deference to the interest of the Erie Canal.[68] "The cars come and go . . . but nothing can be sent by them except small parcels."[69] Governor William Seward of New York asked in 1842 what citizens thought of freight trains on the Western Railroad starting from Albany to Boston every hour of the day and night. True, there were 30,000 boats each year passing through the Erie Canal, but this was a revolution.[70]

Corruption remained in the New York & Erie. The *New York Herald* cut its reform-advancing teeth on it. It was time, the paper wrote in 1842, to have a "ripping up of this shocking concern." The managers had ruined the credit of the state by wasting its aid, and they should be purged: "Let the butchers, carmen, and myriads of mechanics who have been inveighed to invest their hard earnings in this rotten corporation . . . tell their several tales and expose the tricks of which they have been victims."[71]

The crisis was so deep when the Erie suspended operations for three years in 1842 that the railroad was offered for sale at auction for payment of the funds advanced by the state to expedite its construction.[72] It did not help that Horatio Allen, who had piloted *Stourbridge Lion* to introduce steam locomotion to the United States in 1829, became president of the Erie in 1843.[73] "It is a matter of the utmost astonishment to every reflecting person, and every one who desires to see the city of New York prosper," wrote the *Herald,* "that so little has been done towards constructing a rail road direct from this city to Albany. We have had all sorts of schemes on foot by financiers, and stock jobbers, and all sorts of plans proposed by politicians—meeting after meeting—and yet nothing has been done."[74]

The state reentered the fray in 1845, relieving the Erie from its liability to the government provided that it finished the line to Lake Erie in six years, which it did. The state also invested another $3 million in the concern.[75] The *New York Herald* was not sure that was a good idea. New York had the canal, and Pennsylvania and Maryland had systems going to the lake. New ways of cutting ice would keep navigation on the Hudson open later. So why incur this railroad expense? It was, the editor wrote, "for the purpose of getting up a *clique* of officers, superintendents, presidents, cashiers and others, who are thus to be saved from the necessity of getting a living by some other honest mode."[76] The paper dismissed a large rally at the Tabernacle in 1844 as just so much empty blow.[77] Wealthy New Yorkers knew better than to invest in the Erie: it was the domain of young and irresponsible Wall Street plungers, the editor Bennett thought.[78] Such cynicism was not limited to the *Herald* office.

But construction did advance. The New York & Erie reached Binghamton, more than 200 miles from New York City, in January 1849. It sponsored a two-train excursion with 500 guests for dinner. The average cost was less than $50,000 per mile built, despite the most challenging engineering difficulties of the whole route.[79] The fare to Binghamton was $4.50, and the trip took twelve hours. Estimates were that the trip to Lake Erie, when possible, would be thirty hours and cost $10.[80] Passengers on the Erie went through cuts where the tops of the rock were 90 feet above their heads, "and all the time you are comfortably seated, and moving at a rate of thirty miles an hour, with the same ease as if in a large armed rocking-chair in your own drawing-room."[81] The thing seemed plausible at last. "The Erie has passed through its dark days," wrote the *New York Tribune,* "and has now nothing but plain sailing before it."[82]

Dunkirk, the proposed lake terminus of the Erie, grew rapidly, with wharves and depot buildings erected in the early 1850s and connections made with steamboats departing twice daily for Cleveland, Detroit, and Chicago. The Erie, with its 6-foot gauge, had wide and comfortable cars and would soon have a hundred locomotives.[83] Buffalo enjoyed a growth spurt also and expected its hotels to be full when an express train would run from Dunkirk to New York in perhaps fifteen hours. The current of travel that would then run through that channel, a Buffalo editor thought, "will open our eyes with astonishment."[84]

New York & Erie bridge over Genesee River at Portage, New York. Bettmann/Corbis

Riding the Erie was a thrill. The run up to Seneca Lake was scenic and the engineering impressive. One flew at 40 miles per hour for hundreds of miles, "making the momentary stops to catch breath as it were along rivers, up and down mountains, across viaducts, through gorges, and mid-way of precipices, hurried on and on, seemingly faster and faster."[85]

The completion came in April 1851.[86] A passenger could transfer to one of three luxurious steamboats, christened *Niagara*, *Keystone State*, and *Queen City*, and thus make it to Detroit or even to Chicago in record time. The Chicago journey was about sixty hours from New York City, running over what one reporter thought the two best-managed railroads in the country, the Erie and the Michigan Central, with a restful interlude on the Lake Erie boats.[87] When a body of Erie directors and contractors reached the lake on the first train, they cheered. "They felt each one, as De Soto felt when he discovered the Mississippi—they had achieved their object; for years they had struggled on, at one time under great embarrassment and anxiety."[88] The company had been "publicly advertised for sale—a defaulting affair—a doomed and forsaken speculation. It has changed friends—never lost them—it has been denounced—derided—insulted—and from under all this pressure of adversity, the energy of men that knew of what stuff it was made, and they were made, has lifted it up."[89] As Boston held its great jubilee, New York had its excursion to Dunkirk. Ten years later, it had responded to the Western of Massachusetts. The Erie was at the time of its completion the longest railroad in the world.[90]

Pennsylvania and New York had some things in common. Both had invested early and heavily in canal systems, and both were therefore reluctant to jump on the railway bandwagon in a big way as pioneers. But the Baltimore intrusions into Pennsylvania, and the Boston push into New York, made railroad building a defensive necessity to secure trade territory. Both states were relatively late getting under way but showed their colors eventually. The Pennsylvania Railroad, the Erie, and, more impressively, the New York Central slightly later, gave these states premier rail systems and kept them in the forefront as transportation hubs. At first, however, Pennsylvania was more concerned with the activity of the Baltimore & Ohio than with advancing its own rail system.

The Baltimore & Ohio, being probably the best managed of the four westering lines, received the least publicity. Slowly but steadily it seemed to take care of business until it arrived in due course at Wheeling, Virginia (now West Virginia), in 1852.

There were many challenges. The editor of the *Winchester Republican* wondered in 1839 whether the B&O had done enough to justify all the aid that Virginia had given it. "It may well be doubted," he wrote, "whether this is not extending the hospitality of the Old Dominion to suicidal length." The writer was no foe of corporations "in their places" but thought they were "without souls, and consequently without sympathies. They are to be known only by their charters—to be governed by their bond."[91] There was also the old Baltimore nemesis, Pennsylvania. Like New York, Maryland worried about its debt, particularly after the Panic of 1837. In 1840 it owed $15 million, almost all invested in internal improvements, and it had a hard time meeting interest obligations. It rejected the idea of repudiating the debt but was hardly in an expansive mood.[92]

The B&O reached Cumberland, Maryland, in 1842, which gave it 200 miles of railroad and a connection with the National Turnpike Road leading to the Ohio River. A traveler could reach Wheeling by a combination of rail and road in about thirty-four hours.[93] The company put on second-class emigrant cars to haul foreigners, mostly from Germany and often with lots of baggage, into the American Near West. They could rent large wagons at Cumberland for the 130-mile trip on the turnpike to Wheeling and the Ohio River.[94]

The efficient B&O management established four freight rate classes to Cumberland for quantities not less than 1,000 pounds. First class at $10 per ton included ale in bottles, fresh butter, beeswax, boots or shoes, bonnets in cases, beer in bottles, fresh beef, bread, dry goods, drugs and medicines, fish, feathers, fur, and tinware. Second class at $8 per ton included ale in barrels, ashes, apples in barrels, bacon, cotton in bales, livestock in whole carloads, copper in pigs, candies, cheese, and firewood. Third class at $6 per ton hauled brick, barley, corn, grindstones, hides, wheat, and hemp. Fourth class at $5 per ton was meant for butter in firkins, beef in barrels, coffee, copper ore, salted fish in barrels, and tulips. Specie could be transported only in passenger trains and in the personal care of its owner or his agent.[95]

The commission business at Cumberland thrived. The agent of the National Transportation Company there claimed that since the B&O reached his town, his company had received and forwarded 10 to 30 tons of freight every day. Wagon freighters were in such demand that they doubled their rates from Cumberland to Wheeling. A visitor there, however, did not think that the railroad would reach Wheeling in his generation. "Its millions of cost hangs upon the necks of the people like a yoke."[96]

Still, in its seventeenth annual report in the fall of 1843, the B&O reported a return on capital of 4 percent. It was still focused on reaching the Ohio River. "That was the great object from the first."[97] Every intelligent person knew, a writer in Buffalo averred, "that the further a railroad or canal is extended into the heart of a populated region, whose inhabitants possess, as we Americans do, a marvelous propensity to travel every where and to see everything, to say nothing of our wonderful business enterprise, the more lucrative will be the stock of every mile of such improvements."[98]

Western editors pointed out that it was not Cumberland, or even Wheeling, that really mattered. "Experience, dearly bought," wrote a reporter in Chillicothe, Ohio,

> has demonstrated that in the construction of grand works of internal improvement, general interests only should be consulted, and all merely local and petty interests, real or imaginary, be wholly disregarded—unless they can *incidentally* receive attention without detriment to the main objects. In the construction of the successive links of the Baltimore and Ohio Railroad, it should be ever borne in mind that it is not a road from Baltimore to Wheeling or Parkersburg, merely, but a great channel

of rapid communication between the EAST and the WEST, the ATLANTIC and the MISSISSIPPI VALLEY. The road is destined, ultimately, to extend to Cincinnati and St. Louis, and in the location of its various links these seemingly now remote points should be kept constantly in view.[99]

That was one reason the B&O resisted a Virginia law requiring it to terminate its line at Wheeling and experimented with other points on the river, prominently nearby Parkersburg. There was an argument with Pennsylvania, too, which wanted the railroad to terminate at Pittsburgh or at least to build a branch to that city.[100]

D.K. Minor of the *Railroad Journal* in 1850 listed all U.S. railroads by state. There were about 8,000 miles total in twenty-three states by then, with thirty companies in New York State alone and twelve in Georgia.[101] The B&O intended to add to it. In the spring of 1851, there were 4,500 men and 800 horses at work constructing its line north and west of Cumberland.[102] Meanwhile, its articulate president, Thomas Swann, visited communities and state legislatures and lobbied for the company cause.[103]

As it became obvious in 1852 that Wheeling would be the terminus, it had a boom similar to the one caused by the Erie at Dunkirk. A depot went up, as well as many warehouses, four ironworks, a nail factory, and two hotels. One warehouse, owned by Forsyth & Company, cost $30,000 and was claimed to be the largest in the Union. The bridge at Wheeling cost more than $60,000.[104]

On New Year's Day 1853, a train from Baltimore reached Wheeling on the B&O line, "the realization of a great work, planned a quarter of a century ago, and steadfastly pursued to completion, amid the most disheartening circumstances."[105]

There was a celebration, including members of legislatures from Virginia and Maryland, as well as members of Congress. The excursion out was spectacular, going through mountains while being pulled by the most powerful new locomotives the railroad had. "The whole of the mountain glared, as the cars mounted upwards, with the bursting flames of the engines, while the sparkling lights carried up and down the declivities looked as if the stars had fallen from the skies and were sporting upon the verge of the precipices."[106]

Swann spoke at a banquet for 1,000, giving the history of his company. But perhaps most striking was a speech by the engineer Benjamin Latrobe.

We speak of the "array of the conqueror"? Where is there a conqueror like steam? Its panoply, too, is of iron. Man has made it not less than mortal, like the image of Frankenstein, but more than mortal, as it performs the work of one hundred thousand of men's hands. . . . [It] is the precursor of the triumphs, not of war, but of peace, as they build up the fame, not of heroes, but of the people.[107]

It was classic railspeak.

Boston was jealous and caustic in its comments. The managers of the Baltimore & Ohio Railroad, an editor there wrote, had bitten off more than they could chew. Maybe they could manage a short railroad in Maine, or perhaps the old 3-mile Quincy Railroad hauling stone. "But for any more extended enterprises than these, in the middle of this active nineteenth century, they are utterly incompetent."[108] That was, however, only inspired sour grapes. The railroad to the Ohio River was built and working well.

The career of the Western & Atlantic, the fourth of these mid-period pushes to the Near West, cannot be well understood without prefacing some account of two magnificent failures: the Cincinnati-to-Nashville project mentioned earlier (which came to be known as the Louisville, Cincinnati & Charleston), and the New Orleans & Nashville. Both projects, mostly hot air as they were, threatened to leave out Georgia as a vital link in the push to the South and West. That led Georgia to withdraw its support from those projects and to respond with a state-owned railroad of its own tapping the West. Neither did the Western & Atlantic exist in any kind of isolation. Its construction, and the atmosphere that led to that construction, stimulated towns and cities across the South.

As has been emphasized, it is a myth of history textbooks that the South tried to ignore the new technology due to some Jeffersonian nostalgia about the primitive yeoman, or to an incompatibility of slavery with industrialization, or to a disinclination to develop or live in cities. It saw a way to build railroads, advance cities, and continue a slave-based cotton economy with the new technology. In fact the South well understood that it could no longer pursue its regional goals successfully without rail.

CHAPTER 9

Southern Strategy

he Cincinnati, Louisville & Charleston, chartered by the legislature of South Carolina in 1835, had its beginning in discussions as early as 1828. These originated with E.S. Thomas, who had moved from Charleston to Cincinnati. The completion and successful operation of the Charleston & Hamburg, forming a natural first link, made the prospect of a more ambitious western extension seem plausible. Robert Hayne, who had been governor and served in the U.S. Senate, took a special interest and chaired a convention at Knoxville, Tennessee, in 1836 to discuss such large plans. Some 400 delegates from nine states attended. Georgia delegates, worried about being bypassed, walked out. Still, the convention endorsed the Cincinnati project, and that year subscription books for it opened in many southern towns. The $12 million capital needed, and the controversy surrounding the bank that was to help finance it, were obstacles, but success seemed a realistic possibility.[1]

The New Orleans & Nashville was to New Orleans what the Cincinnati, Louisville & Charleston was to Charleston. A corps of engineers arrived at Jackson, Mississippi, in February 1835 on their way to New Orleans, laying out a possible route all the time. Surveys were paid for by private subscriptions at New Orleans, and its supporters traveled up and down the potential line to talk it up and to quash the objections of "a few aristocrats" who were against it. "We are one of the number," a Mississippi newspaper editor wrote,

> who cannot perceive any *disadvantage* resulting from running any rail road through our state, which will increase the facilities of our planters in getting their cotton to market at the cheapest rate. We are in favor of Rail Roads, run where they may; and leave the choice of routes to the planters themselves. They are generally of full age, and sound minds, and competent to judge of that matter, as well as the merchants who transact their business.[2]

New Orleans, always at somewhat of a disadvantage due to its unhealthy location and its propensity for flooding, perceived that the trade the Mississippi-Gulf connection had automatically brought it was threatened by the railroad age. New York City might lose ground to Boston, Baltimore, or Philadelphia, but New Orleans could potentially go from major entrepôt to rural backwater as the railroad changed national trade patterns. Naturally, the Crescent City's promoters hoped otherwise and expressed their desire to get in on the rail revolution. At the same time, they planned for flood control, instituting health measures, installing gas lighting, chartering steamboat companies to extend the trade life of the Mississippi River, and expanding the Port of New Orleans. Capital was abundant, based on the city's past success, and all that was required was to deploy that capital properly to ensure the city's future.[3] There was good potential for new trade connections. A group of Boston businessmen, for example, obtained in 1835 a charter from the Florida state legislature to construct a railroad from St. Augustine to Florida's western coast on the Gulf of Mexico, whence it would be a short sea hop to New Orleans.[4]

The talk stimulated the whole region. "The scheme of facilitating and quickening the intercourse between the extremes of the North-East and South-West," wrote a Virginian, "is, in itself, worthy of the attention of everyone who estimates the value of the Union." The railroad involved no constitutional scruple, and "the wealth, the enterprise, and the energy of New York, the great emporium of the North, and of New Orleans, the great emporium of the Southwest, cannot be better employed than in bringing these two cities, as it were, beside each other, and all the intermediate places will find an impulse given their industry of incalculable value."[5]

The New Orleans & Nashville was to have a track width of 5 ½ feet, which was thought good for carrying cotton. Eventually, when international difficulties with Mexico were resolved, there could perhaps be an extension west to the Pacific and to trade with China.

> On the south we would have facilities of external communication with every part of the world by the gulf of Mexico—by which our merchant vessels, steam ships or boats, would afford a rapid and easy intercourse foreign and domestic. On the east, we shall have a railroad to Nashville, thence to Richmond—which will be short of 1300 miles, thence to Baltimore, Philadelphia and New York—being about 1600 miles, or 400 less than any other route between New Orleans and New York; besides affording a rapid and constant communication at all times for trade and travel.[6]

Such a railroad might cost $10 million, but it would be worth it.[7] The South had numerous advantages for rail construction, a Mississippi newspaper concluded: "The rail roads of the North pass over surfaces very different from the face of the country in Mississippi."[8] Richmond real estate was looking up, the local newspaper wrote in 1835. "How can it be otherwise, when the Fredericksburg Rail Road [Richmond, Fredericksburg & Potomac] is penetrating in one direction—and the great Western communication is opening its arms in another!"[9] In October 1835, an agent went to England to buy $150,000 in rail for the New Orleans & Nashville Railroad.[10]

The possibility of such a railroad was enough to upset towns that might be left out. Lynchburg, Virginia, for example, pointed to the example of Antwerp's historically yielding to Amsterdam and suggested applying the lesson. In 1832 it had seemed that Lynchburg was to become "one of the great pivots on which the trade of the mighty West would turn, as well as one of the immense and immeasurable channels, by which it would pass, *via* Richmond and Petersburg, to Norfolk." But then came an "evil hour" when a local link called the Abington Railroad failed, partly due to the state's idea that river improvement would be cheaper, and the New Orleans project looked like it might bypass Lynchburg. River improvement, a local man thought, was putting the cart before the horse. The railroad would increase property values and provide the taxes needed to work on the rivers.[11]

Other towns had their own debates. Natchez, Mississippi, talked about the proposed Natchez & Jackson Railroad, another potential local link in the cross-country scheme. Too many people in Natchez, a man there wrote, thought only about trade with Europe and could not see the interests of their own county or state. These men had set themselves against the New Orleans & Nashville and thought the whole state would do the same. "It may be that the project of the New Orleans and Nashville railroad is only a bravado to deter us from our praiseworthy undertakings. But it is more probable that the people of New Orleans are in good earnest, but hope to fasten upon our state their odious monopoly by taking advantage of our local jealousies and sectional prejudices." Every section through which such a railroad would pass had to devise a strategy and evaluate its specific interest carefully.[12]

And it would be unwise to consult only local interest. When the Natchez delegation came out against aid to the New Orleans & Nashville as it was debated in the Mississippi legislature in 1836, an analyst thought that there was too much mindless local independence involved. "If the Natchez and Jackson railway cannot exist without the annihilation of other schemes of Internal Improvement of infinitely more importance, not only to the State, but to the nation, we are not its friend." The wealthy Natchez aristocracy should not be allowed to dictate the policy of Mississippi or, by extension, the entire West.[13]

Vicksburg, very near Natchez, promoted its own railroad to the state capital at Jackson and put 400 men to work on it early in 1836. Meanwhile it criticized Natchez and exacerbated that local factionalism some were afraid would interfere with the state's unifying on any rail strategy. Wrote the *Vicksburg Register*, "Let there be no niggardly policy on the part of our State Government—let the Legislature extend, and widely extend, our Banking facilities—let it foster the spirit of improvement which is now abroad, and who can set bounds to the prospect of wealth and prosperity of Mississippi."[14]

An agent of the New Orleans & Nashville wrote in a published circular that he thought there was a great deal of irresponsible rumor. New Orleans merchants did not found the New Orleans & Nashville as a stock-jobbing scheme to draw off the trade of Natchez; it was for broader purposes. They were not limiting themselves to the interests of New Orleans but had corresponded with railroad promoters all over the country about how best to unify potential supporters along a route. The company did not ask for money from Mississippi, only for cooperation. It would expend millions in the state and found towns there.[15]

The editor at Vicksburg warned his readers not to be fooled. The governor's address supporting the New Orleans & Nashville was "a jumble of the stalest truisms, thrown together in the clumsiest manner." As for the rail project itself, "The magnificence of the undertaking, like the scintillations of intellect, may sparkle and dazzle, but should not . . . blind us."[16]

Mississippi continued to argue. The New Orleans & Nashville, far from a sure thing in any event, was planned to pass through Jackson. Mississippians started three railroads to connect other places with Jackson: one from Natchez, one from Grand Gulf, and one from Vicksburg. And then they debated the thing. "Now I fully credit the *sincerity* of all," observed one editor, "but at the same time believe, if the members from the extremes of the east and west, resided on the middle route, the conviction of their judgments would probably be the same as those they now deem in error and delusion." State leaders, he thought, needed to recognize that this was not a plot by a foreign company to prejudice their state companies. The purpose of aiding the New Orleans concern was for the public benefit of Mississippi, not just for the benefit of that foreign corporation. "No one . . . supposes our state was up at auction, or, that we were delivering our citizens into the hands of the Philistines."[17] New Orleans itself argued over its Atchafalaya Railroad and over the same question of the relationship between local and regional and national interests.[18]

New Orleans saw its own interest and pursued it. It worried about the Louisville, Cincinnati & Charleston being built rather than the New Orleans & Nashville. Nashville was still a great market for western produce, "but how long can we hope to continue so, when we let Pennsylvania, Maryland, and South Carolina consummate works of internal improvement which are calculated to take it away from us? We suffer our city to be made a mere agency of New York."[19]

The arguing continued. More and more interests emerged. Editors complained of the "sottish ignorance of some members of the late [Louisiana] state assembly, the interested opposition in Mississippi, the chilling apathy of our merchants, and the reckless speculation of some who had been trusted at the commencement of their plans." The New Orleans & Nashville railroad by the end of 1836 had purchased "negroes, lands, rails, and other property" at a cost of $500,000.[20] But things became ever more complex. The beginnings of the great project went on piles through a swamp and the workers became ill.[21] And more and more the great project was delayed and compromised.

In October 1835, Charleston hosted a public meeting to plan the railroad to Cincinnati.[22] Hayne took a strong role there. He hoped that measures would be put forward to show "that a criminal lethargy has not overtaken us, to the neglect not only of our immediate interests, but our future security."[23]

There were warnings against factionalism. "Whoever is *in* or whoever is *out* of office, the population of the country must grow with every year. . . . Whatever conditions may exist in particular States or localities of our widely extended country, no apprehension, we trust, need be entertained of the continued prevalence of general prosperity." The "patriotic and intelligent" part of the community had to realize that the railroad had made the old political mores and customs obsolete.[24]

There was practical action, too. Charleston sent delegates to conventions at Tuscaloosa, Alabama; Danville, Virginia; Mobile, Alabama; and Knoxville and Nashville, Tennessee.[25] It sent the former head of the board of public works in South Carolina as an agent to Cincinnati and points between to lobby for the Charleston-to-Cincinnati line.[26] The Tennessee legislature took up a bill proposing to appropriate $500,000 for the Nashville & New Orleans Railroad, $750,000 for a railroad from Charleston to Cincinnati through eastern Tennessee, and $300,000 for a project called the Atlantic & Mississippi.[27]

The road to Cincinnati seemed ideal strategy for much of the South. For seven southern states on the Ohio River the highway of communication was only northeast and southwest. From there communication reached the Atlantic in the area between Long Island and Norfolk and thence by the Gulf of Mexico to the delta of the Mississippi River. But between these points of marine connection was 3,000 miles of coast from Virginia to Florida; at the time, the states in the Ohio Valley had no connection even by good post roads. The mail from Ohio to western Georgia and the western Carolinas was sent by way of Washington, D.C., a route four times as long as that proposed for the new railroad. There could be many branches from Louisville south, benefiting at least half the southern population.[28]

But the chartering of little links connecting nearby towns did not seem quite up to the task. Virginia, wrote one man there, "has been living upon glory!—her past glory—breakfasting, dining, and supping on it! . . . She has been stump-speeched to death—she has been fed upon this feeble diet until she is now but a mere skeleton."[29] Another man thought the South was subject to a "fatal submission to mere custom."[30] A promoter of the Louisville, Cincinnati & Charleston thought it was dangerous that the "din of party strife" might cause the South to lose sight of public objects.[31]

The railroad to Cincinnati seemed to gain traction in 1838. It purchased the pioneering Charleston & Hamburg that year and put it under the direction of a local board and an engineer. The States of North Carolina and

Tennessee agreed to a bank charter in connection with the company and to a capital of $8 million. The State of South Carolina pledged its credit to secure a $2 million loan. Charleston's city council loaned $100,000 to the company. The railroad had been in such a precarious position that some thought that most of the stock would have been forfeited had another installment been called for, but these developments made it seem possible the road would be built.[32]

Hayne promoted the line actively, speaking before numerous rallies on the benefits of free trade generally and of this railroad project particularly. "All-conquering steam has indeed changed the condition of the world, and the fortunes of the human race. . . . Fellow citizens! We have every thing to animate our zeal, encourage our hopes, and nerve our efforts in this good work."[33] He wrote to the editor of the *Cincinnati Post* that "such is the spirit of enterprise excited, especially, by the prospect opened to us, of extending our connections by direct trade to Europe; and by railroads to the West, that nothing seems now to dishearten us."[34] Hayne visited the New England railroads in the summer of 1838 looking for "useful hints."[35]

At a rally before the statehouse in Charleston in the spring of 1838, Hayne was at his best. He called the occasion one of the most interesting in history. Commerce, when unfettered, had been a great source of civilization and refinement and linked the nations together by mutual interests. Next to the Christian religion, Hayne said, he knew of nothing that softened asperities and removed prejudices better than free trade. "All conquering steam has indeed changed the condition of the world, and the fortunes of the human race." The Louisville, Cincinnati & Charleston had started by purchasing the pioneering Charleston & Hamburg line, but that was only a start. It had a bank charter, and now it needed public support. Hayne turned over the first earth for the next phase of construction. His speech became a pamphlet, distributed in 3,000 copies.[36]

A letter to the editor of the *Richmond Enquirer* picked up the enthusiasm for this southern push to the West. It would be suicidal for Virginia not to lend aid. "A voice from suffering humanity would urge on; for, then the invalid from any direction, could gain an easy and speedy access to the celebrated mineral waters of Virginia in the summer, and the mild climate of the South in the cold blasts of winter. . . . Old friends, who had, as they supposed, shaken hands for the last time, could in a few days exchange a cheering visit."[37]

That fall James Hamilton arrived in London to sell bonds for the Cincinnati line and to promote direct trade with Europe. A critic in Boston

The engine West Point *with train of cars on Charleston & Hamburg Railroad, 1831.*

thought it was a foolish enterprise, as competing with Boston or New York in European trade was "not viewed as being within the natural capabilities of Charleston; where the nature of the climate, the consequent suspension of all activity in business during the sickly months of the year, and its great distance from Europe, are all against the probability that so southern a port will ever become the grand proposed centre of the western trade."[38]

The response to that sort of talk was vehement. "The people of the South," stated a letter to the editor at Richmond,

> are now only rearing, feeding, fattening, and making insolent, and turbulent, hordes of Northern lions, who in some of the throws and spasms of the political tournament, will be let loose upon us with the boldness of devouring beasts of the forests. They are governed, moved, instigated and acted upon by money. They have been for years, and now are, sucking from the South its heart's blood, like vampires seated upon the body of a sleeping man.[39]

The object of all this passion, however, turned out to be no more viable than the New Orleans & Nashville. Reports in the fall of 1839 were that the great Cincinnati, Louisville & Charleston was stalled and would probably reach no farther than Columbia, South Carolina. The stockholders were frustrated that they could get no unified support and little aid from the states they proposed building across.[40] And, as though to administer the coup de grâce, in October 1839 General Hayne, now the president of the company and the indispensable voice of the project, died, having contracted a bilious fever at a heated meeting of the Louisville, Cincinnati & Charleston stockholders. He was 47 years old.[41]

Historian Ulrich Phillips, in his 1909 book on southern transportation, credited Hayne with great influence. He borrowed $2 million in England.

He single-handedly created confidence enough for the shares of his Cincinnati railroad to rise 25 percent. He recruited plantation owners to donate slave labor and right-of-way. And he had reason to hope that the western extension would work as well as a business as the Charleston & Hamburg had. But in this, the biographer Phillips believed, he was unrealistic, as visionaries sometimes are. Led by Hayne, the backers of the Louisville, Cincinnati & Charleston "went headlong into an immense project for direct transmontane connection, in disregard of the natural obstructions and of their own financial limitations." It succeeded only in burdening the Charleston & Hamburg, reorganized as the South Carolina Railroad Company, with its debts.[42]

It was the threat that the Cincinnati, Louisville & Charleston, the New Orleans & Nashville, or both would actually be built that led to the construction of a much more successful, if less ambitious, southern rail connection with the West: the Western & Atlantic of Georgia.

The W&A originated in 1836 as a state-owned and -operated railway, which "would serve as a great thoroughfare between the counties lying on 'the Western water' [and] the interior markets and seaports of Georgia." It seemed worthwhile from the outset, but, according to its annual report of 1840, "its magnitude appeared appalling, and many denied its practicality." Grading for the projected 138-mile railroad, extending from DeKalb County, Georgia, to a northwest terminus at the Tennessee River, began in 1838. The Panic of 1837 hurt the financing, but Georgia continued to back its bonds in the face of other states that were repudiating. The legislature passed a bill in January 1837 to appropriate $410,000 to the building of the "Great Western" railroad as outlined in a meeting at Macon. And there continued to be expectation of funding. The state appropriated $1.5 million in 1838, and construction was steady. "It is somewhat worse than absurdity," according to the 1840 report, "to pretend that the State of Georgia is destitute of resources—that she is not able to pay off every debt she owes, and place her bonds or Government Certificates on the pinnacle of public credit." The first chief engineer for the road, Stephen H. Long, did a good job with the original fundamentals, though he seems to have been a poor administrator. And Georgia had successful experience with its own private rail lines.[43] Like the Western of Massachusetts, the Baltimore & Ohio, and the New York & Erie, the Western & Atlantic took time to build. And as with the other lines, people despaired of it often. It was offered for sale in 1843 for $1 million but had no buyers. It, too, reached completion in the early 1850s, starting operations in 1850.[44]

Milton Heath, in his 1954 book on Georgia public policy, likewise assigned the W&A great significance. In some ways the W&A was like the Tennessee Valley Authority in the 1930s Depression, serving as a model for what private investors could and should do. Of the $8.5 million invested in Georgia railroads in the first eight years of development, about 50 percent was public money. The rest came from private investors who were doubtless encouraged by the willingness of the state to help all lines in Georgia and to advance a plan that tended to quash the factions. Even though the W&A had its seamy side, Heath thought in the end it was an impressive public achievement.[45]

Georgia, unlike so many states, seemed set on a plan rather than simply allowing capitalists to take any opportunity that presented. When in 1839, banks in Savannah refused to take the bills of the Monroe Railroad Bank, a "subscriber" objected on grounds that the Monroe Railroad was part of a system where the whole was greater than any of the parts. There were 300 stockholders in the Monroe, including some of the most substantial planters in middle Georgia, and the whole of the construction to its connection with the Western & Atlantic was under contract.

> It requires but little sagacity to see that this road forms no inconsiderable link in the chain of Savannah's prosperity. Without it, what will the Central Rail Road be to Georgia? Without it, what will the State Road be? Indeed Savannah is more deeply interested in the Monroe, than in the Central Rail Road; for the river will always furnish, at some season of the year a highway for produce and goods to and from Macon; but nature has done nothing, unless aided by Rail Road, to bring the trade from the West to this City.[46]

The *Georgia Telegraph* in Macon editorialized that "with a phalanx of Georgian hearts, panting in the race for state supremacy, with their enthusiasm properly directed," the state system could not fail.[47] "We look forward in prospect," a Georgia editor wrote,

> to the time when the travel and products of Tennessee, a portion of Kentucky, Missouri, a portion of Illinois, and a portion of Arkansas, will all wend their way through old Georgia, to find their great outlet and to deposit their precious burdens on the bosom of the mighty Atlantic. . . . When that time comes it will speak in tones which will reach from Maine to New Orleans, for the sagacity of our State, and the enterprising spirit of her sons.[48]

Yes, there were divisions, and yes, there was individualism, but many noticed that Georgians were more united on the railroad than on most things. There was waste, to be sure. "If the State had been making an experiment to see how much money could be wasted on a great and noble enterprise, or how it could be expended in a way to produce the smallest possible benefit, it could not have succeeded better." But that was due to the unwieldy size of the legislature and its changing makeup and did not invalidate the goal.[49] With the removal of the Cherokees there was greater opportunity than ever to develop Georgia's resources through railroads.[50] By 1846 the W&A had completed 80 miles of its line and connected with stages for Memphis and the Mississippi River.[51]

Neighboring Tennessee was stimulated by the activity on the Western & Atlantic, not only to think about an extension of that line into their state but also to develop iron ore resources along the Hiwassee River for manufacturing rail iron and transporting them by a mining railroad. Not only would this prevent putting so much money into the pockets of British iron makers; it would add to the economic independence of the South.[52]

The progress of the Western & Atlantic gave Mississippians second thoughts as well, especially after the New Orleans & Nashville fiasco. In 1843 they were faced with surrendering their local railroads after much effort and investment. A Natchez newspaperman advised strongly against it. Mississippi, he wrote, was not rich enough to throw away the money already expended rather than spend a pittance to keep the roads in repair while foolishly waiting for better times. "The only 'better times' which Mississippi, or any other agricultural State will ever know, must come from an energetic cultivation of its never-failing soil, and by affording every facility for the transportation and exchange of its staple productions for those of other parts of this country and foreign climes. The railway is the only great measure for this facilitation in southern Mississippi." It had never been the policy of Natchez capitalists to relinquish useful enterprises. And neither should it have compared itself to Vicksburg, whose railroad to Jackson had been of little use. It was not "romancing" to think of the rail future of Natchez. Look at what Georgia had done![53]

Louisville was definitely enlivened. There was no Cincinnati, Louisville & Charleston, so now what? Colonel T.J. Trezvant, agent for the Memphis & Ohio Railroad, visited Louisville in 1855 and advised proponents what they needed to do.

> You are like a man just getting into pecuniary troubles. Temporizing entangles him, and his difficulties soon surround him.

You will soon be so circumvented by railroads that will pass *by* instead of *through* you that struggling will be hopeless. Sleep on a few more years, while the world is moving with giant strides all around you, and when you do wake up, like Rip Van Winkle, no one will know you if you even know yourselves.[54]

Louisville subscribed $1 million in 1856 to a new company called the Louisville & Nashville.[55]

The reaction extended as far as Philadelphia, where a newspaper railed in the late 1840s about the comparative inactivity of that city in railroads, particularly in building railroads connecting to the South. What a boon it would be to connect Philadelphia with the Western & Atlantic and the branches it was bound to have! The business of Philadelphia, an editor thought, was leaving there "not from any dissatisfaction on the part of customers with her merchants—not from want of means of supply,—but solely from want of *transporting facilities* to the South. It is suicidal to neglect the difficulty longer."[56]

The enthusiasm for rail development in the South, however, was not universal. There was considerable debate in 1847 in South Carolina about the desirability of further rail promotion. One indefatigable writer of newspaper columns in Charleston, using the pseudonym "Anti-Debt," talked about the railroad enthusiasm as a "mania" and felt it was insubstantial and undesirable. It was part of "periodical fits" to which people were subject, and he hoped this one would pass. Beginning in 1817, South Carolina had invested in canals, which cut up valuable lands, spread pestilence, and collected few tolls. No one would take them now as a gift, and yet taxes were still assessed and appropriations made for them.[57] Politics was a poor way to decide such things, as there was a "cuckoo" element in the legislature that acted like an "indulgent parent" when it came to spending for something that might be for the purpose of state pride or the luxury of a few travelers.[58] The statistics cited, the writer thought, were bogus, "false syllogisms" presented under the "specious garb of mathematical figures."[59] And one should not argue that the public good was more important than profits: "The Spartan age has passed away forever. Iron money, public tables, and black broth have gone out with the shield and spear. In the present era of civilization, national poverty is among the very greatest of evils; for in its wake follow disorder, corruption and degradation."[60] "Anti-Debt" claimed he was not against railroads per se. "But I see no reason why the world should go mad about them, and mankind bankrupt themselves to force them into premature existence."[61]

There were responses to the twenty or so newspaper articles written by "Anti-Debt." They included the standard argument that all progress was once thought of as a mania and that civilized people needed a stimulus for action to avoid sinking back into a state of nature.[62] There was quite a movement in 1855 to develop a deepwater port at Beaufort, South Carolina. It was midway between Charleston and Savannah and could easily be connected to both by rail. It could concentrate the hemp of Kentucky, the corn and beef of Tennessee, the pork and lead of Missouri, the sugar of Louisiana and Florida, the rice and lumber of the Carolinas and Georgia, and cotton from the entire region for foreign commerce. There it could be exchanged for the silks and teas of China, the coffee and spices of Java, the gold and guano of Peru, "and all the luxuries and comforts of civilized Europe." One million Yankee dollars would do it. "If the money that is annually squandered by the slaveholders among the abolitionists of Saratoga, Newport and other fashionable Northern resorts, were collected for a single season, it would be sufficient to establish this mart which might prove itself a City of Refuge for the whole slaveholding South in after times."[63]

Yet it was hard to counter "Anti-Debt" entirely. "Why resort to fancy sketches," he wrote, "when the actual landscape is before us, and all can see without the aid of magnifying glasses or perspective tubes?" Had the Charleston & Hamburg or the Charleston & Columbia been so successful? People had been told that Charleston would increase its population into the hundreds of thousands and that the railroad would create a host of millionaires. Had it happened? Charleston, Columbia, and Hamburg had scarcely grown as much as natural increase would have predicted. Ride along those lines and one would see "dilapidation and decay everywhere." Lands had not increased in value and still could be had for 50 cents an acre not more than a mile from the railroad and 40 miles from Charleston. Much of the railroad stock could be purchased at 50 cents per dollar of par value. "Here are facts that are facts. If any doubt they can go and see."[64]

Some of these claims were independently confirmed. The Charleston & Hamburg, another man reported, was strewn with iron in all shapes. Fences were in poor repair, and there was no shelter for the engines. The road needed no more engineers or financiers but rather practical men as managers.[65]

Some of the same ennui existed in New Orleans. There was a "childish" dependence on the river.[66] Too many men there with money, an editor said, left well enough alone.

They look upon all plans for public improvements, however practical or securely based on the experience of practical men, as so many schemes designed to entrap them; in fact, as only a more adroit way at picking their pockets. Satisfied with the capital they have amassed, after, perhaps, a long life of labor and economy, they clutch their gold with feverish grip and exclaim: "Each man for himself!" Leaving others to go where the rest of the proverb sends them.

The "fire of public spirit had dwindled to ashes in their veins."[67] A man at Richmond thought such situations were endemic in the South with its "miserable little jealousies" between towns and regions.[68]

Of course, the doubts in other places did not deter Georgia. In 1849, it was ahead of all southern states in rail mileage and estimated to be ranked third or fourth among all states in the Union.[69] When the Western & Atlantic was completed in 1850, the company was still seeking more state appropriations, and there were still those who thought it could be better managed by a private concern than by the state. But many thought its shortcomings were based on unrealistic public expectations. Compared to most, it was a successful railroad indeed.[70] Wrote the Macon editor: "Great confidence seems to be felt in whatever Georgia lays her hand to. I have often heard it wondered how the citizens of Georgia had succeeded so in building railroads, keeping out of debt, and making their roads pay well."[71] The reason was that Georgia, as its governor noticed in his 1855 address, had a "definite system" and a "uniform principle" in granting railroad charters. It had supported railroads with state aid and management without going overboard in doing so.[72]

Already the myth of southern backwardness was strong in the North. Amid the tensions of the 1850s, which would lead so soon to civil war, the South defended itself partly by pointing out how well it had done in railroad building. "It is fashionable," wrote a man in Louisville, "for a certain class of people at the North to taunt the people of the South with a want of enterprise. It is regarded as necessary to establish the evils of slavery, that it shall be shown that it encourages indolence, and represses enterprise; and to illustrate the truth of the positions assumed, the superior progress of the free States in railroad building is cited as proof positive." History proved that false. The South had built some of the first railroads and some of the best railroads in the United States.[73]

It was also false that southern railroads ran well because northern men ran them or because they used northern supplies and equipment. There were southern ironworks and southern locomotive and car builders.[74] The South argued that slave labor would be a great advantage in railroad building. Just as cities were buying slaves to do urban tasks, so railroads would in the future, and the institution of slavery would become less tied to plantations and the growing of cotton.[75] Northerners were speculators, and eventually there would be proof that the more conservative way the South had proceeded in building railroads was best. It had largely avoided the "chaos of panic and bankruptcy" that characterized northern rail enterprises.[76]

Observers thought railroads had made a big change in southern attitudes. Without the railroad, wrote a Texas paper in 1855, in interior towns farmers "sauntered from store to store" and generally wasted time. They became great talkers and great bores. With a railroad came "hurry and bustle." How could a farmer waste time in town "when he could cash it at home by only raising something—say it was but a chicken—to ship by the cars? How could a man waste his time in loafing, when his neighbors by a little industry are getting along finely in the world, dressing their children better, putting up better houses, getting a nicer buggy, buying more land and niggers than himself? How, we say, could a man sit down as he does and waste half his days, when all this was going on around him?"[77] A man who had visited farmers along the line of the Western & Atlantic in 1837 had found they "moped around," and their children "sauntered about from place to place, as if their highest thoughts were bent on catching rabbits, opossums, or some such small game." What use was it to work when it cost them $2 per bushel to get their wheat to market, where they could only sell it for $1? It was different in 1860—completely different.[78]

Southern railroads were slightly slower in schedule than northern railroads, but they were safer and more comfortable. The food "would be hard to boast of," but it was tolerable. The pace at depots in the South was more relaxed, with none of the "running headlong, with coat tails flying," typical of boarding a train in the North. The conductor boarded the passengers in a leisurely way. Then "the whistle gives a gentle toot, and gradually, as a duck swims against a current, the train moves, and nobody is in a perspiration; no one has lost his baggage, or torn his clothes; no one is left lamenting his hard fate in being a moment too late." Once aboard a train in the South, the passenger found sociable fellows, and the black "servant" who carried water, apples, and oranges through the cars also distributed ice cream.[79] It made travel by rail actually enjoyable.

Far from being a sideshow, railroad development in the South provided a viable alternative to the way things were practiced in the North. Its example gave a strong indication that there was more than one way of adapting to railroads. The technology did not itself dictate its appropriate uses by people and states.

CHAPTER 10

The Prairie and the River

s ambitious as the Eastern Seaboard cities were to reach the Near West, equally vigorous were efforts to create internal communication within the Midwest.

"It is difficult for some minds to keep pace with the progress which the world is actually making in the means of ready intercourses and communication between its different parts," a journalist in Milwaukee wrote in 1842. Those who said that it would be twenty years before there was a railroad across Wisconsin were badly mistaken. It could be accomplished in three years. There had been a money panic in 1837, but there was plenty of capital left in the East and plenty of interest remaining there in developing the West "if we only give them leave and do what little we can to aid the work." It would be a great sight to see a hundred tons of lead "moving across our prairies . . . at the rate of twenty miles an hour!" It would "string every nerve with diligence and enterprise, and add 100 per cent to the value of every farm within fifty miles of the road."[1]

Railroads were not like plank roads and canals. "The construction of a railroad approximates to the greatness of a National work, while neither of the other proposed improvements can be magnified into any thing more than a Territorial affair." If Wisconsin were to have a connection with the Mississippi River, "we want such a work as will secure all the travel and carrying interest which legitimately belongs to the route. . . . In these times of steam-cars and rapid traveling, no one is content to job along in the style of republican simplicity, which a coach and four or slower canal boats 'dragging their slow length along' affords."[2] To enable the producing classes living 30, 50, or 100 miles from Milwaukee to send their products to market more cheaply, something besides animal power and wagons was necessary. That something, one writer in 1848 thought, was "steam moving upon a Rail Road, and the sooner we commence building one the better—more particularly for the wheat growers . . . than for any other class of people whatever."[3]

Every railroad that was made, wrote a man in Ohio in 1845, was the cause of the making of other railroads.

> Some are built because the earlier experiment removes doubts, the existence of which prevented their construction. Others are founded on the principle of self-defense, which causes the people of a particular section of country to contend against a course of events likely to cut them off from a participation in the profits and conveniences arising from rapid traveling and transit of merchandize. Yet others are legitimate continuations of those earliest constructed.[4]

At any rate, railroads were a great thing in the newer regions, as they had been in the old.

Networking the upper Midwest with railroads was a logical next step following the completion of such lines as the Baltimore & Ohio, the New York & Erie, and the Western & Atlantic. Yet, typically for American enterprise, step two did not await the completion and testing of step one before proceeding on its own course. By the time the B&O and Erie reached their northwestern goals in the early 1850s, a considerable system was completed and operating there to meet them.

The fact that Cleveland, Cincinnati, Toledo, Sandusky, Erie, and other cities along the southern shore of Lake Erie should want early to make rail connections with each other and with nearby trade and population points, like Cincinnati and Pittsburgh, was almost a logical given in light of the routes of the B&O and the Erie. The center of all this activity was Ohio.

Geography dictated the nature of the extensions from there. Lake Erie lies more or less east and west; the next of the Great Lakes, Huron, runs

Demonstration of steam engine at Cincinnati. Library of Congress

almost exactly north and south, as does Lake Michigan, farther west still. Thus steamboat connections via the lakes from the western end of Lake Erie at Detroit to the southern and western edges of Lake Michigan, at such thriving places as Chicago and Milwaukee, were very long journeys. However, if railroads could be constructed across Michigan direct from the western reaches of Lake Erie to the southern part of Lake Michigan, initially at St. Joseph, then the traverse was much shortened. This would have been a desirable step even had lake navigation during wintertime not been such a dicey proposition, as it clearly was. There were possible bridge routes through Indiana, but promoters there spent some time arguing whether railroads were superior to canals and lost the initiative.[5] Therefore Michigan became the next focus.

Another desideratum was the connection of the Great Lakes routes with the Mississippi River at places like Galena and Rock Island (Illinois) and Dubuque and Burlington (Iowa). Most promising of all at first was the new southern Illinois town of Cairo. There the Mississippi joined with the Ohio River in an area far enough south that the rivers were ice-free in winter. Unfortunately, the two rivers regularly flooded the low-lying town and infected it with disease.[6] The focus of this third thrust of rail-building strategy (after the Ohio and Michigan initiatives) was largely the State of Illinois.

Of course, St. Louis and New Orleans were long-term destinations. While these cities waited for their connections from north and south, they already planned to tap the hinterlands to the west of them. Although St. Louis did not break ground for its own ambitiously named Pacific Railroad of Missouri until 1851, there was serious talk there in the 1830s of building a railroad to Fayette. Fayette was almost 300 miles west of St. Louis and, it was said, near the eastern boundary of the Far West, "that is to say [the] Western boundary of civilization." It would be only a few years, one reporter thought, before there would be a railroad to the Mandan villages and the mouth of the Yellowstone River.[7] An "Atlantic and Pacific Railroad" would one day "be the name of that splendid whole of which the Baltimore and Ohio rail road is now one of the parts."[8]

Ohio got the railroad fever in the 1830s, when railroads anywhere in the United States were experimental. The editor of the Chillicothe *Scioto Gazette* noticed in 1835 that his region had the spirit of the age and that his town hoped to "step into the lists with her western sisters" in public improvement. City lots were increasing in price on the very rumor of a railroad.[9] That year, grading of the first division of the Mad River & Lake Erie Railroad (chartered in 1834) got under way between Sandusky and Tiffin. The purpose of the line was to connect Sandusky on Lake Erie with Dayton in the south, perhaps eventually with Cincinnati.[10] That would mean a possible connection with the Cincinnati lines being so vigorously promoted by Charleston and Louisville.[11] Also afoot were plans to connect Cleveland and Cincinnati, crossing the entire state northeast to southwest. That road would pass through Columbus, the state capital. Promoters argued that this was a better bet than the Mad River line, which passed through the relatively unsettled western portion of Ohio. The connection at Cincinnati would meet the Ohio River farther south than the B&O connection at Wheeling and, in the mind's eye, form a link in a great chain. Construct a railroad from Cleveland to Cincinnati, a visionary wrote in the fall of 1835, and a relatively quick and easy line of communication would be complete from the Mississippi Valley to New York City. A traveler might make the trip in forty-three hours.[12] A second Ohio railroad, the Little Miami, took a tentative step in the early 1840s between Deerfield and Lebanon, small towns near Cincinnati. It was planned to link with the Mad River at Springfield, northeast of Dayton.

These were "great works" only in imagination. The Mad River was just 38 miles long in 1843 and had gross revenue of only about $2,000 per month. But the vision was powerful.[13] A newspaper at Buffalo pointed out that there was by the mid-1840s a continuous railroad from Buffalo east, more than 1,000 miles. People from St. Louis and New Orleans could get almost "within hailing distance" of friends in the East by the medium of steam. Cincinnati would soon be linked by rail to Boston and New York. "Every intelligent man knows that the further a railroad or canal is extended into the heart of a populated region, whose inhabitants possess, as we Americans do, a marvelous propensity to travel every where and to see every thing, to say nothing of our wonderful business enterprise, the more lucrative will be the stock of every mile of such improvements."[14]

There was early trouble, overspending, and charges of fraud. An audit of the Mad River & Lake Erie Railroad in 1842 turned up some damaging information. The president of the company, John Jones, called the criticism "vague" and claimed that the accounts of the Mad River Company were kept as carefully, at least, as those of the state government. Many people had invested small sums in the company "less with a view to profit on the stock than to secure to their section of the country a means of intercourse and conveyance." The same was the motivation for many land purchases. Jones had received no salary for his first three years as a company official. The company was not exactly a philanthropic concern, but it was a pioneer, and it made the mistakes pioneers made.[15]

Passengers seemed to enjoy the Ohio rail system. A New Yorker visiting in the summer of 1845 intended to stop at Cleveland and then go by stage through Columbus to Cincinnati. But on landing at Sandusky, he decided to try the new Mad River line and then, after a stagecoach ride over a considerable gap, try the Little Miami also. Impressed with the growth of both Cleveland and Cincinnati, he suggested that Cleveland build a railroad to Columbus, 140 miles, to connect with the central Ohio system already under construction. This would "bring the whole of the rich interior of your noble state to your very doors!"

Citizens of Cleveland should follow the example of the shrewd New Englanders who were "fairly paving their country with expensive iron railroads, and they find their interest in doing so, not only by the increase of business in the towns at their termini, but in the direct return in the way of dividends."[16] It did not take wealthy capitalists to do so. The Western of Massachusetts was built by middle-class investors.[17] Cleveland should consider a rail connection with Pittsburgh as well as with Cincinnati.[18]

Other cities would have to react, too. Why should Louisville be jealous of Cincinnati? It should rather become a rival if not a superior. "How can you expect to have much trade with the country unless you manufacture for it and make communications that they may get to you and buy your products and goods? You must make mighty efforts as Cincinnati has and is making." Ohio was filled with "pushing, money-making men."[19]

Two new locomotives for the Mad River & Lake Erie Railroad arrived at Sandusky on the brig *Emerald* in May 1847. They weighed 14 tons each and, like eleven other of the road's locomotives, were made by Rogers, Ketchem & Grosvenor of Paterson, New Jersey.[20] In its fifth annual report in 1848, the Little Miami reported net income representing an 8 percent return on investment. There was a suggestion to put in 14 miles of double track.[21]

"The whole country is railroad mad," wrote an observer in 1850. "It pervades all classes alike; where before the attentions of speculators and capitalists alone were directed, now the farmers and all are taking part in it." Every village, as far away as Iowa, of half a dozen houses and twenty people talked of a branch line, to an extent that was laughable to some.[22]

That growth continued. In 1852, lots in Cleveland that had been worth $100 in 1846 could not be purchased for $1,000. By that time the city, defending its trade territory, had invested $100,000 in railroads. These had given the city new life and saved citizens thousands in expenses. Social life changed, too, as railroads were great practical advocates of temperance. They broke up the "multitude of mean, cold, miserable, dirty, *buggy* taverns that used to stand . . . along the principal stage routes of the land." Railroads carried "light into the dark places of the earth. . . . Along the waste places are now busy towns and beautiful villages, built up by the railroads."[23]

A St. Louis crowd in February 1852 witnessed the groundbreaking for what was planned to be the western extremity of the Ohio & Mississippi Railroad, by way of Illinois. That would connect St. Louis to the Ohio network and then on eastward, and the Pacific of Missouri would bring in Trans-Mississippi trade. "There is enough in what has already been done," said a professor who spoke that day, "to make us all feel that we are at the beginning of an enterprise, the end of which no man can see. I see before me at this moment one of the most remarkable spectacles that ever met the gaze of man." He himself had passed by railroad from Cincinnati to New York City, with only two short gaps of staging. He had gone from Cleveland to Pittsburgh with only a 28-mile gap, and then by railroad to Philadelphia, New York, Boston, and Portland.[24] There was discussion of a bridge over the Missouri River.[25] At an 1857 celebration in Cincinnati of its proposed connection with St. Louis, guests had to be put up on steamboats, the hotels being filled to overflowing.[26]

Iron was ordered for the Ohio & Pennsylvania Railroad.[27] Pennsylvania, it was said, had abandoned the Ohio River as a reliable channel for travel westward several years ago. New York City citizens, however, felt that the mountain travel involved in getting from Lake Erie at Cleveland to Philadelphia would mean that Philadelphia's efforts to promote railroads in Ohio would eventually inure to the benefit of New York City.[28] There was a plan to extend the wide gauge of the New York & Erie Railroad directly into Ohio.[29] Of course, the B&O connections at Wheeling and Parkersburg, both just across the Ohio River from the State of Ohio, gave Maryland status in the competition also. Thomas Swann, president of the B&O, said that an hour's time saving might make all the difference.[30]

The developing wheat lands of Ohio were truly up for grabs as to ultimate markets.[31] Settlers would be well advised, a capitalist in Boston noted in 1852, to buy lands near the railroad in Ohio rather than going into non-railroad counties to try for a cheaper price or a larger spread. Within an hour's ride of Dayton was wonderful land, which could be purchased for $10–15 an acre. Because it was near the railroad, it would increase in value 10 percent annually for many years and yield fine crops all the while.[32]

Cleveland had enough of a railroad iron–milling industry by 1860 that there was an argument over the sickness caused by poor air quality there.[33] There was a car-building shop at Toledo in 1852.[34] "The cars left this morning for New York," wrote a reporter there in January 1853. "Put that in your pipe and smoke it. Here we are a few miles from sundown, and yet within thirty hours ride of the Emporium. All the rest of the world is now tributary to Toledo—and Toledo is tributary to the rest of the world." It was an everyday thing to watch the trains come and go, and yet it was amazing. "We are really the creature of the world. What difference now . . . does it make whether we reside East or West—what's a few hours ride on a railroad any way?"[35]

Now if the state could only clean up its facilities. Thousands of strangers arriving in Cleveland in 1853 got an unfavorable impression by seeing a depot with mud ankle deep, where they were compelled to grope in darkness at night. Paving and gas lighting were needed.[36]

Michigan was not far behind in starting and, if anything, moved more quickly and more impressively than Ohio in the rail field. Michigan became a state in 1835, and its first constitution suggested that the government encourage the building of internal improvements.[37] The *Detroit Journal* reported in the spring of 1836 that companies were chartered to build railroads from Detroit to St. Joseph, from Toledo to the mouth of the Kalamazoo River, and from Detroit to Pontiac. More than 700 miles of railroad might be built for less than the population of Michigan now spent in five years on alcoholic spirits.[38] Government aid would be fine also:

If the business of a barren and hilly country will justify the states in constructing rail roads over the mountains, from inland point to point, and then yield a handsome profit on capital invested, it must be settled beyond a doubt that government would be justified in constructing a railroad uniting the Mississippi with Lake Michigan, where the route passes over a rich and level country, most of which is yet in the hands of the government.[39]

That aid came in 1837 when Michigan appropriated $550,000 to begin work on the Michigan Central, the Michigan Southern, and the Michigan Northern. The state could borrow $5 million to advance these projects. The Bank of the United States in Philadelphia bought the bonds, but the timing —surrounding the national financial panic as it did—was unfortunate. It turned out in the end that the sale of the state interest to Boston capitalist John Murray Forbes in 1846 was a fortunate accident. Forbes was one of the most efficient railroad builders of his time.[40]

A passenger was impressed with the beginnings of construction. "Everything in Michigan is on a grand scale," he wrote in 1838. He rode from Detroit to Ypsilanti on the Michigan Central. His car carried sixty passengers behind a locomotive with a spark arrester. He was amazed to ride without fear of his eyes being injured or his clothes set on fire. He expected the road to push on to Ann Arbor soon.[41] That railroad hauled 150 barrels of flour per day through that year.[42] By the end of 1843, the cars of the Michigan Central ran to Jackson, 84 miles from Detroit and about halfway across the Lower Peninsula. There were sanguine predictions that it would reach Lake Michigan, nearly 200 miles from Detroit, by the next summer.[43]

The Michigan Central, when it came under the control of Forbes and his Boston group in 1846, became a model for what could happen with these western lines under the proper management. A biographer of Forbes wrote that he was an example of a "heroic entrepreneur" and that the age, being one of rapid national and global change, was ripe for his type. He thrived on tension and could hardly sit still. He loved progress, and it was a time when "the excitement of the possibilities overwhelmed the fear of disorder." The Michigan railroad was just right for him and for his operating assistant, James F. Joy. "It seemed," historian John Larson wrote, "that Michigan wanted something it could neither afford nor do without." So outsiders entered the local field.[44]

The revenues of the Michigan Central in 1846 were double those of the year before.[45] The regional press noticed the "Boston style" and predicted that in no time rail passengers would go from Detroit to Chicago in twelve to fourteen hours "with a diminution of hazard and inconvenience which only they can appreciate who have seen the navigation around by Mackinac." Forbes bought the state bonds at 70 percent of their original par value. That seemed on the whole a wonderful deal.[46] The car barn and depot at Detroit, put up by the new management, were to be the most extensive such improvements in the United States. The freight depot there was 800 feet long. "Everything is regular and systematic as clock work along the whole line of the road, and a disposition to find fault in any of its affairs is manifested in no quarter."[47] More than 2,000 men were working along the line in the spring of 1848. There began to be talk that Michigan Central stock was a particularly promising investment.[48]

The journey from Chicago to Detroit was still a three-day jaunt in 1844. Passengers left Chicago by steamboat at nine in the morning and reached St. Joseph at three in the afternoon. There they boarded stages and rode the rest of the day and all night to Marshall, which they reached at four o'clock the following afternoon. Passengers boarded the railroad the next morning at Marshall and reached Detroit after an eight-hour ride. It was a challenge, yet it was far better than earlier alternatives.[49]

However, by late 1851 the Michigan Central had built 30 miles beyond Michigan City, leaving only a short stage hop to reach Chicago.[50] Both it and the Michigan Southern completed lines into Michigan City the next year, filling the state's rail gaps in the process.[51] At Detroit travelers going eastward in those years could board any of three Lake Erie steamers owned by the Michigan Central: *Mayflower*, *Ocean*, and *Atlantic*. They offered carved ottomans, lounges, sofas, and costly mirrors, giving them an air of "royal grandeur." The gold leaf aboard *Mayflower* alone cost $1,600.[52] The Michigan Southern, which ran from Monroe on Lake Erie to Chicago on a parallel southerly route, had three new steamers also by 1852, named *Southern Michigan*, *Northern Indiana*, and *Empire State*.[53]

The Michigan railroads did well financially. The Michigan Central in 1852 was regarded as one of the best investments in the United States. Its earnings were $600,000 per year, up 300 percent in four years, and it moved in 1852 more than 221,000 passengers and 123,000 tons of freight.[54] In 1855 it owned sixty-four locomotives.[55] Piles of merchandise covered the floors of its enormous freight depot on Water Street in Chicago.[56] That depot, jointly erected with the Illinois Central, was 504 feet long, 166 feet wide, and 84 feet tall. There were more than 600,000 square feet of tin laid on the roof, and 2,600 feet of gas piping were needed to light the complex.[57] Nearby, on land that had once been part of Lake Michigan, stood the Sturges & Buckingham grain elevator, completed in 1856 and the largest in the United States. It was more than 200 feet long, stood on 5,000 piles, and contained 2 million bricks.[58] The Michigan Central began manufacturing its own cars in Chicago.[59] Soon, one visionary wrote, the wheat fields in Michigan and Wisconsin would be more valuable than any gold mines and "the independent tillers of the soil, surrounded by their golden sheaves, happier by far than the care worn hunters for gold nuggets in Australia."[60]

William Ogden, a mayor of Chicago and a railroad officer of several lines, by 1857 owned more than 1 million acres of land in Wisconsin and Michigan, which railroads had given a value of $16 million. "The enterprise and energy, and liberality of Chicago capitalists," the *Chicago Daily Tribune* reported in 1857,

> can do everything. They have long since rolled the Mississippi upward, and made its outlet into Lake Michigan; they have now tapped Lake Superior, and will soon draw its trade downward to the same point. Detroit may slumber, Cleveland grow peaches and cherries, but Chicago, regardless of the great inland Lakes and Rivers, has by these railroads secured to herself, beyond all peradventure, a vast monopoly of the wealth and commerce and the manufactures of the Union.[61]

A man who had visited Chicago a quarter-century earlier was amazed at the sights in 1858: "To have foreseen this advancement was impossible. No one could have even dreamed of the means whereby it was affected."[62] Population soared and land values did also. Great fortunes were made—"buy where at whatever price they would."[63] William Cronon, in his insightful book on Chicago, *Nature's Metropolis*, concluded, "By 1860, eastern investors and Chicago railroad managers had succeeded in imposing a new geography on the western landscape."[64]

The entire State of Illinois moved, too. A correspondent writing from Galena in the spring of 1836 reported companies organized to build from Alton to Springfield, to continue to Lafayette, Indiana, on the Wabash River. There was another project from Springfield to Quincy on the Mississippi River, and still another from Chicago to Vincennes, Indiana, on the Wabash River.[65]

Most riveting was the incorporation of the Illinois Central Railroad. It planned, when incorporated for the first time in 1836, to run from Cairo to Galena, both places at that time thought to have more potential than

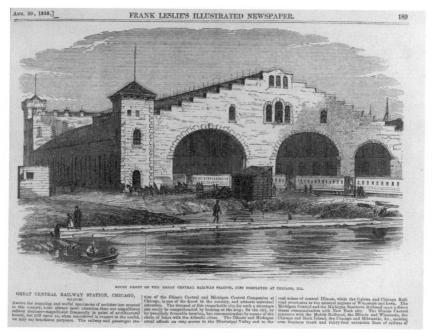

SOUTH FRONT OF THE GREAT CENTRAL RAILWAY STATION, JUST COMPLETED AT CHICAGO, ILL.

GREAT CENTRAL RAILWAY STATION, CHICAGO, ILLINOIS.

Railway depot at Chicago, 1858. Library of Congress

Chicago. Darius Holbrook of Cairo proposed to construct the whole 450 miles on piles at a cost of $3 million. The support was to come from lands. "As a frontier people," historian Paul Gates noted, "Illinoisans had few or no constitutional scruples against the employment of the public domain to aid internal improvements."[66]

The Illinois Central, one man wrote, was "of greater importance to that State, the Government, and the whole Union, than any similar work yet projected." Running north and south through the center of Illinois and to its rich southern "Egyptian" district, it would facilitate communication between the navigable waters of the Ohio and Mississippi Rivers in all seasons. Rivers in the Illinois prairie country froze hard in the winter, and a ride across them on horseback was a formidable challenge. With a railroad, settlement in the empty districts could be pushed and millions of acres of land sold in one-quarter the time it would take absent a railroad.[67]

A second Illinois railroad, the Galena & Chicago Union, organized in 1836, started westward toward the mining town of Galena and the Mississippi River. By 1850 it had reached only Elgin, just a few miles west of Chicago, but it did have the distinction of a Chicago connection, and it paid through the next five years 10–16 percent annual dividends.[68] A third major Illinois line, the Chicago & LaSalle (later Chicago, Rock Island & Pacific), got its charter in 1848 and actually connected Chicago with the Mississippi River before the Galena & Chicago Union reached there.[69] A fourth Chicago line, the Chicago, Burlington & Quincy, started as the Aurora Branch, chartered in 1849, and changed its name to the more familiar moniker in 1855. It reached the Mississippi at Burlington, Iowa, and at Quincy, Illinois.[70]

Illinois boomed. There were 10 miles of railroad built in the state in 1848, 45 in 1851, 390 in 1853, and 1,096 in 1854.[71] Illinois newspapers predicted great profits for the Illinois Central. At its southern terminus, Cairo, investors had built levees that would supposedly protect the town against the greatest known floods.[72] The location of Cairo, wrote a correspondent in Washington, D.C., early in 1848, was at the delta of two great rivers, as was New York City, "and it will ultimately be to Chicago what New York is to Buffalo." When the Illinois Central was complete, it would become the "great thoroughfare between the Southwestern and Western States." Illinois had invested more than $1 million in the line, and it was time, many thought, for Congress to consider aiding it with a land grant. Everyone in the country would benefit from the filling of the Illinois prairie with settlers —ideally, virtuous yeomen, but any kind would do.[73]

A prominent feature of the Illinois railroads was the colonization and development of the great prairies of the region, with aid in doing so by large and controversial grants of land from the federal government. The federal land grant to the Illinois Central in 1850 (2.5 million acres) was the first of a series of such land grants to railroads. These extended over more than twenty years and involved grants to seventy-nine railroad companies and including, had it all been earned, about 200 million acres of the former public domain.[74] The Chicago, Burlington & Quincy also received such a land grant in 1856.[75] There was no underestimating the impact of this means of subsidy. Wrote the historian Paul Gates: "The Illinois Central Railroad, in the first decade of its existence, was primarily a land company and secondarily a railroad company." By the end of 1855, it had sold more than 500,000 acres for more than $5.5 million and was spending $15,000 yearly on newspaper advertising for its lands.[76] Speaking about the Illinois Central land grant, one man wrote: "Considering the grand way we are apt to talk of such things, this does not, at first blush, seem so very large a gratuity." But it was 4,000 square miles, bigger than the states of Delaware and Rhode Island, and it would make a kingdom in Europe.[77]

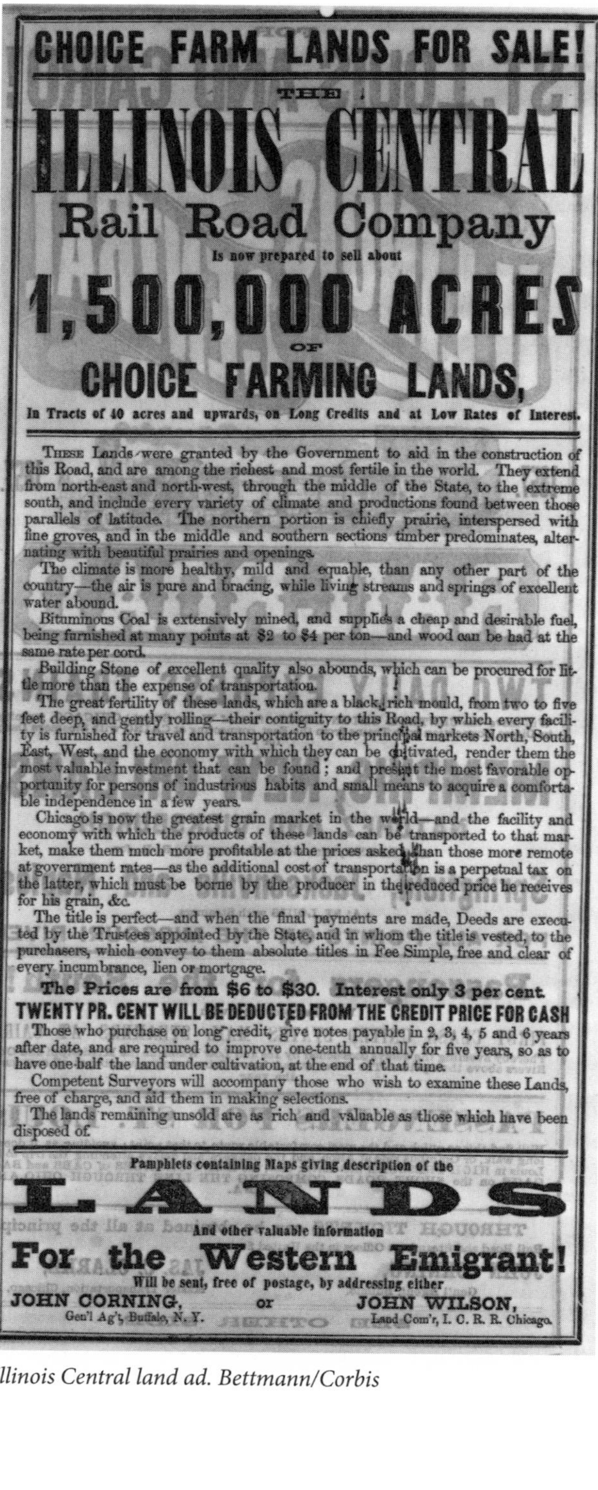

Illinois Central land ad. Bettmann/Corbis

Opinions on the wisdom of the federal action in granting land varied. An editor at Hartford wrote in the fall of 1850 that the Illinois Central grant was a great thing, and the recognition of the principle that it was not only constitutional for the federal government to aid railroads in this way but was its duty to do so "will give satisfaction to every well-wisher of the prosperity of the country."[78] A committee of the Illinois Central held a complimentary dinner at Willard's Hotel in Washington in the spring of 1852 in honor of the land grant and the advancement of construction through "perhaps the finest connected body of land in the world." The residue of the public lands would become more valuable due to the railroad land grant. Daniel Webster wrote those gathered that "God gave the earth to man to be tilled, and land is of no value whatever till the approach of cultivation shows that it is about to become the theatre for the application of human labor, the all-producing sources of comfort and wealth."[79] In 1852, the Illinois Central advertised for 1,000 laborers to be paid $1 per day.[80] A wolf extermination program got under way in Illinois and Indiana in preparation for the tracks and for the farmers.[81] When complete the Illinois Central would be, at 700 miles, the longest railway in the world.[82]

But the nay-saying was always present. It was there in the congressional debates themselves, especially among U.S. senators from the South. "Can Congress give to Illinois," one said, "a million and a half of acres of land, and then turn round and tell the other States . . . we do it in order to benefit the whole of you?" The response to that from supporters was that the government was a trustee of the lands, "created by Providence, bound to administer their facilities to the best advantage, not merely for themselves, but for their fellow men."[83]

Not all were buying that. A correspondent in Georgia, writing in 1851, reported that Congress gave away 30 million acres of land at its last session, most of it to railroads. Were not the public lands pledged for the redemption of the public debt? This seemed to mean nothing, "with the generous representatives who part with them with less indifference, than they do with the smoke of their segars." Would land grants lead to development and settlement? Maybe. Did we need that? No. The United States was already "growing too big for our trousers," and this policy would artificially push a swelling of foreign immigration.[84] An editor at Charleston felt the same way. Congress was squandering the common property of the state "with wasteful extravagance upon a few favored members of the confederacy."[85] A North Carolina man called the Illinois Central grant a "wanton waste."[86] It was one more way in which the South was feeling oppressed.

However, it was not only the South where doubts were expressed about the land grant policy. An editor in Milwaukee thought the Congress in 1853 would be overwhelmed with applications for land grants and that this "grab-game" would not help the West. Wisconsin would get its share, no doubt, but the disorganized method would not be good for an orderly growth. Many in Wisconsin agreed with the southerners that the land belonged to the people of the United States and not to the states and that policy should be more reasoned.[87] The editor of the *Milwaukee Daily Sentinel* hoped that "Congress will set its face sternly against any further squandering of the Public Domain upon reckless and greedy speculators and monopolists." The system, the editor thought, was "unjust, unequal, and altogether mischievous."[88]

A writer in New Jersey agreed. "Railroad-ridden and monopoly trodden" as the New Jersey legislature was, he said, "we are inclined to think that we are not much ahead of the National Congress in this species of 'Democratic Progress,' which yields humbly to the mandates, and, we may say, the substantial temptations of the 'lobby.'" There were eighty lobbyists in Congress in the 1854 session who had prepared 100 railroad land donation bills involving $300 million worth of public lands. Many were using the lands as the basis for stock-jobbing schemes in large cities.[89] A newspaper in Racine, Wisconsin, said land grant railroads had "lost the confidence of the honest portion of the community" and had for years "practiced fraud as a profession." Railroads had been used as a "vast political engine" and had sought "to mold our Legislature so that they would move at its beck and nod."[90] Such critiques presaged the land-reform atmosphere that eventually ended rail grants of land in the 1870s and led to federal railroad regulation in the 1880s.

As lands sold and farmers moved, the criticism became quieter. A North Carolina paper admitted in 1853 that the land grants in Illinois had allowed construction with little expense to the stockholders. Under the Locofoco Party rule in the South, "we are forced to build our roads, whilst the *anti-slavery* States have roads built for them."[91]

What had been nearly worthless lands on the prairie sold by the mid-1850s for $2.50–5.00 per acre on average and $20.00 per acre for the best lands.[92] Illinois railroads thrived. The Chicago & Galena Union erected a large depot in Chicago in 1853 that was 280 by 57 feet and supported by forty-two iron pillars.[93] The Rock Island that year hauled 800 passengers a day and collected $2,000 from them.[94] The credit of the Illinois Central was so good that none of its 7 percent bonds sold at less than par.[95] Chicagoans talked about a Pacific railroad to join its system with those farther west.

But its system by itself was marvel enough. It could be compared, said a local writer, to a wheel, "say an iron steamer wheel, with one side dipping in the wavy outline of the Atlantic and the Gulf, and the other sweeping around to the base of the Rocky Mountains on the West, and to Lake Winnipeg and Hudson's Bay on the North." This was the iron wheel. "Lake Michigan might represent the ponderous crank; the other lakes, bays, rivers and falls, the walking beam, cylinder, piston, pipes, and valves." Like the locomotive itself, the Chicago rail system was a kind of giant machine.[96]

Chicago was a wonder to travelers. "R.K.," writing to a Milwaukee newspaper, said that one could not admire its location, but there was no denying that it thrived. "The scream of the Locomotive has got to be one of its 'city cries,' and its Rail Roads are almost as numerous as its streets." There were good hotels there made of Milwaukee brick, and the visitor called on two newspaper offices.[97] There was a locomotive factory in Chicago and business enough, one man said, for fourteen more such establishments.[98] Its census showed a population of more than 60,000, double that of three years earlier. Its rail tracks handled seventy-four trains per day.[99] It was planning a city railroad to connect its trunkline depots.[100] In 1854 it claimed thirteen railroads: the Illinois & Wisconsin; the Galena & Chicago Union; the Beloit Branch; the Galena Air Line; the Chicago, St. Charles & Mississippi Air Line; the Chicago & Aurora; the Chicago & Rock Island; the Chicago & Mississippi; the Great Western; the Illinois Central; the Michigan Southern & Northern Indiana; the Michigan Central; and the New Albany & Salem.[101]

The writer "Chicago Militant" seemed threatening to Milwaukee. Having waxed fat, Chicago was beginning to kick. "Not content with swallowing Milwaukee, and threatening Detroit, it is now shaking its fists at Cleveland and trying to bully Buffalo." Milwaukee had some railroads of its own, and a lot of dreams. "*Our* little Lake Shore road is voted and forgotten long ago in the magnificence of this Air-Line-Boston and Astoria-Grand-Trunk-Atlantic and Pacific-Junction-Slam-Bang-Rail-Road. But tell it not to Chicago, lest they should thrust in their hateful pod-auger somewhere and let the whole stream of commerce and travel down (or up) into their already stuffed mud."[102]

Detroit thrived almost as much as Chicago. In January 1854 a banquet took place there in a dining hall prepared by the Michigan Central. The room was 200 feet long and 177 feet wide, warmed by four immense stoves, one at each corner, and hung throughout with tapestry. There was a large banner with the motto "New York Central, Great Western, and Michigan Central Railroads. We United Them All." There was a painting of a locomotive and tender illuminated by twenty burners. Near the center of the room was an orchestra surrounded by 4,500 yards of bunting and 1,000 yards of evergreen wreathing. There were nine tables of 160-foot length each and two that were 50 feet long. Only in railroad America![103]

Similarly elaborate was a great excursion celebrating the completion of the Rock Island in 1854. Two trains of twelve cars each left Chicago loaded with 1,300 people to the cheers of a vast crowd. They proceeded through the prairie and stopped for people to gather wildflowers and grasses and to observe the substantial stone houses and gardens already established along the line. The prairie, a traveler on that train said, "was in its way as grand as the White Mountains, or Niagara Falls." Arriving at Rock Island and the Mississippi to a cannonade, there was a banner at the depot reading: "The Mississippi and the Atlantic Shake Hands." Drawn up to the wharf were six of the largest Mississippi River steamboats—*War Eagle, Galena, Lady Franklin, Sparhawk, Golden Era,* and *Jenny Lind.* Each had a band playing on the upper deck.[104]

The "Conquests of Civilization" looked especially impressive that day, comparing favorably with any military conquests of old. Wrote a man celebrating the excursion opening the Rock Island: "Our invasions, instead of desolating and laying waste the regions into which they are carried, spread fertility and abundance on their track, and they bring us back, instead of weeping captives to minister to our ostentation and pride, the fruits and riches of the earth, garnered from the most distant climes and kingdoms."[105] The Illinois Central Company was bigger than the U.S. Army. That army had 10,000 in 1854. The Illinois Central railroad employed 19,000 who earned a total in wages of nearly $4 million per year. In three years it would build 700 miles of railroad, whereas in thirty years the federal government had spent $200 million on the army "for which they have nothing to show but some old forts, guns, battered uniforms, and demoralized veterans."[106] Soon enough, in 1856, trains passed over the Mississippi on the great Rock Island Bridge, 1,581 feet long with a draw in the center.[107] "Yes, the Mississippi is practically no more. It is spanned by the mighty artery of commerce and enterprise—the railroad."[108]

The uninhabited prairie might be sublime and a "solemn" sight, but seeing the plains of Illinois divided into farms was more exciting still. The fields would "drop fatness" when in time "the old fogy sod, matted conservatism of centuries, is overturned by the revolutionists, the ploughshares, and penetrated by those radicals, the grain roots, and the wheat fields stretch out green and wavy as the seas."[109]

A man on an excursion across the Illinois prairie in 1855 could not believe what he was seeing:

> The iron horse struck out upon the boundless prairie towards
> the Father of Waters. To those who have crossed this limitless
> ocean of land, nothing need be said, for they know words cannot
> convey a realizing sense of the beauty, the majesty, the grandeur
> of the Illinois prairies. To those whose eyes have not been
> strained in fruitless attempts to take in such a landscape, I can
> but say, that seeing is believing, and he is a foolish man who has
> the vanity, and a reckless man who is willing to risk his reputation
> for truth and veracity in an attempt at a description of a
> trip from Lake Michigan to the Mississippi. As far as human
> vision can reach, God has laid out a giant bed and covered it
> with a boundless "spread." Man has adorned that spread. Here,
> in the fresh-turned earth, is a huge stripe or square of rich black;
> there, a bright green patch of waving wheat; again a dotted strip
> of corn; and here and there a more sober shade of natural grass,
> mottled with bright flowers of every hue and tinge. Groves of
> oak and of cultivated locust trees, relieve the monotony; and
> herds of cattle, flocks of sheep, droves of horses roam and fatten.
> Pigeons, and quail, and prairie chickens flit over and around;
> and the eye wearies, and the mind tires in vain attempts to take
> in the beauty of the scene. The burning steed dashes on, screaming
> like a demon in his triumph.[110]

The West was thought to be the fulcrum of the country. "We have outstripped the Arithmetic of our Ancestors," an Ohio editor thought, "and have reached the twentieth century at the middle of the nineteenth."[111] The proof was the Illinois Central. When it was completed to Cairo early in 1855, Chicago was "united to perpetual navigation on the Mississippi," and the North effectively united with the South, at least commercially.[112] The governor of Illinois, in his 1855 message, referred to the railroad progress with satisfaction and said he was confident that the interest of his state "could hardly have been entrusted to a class of men with greater energy, or more regardful of the rights and interests of the state" than the managers of the Illinois Central.[113] The railroad had opened up large sections of the state "hitherto inaccessible and uninhabitable."[114]

Not all went smoothly in this new prairie world. The winter of 1854–1855 was particularly severe, and it interfered mightily with rail operations in

Illinois. Newspaper accounts abounded of trains trapped for days by snows in spots so isolated that the passengers worried about starving or freezing before rescue might come. In February 1855 the delays were constant, and mails were stopped entirely for days at a time. A man wrote from Chicago on February 4 that he had gotten that far but would stay put. All the lines from Chicago were closed except the Michigan Central, and "passengers are scattered all along the route . . . and can't get either way." Chicago was jammed with snowbound passengers, and the correspondent himself was on one of five trains frozen in near Chicago, where there was no food for forty-two hours. "I thought I had seen snow . . . but it remained for me to see the elephant on this trip. . . . Locomotives and tenders looked more like icebergs than anything else—some of them covered entirely up, buried and forsaken."[115] A general snow embargo that February lasted more than three weeks.[116] It was a "real Russian winter in the West."[117] Wrote one man: "There never was a time of such general suspension and disarrangement of travel since the day railroads were invented."[118]

Accounts from the snowbound were as harrowing as those from accident survivors. One wrote from a hotel in Mendota on a Saturday morning, "day of month forgotten," that they had been four days and nights on a passage from Springfield and were still more than 80 miles from Chicago "with the railroad closed upon on the north and unfathomed banks of snow on the south. . . . At present we are about as much cut off from the world as poor Sir John Franklin and his men." Illinois Central crews had rescued them from their trapped train and carried them by sleigh to the town of Mendota.[119]

Another account told of snow over the tops of cars and passengers helping with shovels in a cold wind. A letter from a passenger, published in the Kankakee *Gazette* in February 1855, said he had been an admirer of the prairies, but being cold in a tempest was not the most attractive feature. "We behold ourselves in the midst of a vast ocean of prairie, wild and stormy—our windows covered with a thick glazing of ice, and the snow driven into the cars at every crevice. Passengers gazing upon each other with anxious faces; the cold and storm too severe to venture far from the cars; one of two houses seen miles distant; no wood or timber in sight." Hunting a deer seen on the prairie did not yield food, so the group survived on cheese and crackers and a few tins of oysters.[120]

It did give pause among the excursions and the dividend notices. If it could be this grim in Illinois, what might be the case in the more remote West of America? "These Illinois snow drifts have put a quietus to the

Snowbound on the Michigan Central. Library of Congress

Pacific Railroad by any other than the extreme Southern route. And there the howling volcanic deserts which we have purchased of Santa Anna, without rain, or wood, or water, are as terrible to the traveler in summer as the snow drifts of the South Pass can possibly be in winter."[121] Maybe Thomas Hart Benton would create an artificial climate on "chemical principles" or invent in his oratory wonderful snowplows. But to practical people, there were major problems in even considering pushing into Kansas or Utah.[122] But then there was a time when the Patapsco River valley in Maryland had looked impregnable and impossible for the steam horse. Change was a tonic that was being deeply drunk.

CHAPTER 11

Panic

ll the euphoria seemed for a time to drown out concerns about the risks of railroad building, particularly the financial risks of raising the enormous capital required. The Panic of 1837 had been an object lesson, but it had come and gone, and the booming U.S. economy seemed none the worse for wear. Perhaps cycles were mere adjustments, and the slight corrections made in response to the last one would be sufficient to ameliorate things in the future.

However, to the wary there were continuous warning signs concerning the instability of the new rail world. In addition to the problem of state debts, there arose in the 1840s the specters of corporate bankruptcies, poor rail management, and personal dishonesty among company officers.

Did not corporations have a public responsibility, which they were badly abusing? They derived their existence and maintenance from the public, "and it is to that public as well as the individual stockholder that they are responsible. We do not subscribe to the doctrine that because a road pays *ten per cent* that the stockholders and public have nothing further to do with it." A newspaper editor in New Hampshire said that he was an advocate of corporations "because we hold that there are interests that can be better advanced by associate or corporate wealth than in any other manner, but because we hold to corporations it does not follow that we are to be the apologists or remain silent upon *corporation abuses*."[1]

The trouble was, the public knew little about railroad corporations "and all who invest in them do so blindly." Everything was "wrapped in mystery, and the first developments made, we fear, will be in the shape of an explosion."[2] Banks and canals had had their day of exposure and reform, and it was time for railroads to "pass through the same ordeal before they become purified and placed upon a proper basis."[3] One editor noted that the United States was in a "curious" and unprecedented financial condition, with wheels within wheels of complications. When a reforming journalist tried to investigated a railroad "we [were] stopped at the very threshold by statements, figures and reports which no man living can understand."[4]

During the mid-1840s rail mania in England, a man named George Hudson became famous as a "fashionable swindler," one who lived well on the proceeds of thoroughly dishonest practices, paying no attention to the interests of the stockholders whom he supposedly represented. Such practices seemed to be taking hold in the United States also. Criminals could not necessarily be recognized in the new corporate world. They held high positions, "standing at the head of social and fashionable circles, rolling round the country in their splendid equipages, and dealing out damnation to all those who venture to whisper a word against the corrupt and fraudulent system by which they thrive."[5]

The equivalent of Hudson in the United States was Robert Schuyler, grandson of a famous Revolutionary War general, nephew of Alexander Hamilton, graduate of Harvard, and the first president of the Illinois Central, among many other rail interests.[6] In 1854 Schuyler was the principal in a scandal involving an overissue of spurious stock of the New Haven Railroad and a consequent disastrous fall in its value. Schuyler resigned as president of the New Haven. But soon a similar scheme was discovered at the Vermont Central.[7] Schuyler's operations extended into the West, where it was discovered he had swindled the little Racine & Beloit Railroad in a crooked deal as agent to buy rails for it. That company, an analyst said, had found "Wall Street a 'hard road to travel.'"[8]

Railroads had done much for the country, the *New York Herald* commented, but "have been the means of developing the knavish propensities of some of the greatest rogues the world ever saw." Schuyler was a prime example and had wielded great influence in the business and social worlds before his exposure came. Even when it came he "continued to plunge his hand freely into the public pocket; always hoping, doubtless, that better times would enable him to make good what he had taken."[9]

The most disturbing thing about it was that many seemed little bothered by the Schuyler story. Railroad enterprise was tempting, even "seductive," to ambitious people "who have more enterprise and recklessness than firm moral principles." Accounting was not very transparent, and those with access to the books could get away with a great deal. Discretionary authority often went to those with few qualifications.[10]

> In a city in which three-fourths of the mercantile and trading classes are living beyond their means, and indulging extravagant tastes at the expense of others, it is not to be expected that commercial ethics should be over strict, or that offenses like that of the late President of the New Haven Railroad Company should excite either excessive astonishment or reprobation. It is only the consummation, on a gigantic scale, of what each in his turn expects to accomplish in a more humble way.

There was even respect for the coolness and audacity of Schuyler.[11] "The dignity of swindling to the amount of millions inspires awe."[12]

Schuyler escaped the country and bought property on the Rhine River to spend his winnings until he died late in 1855.[13] There were plenty of copycat crimes, large and small, suggesting that Schuyler had "debauched the public taste." A financial villain was hardly worth his salt unless he had robbed enough to build a city. Yet the petty thief went to jail, and these men often escaped punishment.[14] The comment of Schuyler himself was that, like so many, "his ambition overleaped his capacity for steady industry, and in his anxiety to grow rich he forgot to keep honest."[15]

It would be one thing if the problems had been merely a matter of high-profile personal dishonesty. But it went deeper than that. There was suspicion that fraud and financial panics as well were endemic to the American capitalist system. The *New York Herald* reported in 1854 that people in trouble tended to stay away from the source of it. They thought the big sums put into rail construction were the cause of the monetary tightness, and so they refused to invest in rail securities, further reducing their value. These were unsophisticated investors, the reporter thought, who did not so much make a mistake in investing in the first place as fail to predict that "the relations of things are changing," which was normal in finance. "In the United States, where entire freedom is allowed to every impulse, it is natural that the pendulum of public opinion should oscillate beyond the boundary that marks the limit of its healthy movement." Passion for railroads had exceeded "the harmonious development of all our great interests," and there had to be a painful corrective. Railroads were the "great fact of the physical progress of our people," but they were not predictable, and investment in them could be dangerous.[16]

The *Charleston Mercury, Louisville Daily Journal,* and *Hartford Daily Courant* took a similar tack. American nativist optimism was simultaneously attractive and dangerous. These newspapers concluded that railroads had been built too fast, diverting money from more legitimate channels. "We have anticipated results which have not yet arrived; in fact we have provided means of transit for the produce of unsettled counties and untilled lands." Frauds like that of Schuyler and his like only accelerated a crisis that was sure to arrive. The acts of criminals were produced by the times "and the viciousness of a highly speculative period."[17] Railroad stocks declined about 30 percent on average in 1854, which was not even an official panic year. As soon as one railroad was finished and doing a fair business, then a rival one was ginned up, "and the result is that when one road would have proved a profitable investment, the two are sinking concerns."[18]

It was complicated to assess properly the contributions of railroads in the broader economy. Wheat was carried at 9 cents per bushel from the Ohio River to Hartford, Connecticut, as contrasted to 75 cents before railroads. Passengers rode at one-fifth the cost of the stage. But the enterprisers who had built the roads lost money. If expansion could be slowed, and if there were more careful planning of the need for routes, rates could be brought into line with what railroads needed to prosper.[19] The current situation, however, was chaotic. "Borrowers cannot get money or repay that which has already been used. Railroad operators cannot get money to finish their works, and thus prevent that which is already laid out from being sacrificed. . . . Everything goes wrong. It is a time that tries men's honesty as well as their purses, and peculations and embezzlements occur, adding their evils to the difficulties around us." There was a general distrust, which hurt the credit system. "If it only buried the fraudulent in its ruins, it would be less to be lamented, but men of honesty are liable to be crushed when it falls."[20]

Railroad bankruptcies seemed to confirm such an analysis. The New York & Erie went into receivership in 1842 and suspended operations, apparently indefinitely. A New York paper said that was due to the influence of "pipe-layers" in the management of that corporation and in the state legislature. These people rented a splendid suite at the Astor House and entertained influential friends with money that should have been spent up-grading the rail line. They borrowed money from anyone "who could be induced to trust them," and they had ruined the railroad.[21] "Nothing *freezes* a New Yorker," wrote a newspaper there, "like a proposition to undertake an improvement that may not promise an immediate speculative return on his investment." Boston was more prudent, but in New York "factious obsti-nacy and miserable folly rules."[22]

The Philadelphia & Reading Railroad was not much better off. In 1844 that line expended $1.7 million while hauling only 218,000 tons of coal, 17,000 tons of merchandise, and 26,000 passengers. None of its promises to investors and the public had been realized.[23] Its rails were light, its bridges flimsy, its operations inefficient. Meanwhile, it borrowed ever more, so much that it lost its credit altogether. No "cunning financiering—no stock jobbing" could make up for the failures.[24]

The newly organized Pennsylvania Railroad struggled also, and Penn-sylvanians did not seem to recognize how important completion of this line was for Philadelphia to compete successfully with Baltimore. "Those of our citizens who remain inactive at home, or waste their summers amid the inanities of fashionable resorts, can neither realize the immense losses sustained by Philadelphia commerce for want of this road, nor the inconve-niences to which its absence subjects our Western friends."[25] When J. Edgar Thomson, formerly a civil engineer, became president of the Pennsylvania in 1852, there was rejoicing that finally a practical and honest man had taken the office, rather than the former management, who took "counsel from [their] passions rather than from justice or truth."[26]

The Charleston & Hamburg was deteriorating, and it needed ever more maintenance as engines grew heavier and faster. This did not seem to be forthcoming. People should not expect perfection, or easy profits. It was a matter of long-term commitment and discipline. "Timber will rot, iron wear, screws and wedges work lose, ditches fill up." These ordinary things needed to be attended to, and the shops needed reorganizing. This would not be done by speculators in the stock.[27] The "insane outcry" over taxes would not help either.[28] "As a pioneer in the Rail Road system," one journal-ist commented, this line had "to pay heavily for the experience incidental to all early enterprises."[29]

A New England pioneer suffered equally. Boston & Worcester stock de-clined rapidly in 1849. It had at one time sold for a 30 percent premium. The line had double track and seemingly a good deal of traffic, but there were things the general public could not know. Dividends were declared, but not really earned, and were based on borrowing. Accounting reports were inadequate. Such failures as that of the venerable Boston & Worcester caused people to distrust all railroad corporations.[30]

The Western & Atlantic, once the pride of Georgia, fell on hard times by the early 1850s. The legislature appropriated $500,000 in 1852 for its repair, but that was thought not sufficient.

> No subordination seems to exist—no acknowledged head, no recognition of the immense responsibility assumed in transporting passengers over an unsafe road with still worse management. The frequency with which accidents have occurred within the last few weeks had been such as to excite a thrill of alarm sufficient to deter any from passing over the road unless impelled by necessity. Horses, cattle and hogs are run over as if it was but school-boy sport—engines run off the track almost daily—trains are running in time and out of time, without any apparent regularity of system, but rather as if governed by the whim of the director or engineer. Cars and locomotives are smashed up as fast as they can be replaced.[31]

There were lessons to be learned, but there was also a fear they would not be learned. The country had pursued a "radically false policy," many wrote, but people would never learn, even when they suffered.[32] They complained and then went right back to acting as before. "Railroads," wrote a New York observer, "are generally beneficial to the country, but largely disastrous to individuals." The original owners lost money in behalf of the general good. It was a question whether better planning would make these things more predictable, to put railroads on "proper and reliable bases." But railroad finance in the 1840s and 1850s was hardly the science that locomotive building had come to be. The "philosophers of Wall Street" did not trouble themselves with the data relating to the profitability of a railroad company. "All they desire is a respectable list of respectable directors, respectably empowered with respect to issuing shares in a respectable way. This being done, whether it is Erie this or Erie that, is all the same to them. They speculate with pieces of paper, the nominal value of which, rise or fall, as the bulls and bears are transported upon the road. . . . Their only question is, who will buy—who will sell?"[33]

Nevertheless, there did arise a call for reform of railroad management in the wake of news of such dishonesty. "Under the present system," wrote a reporter in Boston, if a man blunders into the possession of a hundred thousand dollars, and will invest a few thousand in a corporation, he is made a Director thereof, and with an equal amount of complacency and stupidity will lounge about the offices, talk oracularly about the financial world and of the prospects of the corporation of which he is a Director—while the Clerk, Cashier or Treasurer is embezzling, year by year, thousands or even hundreds of thousands of their capital.

Those who supposedly were auditing the books were incompetent. "They never had the capacity to detect any fraud which a clever scoundrel might attempt to practice. Their intercourse at the office of the corporation is nothing but a continual swagger; and weak and vain, as they are swaggering, a dishonest officer flatters their vanity by soft soaping them and then pockets the money of the corporation." Rich directors could hardly read or write. "In this oscillating age, when the revolving wheel of fortune sends man to the top to-day, and whirls him to the bottom to-morrow, nothing can be more stupid than to suppose a man becomes competent to manage the affairs of a corporation, because he has stumbled upon a fortune."[34] Boards of directors were incompetent, too, often corrupt, and only hamstrung the president. It was not enough that officers were often stockholders. They could make money by trading on negative inside information to sell stock short as well as by doing things that benefited the corporation generally and in the long run. Sometimes the railroad president was nothing more than a representative of a group of brokers trying to make money on stock manipulation rather than by increasing the health of the company. In any case there was a premium on volatility and sudden fluctuations in the stock. This was a kind of swindling, yet the stockholders and directors practically licensed it by paying small salaries and allowing officers to own stock.[35] Officers always had a "retinue of relatives and dependants" who flattered their vanity and got appointed to subordinate situations in the company, "the sole qualification for which . . . is that they will practice toadyism towards those from whom they receive their appointments." It was one thing for a man to put such people in a company he owned personally, but limited liability corporations needed more professionalism.[36]

It was remarkable, one journalist thought, that the American people, with all their intelligence and ingenuity, had not discovered a better system of management.[37] There was, another said, "no well defined, well understood Railroad system." Yet there was no reason why there should not be.[38] It was remarkable that better managers could not be attracted. The first stockholders of every railroad seemed to be deceived by the first managers, who tried to make money through shady deals with contractors to the detriment of the long-term health of their company. Perhaps this was actually necessary to get the railroads started, but stockholders suffered, and conflicts of interest among managers and contractors were rife. Railroad managers seemed pious indeed when it came to going to church. "If they cheat and shave the stockholders . . . during six days of the week, they are pious, laying up large amounts of stock in the kingdom of heaven."[39] It was a system of "fraud and imposture," and everyone had a finger in it. One heard it talked about on Wall Street with a wink.

Through all, the public seemed silent or impotent.

> There is no more extraordinary phenomenon under the sun than a "Public." Its character is as undecided as the color of a chameleon. . . . A public may be humbugged and wheedled in a manner that would bring disgrace and ridicule to the veriest idiot. . . . An "enlightened public,"—a "discerning public"—a "humane public"—a "reading public". . . . in fact every description of "public" is appealed to and used as the most effectual shield for impostures of every kind by knaves of every hue. The Public was the "most patient and stupid of asses."[40]

Railroads had become too important to escape regulation and the application of science to their management. Everything about them affected the whole community.[41] Railroad reports should be understandable. Instead they were presented in a way that "no man living can understand."[42] The public should not bear the losses from bad management. "Blinded, hoodwinked, helpless—and that by the act of the company—they [the public] committed no single act from which any such want of precaution or prudence could be inferred as would justify throwing the burden of the loss on them." It was time to stop discussing these matters as lawyers, looking at the technicalities only, but as "men, as men of business." Such frauds as that perpetrated by Schuyler were inevitable, but the courts needed to work out the consequences fairly. Should foreigners "be entitled to consider our railroad companies properly typified by Schuyler?"[43]

The "wholesome restraints of the law" were needed more than ever. That was the mark of true civilization, as contrasted to the free exercise of appetites and passions. Public opinion was not a good regulator.

It does not sustain and promote the growth of virtues of any sort. It stifles all of them. It is supremely false and corrupting. It is a radically vulgar public opinion. It is fascinated and won by might against right. It elevates show above reality, extravagance above elegance, pomp above beauty, form above simplicity and culture, and barbaric tinsel above refinement. It sneers at the substance and kindles all the wild, untamed energies of the human spirit in a vain race for the shadow.[44]

The wise were consequently suspicious of newspaper promotion and boosterism. Perhaps the editors knew enough to take their claims with a grain of salt, but it was not evident that the public did not swallow much of the rhetoric whole. It is well-known among historians that behavior among the masses (and maybe even among college professors) is not driven by a sophisticated understanding of reality but rather is influenced by stereotypes projected in media stories of questionable reliability. This is particularly true when one proceeds far from one's area of personal expertise, as most ordinary railroad investors did during the pioneer days of railroading. The newspapers were the major information channel for most, and they had conflicts of interest and problems of source reliability at best in conveying information accurately.

There had been warnings for some time that another financial panic might be in the offing. "The pulse of our financial and monetary body is most unfortunately located in Wall Street," a Cleveland man complained.

As the heart-current ebbs and flows in that gambling den, so pales and flushes the extremities. It has been noticed that the stock-brokers—than whom there is not a more desperately reckless class of operators alive—have had their figures sadly disarranged by the continued "gloom and hesitation" of the money and stock market. . . . If the gale only sweeps through Wall street, no body will care a straw, for the contest there, is bull on one side, and bear on the other; and it matters not which whips. To the honest business community it is hardship thus to be swayed by the current, in Wall Street; but nevertheless it is so, and if forewarned, there is no excuse for not being forearmed.[45]

Early in 1857 there began to be warnings that something more than "hard times" was on the way. There was likely to be a crash on the scale of 1837. The United States had built 26,000 miles of railway at a cost of $1.2

billion. This was distributed between stocks and bonds, with and without backing security. A large portion of this was held by cities and counties and was taken not as an investment but to encourage the projected roads and gain indirect benefits. Landholders along the line had similar interests and held much of the stock. Wall Street speculators owned the rest, and their interests were definitely short-term and subject to the daily news and their own psychological makeup. The goals of making money in the short term and of developing the country were incompatible. "We have wanted to get two profits out of the same money." The financial, social, industrial, and political "excitements" would come to roost, a New York editor thought, in "one concentrated crisis, perhaps in two or three years."[46]

A Chicago reporter analyzed the trends in June 1857. Speculation, he wrote, had caused many stocks to fall below what they were intrinsically worth in the battle between stock-market bulls and bears. Also, there was the building of rival lines to excess; dishonest management; bad financiering; construction of nonpaying branches; casualties by accident, fire, and flood; and construction fraud. Few rail stocks were selling at par, and most were below 60 percent. Contractors had taken stocks and bonds as part of their pay, then sublet the work to "sharp, driving, Irish and Yankee 'bosses.'" This pressed the construction to be accomplished with the actual cash at hand, a fraction of what the work was originally estimated to cost. Directors converted their county and town subscriptions into bonds and sent them to New York or London for sale. There they might settle for 75 percent or less of par. Then there was the yearly interest load. Dividends were sometimes paid out of borrowing, and often paid in stock, which expanded the capitalization but did not get the road built. Iron and rolling stock were purchased on the same kind of basis. Often the company issued second mortgage bonds for that purpose "at a heavier shave than on the first bonds." The earnings of the first few years of operation were consumed in ballasting, fencing, rebridging, laying sidetracks, and building machine shops and depots. Then came maintenance. Net earnings went to meet bond interest and "to kite along the floating debt," which meant short-term borrowing at high rates of interest. Then the road sold more stock to provide more equipment. "By a vigorous system of puffing, and skillful misrepresentation of earnings, expenses, and prospects, the new stock is got off at a high price, enabling the road to finish itself and the 'knowing' stockholders to sell out before the decline overtakes the stock." Finally, when the stock and bond issues were more than double the amount actually spent, the stock declined "with a run." The officers were "ex-officio" stockjobbers who might sell short, hoping the stock would decline. These were the tricks of the trade.[47]

In August 1857, amid news of breaches of trust in the stock issued by the Michigan Southern Railroad, the announcement came of the suspension of the Ohio Life & Trust Company of New York. The capital of that trust company was $2 million, and the last report indicated a surplus of $200,000. It was paying a dividend of 7 percent semiannually. But suddenly its stock value fell by 85 percent. Such a surprise led many to lose confidence in all financial institutions and in any kind of investment. It seemed they were a pure gamble and the information that might be studied about them a sham.[48] It was noted that Ohio Life had loaned heavily to railroad companies, most lately the Cleveland & Pittsburgh.[49]

Some felt complacent about it. The "bursting of bubbles in New York," wrote a Chicago journalist, should not worry anyone in the West. The prosperity of that region did not depend on the activity of bulls and bears on Wall Street. "So long as corn and wheat grow, and cattle and swine fatten on the broad prairies around us, Chicago will be able to do a safe and sound business."[50]

The South was smug also. The breaking of banks and the collapse of great firms in the North should not worry the South. Tobacco was selling for a good price, and there was another large crop in the ground. The same was true of wheat. The crash might be healthy for the country, showing as it did the instability of business as it was done in the North, rich as it was in "fictitious values." Railroads into the wilderness and paper towns were useless things—as useless as "railroad bubble stock."[51]

Such claims seemed logical enough. However, the facts were that the financial panic affected railroads and regional prosperity everywhere. The crash was based on deception and mismanagement, certainly, but the causes were too complex to be cured with a sermon or two. The Chicago press admitted in September, "We have not yet touched bottom in our railway explorations. . . . There is still another depth of rottenness which has not been probed."[52] It was all very confusing. The Ohio Life & Trust Company "seems to have gone down, like the city of Sodom, into the yawning earth . . . leaving no one to tell the tale of its disaster." Some of the ablest financiers in the country were blind to the signs of the disaster. They were perhaps as gullible as the country bumpkins about keeping their fingers out of the fire.[53] Arrogance was so strong that the Michigan Southern sued the *New York Herald* for libel concerning the newspaper's reporting about that railroad's shaky finances.[54]

The boom now appeared to have been a masterful piece of propaganda, based on a truth, but not as glorious a one as advertised. Many "unsophisticated" stockholders had gotten involved in the market, and railroad stocks were found in every farmhouse and village. There were "a thousand Chicagos in embryo" in the presentations of securities agents. The opening of Kansas would check the slaveholders and at the same time fill the pockets of investors. "Thus railroads, freedom and the gospel were beautifully mixed up, till the result was that every man who had a dollar laid by felt that he was not only assisting humanity and religion, but bettering himself by an investment in the 'West.'"[55]

What were the lessons? A simple one was that no country could prosper on wind, on confidence, and on vanity. When everyone in every grade of society "was straining to the utmost, to make the greatest possible display, these financial pressures must be expected."[56] A second one was that banks should not be operating in risky railroad stocks and bonds using people's savings. Ohio Life had its headquarters in Cincinnati, but it also had a branch house on Wall Street, coupled with influence everywhere to draw others "into the vortex." It was not content to make "fair profits" but had to speculate in the much-hyped railroads. Ohio Life had advanced $600,000 to one railroad in Ohio and $200,000 to another, both loans made with no security at all. The moral, according to the *New York Herald*, was to have nothing to do with railroad securities. "When they ruin a company with an almost unlimited command of capital, and possessing the very best means of judging their worth, what chance have small capitalists to escape?"[57]

It might be nice to learn from economic history, but there was small prospect of that. The New York press noticed the similarities between the Panic of 1857 and the Panic of 1837.

> There is the same exaggerated value of stocks, the same high prices of the necessities of life, the same wild speculations in real estate, the same gradual tightening of the money market . . . and the same growing distrust in the minds of all men. This is because the causes that have led to the present state of things are identical in their nature, though different in form, with those that produced the crisis of 1837.

But so long as people made money in the short term, and lived well on it, no lesson would be learned.[58]

The best minds were deceived, however "strange" that might have seemed to some.

It has been a perfect piece of fascination. Men who wanted to sell their bonds, would come here with the most extravagant representations, which they must have known to be false—statements about the case with which the road could be built, always under-estimated—statements about the business of the road and the character of the country through which it would pass, always over-estimated—statements showing that the ten per cent bonds could be met twice over, and would be met punctually. All these over-wrought representations were implicitly believed by our long-headed men.

Was it likely that the "present burning of their fingers will teach them hereafter to keep out of the fire"?[59]

Indeed, the historical repetition of financial disaster was disturbing. In the midst of the financial downturn, people were cautious about officers and their representations. "Every one distrusts them; but the wonder is that any one ever had any confidence in their securities, and the greater wonder is that any one ever should have again, as they certainly will, and the same career of headlong credulity, to be followed again by headlong disaster, will be run."[60] Perhaps railroad securities would be better named railroad "insecurities."[61]

Gambling and untoward risk seemed to have a deep psychological attraction. Many in New York City, both in fine brownstones and in cheap boardinghouses, worried over the panic "because they are blind, inveterate, irreclaimable gamblers." Alexis de Tocqueville had said that the besetting sin of Americans was a desire for material luxury, however it might be obtained. And the quicker it was obtained the better. Women pushed their husbands to more risk and bought at the milliners and jewelers "on the faith of their husband's good luck." But when luck came, it was not seen as luck but as power—the second great desire of everyone. "To ruin somebody, overwhelm somebody, crush somebody, kick somebody out of the way at whatever cost, is everybody's great aim."[62] That was a deep and dark irrationality, and its results were not to be contained by rules.[63]

Many knew generally that by some subtle hocus-pocus, called *financiering*, railway managers were able to get large sums out of the public and into their own pockets; but few did or do know to what an extent this new system of financial ethics prevailed; —now the essence of railway skill consisted in making false but plausible statements—how much money was spent in manufacturing "public opinion"—how the "cooking" of reports became a science—and how the principles of sound business and honest dealing came to be neglected and despised.[64]

The straight facts were dark enough. The Erie and the Illinois Central suspended payments on their debts and appeared so weak as never to rise again.[65] The Michigan Central, of late the most prosperous and admired railroad in the country, suspended also, and John Murray Forbes sailed to England in search of a $2 million loan to keep it afloat.[66] It laid off more than 1,000 men and reduced wages and salaries 25 percent.[67] A man who recently had headed a firm clearing more than $1 million a year, and whose own estate was valued at $2.5 million, died in an insane asylum after his firm went under. One asset in his estate was 1,000 shares of Illinois Central Railroad stock, which went from a worth of $800,000 to about $50,000 in the months after his death.[68] A lifetime investor in rail securities offered 13 bushels of "engraved paper" for sale at a price competitive with wallpaper.[69] A defaulter poisoned himself with laudanum in his suite at the Metropolitan Hotel.[70] Yet there were reports of laughter on Wall Street, with parties "as though a threatened general suspension of payment were a gigantic practical joke."[71]

The French were chuckling also. *Le Constitutionel* wrote in January 1858 that the causes of the Panic of 1857 were the credit system and the excessive speculation it had caused.

> They have created a crowd of banks, and to the aid of these banks they have accumulated enterprises upon enterprises. They have commenced a multitude of railroads, without the capital to complete them, and suddenly, without a note of warning, this great financial edifice, built upon the sand, falls with terrific din—the railroads carry the banks in their train, and the banks in turn involve the commerce and industry of the entire Union in the general disaster.

Disasters always resulted from such abuse of credit, and the United States should have expected it. There was no moderating by government, and maybe now there should be. At any rate, something had to be done with the enterprises of men, "feverishly excited by the spirit of speculation," to make sure their aims were reasonable and financeable.[72] Otherwise there would be one panic after another, and the suffering would be a continuous accompaniment of American railroad progress. But, many agreed, "there is nothing which Americans so soon forget as the lessons of adversity."[73]

Perhaps a foreigner could see the pattern better than an American, so much in the midst caught up in the whirl of money and machines. The two panics of the antebellum rail era were not to be the last. The temptations remained, human nature remained, and the combination was volatile. The compensation available to comfort those who risked loss, ruin, dishonor, or all of these became ever greater. The measure of a man in the United States was increasingly his portfolio and the lifestyle it would buy. A generation had matured on it, and their children would be born to it. To say that the locomotive had modified the culture was an understatement. The raw material had always been there, but the opportunities were now so manifest that there was no use preaching about the ills of plunging. There was only one form of gambling, a reporter in Hartford wrote, and it was an ancient one. It consisted of getting money without service: "They are not content to take the share of the gifts of Providence to which they can entitle themselves by honest industry, but they desire to get some other man's share without paying for it. They forget that the value of a fortune is just what amount of honest and virtuous endeavor it costs to get it, and not a cent more."[74]

The Panic of 1857 was perhaps less a deep shock than that of 1837 had been. It was as though the new world had become accustomed to such things. Ambition seemed only to feed on possibilities to which these reverses only represented a mild hiccup. Should railroad enterprise divorce itself from Wall Street? An editor in Cleveland thought so. He wrote that

> until Railroad companies cease to seek officers in the fetid atmosphere of Wall street, they will be but foot balls to be kicked back and forth as these Wall street managers see fit. When Railroad officials have only in view the interests of their stockholders and their own reputation, a new era will visit our Railroads, and the dawn of that era will be when Wall street is "cut," and only practical, honest men, residing on the line of the road, are selected to manage these great interests.[75]

But the realistic chances of that actually happening were slim, were panics to come oftener and last longer than they actually did.

CHAPTER 12

We Fly by Night

elcoming the railroad was one thing; assimilating it, or adopting it in full—integrating it in all its expected and unexpected effects into American society—was another. With the excitement came blindness, with the promise dangers. Some of the latter were so distant from the track and operation proper that they seemed at first coincidental and only distantly related. But the matter of who was to do railroad work and on what basis impacted the entire labor movement in the United States, as well as affecting the mix of immigration. Various standardization questions, from locomotive design to gauges to time, schedules, and work rules, were part of a trend toward centralization and scientific homologation. Each detail of the emerging mature railroading picture, from better heating and lighting for cars, to the elimination of picturesque but primitive inclined planes and masonry architecture, and to issues more remote like city livability, the carriage of the mails, land speculation, and race relations, was part of a partly unconscious development in response to unexpected challenges. As changes took place, the railroad could be said to be no longer an experiment but at last established, if not fully comfortable, in its American home. There was hardly a part of anyone's daily life

that it did not, by the 1860s, regularly touch and deeply influence. But, as one journalist put it in Latin, *nocte colamus* ("we fly by night")—not only on the express trains toward Chicago but also aboard an industrializing society driving with obscured vision into an uncertain future.

This was definitely true of the workingman. Railroads became the largest employers in the United States. They employed many types of workers with a great range of skills, and the relation between these workers and rail management had a good deal to do with the emergence of the rail brotherhoods and of the union movement generally.

The labor issue was early on strongly connected with the great influx of Irish. The Irish became the quintessential railway workers as well as New York City policemen, for better and for worse. Their adventures on the railroad influenced stereotypes of their nationality as well as of the corporations by which they were employed. Part of the Irish stereotype was that they were pugilistic, especially when drinking heavily, as they were prone to do. Violence was not something Americans wanted to see as endemic to their form of society or to new forms of labor relations, so it was convenient to blame that violence on resident aliens who happened to work cheaply at dangerous jobs.

Late in 1834 there was a murderous "riot" among Irish workers building the Baltimore & Ohio to Washington, D.C. One of the construction superintendents, unpopular because of his "driving and arbitrary manner," was dragged from his bed and bludgeoned. Firebrands were poked into his mouth and eyes. Then, leaving that man for dead, the crowd attacked two other managers, breaking in their skulls and even killing a dog belonging to one of them.[1] "Great numbers of these ruffians," a Boston reporter wrote, "are still lurking in the adjoining woods, from which they issue forth at night to burn, massacre, and lay waste." An innkeeper in the area was moving his family and furniture after the "infuriated wretches" burned down his barn and threatened him. Militia members arrested 250 Irish workers.[2]

Local people said that the Irish had been arguing among themselves all summer and that whiskey was the cause of their violent temper. Contractors passed out spirits under the impression that they could get more work that way, providing it freely to the men several times a day. One correspondent averred that such things would never happen on the New England rail lines, where liquor was not allowed.[3] However, there had been similar disturbances in Pennsylvania earlier in the year.[4] The events were a shock to those who were thrilled by the progress of the railroad and the seemingly contented and industrious workers along the tracks. Now all changed. The noisy activity of daily labor, the hallooing of the workmen, the rushing of the cars upon the temporary railroad, and all the picturesque bustle of a great public work were now no longer visible. The workers' shanties along the road had been torn down as a security measure.[5]

When, however, the dangers of construction work were taken into account, the public was more tolerant of the Irish. In the spring of 1835 four men were killed and eight mangled while excavating for the Boston & Worcester. As workers approached, thinking a charge was entirely spent, a second explosion occurred. One man was entirely divested of his limbs and thrown into the top of an oak tree, his body lodging 40 feet off the ground. All but one of the victims, the press mentioned, were Irish.[6] While there was talk that they were drunk and that the accident was their own fault, 100 other workers refused to return to work on the grounds that the company was not concerned enough about safety.[7]

"There is no class of our population so much abused as the Irish," commented a Boston editor. "But we Yankees are immaculate. We never do any wrong and we never did. We never hung a witch or burnt a convent. We are exclusively liberal, exclusively benevolent, exclusively industrious, exclusively temperate, exclusively honest, exclusively patriotic, exclusively righteous. . . . We have a charming opinion of *ourselves*, and that is reason enough why we should be thought most highly of by others." Look at the bridges and railroads and wharves the Irish had built; they were hardly a lazy people. The records of the savings banks showed they were a thrifty group as well. Were they not serving here as a scapegoat for the dark side of railroading that the public was not willing to recognize?[8]

In the wake of the Panic of 1837, low rail wages became an issue. How could one expect careful work in either construction or operation of railroads when the labors of U.S. rail workers and Cuban slaves yielded about the same wage? Some U.S. rail workers in 1840 were receiving 62 cents per day to support a family. There were suggestions to reduce that to 40 cents daily, or about $125 for the entire year. "*Forty cents*, for wheeling dirt twelve or fourteen hours in the broiling sun." President Martin Van Buren, the "poor man's friend," earned $25,000 per year.[9]

Low wages seemed the result of a conspiracy to some. "Our Government and Corporations seem to go hand in hand in their war upon labor." When rail workers on the east side of Boston learned in 1842 of a stiff wage cut, they all quit work. "The mask is fairly off now," wrote a Salem reporter. "The federal monied aristocracy seeks to crowd down and degrade the classes that honestly labor for subsistence." Railroads had benefits, such as tariff protection from the federal government, and it seemed to some they should be the last to take advantage of laborers. Daniel Webster had once said that the government should take care of the rich and the rich would take care of the poor. But this early "trickle-down" theory did not seem to be working. Newspapers asked in 1842 whether the president and officers of the Boston railroads were taking pay cuts also.[10]

Organization and strikes were the inevitable result. In September 1842, hands on the Philadelphia & Reading Railroad went on strike, some having received no wages for four months.[11] Workers at Northampton, Massachusetts, left work in March 1845 in protest against a daily wage of 55 cents, with no compensation for inclement days when they could not work. They paid $2 a week for their board, leaving them, if the weather was fair, $1.30 as their weekly net pay. They asked for 75 cents with an eventual raise to a dollar a day.[12]

Some saw the irony in allowing railroads to combine, set rates, and make profits while workingmen suffered. If workers raised their rates when rent and food went up, they would be denounced as enemies of society waging war on capital. "There is neither good sense, or common humanity in making or in recognizing such distinctions," wrote the *New York Daily Times* in 1854. The railroad combinations were no more or less than strikes by corporations that were created to be competitors. The main stockholders of the Hudson River Railroad got their profits from the enhanced value of real estate. Meanwhile, "the 'poor' stockholders, the carmen, retail traders, butchers, &c, who were induced to invest their savings in the road, by promises of large increases in business from the cheapened freights and fares, have not as yet . . . been able to 'realize' their expectations."[13]

Higher wages would attract more competent employees and be a benefit to the public. Most engine drivers, wrote one in 1855, did not know anything about the construction of the locomotive. "They know that by pulling a lever the engine moves, and have some sort of idea that steam moves it; but of the principle upon which it operates he is entirely ignorant. Like a man catching fish, he feels the bite, but does not know what is on the end of his line." People came to the railroad shop directly from a shoe factory or a logging swamp and may never have seen a locomotive. Then after a few months as firemen, they were promoted to engineers. Engine drivers should be skilled mechanics and be suitable types to take the enormous responsibility they were given.[14]

Another class massively affected by railroads was African Americans. This became evident in the situation of slaves, and also of free blacks.

A number of southern railroads used slave labor, either hired out from plantation owners or owned by the railroad itself.[15] In 1841 the "Negro Harrison belonging to the Carrollton Railroad Company" was charged with assaulting a white man and sentenced to seventy-five lashes.[16] A Natchez newspaper in 1852 contained notice of the sale of "Negroes and stock belonging to the South Carolina Rail Road contractors." There were ninety-seven men aged 20–40, who sold at an average price of $847. There were eighteen boys at $656, four women at $555, and two old men for $528 each. At the same sale eighty mules sold for an average price of $95.[17] The Tennessee & Alabama Railroad, projected southwest from Nashville in 1856, proposed in its annual report to purchase "niggers" to build the road. About 400 were to be purchased at first, costing $1,000 each. Intending to train many as masons, the railroad would become a "nursery for slaves and mules."[18] In the spring of 1861 a contractor for the Mobile & Ohio Railroad sold his force of seventy slaves for $1,370.50, on twelve months' credit with interest.[19]

The southern press argued that not only would railroad work strengthen and expand the institution of slavery even into areas where cotton, tobacco, and rice could not be grown; it would also be a boon to southern railroad building in competition with northern enterprises. The effort to build a southern transcontinental across Texas to southern California was to be enhanced by the purchase and use of slave construction crews. A Texas editor thought, "A Southern road to the Pacific, built upon slave soil and by slave labor, would be a great creative agent in rapidly germinating the elements of slave states on territory contiguous to this stupendous work." Six or eight new slave states could come out of the effort, something "the freesoil politicians of the North, and the abolition organs in their pay have long since discerned."[20]

There was concern that northern railroads, too, might indirectly support slavery. The Boston & Providence Railroad owned land in Virginia from which it cut wood for its engines. The company hired slave drivers and slaves to do it. A Boston editor thought that was passing strange in a company in which churches and the City of Boston owned stock.[21] But it belonged to that class of unintended social consequences of an important new technology that could hardly be totally avoided.

There was concern that runaway slaves would use railroads to their advantage. In 1842 three such persons arrived in Boston on the Boston & Worcester Railroad. Their master from Georgia was waiting at the depot. Two were secured, but while irons were being put on a third he knocked down his master and ran through a crowd of surprised spectators. He hid with some abolitionists, first at Salem and then at Newburyport. The master of an eastern coaster declined to take him on board, but well-wishers finally got him on a steamboat named *Huntress* bound for St. John.[22]

The concern went beyond runaways proper. In 1854 there was a report that thirty blacks came to Louisville on the train from Lexington. They had been emancipated, were on their way to Liberia, and had been given free passage by the railroad company.[23] Southerners worried that this could get out of hand. Since the construction of so many railroads in the South, one wrote in 1861, "the social privileges between slaves in distant localities have been increasing far more proportionally than those of the white population." This should be curtailed out of "proper regard for the safety and peace of the country, as well as humanity for the slaves themselves."[24]

There was criticism in 1854 of the Jeffersonville Railroad for attempting to "introduce slavery and slave-driving laws" into the free State of Indiana. The *Louisville Journal* defended the railroad for accepting blacks as passengers, no questions asked. It should not be required even under the fugitive slave laws to ask a black person if he were a runaway slave any more than it had to require proof from a white person that he was not a runaway apprentice or a fugitive from justice.[25] It became common late in the 1850s to issue monthly passes to slaves traveling through the South. These passes, a New Orleans writer thought, "make the slave, for the time being, virtually free. They remove them from the restraints of masters, and bring them into contact with the worst classes of society."[26]

Many railroads, in response to criticism, required that only whites be allowed to purchase tickets for blacks. An editor in Augusta, Georgia, thought there should be a stricter rule: that tickets should be purchased only by the master of the slave traveling by rail. "We are not aware if any distinction is made at the rail road offices between the half tickets sold for children and those sold for negroes, if not, there should be some distinctive mark on the tickets, for nothing is easier than for a negro to procure some of the idle white boys, loafing about the depots to buy a ticket and make the transfer to himself."[27]

Perhaps the railroad would affect slavery also by bringing northern farmers into the South to compete with the institution. "These swarms from the Northern hive," an abolitionist paper wrote, "will drive off the effeminate and lubberly lordlings, or make them hewers of wood and drawers of water, in a single generation."[28] Or it could give slaves ideas by mixing them with whites on the railroad, where it was a custom for a master to bring his slave on board an integrated car, where free blacks were not allowed.[29] Free blacks were often regarded in the South as a "baleful influence" on the slave population. If they would not go back to Africa, they should be put to work on railroads where they would be out of the way of the general population.[30] A paper in the North quoted one in the South to the effect that the head of an African American had been picked up along the railroad. The owner could claim it by paying for the advertisement. "What savagery!" the editor commented.[31]

There were some touching accounts of loyalty. A lady leaving New Haven in the summer of 1850 found that her slave nursemaid was missing. Some said she had escaped. But some days later she appeared again. In changing cars she had gone back after something one of the children had left and missed the train. She followed the railroad line on foot, walking for two days to catch up with the family.[32]

Of more concern than the impact of railroads on slavery was their impact on the social and political relations between whites and free blacks. Right up to the 1896 U.S. Supreme Court case *Plessy v. Ferguson*, the issue of integration versus segregation of railroad cars had been key in defining U.S. policy toward racial integration. Before the Civil War there were particularly strong expressions of opinion on this. Incident after incident on railroads was publicized as an example of injustice to African Americans and unsatisfactory policy for a country based, supposedly, on equality of opportunity.

A Louisiana man, riding the early railroad from New Orleans, wrote that his pleasure while riding was diminished by the policy of placing blacks in the same car with whites. Surely it was an oversight by management, who would not "sanction a thing so totally at variance with the distinction necessary between the white and colored population."[33] On another New Orleans line, where there were separate cars for blacks, there was a disturbance in 1833 when a "gang" of fifteen African Americans tried to board a car for whites and were forcibly removed by the passengers.[34]

The controversy in New England was more vigorous. During the debate in 1841 over a bill to allow the Eastern Railroad to extend its wharves, George Bradburn, a representative from Nantucket, complained about the company's treatment of African Americans. It enforced, he said, an "odious and unjust discrimination of passengers, on account of mere differences of complexion." His fellows in the legislature laughed out loud when he said that. But he went on to say that the railroad was built partly using credit from the state, "a credit which was constituted by the labor and capital of the colored, in common with those of the uncolored, citizens of the Commonwealth." The representative from Salem demurred, saying that African

Americans were treated the same as whites, only transported in separate cars. A Virginian present at the debate wondered why Massachusetts people were so squeamish about riding with blacks when they were the ones who had given them rights.[35]

There was a considerable exchange about the policy of the Eastern Railroad in the columns of William Lloyd Garrison's abolitionist paper, the *Liberator*. Bradburn wrote that not only the Eastern Railroad but also the Boston & Providence and other companies were "guilty of the same scandalous and cruel conduct" in segregating their cars. Returning home from Boston on the B&P in 1841, Bradburn observed "an elderly and very respectable looking colored man" being asked to leave the car. A southerner on the car commented that nowhere were African Americans treated so shabbily as on New England railroads. They allowed the most disreputable whites to occupy the cars with "our most fastidious epidermis-aristocrats" while they thrust out blacks, however educated, talented, and virtuous.[36] The same year as Bradburn's experience, David Ruggles, an African American traveling from New Bedford to Boston, was shown the printed regulations and expelled from the car. He brought suit for assault and battery, but lost.[37]

Some in New England saw this racial discrimination as more evidence that corporations had no souls and needed to be brought under stricter regulatory control by the state. Railroads were purely selfish, and the more they were able to indulge this selfishness, the more the liberty of others would be compromised. "They are sure to take all the power they can get without regard to the welfare of the people or the rights of individuals." This must not be allowed to happen by accident. "If we *must* be enslaved, give us a tyrant in his private capacity, and not in the shape of a servant to a corporation." The "negro car," the newspaper at Lynn, Massachusetts, wrote, was more inexcusable than slavery itself.[38] It was a reproach, the *Colored American* wrote, "to the land of the pilgrims."[39] If the railroad attached itself to the defense of slavery, wrote an editor in Quincy, it would be crushed when slavery and "its accompanying abominations" fell, as they surely would.[40] There was even a proposal in the Massachusetts legislature in 1842 to require integration of railcars. What next, asked a Georgia editor, forcing blacks and whites to share the same bed at hotels?[41]

Slowly practice in the North did change. African Americans boarded white cars and were often allowed to stay as prejudice declined "and a right feeling toward the colored people" gained ground. Several railroads rescinded their rules about segregation by the early 1840s.[42]

Many in the South objected violently. A correspondent of the *Richmond*

Whig, writing early in 1843, said this change in practice was the center from which "all radical and disorganizing influences go forth." There was no respect for tradition and no disposition to learn from history. Instead there was a cry of "reform." Race mixing in railroad cars would lead to intermarriage and "the milk and molasses color will hereafter be fashionable in the Bay State." State regulations to oblige conductors "to stuff negroes and whites together in the same cars" would lead to "fragrance" being added to the other delights of rail travel.[43]

The change was slow. On the Little Miami Railroad in Ohio in 1857, a family of African Americans boarded the train shortly after it left Columbus. The man had a gold-headed cane, and the woman was well dressed. It was the custom to furnish passengers with ice water, and a black man delivered this. He came into the car from the rear and began serving the passengers there first, which happened to include the black family. A southerner sitting at the front objected to the whites not being served first. The porter responded, "We don't sort people in this State."[44]

In 1860, however, when a train over the same railroad reached Xenia, Ohio, two African-American men, a bishop and a minister, got on board and took seats in a sleeping car nearly filled with passengers. The person in charge ordered them to a forward car. When they refused to move, the agent told them that although chair cars might be integrated, the sleeping car was private property and the owner had the right to restrict use. A "wordy conversation" ensued and the two were forcibly ejected "much to the relief of the passengers who had been disturbed." The men sued, but a Cincinnati paper doubted whether any jury in the country would sustain them.[45] The same year, however, a judge in Cincinnati ordered that blacks be allowed to ride the city railroad there so long as they behaved properly and did not have an infectious disease.[46]

It was not only in direct labor-management relations or as customers that the operations of the railroads affected the common masses of people. The effects of the railroad on urban areas, always an issue, led to some outright riots. There was a considerable one in Philadelphia as the Philadelphia & Trenton road made its way into the city in 1840. Citizens attacked workers, and a general fight ensued. A mob of more than 500, a good part of them women, set fire to the house of the president of the railroad company and burned it to the ground. It also tore up the rails and broke doors and windows in a number of houses. There was a running battle with 100 police, leading many to wonder whether this seemingly beneficial new method of transportation was so benign after all.[47]

Ever since the B&O had run its tracks down Pratt Street in Baltimore in the early 1830s, people in cities had argued about how best to adapt to and accommodate the railroad. The Canton Company in Baltimore, incorporated in 1829, was a land development company closely tied to the directorate of the railroad. It laid off more than 1,000 acres with 11,000 building lots, and it controlled more than 3,000 acres. This land would have sold for $100 per acre as farmland but would yield $30 million in lot sales. And even though most did not begrudge the company this profit from developing the city, some questioned whether such expansion was properly planned or aimed mostly for speculative gain.[48]

There was a similar debate in 1835 over a land development corporation in Boston. That company was literally changing the topography by tearing down hills and filling in parts of the bay. It also tore down numerous old colonial homes. But the majority of the population seemed to accept this as the price of progress.[49]

Stock in the Canton Company of Baltimore rose in one month in 1835 from $50 to $200 per share. Shortly it was $1,000. The Boston concern, named the South Cove Company, was expected to do as well.[50] If the Harlem Railroad extended to Wall Street, stated a New York newspaper, financiers would live in Harlem and commute, booming real estate both downtown and uptown.[51] True, the developers did not always have time to put in adequate streets and sewers, but these would come in time.[52]

There was much comment on how gratifying it was to see people alert and seeming to move purposefully down the crowded city streets. An Ohio observer saw 25,000 in motion one day in 1851 on the streets and about the hotels in Columbus. People from the hinterlands could come to the city for a day of shopping and then return home by night, carpetbags in hand. It seemed a "magic influence." The reporter was "forcibly impressed with the great social effect which railroads exert upon communities."[53]

When the effects of the actual operation of city railroads were concerned, there was less unanimity. The City of Richmond in 1838 ordered that no railroad vehicle in the city be allowed to remain stationary in the street for more than one hour after its arrival. There were complaints about the unloading of freight. The merchants wanted it unloaded convenient to their stores, but their competitors and travelers on the street did not care for it. The Richmond, Fredericksburg & Potomac Railroad said it would like to comply with the city's wishes, but there was a shortage of space and business was increasing.[54]

There were compensations. By means of the railroad, a New York editor noticed, the vast amount of manure accumulating on the streets of New York could be reduced as horses diminished there, and what was left could be hauled by railroad to the country to be used as agricultural fertilizer.[55]

Still, there was clearly an increase in hurry, stress, and danger with steam railroads operating in congested parts of a city. To elderly people who were only visiting the city and whose reactions were slow, the steam railroad was a hazard. "From the moment the cars begin to move, the countenance assumes a troubled and anxious aspect; the eye is eagerly watching for the next train which is to sweep every thing before it, and not unfrequently a low whispering in the vicinity of the door betrays a half determination to escape while there is yet a chance of safety." One old man commented that he thought the railroads cared no more for a person's life than for that of a dog. Older people were often shocked at the equanimity with which the young adapted to the pandemonium in the streets and at the railroad depots.[56] Even those fleet of foot worried about getting out of the way of the fast trains of the Brooklyn & Long Island Railroad, where some did not dare trust their families or horses along Atlantic Street where the tracks ran.[57]

City rail service could be awful, and it was inevitably overcrowded. A rider of the Harlem Railroad wrote in the fall of 1844 that there was no protection from inclement weather and, seemingly, no set schedule. The cars ran at the caprice of the conductors, whose only aim was to fill the cars to their capacity and beyond, whatever the effect on the comfort and nerves of the customers. The commuter had to stand on the end of the car "in a crowded, inconvenient, often dangerous, situation, subject . . . to the annoyance of tobacco smoke, and having to make way for the egress of passengers often by jumping off." The progress on average was no faster than walking pace, and the riders cursed at the bumps.[58] Etiquette on railcars, which might have softened the experience, was a "new science." People would not give up their seats to women or to the elderly or trade seats on the shady side of the car with someone more in need of relief.[59]

As a result of these shortcomings, when railroads applied in 1852 to build down Broadway in New York City, there was considerable objection before the city council. The attorney for the railroad company, David Dudley Field, had to make an extensive argument that the city railroad was a positive force and that it was good riddance to the omnibus. "Instead of these heavy, noisy, racing vehicles, on high wheels, which now encumber the

Elevated railroad in New York City. Bettmann/Corbis

street, stunning you with their noise, battering the pavement, and tearing from one side of the street to the other, we should have cars, on low wheels, moving upon smooth iron rails, on a fixed line, making little noise, and doing no injury to the pavement." The railroad would provide cars holding sixty people and move them with two horses at 6 miles per hour. Congestion would be lower. Transport would be cheaper. Broadway was crowded as it was with 6,000 omnibuses passing along it every day and more than 9,000 other vehicles. The railroad would reduce the number of vehicles, substituting sixty cars carrying 3,600 passengers an hour and drawn by 122 horses for 527 omnibuses drawn by 1,054 horses. Field argued his case for hours and not without considerable opposition.[60]

The *New York Herald* wrote of a "mania" for city railroad building. There were only three lines at the end of 1852—the Harlem Railroad, the Sixth Avenue Railroad, and the Eighth Avenue Railroad. But many more were before the city council. When all were completed the streets would "present the strangest and funniest spectacle that any city has ever exhibited."[61] In the mid-1850s, New York moved to regulate and reduce fares, citing the unusual high profits of the street railroads. It also suggested licensing to ensure better service.[62] The city authorities in Boston at the same time suggested denying approval to any further city railroads.[63] They admitted that the city railroads allowed commuting to the more healthful suburbs, at least by the middle class. But early and late trains only made these people labor longer at their desks and enjoy their suburban retreats less.[64] Chicago was similarly reticent. "The great barrier in the public mind, to railroads entering the heart of the city," wrote the *Chicago Daily Tribune*, "is that they endanger life and interfere with other kinds of business."[65] A promoter in Louisville admitted in 1859, "It is astonishing to observe the amount of uninformed prejudice which exists against them [city railroads] before their operations and utility are tested."[66]

There was much talk of corruption when railroads and cities operated together. Many thought that needed to change. The public should be consulted in everything when the railroad ran through a crowded city. Was it not the public who had allowed the city railroad to prosper? "Their gains have increased, they are stuffing the half dimes in their treasuries by the peck, and far from showing any gratitude to their customers, they act as unprincipled quacks are said to do, and deteriorate the quality of what they sell because . . . the wares will sell just as well as if they were good!"

The person who paid for a seat should have a seat. There should be arms or rails between every seat and no standing. People should not have their coattails in their faces and worry about how to get on and off the cars. Anything less would be unsatisfactory and should not be allowed.[67] After all, in 1860, New York street railways carried more than 32 million passengers under unsavory conditions. Passengers were subject to a "rail car poison," which, some said, shortened the lives of commuters one minute for every mile rode. Meanwhile, the carriers made enough profit to have a nefarious influence in lobbying the state legislature.[68]

Adapting the railroad to the city was a case where what seemed a boon was not without difficulty in proper implementation. The same was true of the questions of a standard gauge or of standard time and, surprisingly, of railway mail service. The increased speed with which railroads could deliver the mail as well as newspapers and magazines seemed to make it a certainty that all such carriage would quickly be by rail. But it was not that simple.

Postmaster General Amos Kendall, serving under President Andrew Jackson, came into conflict with railroads in the mid-1830s over the question of the prices they charged for carrying the mail. The reaction in most of the press was that it was important for the government to be economical, but prompt, speedy, and reliable conveyance of the mail was a far greater public boon than extinguishing the debt of the Post Office Department a year or two earlier.[69] Also offensive to many was the federal postal bureaucracy. An individual could not carry a letter as a passenger on a public vehicle, and there was the fear that passengers could be searched to see if express companies were trying to get around the regulations by having passengers carry parcels.[70] Most thought that newspapers should be exempt from postal regulations and the penny press allowed to distribute its papers by rail in bulk without going to the Post Office at all. "A system which is designed to promote the public convenience and the prompt transmission of intelligence, ought to be so regulated as not deliberately to counteract these objects."[71]

In 1842 there was such a crisis over rates that the Post Office Department began sending mail by stagecoach. A man in Boston thought this would cause great trouble, "and one of the most important public advantages expected to result from these new modes of conveyance will be lost." People would not wait for two or three days for transmission of their letters and papers knowing that it could be done more quickly. Could not some arbitration be had between the Post Office and the railroads? Should high-tech railroads have to carry mail at the same rate as wagons and stages had? And what claim had the U.S. government on any railroad? "Have they lifted a finger, or spent a dollar, to aid it?" The nation was obligated to the railroads, not the other way around.[72] The government should get no better rate than an individual shipper.[73]

Some felt otherwise and thought railroads were being arbitrary and "arrogant." The Western Railroad of Massachusetts wanted to charge $200 per mile or $11,800 annually to carry the mail from Worcester to Springfield. The Post Office, which could buy the carriage by road for one-third that price, offered three-quarters the rate and was refused. Maybe the federal

Carrying the mail. Bettmann/Corbis

government had not helped the railroad, but the state had, and it was residents of the state who wanted their mail delivered.[74]

An order by the Post Office that newspapers be carried with the mails caused an uproar in the press in 1843. Harnden & Company, an express carrier, was sued that year by the order of Postmaster General C.A. Wickliffe for carrying newspapers outside the auspices of the U.S. mail. Wrote the *New York Herald*:

> We presume the next step will be to appoint a corps of officers, such as are met at the entrance of all European cities with a sword under their cloaks, and a log wire pricker in their hands, which they thrust into all bundles, packages and boxes, to as-

certain their contents, to be stationed at all railroad depots, and steamboat landings, to turn every body's pockets inside out, examine the bandboxes of the ladies, thrust their fingers into the reticules, ransack their trunks, and analyze every protuberance about their persons, to see if perchance the printed lucubrations of some unlucky editor are not in the act of being transported in a manner contrary to the decrees of a successful officeseeker.[75]

With "cool contempt" for public opinion, according to the *Herald*, Wickliffe stood on the constitutional right of Congress to establish post offices and post roads to "manufacture" the claim that no letter, newspaper, or package could be sent otherwise. That was a right that was not yet then established in the law, and it seemed odd to many Americans.[76]

Yet the order was enforced. A traveling agent of the American Mail Company was removed from a railroad in Pennsylvania in February 1844 after a search of his valise revealed that he was carrying mail.[77] That summer Judge Joseph Story adjudicated the case of Windsor Hatch, charged with carrying private mail. In that case Hatch escaped on a technicality, but there were appeals.[78] Postmaster General Wickliffe said he would fine the railroad companies $50 every time they transported an item through the Pomeroy Express Company. Meanwhile, that company threatened to sue the railroads for damages whenever they failed to convey its agents who had purchased a ticket.[79] In response several cities held public meetings protesting the Post Office monopoly and demanding to choose the cheaper rates and better service provided by the private express companies.[80]

The histories of such "adjustments" could be detailed indefinitely. One by one, there came to be regularity and standard expectation about all of them. That was true also about rail technology and the standard of the operation of railroads, which became more sophisticated and efficient by the 1850s than they had been earlier. The manufacturing establishments ancillary to railroads were attractive places for visits. By the early 1840s, American locomotive manufacture was dominating the world, as were American rail engineers. J.G. Bennett visited locomotive works at Lowell and Philadelphia in 1841. He was especially impressed by the Norris Locomotive Works at Philadelphia, though he found it difficult to describe the complex process of building an engine. In one large building, he saw forges "all blazing, hammering, and smoking together," and in another "the wheels, cogs, pullies, screws, and the various pieces of the machinery were made in every variety of way and method." In a third building there were locomotives nearly complete and being packed to go to Prussia. There was a miniature engine, capable of drawing 5 tons and built at a cost of more than $4,000, that was going to the royal museum in Berlin. It was similar to the gift Norris had made to the emperor of Russia, and another he provided for King Louis Philippe of France. The Norris works employed 300 men and could build a locomotive to order in a month. In 1841 it planned to build fifty engines.[81] By 1855 it was building sixty-five engines a year and employing 600.[82] The firms of Baldwin and Rogers also developed into well-respected American makers.[83] By 1842 there were plans for the manufacture of refrigerator cars and hopes of getting fresh halibut from Massachusetts to Chicago.[84] There were even experiments with containers that could be packed with merchandise, carried by wagon to the railroad, and then loaded and unloaded from the cars intact.[85]

Iron smelting was a growing American industry in the 1840s, and there was a hope of ending the expensive importation of rails.[86] The only problem there was considerable objection to a protectionist tariff to protect the infant industry. "No subjects of any absolute province . . . are taxed as we are taxed for the sake of a dozen men in this country who manufacture iron for railways."[87]

The trials of the early rail passenger became relative as the problems of dust and discomfort, nighttime travel, and dining and sleeping aboard were met with improved trains and service. The passengers of 1860 might complain of boredom, but they were hardly the fearful persons on an adventure of twenty years earlier. More modern stoves, though still dangerous, reduced the problems that burned several women in 1837 when a hot brick used for heating set fire to the straw on the floor of a car.[88] Spark arrestors diminished the fire danger to the landscape, as did the increased use of coal for fuel rather than wood.[89]

By 1838 a man from Wilmington, Delaware, who had said he would never travel west again until he could "travel in railroad cars with fires in them and beds to sleep in," thought that time had come. There were stoves that rendered cars "comfortable as a parlor," and a few night trains had beds in which the passenger "however indisposed to sleep is soon wrapped in its embraces by the composing motion of the car." There were ladies' cars with private dressing rooms. "With all these appurtenances," one observer noted, "we know not where a man of leisure could *live* more pleasantly or healthfully than on a railroad."[90] There was not perfection yet, someone wrote,

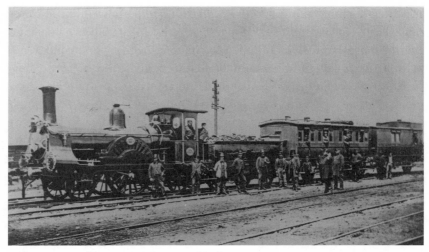

Pullman cars and locomotive. Bettmann/Corbis

but improvements were regular. When an automatic water pump to supply engines was invented in 1838, the comment was: "We shall next have locomotives trained to picking up passengers when cars overset, setting broken bones, mending holes burned in clothing, and picking uncomfortable cinders out of eyes! Rail roads may then become popular."[91]

By the late 1850s there were many compliments on the smoothness and convenience of rail travel, especially by those who had watched the changes over a decade. A woman riding the sleeping cars on the Michigan Central in 1858 from Detroit to Chicago wrote: "You can hardly imagine what a luxury it was after so much sitting, unless you have experienced it. We had nice white linen pillow slips, and the *darkey* even came along and brushed our shoes. We had a wash basin, clean towels and nice ice water, with a bright fire and a cheerful lamp burning all night." The extra charge for such luxury was only 50 cents.[92] Some thought the sleeping car would introduce class differentiation on American railroads, as in Europe, and that would be a good thing. All persons were not of the same taste and did not live in the same style in home or hotel, so why should they be equalized on the railroad?[93] Also attractive for night travel was the introduction of gas lighting for car interiors and hydrogen-powered headlights backed by parabolic mirrors on locomotives that allowed one to read a newspaper a quarter-mile away.[94]

Comfort was a priority. Describing the "perfect" sleeping car on the New York & Erie in 1860, a traveler noted that it was 75 feet long, 11 feet wide, and 8 feet high. It had seats for sixty that could be changed to double or single berths to accommodate fifty-five sleepers. The woodwork was of St. Domingo mahogany. The backs and cushions of the seats were upholstered in royal purple plush, the berths enclosed with satin damask curtains. There were Brussels carpets on the floor, finely crafted gas lamps, and two washrooms. Heaters circulated even warmth through the cars, and there was a sophisticated ventilation system. A body of water under the car was forced up either side into a recess encased in glass where it would break like the spray of a fountain. Entering air passed through this water and was cooled and purified of dust and then entered the car through ventilators between the seats. Most elegant![95]

Little by little, issue by issue, the annoyances of railroad operation were smoothed even as the track itself was. If the rolling society was out of tune with the broader society that supported and surrounded it, adjustments happened on both fronts. Americans came to feel at home with their railroads, which had become ubiquitous. They were taken for granted as benign tools whose erratic history was largely forgotten. The great landscape modifiers were now part of the landscape, and it seemed the only problem was that there was still an American landscape, the Far West, that was not yet covered with them. But the remedy to that was at hand.

CHAPTER 13

Mr. Whitney's Dream

There had been some talk of a Pacific railroad ever since railroads themselves were envisioned. But people considered that it was decades, if not generations, away in execution. Then suddenly in 1845, and in the midst of all sorts of rail challenges nearer at hand, all that changed.

That change was clearly the result of the strength of character, articulate speaking ability, and single-minded dedication to the cause of one individual—Asa Whitney. His proposal to build a railroad to the Pacific seemed at first a pure dream, an entertaining interlude, almost an interruption to the serious and yet unmet challenges of trying to build a rail network connecting the Eastern Seaboard with the Mississippi River. But it was at the very least a fascinating concept, with enough detail to stimulate a debate on ways, means, and routes, which was to occupy a great deal of public attention for two decades. It would no doubt have been surprising to people in the 1840s that it was accomplished by the late 1860s using several of the techniques that Whitney suggested. But some began to think it could be done "at no very remote period." The "stupendous" project of a railroad across the Rocky Mountains to the West Coast was wrote an editor in the spring of 1845, "among our pleasing anticipations."[1]

Whitney emerged on the scene in January 1845 when he composed a memorial to Congress proposing to build a railroad from Lake Michigan to the Pacific Ocean "with a view to the establishment of a direct intercourse with China &c., and asking the government, for this purpose, thirty miles of territory on each side of the railroad."[2] The most prominent feature was that no financial aid would be required, only that the government devote an enormous amount of its now nearly valueless western "desert" lands to the purpose of paying for the improvement that would give them value. There had been some move in U.S. land policy in the direction of using western lands to encourage settlement rather than for revenue only, but this was one of the early specific suggestions of tying lands to railroad building in the way that eventually led to the enormous federal rail land grant era of 1850 to 1871.

Whitney's memorial emphasized many points that became part of the Pacific rail debate for the next twenty years. The advantages, he wrote, were "far beyond the imagination of man to estimate," but they included the ability to concentrate military forces quickly, to unite people, to advance international trade, to settle the West, and to employ thousands.

> This road will be the great and desirable point of attraction; it will relieve our cities from a vast amount of misery, vice, crime, and taxation; it will take the poor unfortunate to a land where they will be compelled to labor for a subsistence, and as they will soon find that their labor and efforts receive a just and sufficient reward, finding themselves surrounded with comfort and plenty, the reward of their own toil, their energies will kindle into a flame of ambition and desire, and we shall be enabled to educate them to our system—to industry, prosperity and virtue.

All this could be done for $50 million, none of it required in cash.[3]

It seemed a long shot but was specific enough to be taken seriously. U.S. House member Zadock Pratt of New York, the chair of the Committee of Public Buildings and Grounds and owner of a tannery and a banking business, introduced the memorial.[4] He was well regarded as a practical man, and many thought that was a recommendation for Whitney.[5] The subject was important, a man in Baltimore wrote, "however extravagant and visionary it may seem."[6] Whitney called it "alike valuable and magnificent." The manufactured products of the United States might, with the railroad and its steamship connections, be transported to China in thirty days "and the teas and rich silks of China, in exchange, come back to New Orleans, to

Charleston, to Washington, to Baltimore, to Philadelphia, New York, and to Boston, in thirty days more. Comment is unnecessary." It would revolutionize the commerce of the world and do it now using American land resources. Otherwise, it would be delayed for "ages to come."[7]

Henry Nash Smith, in his famous 1950 book, *Virgin Land: The American West as Symbol and Myth*, spoke of the great psychological and mythological impact on the American mind at the time of the "highway of nations" and "passage to India" concepts that Whitney's proposal engendered.[8] Surely, too, it is important to remember that with the election of James K. Polk to the presidency in 1844 the era of Manifest Destiny and expansionism gained strength, culminating in the Mexican War two years later. Through that war the United States acquired fine ports in California and a southwestern empire whose commerce and political importance made some sort of transportation and communication link all the more important.

But what is sometimes less emphasized was that Whitney, and many others at the time, considered it an immediately practical project. It would take decades to accomplish, not generations. Whitney was a New York City merchant involved in the China trade and, during visits there, actually calculated the volume of trade that might be expected.[9] *Hunt's Merchant Magazine* in spring 1845 suggested that because the supply of cotton from the United States, including the new State of Texas, was far more than the domestic market could absorb; because the Sandwich Islands (Hawaii) would come to be a U.S. possession; and because American whalers dominated the Pacific, the railroad fit perfectly. "Those persons are now living who will see a rail-road connecting New York with the Pacific, and a steam communication from Oregon to China. For the last three centuries, the civilized world has been rolling westward; and Americans of the present age will complete the circle, and open a *Western* steam route with the *East*."[10] Whitney organized a surveying party right away, as though letting the first construction contracts might be imminent.[11] Young men from nineteen states volunteered to sign up for the party at their own expense.[12]

Whitney began touring the country and giving well-attended speeches. He stopped in Milwaukee on his way to the western survey. He told crowds there that their own city was a wilderness ten years earlier, yet now had 8,000 people. Chicago had grown from nothing to 10,000 in the same period, and now it had all the luxuries and refinements of older cities. Any doubts Whitney had about the ability of land sales to provide for construction of the road through their development and increase in value were removed by seeing the example of Milwaukee.[13] A reporter in Milwaukee, after an interview with Whitney, commented, "He has evidently thought much upon the subject, and is very sanguine as to the success of his scheme." He was no more impractical, the reporter thought, than Robert Fulton or Oliver Evans were once thought to be.[14]

Others were less impressed. Whitney often pointed to the success of shorter railroads and said that if you could build 1 mile of railroad, you could build 50 or 3,000 miles. This logic, the *New York Herald* man commented, was as good as saying that if you could jump 2 feet high, you could jump to the moon. "The whole project is ridiculous and absurd. Centuries hence it will be time enough to talk of such a railroad."[15] There had been many explorations of the American West, the *Herald* editorialized, conducted "by competent men, and with proper motives." But this Whitney survey was done "in such a ridiculous way, as to create laughter instead of respect." Whitney's plan was a "perfect farce." Someday, perhaps, after Oregon was settled and developed, a railroad would be built there funded and operated by the government, but that was far in the future.[16]

They laughed in Louisville, too.

> We think it was that surprising genius, Baron Munchausen, who projected the magnificent scheme of a bridge from *terra firma* to the moon. We are not aware that the Baron memorialized any public bodies for assistance or undertook to procure subscriptions to a stock company, to enable him to perfect his vast enterprise. He was probably content with the fame of his prodigious conception, leaving to men of inferior powers the task of executing it. In this respect, the Baron compares favorably with Mr. Whitney who has projected the great scheme of a mammoth railroad to connect Oregon territory with the United States.

Whitney seemed to think the difficulties would vanish "like Lapland witches before sunbeams," but he had not taken into account even the simple possibility that roving Indian tribes might tear up the rails and diminish the delight of the first excursionists.[17]

In 1847 a letter writer at Louisville took up the caustic theme. From the time Eve ate the apple, he said, man has been gullible. The writer read John Frémont's exploration reports. But he was discouraged by them about the possibility of a railroad over the Rockies, not encouraged, as Whitney seemed to be. Maybe the "luminous mind" of Whitney could convince him were he to meet the man in person, and then the correspondent would be able to see rice being sent to Japan, cotton to India, ice from Boston to

Bering Strait, and live hogs from Kentucky to China, but for the moment that seemed unlikely. Whitney's highway of nations seemed to this man "all slops and dishwater." Whitney himself was a kind of sincere but misled Don Quixote de la Mancha. The facts were that California could produce wheat more cheaply than it could be shipped there—and so could most other places; wheat sold in Rangoon, Burma, for 12 cents per bushel; and the price was similarly low in many other places. Whitney enthusiasts were the victims of a "plausible fraud."[18]

There needed to be less froth and more beer in all discussions of the Pacific railroad, "fewer words and more arguments, less rhapsody and more reasons." Americans were a thinking, utilitarian people not disposed to accept opinions for arguments, "even though they appear in the gaudy trappings of labored language that doth 'Amaze the unlearned and make the learned smile.'" Why must we have a route of our own, and what would draw trade to it? "Commerce is a cosmopolite; it worships no God but Mammon; it obeys no laws but its own; it opens its arms to the embrace of the Pope and the Pagan, and it serves alike the Republican and the Imperialist." Railroads were only an "appliance of trade," not the proper subject of hopes and dreams about a better world. The idea of a "political railroad" was absurd.[19]

Of course, New Hampshire was against the Whitney railroad. That state broke up, one observer wrote, the "flattering unanimity" that had greeted Whitney. Resolutions condemning his plan passed the New Hampshire state senate.[20]

Whitney kept the project before the public. He wrote a series of letters to the press from his surveying expedition of the country along what was to be the first part of his railroad. He reprinted letters from Indian agents about the suitability of the topography of the Far West for his railroad.[21] "I have found all I desired, and far more than I expected." If he could get a land grant, he *could* build the railroad, starting in a few months. Then "we shall have the whole world tributary to us. . . . The whole commerce of the vast world will be tumbled into our lap." The West would become a garden "feeding, clothing, comforting and enlightening millions, who are now starving, homeless, naked, ignorant and oppressed." Who could oppose such a work? Any intelligent person could study it, Whitney wrote, and see that he did not exaggerate. It was not "chimerical," and half the results had not been mentioned.

> No man's rights to be abridged! No man's taxes increased, and
> not even one cent asked for from any man. All I ask is that which

is now a great part of it useless, and ever must be without this road; and I do not ask that without pay in money, for the whole cost of the road is to be expended for materials and labor, and the products of the earth to sustain the labor amongst, and paid over to the people, to whom the lands belong. Though it does not go into the treasury of the United States, it goes into the pockets of the people, directly to whom that treasury belongs, and a sum too, more than double of that which will be received for the same lands in any other way.[22]

Some in the South took Whitney seriously. At a convention in Memphis in the fall of 1845, there was concern about the northern route Whitney proposed. John C. Calhoun, who presided over the Memphis gathering, had talked for twenty-five years about the South's trading with China by an inland route to the Pacific. The distance from Charleston to the mouth of the Gulf of California was only 2,000 miles, and part of that distance was already covered by railroads. Might it be best to move for a southern Pacific route now before Whitney made any more progress?[23] Whitney tried to attend the Memphis convention, but his boat was detained and he arrived too late to address the gathering.[24]

One of the participants in the convention, James Gadsden, would eventually be chief negotiator for a purchase of Mexican territory to help make such a southern railroad to the Pacific possible. Gadsden said that the spirit of free institutions meant that there was no limit short of the Pacific to the enterprise of U.S. citizens.

It is not by the right of Spanish and French discovery; it is not by premature explorations of wilderness before our population are prepared to occupy; it is not by conflicts on the Ocean, or military invasions by land, by war, or bloodshed, that the American claim to the North-American [continent] is to be maintained or confirmed; but by the silent, slow, but certain influences of our liberal institutions, spreading their peaceful wings of protection over our population as it progresses. . . . The Mississippi Valley is no longer a frontier; it is the centre of the Union.[25]

The discussion of a Pacific railroad on a southern route was the beginning of an element of the sectional controversy that peaked with the Pacific Railway Surveys of 1853 and continued right up to the Civil War.

There was excitement, too, in Europe. A politician in Germany went so far as to send a copy of one of Whitney's pamphlets to the czar in Russia with the hope he might extend his railroad across Siberia to China, there to complete the great global route that with steamships and land bridges would tie the world together as trading partners. "Corn laws and all other restrictions on trade and international intercourse would be trodden under foot of the world's great IRON HORSE."[26]

Proposing Pacific railroads became an industry. George Wilkes published a pamphlet proposing a government-built Pacific railroad employing 20,000 people. Dr. Hartwell Carver put forward a scheme. So did Stephen Douglas of Illinois, Thomas Hart Benton of Missouri, and John Plumbe and P.P.F. De Grand of Boston.[27] "While government officials and babbling politicians are busily arranging and rearranging, tearing down, and building up tariffs and systems of foreign policy, the master minds of the age are contemplating the most magnificent enterprises that ever were conceived." The great attraction was that the railroad was "bloodless, righteous, and peaceful," a way America could take pride in proceeding.[28] None, however, had quite the drive of Whitney. "This project, I may say," he wrote, "is the object of my life."[29]

Congress took up the debate in earnest in 1846. The issue divided opinion with great emotion. There were questions about the power of Congress, about the extent of trade, and about the effects on the United States "in a moral, political, and military point of view." The Senate's Committee on Public Lands thought there was something to the idea of using lands to subsidize a railroad, if not this one under these terms, then another under other terms. It would encourage settlement, and that was in the interest of the United States. There would be no tax, and that was wonderful. But Congress did fear that the land sales could become a vast speculation and thus suggested limiting entry to settlers only. Whitney had proposed that people could buy lands for half cash, and take out the other half in working on the railroad, making it a great democratic experience in several ways.

> Thus every man [almost,] on the Globe may have a home, a farm, and if he will work a comfortable living, and in fact the land does not cost him anything, for the money which he gives with his labor, is not taken from him, but expended upon the Road which allows him to send his produce to all four corners of the earth, in exchange for necessities and luxuries which he cannot produce, and which he could not get without the Road.

It allows him to communicate with all the earth, himself in the center, surrounded with plenty, comfort, and happiness, which can be produced only by this road; for were the land given him without price, there could never be a concentration of means and persons to construct such a work.[30]

What could be more wonderful? *Knickerbocker Magazine* commented that there were no insurmountable barriers of any type that had not already been overcome farther east. And what treasures would be uncovered!

The granite mountain will melt before the hand of enterprise; valleys will be raised; and the unwearying fire-steed will spout his white hot breath where silence has reigned since the morning hymn of young creation was pealed over mountain . . . and field. The mammoth's bone and the bison's horn, buried for centuries, will be bared to the day by the laborers of the "Atlantic and Pacific Railroad Company." . . . The very realms of chaos and old Night will be invaded; while in place of the roar of wild beast, or howl of wilder Indians, will be heard the lowing of herds, the bleating of flocks; the plow will cleave the sods of many a rich valley and fruitful hill.[31]

Some in Louisville came around to it. If those accepting Whitney's arguments were gullible or foolish, they included a committee of the U.S. Senate, the chamber of commerce of New York City, and the members of many town conventions. Were they all simpletons, or Locofocos?[32] The climate in Panama was bad and the planned railroad across the isthmus would not be controlled by the United States. Engineering was now capable of building such a project, and railroads had become "necessities of existence to every trading people."[33]

At a Whitney meeting in November 1846 in Cincinnati, resolutions favoring his railroad and recommending it to Congress passed. Now was the time, the convention reported. The railroad could be built now without the slightest inconvenience or constitutional compromise. Delay would mean that private owners would take the lands now in the public domain. Their value would increase, and the whole idea of getting the right-of-way for nothing and building the railroads with the proceeds of development would not work. The spending on the Pacific railroad of $2 million or more yearly would be distributed over the country and help the economy generally. The desert would literally bloom.[34]

Whitney began to use a large map as a prop and expanded his standard speech to more than an hour. At the courthouse in Columbus, Ohio, on November 26 he said that the great commercial, manufacturing, and business part of the world extended in a line east and west around the world at the latitude of the United States. The effects of the railroad in bringing moral light to "the cannibals, the slave, and barbarians" would be "wholly indescribable."[35] He crossed Indiana that same month with the same message.[36] Returning to Philadelphia with his map in December, he addressed a crowd at the Chinese Museum.[37]

He then proceeded to speak to the Connecticut state legislature. Whitney there compared his idea to the Baltimore & Ohio goals as they must have looked in the late 1820s. As soon as the road was commenced, the means would come forth to accomplish it. He was, he said, a "plain business man." There were no dividends to earn. "The route is an entire wilderness—the earth the capital stock—and the labor of man applied thereto, to bring forth the abundant means for its accomplishment." His map showed that the United States was at the center of the world, and its population was increasing fast. Its frontier was what gave his scheme its leverage. He personally was not going to have any power; Congress could repeal the authorizing act or change it at any time. Meanwhile he would generate $70 million in construction costs from developing 92 million acres of wasteland.

> It will probably (if I succeed) require all my life, and were I to gain millions it could do me no good. I have undertaken it for the good of the country first, and after, that of all mankind. I think the work is wanted by the world at large. The time has come—the surplus population of all the world are driven by necessity to our shores. The God of our fathers has given us this rich inheritance, not for ourselves, but for all mankind, under our guidance and governance.[38]

The critics in Louisville even disdained to attack Whitney personally. "Mr. Whitney's character has been without a stain."[39]

Although Whitney was thought to be convincing, he was not necessarily articulate or entertaining. Jerome Cotton, who heard him at Cleveland one Saturday evening in January 1851, said the audience at the National Hall was small, and perhaps that was just as well. There was a cold wind.

> The hall was poorly heated, and as the speaker had no animation to warm up the hearers, they came as near freezing to death

as was advisable, or perhaps possible. Mr. WHITNEY has very little fluency of speech. His gesticulation is wanting. His enthusiasm is small. His imagery is meager. It is all straight forward matter-of-fact with him. It is yet that kind of matter-of-fact which is shaped by policy. He has a facility for suppressing what may be deemed unfavorable. This is worth more than oratory. He would not be deemed an interesting lecturer. But the great project he explains, and the fact that it is *his* project will make men hear him.[40]

There was a meeting in California, which quoted Napoleon Bonaparte to the effect that nothing was impossible. The termination of the railroad should not be in Oregon but in San Francisco.

> We are bewildered in the contemplation of so grand, so magnificent an enterprise; but when the rich plains and fertile valleys of California [are] filled with an industrious population, the numberless streams of the mountains occupied by machinery, and the innumerable mines actively works, and the great Bay of San Francisco whitened with the commerce of every maritime nation, there will not only be means, but willing hands to perform this noble enterprise.[41]

Late in the decade, interest in a Pacific railroad was further enhanced by the performance of the new invention of Jedediah Morse—the magnetic telegraph. The *New York Herald* reported that it had acted as a spur to the spirit of improvement. Businessmen were now able to send a communication to Cincinnati, St. Louis, or Petersburg and receive an instant response "in as short a time as if their billet went only to the next street and returned." That being so, it was difficult any longer to support the idea "of creeping with their merchandise through thousands of miles of rough sea, in order to gain access to ports on the western side of the continent."[42] Maybe someone would soon invent a balloon to go over those mountains even faster.[43]

So also, many felt that the constant discussion of the matter of a Pacific railroad was itself assurance that, seeming real to the public, it would eventually become real.[44] The mind was led to "many reflections" by all the publicity. People were much the same everywhere, an essayist wrote. "A remove of one generation from ignorance and suffering will, in the offspring of the next, be strikingly manifest." There would be an "intellectuality" where before there was gross animal influence. Circumstances thus affected the destiny of mankind, and commerce ameliorated the condition of man, while technology extended the "facilities for human happiness."[45] The work "creates for itself the 'meat on which it feeds.'"[46]

But deep doubts remained. A writer for the *New York Herald* in 1848 thought the line was likely to cost far more than the estimated $20,000 per mile. "The grading of the mountains, the opening of the gorges, half filled with volcanic debris, the bridging of deep chasms, and the transportation of supplies, would augment the expenditures to at least $100,000 per mile." It might take sixty years to build, as one would wonder how more than 50 miles per year could be built under the best conditions. There were 2,000 miles of empty space without population, timber, water, or many resources of any kind for the agriculturalist or the railroad builder. There was only the salt of the Great Salt Lake. A railroad or ship canal through Panama would be better "or a line of Arabian camels and dromedaries from St. Louis, via Santa Fe and the Gila, to Monterey or San Francisco." Let a half-dozen states be formed west of the Rockies before considering a Pacific railroad.[47]

Some believed that the railroad would be long in arriving and not too satisfactory when in operation. Whitney thought it would take at least fifteen years to build; others thought much longer. What would happen to the trade with Oregon and California in the meantime? The water route via Panama was only about 5,600 miles, whereas Whitney's route might not be too far short of 3,000. Even supposing the railroad could be built across the continent without a gap requiring a change of cars, there would still be four transshipments before reaching New York City and five before reaching London. The Panama railroad could be built in two years. Ought that not to be done in any case?[48]

The South objected to any interference by government in either a promotional or regulatory way. There was little to choose from, a Natchez editor thought, among the four or five projects before Congress in 1849, but maybe Whitney's was the worst of them. It was "monstrous" to grant so much to a single man or company. The Tehuantepec and Panama projects were objectionable because they were on foreign soil. It would be best to have a private company build in the United States, giving the nation and its free settler-citizens the right to become "law-givers to the whole world."[49]

Still Whitney traveled and worked, and still he got grudging respect. By 1849 he had visited most of the states of the Union and lobbied with their legislatures. Whether his name was linked with any successful company ever, most agree that he deserved credit for perseverance and enterprise.[50]

The year 1849 was a productive one for Pacific rail conventions, the most prominent being at Memphis and at St. Louis. Memphis had an interest in being the eastern terminus of a central line to the Pacific but found Senator Benton and his St. Louis constituency to be a kind of nemesis there. The New Orleans press damned both schemes but expressed hoped that the conventions would at least put the quietus to the Whitney idea. The barrier of the Rockies would end the central line idea on its own, and then, New Orleans hoped, attention would turn to a southern route.[51] The Mexican War, unfortunate as it was, might have been planned by providence, wrote an editor in Louisville, to bring about that same result.[52] Are we to be excluded from the territories newly acquired from Mexico, wrote John Calhoun, after the South had expended blood and treasure to win them?[53]

That hope, helped as it was by the barrier of the Rockies, was hurt by the growing prominence of San Francisco and its suitability as a terminus. A traveler there from New Orleans had to admit it was an impressive and cosmopolitan place:

> You can form no idea of the bustle, excitement and confusion in the streets here from morning till night, and if ever there was a Babel on earth, or a very close imitation of one, then it is this delectable place of San Francisco. In my satchel-carrying, apple-munching, birch-tasting, brain-cudgelling days, I used to gaze in wonderment upon the plates representing the inhabitants of all parts of the globe, but now they can be seen "free gratis" in the streets of San Francisco. All descriptions of the human species, or of the animal approaching the human, from the ourang-outang to the highly polished European, are here.[54]

What was becoming clear by 1850, however, was that, whatever unity the nation found in its vague fascination with the ideas of Whitney, it shattered amid sectional jealousies as myriad other Pacific railroad ideas emerged. A Boston paper concluded that Whitney's route was impractical because of the inevitable delays and the great uncertainty of its success. It would take a century if it could be done at all. Benton's St. Louis–to–San Francisco route was not practical either. P.P.F. De Grand might have the best idea, as it involved the most government funding and control and could be done most quickly. However, that was not likely to gain enough support either. The Pacific railroad question, the writer thought, would be "subject to the caprices of the changing elements of the political world; made a shuttlecock for the battle[s] . . . of unscrupulous partisans . . . and exciting them for violent and useless debate." Many politicians would be "fleshed in the bleeding body of the National Railroad" before anything concrete would be done.[55]

Alas, it was so! Over and over through the 1850s, commentators pointed out how much more useful it would be to build the Pacific railroad than to argue over slavery, and how much cheaper it would be to build it than to finance a war between the regions. But disunion was to come, and the Pacific railroad, north or south, privately or government financed, could not be separated from that larger trend. The rueful later history of the issue right up to the passage of the Pacific Railroad Act of 1862 was complex and engaging. However, with the failure of the Whitney initiative failed the last realistic chance of much antebellum progress. Men were turning the subject "into as many shapes as Proteus could assume."[56] There was a "sublime conception" at the outset but then somehow a "monster" had been fabricated and would not disappear.[57] The report of the St. Louis convention of 1849 concluded that its object had been "simply to embody public sentiment on the subject of the magnificent project of a Railway communication with the Pacific . . . to draw forth the various plans, ideas and wishes of the different sections of the country." It was beyond the "moral or legal power" of the convention to do more.[58]

Maybe it was moot anyway. One editor thought all the "railing" about the Pacific railroad was "confined to the leaden columns of a few stupid newspapers." It was probably a quarter-century in advance of its proper time to make such a railroad other than on sheets of paper "where the coulds and woulds of man's ingenuity may be exemplified without material interfering with any people, or the finances of the nation." Whitney had produced "some grand ideal views in the brains of a small class of brokers and capitalists," but he produced nothing tangible.[59] Convention would follow convention, and there would be talk upon talk.[60] The Pacific railroad plan was "a big gun aimed *point-blank*, but it wants caliber, and the main ingredients, powder and ball."[61]

It was hard, wrote a Milwaukee writer, to reason calmly about Whitney's project. "Its magnitude confounds the mind, and bewilders the senses. It is strange that it has not already crazed the projector himself."[62]

CHAPTER 14

Pacific or Bust

hitney's initiative faded in the 1850s. Sectional tensions became stronger than ever. But the Pacific railroad project remained an exciting public issue. "Looking over the immense region which Providence has given us to occupy," wrote a man in Cleveland, "the mind is lost in the immensity of the greatness which awaits us, and the heart is stricken with awe at the vast responsibility which must rest upon us as the people who hold in trust the accumulated results of all preceding civilization."[1] A visionary wrote, "It seems as if the good Providence, which has always had in its charge the welfare of this nation, had, by these seasonable inventions, (the engine and the telegraph) been providing securities against its greatest danger." These technologies would unite the republic, no matter how large the distances involved.[2]

The press called for a more rapid resolution, more "striking boldness." The road needed to be built "not by inches, not alone for our descendants, but for us." The United States was gathering strength along with moral and political importance in the world at the same time the "golden treasures" of California were flowing into national coffers. "The present great movements of our country are those of preparation for a Future, the rush of whose mighty wings we already feel."[3]

The situation required not only expansion of engineering skill but also broadening of public ambition and vision. There had been seeming impossible advances in other fields, such as printing. Nothing was impractical because it was stupendous. "That might have been said twenty-five years ago, but it does not convey a meaning in the year 1850. To material enterprises, whose use is plain, the words 'impracticable' and 'impossible' are no longer applicable. Human genius and energy have abolished them."[4] "Who shall declare the extremity of human attainment—who will venture to set up the standard of perfection?"

There needed to be cultivation of the public mind. There were "engines by which the people must be eventually elevated to that position in social appreciation which is their right." But that was not enough. "They must come to their inheritance prepared to receive it and use it to advantage." This required abandoning the "contracted policy which has heretofore governed the intercourse of men."[5]

To form effectively the proper images, stump speakers harped regularly through the decade on certain common themes. Among these were that the railroad would hold the Union together, that it would be a "highway of nations" and bring the nation world trade, that it would change the weather in the western deserts for the better, that it would prove the worth of republican government, that it would improve the efficiency of the U.S. military and diminish the need for fixed forts, that it would bring religion to the heathen, that it would establish the place of the republic in history, and that it would provide an example of the triumph of human will over material adversity. The repeated word patterns were important. One editor wrote that what passed for public opinion on an issue like this was "reason on leading strings. Like a . . . locomotive, it travels fast. . . . But its course is only along the prescribed route, over the rails that have been laid by others."[6]

Not all the speeches made sense. Thomas Benton, recently retired from the Senate and practicing law in Washington, rejected both the idea that the exploration of his son-in-law John Frémont might not have marked out a good route for a railway over the central Rockies and that scientific engineering was needed at all. The bison was the "first and best of engineers," he said, and all the rail crews had to do was follow the trails of wild beasts through the West. An editor in New Orleans called that nonsense. St. Louis was not a salt lick or San Francisco a pasture, so the strategies of the bison in reaching animal goals were not appropriate for humans building a railroad.[7] Benton opposed the various Central American railroad schemes so that the country might concentrate wholly on an American transcontinental. This received as many jeers as his ideas about bison trails.[8] The fact that a company calling itself the Pacific Railroad of Missouri had built a few miles of railroad in his home state and put the first locomotive west of the Mississippi on rails was not a particularly impressive achievement.[9]

But even the most seemingly scientific of investigations and publications might be flawed. It was an easy task, a southern promoter wrote, to "plan out on maps where a railroad should run or how long it should be." One could even estimate costs per mile, the possible number of passengers and tonnage of freight, the projected annual revenues. But were these figures not just as speculative, maybe even fictional, as the visions of the stump speaker? These statisticians were dreamers, too. "It is a task of no moment to them to put a girdle of railroad iron around the earth in ten years, or ten minutes, as it is required; it costs them but the stroke of a pen, or the delivery of a dozen words, to tunnel the Alps, bridge the Mississippi, embank the Pacific, and place China and Sardinia in twenty-four hours proximity to each other." One journalist thought they were the descendants of the genii who built palaces in a night in Eastern legend. Maybe before the Texas railroad convention should plan an extension to the Pacific, it should try building some actual railroads between certain Texas towns.[10]

That hardly slowed the rhetoric. The Texas convention of 1851 proposed a railroad across Texas and to the Pacific through country of "unsurpassed loveliness." Texas could support it with a grant of some of the more than 100 million acres of land it owned. It would create an immense business "and the travel of the world would be through Texas." The North would be pushing a Pacific railroad, and the South must also.[11]

A large convention at New Orleans in January 1852 devoted itself to the same matter while admitting a convention would never build a railroad.[12] New Orleans and its northern rivals were in a "great chess game" in the American landscape, and the prize of the winner would be the seat of empire. The loser would be stuck with commercial dependence. Enterprise could "outbid Nature."[13] It was a matter, as a California publicist put it, of properly guiding the public interest and the press so that it became a "vigorous and efficient demand."[14]

William Gwin of California introduced a bill in Congress in 1852. His justification was primarily to link California more solidly with the East.[15] It was a bill to please everybody with two lines, one starting in the South and the other in the North, to join farther west. "Fancy a railroad station at Santa Fe or James' Peak—a terminus in the silent depths of the primeval forest, or close by the wigwam of the Choctaw chiefs!"[16]

Some thought a more promising direction than a government monopoly and construction by the lowest bidder was to back a private company offering the most stupendous proposal of all: the Atlantic & Pacific Railroad Company of New York. The A&P, chartered in 1852 in New York, was the brainchild of Robert Walker, former secretary of the treasury during the Polk administration and shortly to be governor of the volatile Kansas Territory.[17]

Everything about the A&P was outsized. Its capital was set at $100 million, an unprecedented figure. Press reports were that it was backed by "men of the most enterprising character, and the greatest amount of practical information, and the widest influence and credit and the largest wealth in New York." It required no land grant, only a thirty-year, $30 million loan from the federal government.[18] There were reports in February 1853 that the A&P had actually ordered locomotives from the Norris works and made contracts to build 1,000 miles of 6-foot-gauge track within twenty-one months.[19]

The Pacific Railway Surveys carried out by the War Department in 1853 added immediacy to the plans of the A&P and others. The federal government published twelve magnificent, well-illustrated volumes, including all the information collected by congressionally funded parties sent out to explore four possible Pacific rail routes, from the far North to the far South. Secretary of War Jefferson Davis expressed a preference for a fifth route along the 32nd parallel across Texas, which was not included in the government volumes at first but was later the focus of supplementary surveys by the federal government. William Goetzmann, the great twentieth-century student of army exploration in the West, pointed out that the Pacific surveys held the promise of an "impartial solution to what had become . . . a well-nigh insoluble problem of infinite political complexity." But in the end they were too vague and biased to be of much use in breaking the deadlock.[20]

The A&P tried to obtain a large land grant from Texas, gain the support of the South while drawing on capital and expertise from the North, and be the first in the field in serious construction of a Pacific railroad.[21] The press superlatives describing the surveys and about the A&P, however, had hardly begun before the plans began to unravel.

The shenanigans of the A&P management became national news. Walker, though experienced politically and with a Mississippi upbringing that might inure him to the South, had an unsavory financial reputation. He was considered a man who promised much and accomplished little. Lately he had been in England supposedly negotiating a $17 million loan for the Illinois Central Railroad. But the loan did not materialize, and reports of it were said to be merely "fabulous."[22] Walker personally subscribed $10 million in A&P stock, which astonished everyone who knew his financial situation. There was similar surprise at other large subscriptions by financial bit players, suggesting that the whole thing was a ruse.[23] Walker had just turned down a possible appointment to a diplomatic post in China, being unwilling, one letter writer thought, "to surrender the sumptuous living at New York, for the rats and birds-nest soup of China."[24] Goetzmann, writing in 1959, suggested that Walker and associates planned either to sell their shares among southerners as the railroad was being constructed or to create a huge watered stock company using federal subsidies and Texas land grants.[25]

Criticism thrived. One man thought it was absurd to

> take the United States in tow, create a stock company with ten times the power ever enjoyed by the old U.S. Bank, borrow the credit of the Government, pay no interest on the money thus obtained for thirty years, and then take possession of the greatest monopoly in the known world, in comparison to which the privileges of the British East Indian Company, as it now stands, would themselves sink into insignificance.

But one could never tell what Congress or the State of Texas might do.[26] The New York scheme, wrote another, "surpasses all former contemplated spoliations of the federal revenue." The purpose of Walker and associates was, "while duping the public into small subscriptions," to monopolize the A&P stock, then levy assessments on the outsiders "to be spent in boring Congress for appropriations of land," and finally to sell their shares at an advance, pocket the profit, and retire from the business.[27]

There was some outright hooting. It was a bubble, wasn't it? So why take it seriously? Existing "fancies" had gone underwater and benefited only the bears, so the bulls would play with this one, making the eyes on Wall Street glow. "Brokers will buoy it up; newspapers will speak of the noble enterprise, so well worthy of the American nation; Senators and Congressmen will utter irresistible orations showing that the Union had better be dissolved if a few millions cannot be spared for Mr. Robert J. Walker and his colleagues." But the A&P proposal was really as foolish as attempting to bridge the Atlantic.[28] The New York Tribune called the A&P the "Moonshine" company.

It was a self-acting machine, which could be carried on indefinitely "without external supports or an ultimate landing place." Meanwhile champagne and chicken would be passed out to all comers, and the company's rooms in Washington would be well lighted at night during the winter. Soon, however, as the balloon inflated, it would become obvious to some whence came the gas.[29] It was a "hotel" scheme to build a railroad without money and would "deceive no one whose real capital is worth caring about."[30] Under its current management, the company would simply make itself ridiculous. The more it paraded before the public, the sooner it would be laid aside.[31]

What a fraud anyway was the very idea of a Pacific railroad? It was a sham as much as the A&P was a sham, thought the *New York Herald.*

> A railroad to the Pacific must be viewed in the same light as a railroad to the moon, for the next quarter of a century. Neither this government nor the people of this country, nor the people of England, nor any other person or people that we know of, can afford to sink one hundred millions without hope of returns. Without sinking this, or a larger sum, no railroad can be built; even if reliable scientific men should discover a suitable route.[32]

It was no surprise that again no Pacific railroad bill passed Congress in 1854, although "there are at least a dozen different squadrons of speculators, each watching to urge this or that scheme for it, only in the hope of making money for themselves out of it." Politicians hoped to ride the Pacific railroad "hobby" into more turns in office.[33]

In the spring of 1854, Cornelius Peebles published a pamphlet attacking the Atlantic & Pacific. He said only $25,000 had actually been paid in by stockholders and that the top fourteen stockholders, who subscribed to $7 million in stock, were not worth $500,000 among them. Walker was a "flibberty-gibbet" and so was his partner Thomas Butler King and their erstwhile agent Jeptha Fowlkes. They were on the executive committee through "extraordinary activity and hypocritical subserviency" only. "There is nobody to pay.... It is a rotten affair, kept on foot by a few seedy, hungry vampires in bread." The company principals tried to defend themselves by saying they would rely on goodwill and 12 million acres of Texas land to see them through.[34]

Actually, the Texas initiative had a realistic chance. Walker had friends in Texas from his pork-distributing days in the cabinet. He had helped finance the Mexican War, a fair-sized project. King had experience building railroads in Georgia and was successful at it. The two proposed to use slave labor, and that seemed to some in the South both practical and politically desirable.[35] Texas had, in what one paper called "a moment of madness and folly," passed a bill offering twenty sections of land per mile to any railroad that built a road across its territory along the 32nd parallel, deposited $300,000 with the state treasury, and started the work by August 15, 1854. As the company built each 50 miles, it could draw its land. The value of the land was about $100 million, exactly the capitalization of the Atlantic & Pacific Company.[36] There were claims that the ore in eastern Texas could be smelted into iron rails, thus multiplying the benefit to the state and the company.[37]

Walker and King deposited the required $300,000. It was not submitted on time and not in cash (they offered $1 million in Texas bonds). But they did respond to the Texas land grant act.[38] The governor of Texas refused the deposit they offered as unsafe, but the state treasurer, who had an interest in the company, accepted it. The debate went into the state legislature and the courts; papers in Missouri, where Benton was actively promoting a more northerly route, said that the "impudence is amazing." The promoters of the A&P were a "nest of insolvents, now and for years inaccessible to executions and notorious for speculations at the expense of the public and individuals."[39] The Pacific railroad had but one bidder, wrote a Texas journalist in Austin, and that bidder failed to comply with the exact provisions of the law. The danger was that the state, in its eagerness for a railroad, would bend the law and resort to "wild excess."[40]

Despite these handicaps, the Atlantic & Pacific, under that name and also under the names Texas Western and Southern Pacific, built considerable railroad line in Texas. It was easily the company that made the most actual progress on a Pacific line before the Civil War, and it is an interesting speculation what might have been the situation had the war not intervened.

Dr. Jeptha Fowlkes eventually gained control after wrangling between the old company and a new company, a court battle on forfeiture of the land grant, and public debate over the desirability or legality of that grant. The more controversial directors stepped aside, the capital was reduced to a more reasonable figure, expenses (including salaries) were pared, and the company built 50 miles of line by the spring of 1859.[41]

A Louisville editor thought Fowlkes was a brave man, one who had encountered

> difficulties and personal dangers which would have deterred
> most men prosecuting the enterprise he took; he has been as-

sailed by calumny and loaded with reproaches; his motives have been misrepresented, his integrity has been impeached, and his life threatened by those whose game it was either to destroy him or raise the prejudice of the State of Texas against him so that its legislation might be brought to the aid of their scheme.

He got the company to a state of "disembarrassment," which was a considerable achievement in itself.[42] Had the charter been annulled by the courts on "mere technicalities," according to a southern commentator, "Texas would have been dishonored and one of the greatest enterprises of modern times checked most disastrously." The people of Texas had been "warmly attached to the company" all along—and so had many in the broader South.[43]

The road to that modest achievement was rocky, to be sure. A New England paper commented when the $300,000 deposit was supposedly made that "this company, started upon moonshine, will become the owners of the largest capital ever held by a corporation, and the people of Texas will have sold their birthright for less than a mess of pottage."[44] A New Orleans writer did not think better of it. The idea of giving Texas land to build a Pacific railroad along the 32nd parallel was, he said, an act "of madness and folly unparalleled in the annals of legislative insanity."[45] At a Texas meeting to discuss the road in December 1854, Walker did not appear and King spoke in generalities. "Not one word on the very foundation stone of the project; not a sentence to show that the company had any rightful expectation of securing that thing without which the Pacific Railroad Company is a bubble too attenuated even to amuse us with a show of prismatic colors!"[46]

Shortly, however, and as the problems came to seem less severe, the press in the South began to back any southern Pacific line. A writer in Louisville early in 1855 thought it would change the commerce of the world and that the men promoting it did not deserve the abuse they had received. Much of the criticism was instituted by northern interests and rival companies, the writer thought.[47] Walker had been a cabinet member, King a member of Congress. "The idea that such men, at their time of life, with a clean record of thirty . . . years behind them, should engage in a wild scheme of speculation, is most ridiculous. Such a supposition, independently of the facts of the case, contravenes all the motives that ordinarily prompt men to action."[48]

King went on a speaking tour, appearing on Wall Street, among other places, arguing that it was unwise to push several Pacific railroad plans at once. The northern routes were too much impeded by snow and mountains, and there were no companies pursuing them as sound as the one of which he was a part.[49] If a northern transcontinental were built through Salt Lake City, new states would appear along its route settled by northerners, who would "pattern their domestic institutions after the statutes from which they are settled." New York would forever outdistance Charleston and Savannah as a commercial city, and the cotton business would pay tribute to the North. A southern Pacific system, connected to the East and the North through the Fulton & Cairo, Memphis & Little Rock, Louisville & Memphis, and Ohio & Mississippi, could provide a different future.[50]

The first annual report of the reorganized Atlantic & Pacific, renamed the Southern Pacific Railroad, issued in December 1856, was encouraging. Although speculators were pulling wires in Washington over a congressional Pacific railroad bill, the report said, this company was pressing forward. It would be complete to El Paso, more than halfway to the Pacific Ocean, before any bill emerged from Congress. How much better it was to concentrate on this single line and extend it on to San Diego than to launch huge projects of building two or three parallel lines in the north—"rash schemes to fill the coffers of unscrupulous speculators and place-men, and to deplete the public treasury." The Southern Pacific was now a sound company. It would receive 25,600 acres of land, worth $5 per acre, for every 5 miles it completed, and it was claimed it would yield a 33 percent return on its eventual $14.5 million cost. Horatio Allen, the man who ran *Stourbridge Lion* in the first locomotive trip in the United States, and had later experience with the Erie, was now a director of the Southern Pacific.[51]

Robert Walker said that by connecting his "humble" name with the enterprise, he had expected assaults but also to see the truth "vindicated by time and actual results."[52] Those who criticized the Southern Pacific, wrote a Louisville man, should look more closely at Benton's scheme for following bison tracks through the snow.[53]

A paper in Knoxville admitted that the Southern Pacific's annual report was an able document and that newspapers all over the South supported the company on the basis of it.[54] "There are a thousand reasons of expediency, interest, and political advantage," wrote a New Orleans reporter, "which combine to make this Southern line of a Pacific route of the deepest consequences to the Southwestern States."[55] Why not build it? "Neither Arctic winters nor tropical heat will interrupt the transit over this line. Nature itself has broken down the mountains, which form the backbone of the continent, to afford an easy grade." The Southern Pacific ran its whole route through slave territory where slave states would be created. "The emigration into Texas, New Mexico, and the yet unnamed wilds, will be a people Southern in their habits, their customs, their opinions, and their social institutions."[56]

Some in the North agreed that the Southern Pacific had a head start. The *Daily Missouri Republican* in St. Louis wrote a piece late in 1858 saying that although the Southern Pacific was not the route that was best for St. Louis, there were too many delays on the central route. "There can be no harm in wishing success to private exertions of individuals, aided by the State of Texas, which promises to insure the country a road to California, even though it fails to follow the precise track our desires would have marked out for it." It would connect through Arkansas with Missouri's Iron Mountain Railroad, and a bird in hand was desirable.[57]

In the summer of 1859 all the lawsuits demanding the forfeiture of the charter and land grant of the Southern Pacific were dismissed.[58] There was a rumor that J. Edgar Thomson of Pennsylvania, a well-respected railroad operator, might become president.[59] The company proposed to sell 1.5 million shares of stock to purchase 1,000 slaves as rail workers.[60] The 1859 annual report claimed that the debts were paid and the feuds settled. "The only parties who now entertain any opposition to your Company are the men whose efforts to defraud you detected, exposed and defeated—men whose noise is as valueless as that of any empty vessel."[61] A letter from Memphis noted, regarding Texas, that "the slaves, the cotton producers . . . are swarming into this region already."[62] A locomotive, *Sam Houston*, went to the Texas railroad early in 1860, and the Texas legislature voted to change the company name from Southern Pacific back to Atlantic & Pacific to make it seem less sectional in character.[63] A railroad meeting was held in San Diego in January 1860 as that city began to feel a realistic hope that it, rather than San Francisco, would be the terminus of the first completed railroad to the Pacific.[64]

In the spring of 1860 the railroad had built 135 miles through Texas.[65] The *Daily National Intelligencer* in Washington, D.C., writing of this project, noted that the North had long underestimated the South, thinking it a raw and undeveloped region a half-century behind in civilization. But its railroads, including the one moving toward the Pacific, were "a standing refutation of all such misconception."[66]

Given the checkered history of the debate over the Pacific railroad, there is every reason to agree. The prospect in Congress for support of any northern railroad was early in 1855 called "bewildering." It seemed a question of which clan of speculators would get the plunder, and the proceedings of Congress over it were characterized by one southern paper as "legislative self-stultification." The U.S. House was called a "fat marketable ox" pursued by rival parties of butchers determined to hang the meat in their own stall. Bills emerging were "as much of an abortion as the proceedings." Like P.T. Barnum's mermaid, they were the patching together of two animals "wherein it was found necessary to preserve the stomach of the monkey above, and impossible to get rid of the stomach of the codfish below."[67]

There were real challenges on the northerly routes. Snow was one. As the hard winters of the mid-1850s closed in, writers imagined what it might be like far to the west. On the route suggested by Frémont a trapped train would stand "little more chance of extrication than a ship's boat in the mid-Atlantic." Could Benton change that? Perhaps he could claim to, but he could hardly "sow an artificial climate" or invent through rhetoric a better snowplow. Several of the routes seemed too far north.[68] Benton's idea of a tunnel through the central Rockies did not add up.[69] "The scheme is poetry and nothing more."[70]

There remained, however, reasons to pursue the Pacific rail project along some trajectory. The federal government in 1859 spent more than $25 million per year for the military service, mainly west of the Mississippi. Nearly half of that was for transportation. Every regiment employed in hostile territory cost nearly $1,000 per man per year, nearly half of which could be saved if a Pacific railroad existed. The mail would gain an important advantage. The social, moral, and intellectual blessings of such a line were largely unquestioned.[71] The existing commercial lines to the Pacific states were "circuitous, exterior, and oceanic, passing through foreign States by no means friendly to us." Congress surely would have the right to build a Pacific road under its power to ensure the domestic tranquility.[72] Still, there were those who would opt for a good road or the Pony Express to do part of these things at less expense. "Shall we punish ourselves by refusing twelve miles an hour because we cannot have thirty?"[73]

The sectional political problems, of course, became only more intractable. One version of a Pacific rail bill offered in 1860 suggested federal grants to two companies to build to the Pacific, one from the west boundary of Texas south of the 35th parallel and one from the Missouri River north of the 38th parallel. The grant to the southern version of the railroad would be made to the president and directors of the existing Southern Pacific Railroad.[74] There were numerous bills each session, and all met opposition.[75] The People's Pacific Railroad alternative, proposing that a million Americans contribute $100 each, did not get far either.[76]

This was frustrating to many who thought of the glory of the accomplished work. "The great heart of the Nation pulsates with unceasing and increased vigor," wrote a reporter in Omaha, "and this Republic *must* progress, *must* advance, with rapid strides, towards that prognosticated and certain glory, which no other Nationality or People have ever attained, or even hoped for." There was too much talk about black people, the writer thought, and not enough about what could be done for the white people of the "Yankee Nation." Congress needed to stop talking about the "*wooly* head of the *punished* African for a time, and devote your attention to the Iron Horse."[77]

That the passage of a Pacific railroad bill after the commencement of the Civil War was politically easier is obvious. For one thing, there no longer existed the necessity of promoting two railroads at once in order that one might run through the South. However, the fact it was taken up at all amid such a crisis was, one journalist said, evidence of the "indomitable courage with which the country regards its future."[78] Benton had said it well in a speech in 1854: "Here is an enterprise worthy of your energies—worthy of your wealth and fame—worthy of the helping hand of merchants who know how to combine the character of merchants and statesmen, and how to aggrandize their country while enriching themselves.[79] The debates leading to the Pacific Railroad Act of 1862, instituting the famous competition between the Central Pacific and the Union Pacific, were almost anticlimactic. The question of whether some line should be built had long ago been decided; it was now just a question of how. Amid tedious discussions of individual clauses and struggles over the exact route, the most interesting comments were sometimes those that were off the point.[80] It was obvious, as one representative put it, that the road "could never be constructed on terms applicable to ordinary roads" or at a corresponding reasonable cost.[81] But everyone had long known that.

This history ends where most histories of the building of the transcontinental railroad begin. As Maury Klein, the historian of the Union Pacific, noted, the Pacific railroad and railroads in general in the United States had advanced by 1862 from the visionary to the purely practical. They were hardly any longer considered as "adopted," or in process of development, but almost as an axiomatic part of American life. The "hour had come," Klein said, to advance the big project. The Pacific railroad was something the American public was almost tired of, and it "bore the scarlet letter of suspicion from the beginning." There had to be compromise. The "vision of a transcontinental road had been transformed into legislation, which is not

Rail yards in Virginia 1860. Bettmann/Corbis

to be confused with reality."[82] Still, it was time to stop working on the tools and begin using them.

There was excitement. The *New York Times* commented when the cumbersome 163-member board was appointed to oversee the transcontinental project that it was "one of the most extraordinary spectacles of this time, and an event which would have been regarded as prodigious in any other time." The social and political implications were vast.

> The very foundations of the government are moving, its firm set pillars are tottering and reeling, and the whole vast frame of society is heaving and rocking with a mighty convulsion; and yet in the midst of it all, with an unconsciousness, or disregard of the threatened catastrophe, that it would seem could only be the fruit of some strange blindness or fatuity, did we not know the sublime faith in popular institutions and in the perpetuity of the Union on which it is built—men come quietly and hopefully together to lay the foundation of a stupendous work of internal use and strength, which is to open a continent, and mould together into one living and glowing mass of social intercourse and commercial harmony, Asia and America, the East and the West.

Amid a damaging war, it was encouraging that the arts of peace still proceeded and offered hope of a peaceful future of business enterprise. The dream that began in the 1830s, as the Baltimore & Ohio started west and *Best Friend of Charleston* puffed along its southern track, would yet be fulfilled when channels of commerce, business, and social relations would be reestablished though now "rudely broken to pieces and trampled in the dust by the onward march of armies."[83]

San Francisco had a celebration in mid-July 1862. It was in honor of the passage of the Pacific Railroad Act, but in a larger sense it was in praise of the growth and development of the railroad in the United States that had allowed such a thing to come to pass. Banners read:

> The Locomotive—he chaseth the sun in his course; he speedeth like an arrow from sea to sea; The Locomotive—His prow is wet with the surge-foam of either ocean; His breast is grim with the sands of the desert; The Locomotive—His neck is clothed with Thunder! The glory of his nostrils is terrible! He rusheth over the valleys and through the mountains, and rejoiceth in his strength; The waste places shall be made glad! The Wilderness shall blossom as the rose; The American Union—It strides to power and glory with legs of iron; its loins are terrible in strength; in its breast there is nourishment for the nations of the earth; its arms are of steel and on its head is a crown of gold.[84]

It was an old song by now, but the United States had some real reason to be proud. It had more than 32,000 miles of track in 1862.[85] People rode these lines in comfort and convenience. The country could now aspire to more in its transportation system with confidence. The American railroad had come a long way in its suitability and service to Americans. And Americans had done a great deal of adapting to the new, perfect machine.

CONCLUSION

Adapting to the Machine

hy do our clothes not fit so well? It results from a chain of circumstances the origins of which are obscure to most and the direction of which was partially accidental. Early in the nineteenth century, inventors came up with an automated loom, and businesspeople put these to work in England and in such American industrial cities as Lowell, Massachusetts, turning out cheap cotton cloth. This, along with the application of the cotton gin to cotton production, revitalized slavery as well as creating an incentive for inexpensive ready-made and therefore not specifically tailored clothing.

Such long-range deep impacts of technological and business developments have long been studied. Lynn White, in *Medieval Technology and Social Change,* documented the enormous impact of clocks, heavy harness, and stirrups on population growth, shock warfare, and the age of exploration.[1] Siegfried Giedion wrote in his *Mechanization Takes Command* of what he called "anonymous history." Who can estimate the impact of the invention of the toilet, or the assembly line in food production, or household machinery on the status of women?[2] Langdon Winner observed, "Developments in the technical sphere continually outpace the capacity of individuals and social systems to adapt. As the rate of technological innovation quickens, it becomes increasingly important and increasingly difficult to predict the range of effects that a given innovation will have."[3]

A recent touring art exhibit called "The Railway: Art in the Age of Steam" reaffirmed the impact of that technology on perceptions of life and landscape. "The application of steam power to motion," the catalog noted, "came as a startling turn of events." Some found it wondrous, "but for others it heralded a frightening, almost demonic energy." There was something supernatural about it, even extraterrestrial. It made middle-class people "physically and psychologically susceptible to impersonal and potentially lethal industrial machines."

Some modern analysts think the impact of the railway, especially in literature, amounted to no less than the "de-realization of consciousness that can occur under the conditions of modernity."[4] Regularly, newspaper editors of the nineteenth century spoke of the "bewildering" effects of the railroad. They seemed to think that was wonderful, but there has been much questioning since then whether it really was. Being baffled and disoriented, according to Langdon Winner, is not desirable. "What we lack is our bearings." There is a disconnect between reality and our understanding. "And without our bearings, not only may it be true that we do not control the technology we supposedly created, but it might also be true that *it* controls *us*."[5]

Think of the social and psychological changes wrought by the telegraph, electricity, the phonograph, the automobile, the airplane, radio, television, the computer, the Internet, the long-playing record, video games, the cell phone, fast food, the shopping mall, and the iPod. And think of how "baffled," in many ways, we are by them and by how they should fit in with the rest of our existence. These devices have become ubiquitous parts of modern life. An age when they did not exist is nearly unimaginable to many, while an age where they do exist is unendurable to others.

Such ruminations about technological dominations and cultural decline were present in the nineteenth century. Henry Adams was famous for his muckraking articles on the Erie railroad scandals of the 1860s and for his portrayal of the dynamo as the nineteenth-century equivalent of the place of the Virgin Mary in motivating people of the Middle Ages. But Adams found the new machine age mostly depressing. This was not because the machine was not wonderful, but because its effects on society had not been well anticipated or dealt with properly. Adams wrote to his brother Charles, who would later become president of the Union Pacific Railroad, in 1862, just as that railroad was being organized. His conclusions did not share in the general euphoria: "Man has mounted science," Adams wrote, "and is now run away with. I firmly believe that before many centuries more, science will be the master of man. The engines he will have invented will be beyond his strength to control. Some day science may have the existence of mankind in its power, and the human race commit suicide, by blowing up the world."[6]

Ralph Waldo Emerson expressed similar views. "Many facts concur to show," Emerson wrote, "that we must look deeper for our salvation than to steam. . . . Machinery is aggressive. The weaver becomes a web, the machinest a machine. If you do not use the tools, they use you." Later, economist Thorstein Veblen noted, "The machine discipline acts to disintegrate the institutional heritage, of all degrees of antiquity and authenticity."[7]

Lesser minds perhaps saw less dire consequences, yet they wondered, too, about the consequences of railroads. Henry Harrington wrote in 1840 that the United States was losing its simplicity, thanks to the railroad. "Improvement has trod over its highways and byways, and made its loneliness resound with the din of business, and the clamor of a crowd." The railroad, Harrington wrote, was "a noisy, unromantic invention," visiting its "dazzling newness" on everything, whether welcome or not.[8]

In the old days, wrote a poet in the 1840s, men rode "noble steeds," but now they were pulled by this iron one that neither needed nor would brook any rein while traversing its "level" way. "But the IRON HORSE, there was none like him! / He whirls you along till your eye is dim / Till your brain is crazed, and your senses swim, / With the dizzy landscape on either side!"[9] Americans had acquired the railroad "habit," and it was in part a stressful one.[10]

Peter Gay once wrote in thinking of the nineteenth century: "All change is traumatic, even change for the better. The very gratification of wishes generates dislocations." There had always been "buccaneers" breaking dull routine. "But," Gay wrote, "in providing a battery of realistic hopes, the nineteenth century lent the double idea of resourcefulness and autonomy new prestige, and, with that, released a flood of energies."[11]

Winner confirmed that thought. The concept of need, he wrote, has two meanings: necessity and desire. There were many things not strictly necessary, but they were wanted for the satisfaction they brought.[12] That newspapers generated desire for railroad travel, as well as trying to document the practical uses of that technology, should be clear. There was an element of play in it all, as well as serious good sense.

More than a few times in thinking about railroads, writers had been reminded of the myth of the young and headstrong Phaeton, who, thinking of the fun he might have, took over from his father, the sun god Helios, his horses and chariot for a ride hauling the sun across the sky. Warnings aside, the boy delighted in the experience, only ultimately to crash while literally playing with fire. There was hubris involved, to be sure, when writers talked about the species evolving with the aid of their "skillful friend" the railroad, until *Homo sapiens* was freed from his ape ancestry and from the bonds of "mere sense" to become exalted in the scale of being to near-divine status.

Modern critics have argued that technology has created an artificial or simulated environment, isolating modern people from nature and from nature's reality. James Howard Kunstler, in his book *The Geography of Nowhere*, blamed the United States for allowing profit-making corporations to create a "tawdry" landscape and a meaningless, commuting, suburban lifestyle based around the automobile and concrete. There existed, Kunstler wrote, a "creeping-crud economy," which was accompanied by a "lamebrained notion of the good life" that was perfect for those with goods to sell. Aesthetics and taste suffered until "every town hall built after 1950 is a concrete-block shed full of cheap paneling and plastic furniture, where courthouses, firehouses, halls of records, libraries, museums, post offices and other civic monuments are indistinguishable from bottling plants and cold-storage warehouses." It was what the automobile demanded, and Americans came to love the automobile.[13]

There is currently no lack of critics of the world that, one could argue, the railroad created. Novelist Mark Helprin, in a book defending copyright, has spoken of the "digital barbarism" that has resulted from the ultimate technological mediating environment. "Man," he wrote, "need not model himself, the way he lives . . . after machines." Extending our sense has been exciting but also damaging in that people have thought to abandon the limits of their own natures and become in their mind's eye multitasking superpeople. In the process of annihilating time, space, and isolation, humankind has given up things it desperately needs. Overloaded with instant information, people have found a new kind of stupidity. The promise has been largely false. "It would be one thing," Helprin commented, "if such a [technological] revolution produced Mozarts, Einsteins, or Raphaels, but it doesn't. It produces mouth-breathing morons in backwards baseball caps and pants that fall down." What hath God wrought, he asked, and why didn't He stop with the telegraph?[14]

The artificial, technologically mediated environment engendered, according to some, a class of subhumans. No twentieth-century critic was more severe than the press in the nineteenth century when it stated that the new opportunities for corruption brought by the railroad only made it more clear that the public was "the most . . . stupid of asses." The merely legal, perhaps even the merely honest, were as limiting and as boring as small-town life, the repetitive cycles of the farm, or slow travel. Here were new thrills, constantly new, and potential for gain or ruin beyond one's wildest imagination in former times. People doted upon Wall Street, were fascinated by speculation, and awaited the next boom while at the same time eagerly consuming invective against the plungers and looking for government relief at periods when the results were ruinous. The extremes seemed wrong only in that the jealous small-timer had not been able to reach them. Maybe next year!

The environment in which imperfectly educated, partly civilized people lived also changed, and they went along with it. John Senior, in his book *The Restoration of Christian Culture*, concluded from a religious perspective something not unlike what Helprin did from a secular point of view: "Generations brought up in centrally heated and air-conditioned homes and schools, shot from place to place encapsulated in culturally sealed-off buses, who swim in heated, chlorinated pools devoid of current swirl or tide. . . . Poor little rich suburban children . . . living in constant fluorescent glare, have never seen the stars."[15] Railroads, in building across the eastern United States, actually created their own nature, independent of the limitations of biology. That modified nature, modified again and again since then, is still with us.[16]

A friend of mine recalled a visit to his school in the 1930s of a man demonstrating "high fidelity" sound. By "high fidelity" the man meant more faithful to the sound of live music performed on actual instruments. He asked the students to compare the sound from a standard 78 rpm shellac record with his new version. Overwhelmingly, the students preferred the artificial sound to which they had become accustomed to the more "real" version. Why refer to the so-called real at all?

John Stilgoe's book *Metropolitan Corridor: Railroads and the American Scene* well demonstrates that railroads in effect carried American eastern urban civilization with them into the wilderness. The railroad, he wrote, "reshaped the American built environment and reoriented American thinking." One saw actual Native Americans and actual wilderness—but through the windows of a Pullman car. It reminds one of high-tech camping, where one can appreciate nature, but only within proximity to the air-conditioned car and the hot bath. Stilgoe reported that the railroad, in its actual and in its model form, came to fascinate generations of boys like nothing merely natural ever could.[17]

The railroad and its accoutrements had a physical effect on people, an effect that was unaccustomed, novel, and exciting. Like drugs and rock 'n' roll, rapid rail travel, bustling cities, and rapid change affected people in an obvious way. It was easy to believe that the effects represented something fundamental, positive, and profound. Speed and power were a kind of aphrodisiac. The railroad was the perfect slave, submissive to the male will and organization in the way that African Americans and women no longer were. People identified with it, as they did in later times with sports teams, imagining that the impressiveness of the railroad made its patrons somehow more impressive and powerful also.

We think that the United States took so well to the railroad because we had a materialistic, progressive, risk-taking culture. But it might well have been the other way around. That culture may have developed partly as a way of adapting to the railroad, which exercised such a powerful pull. The new, or at least modified, culture did not develop over time and was not evolved by thinkers considering the eternal verities. It sprang up quickly as a reaction to a relatively temporary phenomenon, and it was most democratic in its effects, for better and for worse. "The attraction is strong," Helprin wrote, "the need is real, the marvels truly marvelous, and there is no going back." Often a change in history, like the railroad, had its "own internal logic, pulling everything after it."[18]

Such innovations affected hopes and dreams. Joseph Corn, in *The Winged Gospel: America's Romance with Aviation, 1900–1950*, argued that the way people imagined themselves and their future was influenced not only by the airplane itself but also by the way the public came to understand the possibilities of flight.[19] The electric world, the paperless world, and the global village similarly became, once some new technology was in place, as much dream as reality.[20] "Railroads are a new power in the world," a journalist wrote in 1858. "Their introduction has led to new modes of business and thought."[21]

It should be emphasized that the dark side of technology was prominent in the minds of a small minority in 2010—and also in 1855. The mass of people in the early twenty-first century happily talked on cellular telephones, surfed the Internet, watched high-definition television, and jetted across oceans with hardly a thought that they were losing anything. They did not seem to miss starlight, or quiet, or clean air, or knowing their neighbors. After all, they had 5,000 friends in a virtual Facebook network or could tweet to everyone on any subject. Perhaps they were less reflective than the intellectuals, or perhaps their reflections just led to different conclusions. Had not life on the farm or in the village been a colossal bore?

People in the middle of the nineteenth century perceived drawbacks to the railroad. Some, like the residents of Salem, Massachusetts, or of the State of New Hampshire, presented a fairly uniform front against railway abuses and seemed willing to sacrifice the benefits altogether if the drawbacks were not corrected.

The South made an effective effort to put the railroad in its place as part of a set of preexisting cultural assumptions, arguing that it was a supplement to things as they were, not a replacement for them. And lest there be too much stereotyping about the unitary nature of regions, one should read the speeches of southerner William Hayes, which would bear comparison in hyperbolic apotheosis of the railroad industry with any northern promoter. But the experience and accomplishment of the South showed that not all the social effects—including prominently huge debt, lack of coordinated planning, federal land grants, and free labor—were inevitable parts of the package. The series of articles by "Anti-Debt" in the Charleston papers in the late 1840s are demonstration enough of that. That writer was not against railroads but saw no reason "why the world should go mad about them, and mankind bankrupt themselves to force them into premature existence."

The rail system of the South, constructed with different political and economic assumptions, was at a healthy height in the 1850s. The section had changed in many ways, but not in every way—taking, it thought, most of the good with minimum of the bad from a rail system that its leaders seemed to recognize contained potentially a good deal of both. They would have said that the North took the railroad, as it took so many things, as almost a fad or mania and badly overdid it.[22] The southern rail system declined only because of the Civil War, not due to the weight of any practical considerations.

As the example of Hayne shows, individuals could exert a considerable influence on the goals and terms of the railroad debate. Notice the critical impact the energy and enthusiasm of Asa Whitney or the nerve of Robert Walker had on the Pacific rail situation. The pecuniary escapades of Robert Schuyler led to an era of demoralization.

It is also clear that the manner of speaking and arguing of individual promoters was as critical as the facts and arguments they commanded. It was important, too, how their appearances were reported and the manner of their critics in making of them either a credible or risible spectacle. Thus, speeches and editorials have often been quoted here for style as well as substance. All this suggests that no particular framing was inevitable. The Marxist conclusion that ideology was a simple reflection of economic conditions and requirements is belied by the complexity and the variability of the social response to early American railroads.

Most, however, did not feel any necessity to slow or modify the coming of a new world and a new machine in any way. Railroads, even to an intellectual like Emerson, represented a new poetry in progress. Progress, like growth, was such an axiomatic boon that it hardly lent itself to serious question. Perhaps money was not the measure of all things to a philosopher, but to the man on the street it seemed that the age of outright materialism in finance as well as in technology had come. Numbers and statistics were what counted in measuring progress.

Again and again, newspaper writers reminded readers of the pains and inconveniences, the inefficiencies and dangers, of the older modes of transport—and thanked their stars for the railroad. Indeed, nineteenth-century Americans were much closer to raw nature than those in the twentieth century, but rather than being more attached to nature, or more nostalgic about its loss, they were glad to be rid of some of its banality and horrors. Yes, the American public had to go through an adaptation process to the railroad, but the outcome was never much in doubt.

Credit came with steam. Along with the nation's first big business came big financing, big financiers, and large debt. The antebellum years were not quite yet the age of the robber barons, or the time of the merged giants, or of multinationals and hedge funds, but the trend was in that direction. The federal debt remained remarkably small in this period, despite the watershed change of large and controversial land grants in the 1850s. Individuals had not quite entered upon the credit rampage that was typical of later times. But states definitely took the plunge into massive borrowing on an international scale as well as occasional default, and the stock market became a nexus of large-scale and risky speculation. Steve Fraser, in his recent book *Every Man a Speculator: A History of Wall Street in American Life*, has documented the rise of the "Confidence Man" and claimed that "antebellum America ran a traveling school for amateur speculators."[23] Railroads engendered not only speculation in the rail companies themselves but also speculation in lands, whose value had suddenly become fluid, and in city lots. The instability of such speculation led to two financial panics during the period, in 1837 and 1857, and the pattern continued to feed the cyclic nature of the American economy to this day. Fraser calls the dreams of instant wealth on borrowed money "fatal fantasies."[24]

It might be noticed also that the chartering of railroads in connection with banks, for the express purpose of increasing their capital with a captive donor, was the origin of the currently controversial business of investment banking by conventional banks of deposit. It was also the origin of "flipping" urban real estate purchased with borrowed money. The concept that gambling was a sin waned as the rewards of gambling increased. The farmer, once regarded as the foundation of the economy with his steady small gains from hard work, now seemed, in the penny press at least, a rustic fool.

The railroad mania seemed to some "too much like fever to have a happy result." Others pointed out that this fever seemed to affect mostly the middle and upper classes and that working people, including the Irish and African Americans, who actually built the lines, were surviving on starvation wages. But such challenges as uniting the Union all the way to the Pacific, trading with China, unlocking the wealth of the West, and compressing time while rushing off on pleasure trips at 40 miles per hour were irresistible. Those changes that seem in retrospect attractive, such as the classlessness of the cars, better mail service, standard time, and eventual racial integration of railroad cars, arose out of the economic necessities of the railroad rather than the requirements of the surrounding society. The optimists, the centralists, the developers, the entrepreneurs, the engineers, and the futurists held the field. The ancillary benefits to railroads, from iron making to the development of a native engineering profession, were nearly incalculable. The protest was moot. As the Salem protestors put it in the 1830s, speaking as they did for the corporate regulators, strict constitutional constructionists, intellectuals, agrarians, village aficionados, environmentalists, primitive moralists, bank regulators, safety advocates, historic preservationists, defenders of individual freedoms, advocates of racial equality, and those worried about eminent domain or the power of the "soulless" corporation: "This is a point which the rest of the world have settled for us."

This book is a history, not a sociological study or a philosophical tract. But it is a history of the interaction of technology and public opinion, which involves learning in some detail how something was sold and how it was bought. Adaptation to the railroad involved extensive discourse carried out through the media for many years. That resulted in a balancing by the public of railroad benefits and drawbacks, which led to the conclusion that the Iron Horse represented progress perhaps better than any development ever yet had. Not only was the railroad accepted in the United States; it became a quintessentially American business.

Some maintained, wrote a Savannah reporter in 1850, that the railroad had ruined towns and villages, destroyed the old America. "This opinion arose from the abstract reasoning of those who only looked at *one* side of the question. It has been left to Rail Roads themselves to work out their own problems; and such are the results that the old idea is now completely exploded."[25]

Yes, there were those who claimed that "practical ideas must have their due weight even in the midst of the most fascinating excitements," but fascinating excitements always held the trump card.[26] The simple facts themselves were "surpassingly sublime" when processed by the imagination of an "*enlightened* world," held in thrall and in awe at this new appearance.[27] People felt "a thrill of amazement in every nerve" at the "mighty consequences" that would come from the railroad. The Mississippi would become a neighbor of the Hudson, and the Gulf of Mexico would be in touch with the St. Lawrence River. Doubters would in a few years be "swept away before the brooms of the Iron Horse, who with nerves of brass and sinews of steel and breath of flame, will . . . be coursing over every valley and hill . . . and scattering in his train the lights of religion, of education, of refinement, and all the blessings that flow from a higher civilization."[28] No wonder was beyond the railroad. Maybe in the future, a man wrote in 1852, the trains would be run by the power of thought, without the danger of bursting boilers or wear on wheels.[29]

"This age is a practical and utilitarian one," wrote a newspaper in Kansas in 1859, "and it makes sad havoc among the romantic notions of our grandfathers." No one, however, regretted that.

> The age of steam and electricity, of freedom and education, of labor and progress, is the true golden age of the world, and this nineteenth century sees the world in a much prouder condition, and mankind in a much happier state than any century that has preceded it. . . . The inventor of the steam engine did more for the human race than all the knights that ever lived.[30]

A man writing in 1845 concluded that "man is destined to advance in progressive development of the powers committed to his hands, himself the constant source of a more profound knowledge of that infinite wisdom, which has adjusted and adapted the works of creation."[31] As every new business aspires to be so well integrated into the society where it operates, the study of the American adoption of the railroad is especially germane.

The maturation and adaptation of the American railroad system were the result of a series of experiments and decisions, as well as years of constant acquaintance with a new world by the American public, either through direct experience or through media discussions or both. The world as known went topsy-turvy, and adjustment could not be instant.

The corporate form itself was initially suspect in some quarters. It was unclear whether the railroad would represent stone architecture, as in England, or use more practical, if less monumental, materials. Was it safe? Who was responsible if it were not? Was it convenient? Was it comfortable? How could there be a meeting of changes and acclimation that led to placid, if not exactly happy, travelers? How universal would railroads be? Could they carry heavy weights at low rates? Could they cover the vast distances of the American West? What would be the effect of railroads in cities and upon cities in their trade competition with each other? How were these vast enterprises to be financed, and would their financing endanger American standards of morality and economic stability? How would governments be involved in railroad building, and how would that modify the political workings and the sectional balance of the American republic? How did they change the local landscape, and was that acceptable? What was to happen to land values and to whose benefit?

And there were broader questions still. What was the right relation between labor and management? Between man and machine? What were proper human priorities, and how might they best be served? What is valuable and how is it to be valued? In short, railroads affected much about American life at all levels, from the stress of ticket buying to whom you might sit near on the cars.

The answers to those questions affected society ever more deeply. Wrote a Kansas City editor in 1887:

> We live in an age of unparalleled "passion, pulse, and power" —an age with gigantic problems suddenly laid on it. Our civilization is chiefly industrial, and the railway, the factory, and labor organizations are the largest elements of our social life. Would any one believe a priori that under these circumstances our colleges would still be haggling over the Greek and Latin question, and that only one of them in the entire country should give instruction on railway transportation?[32]

There were few by then to doubt the sensibility of that kind of suggestion.

Answers developed, evolved. And it is not only the final result that counts but also understanding the nuances of how a free society incorporated such changes and why. The medium of the exchange was largely print, and the tenor of things was the domain of the editors, the reporters, and the readers of the daily and weekly newspapers across the nation. There was a pamphlet literature, there were letters and reports, and there were the records of formal political debates. But anything of significance that involved a public decision came eventually to the pages of the local newspaper.

Everyone read the paper, often in an increasingly nervous way. Some noticed the artificiality of this. There was a kind of "effervescence" in American society, a journalist in Boston wrote in 1853, affecting all classes. "It seems as though all our fellows had by some unaccountable arrangement been placed in the respective positions for which they are peculiarly unfitted by nature, and that in their endeavor to right themselves they meant to push the very few contented souls which they find out of the spheres they respectively occupy." Anglo-Saxons lusted for power and wealth and "must have something to devour." The market ruled—and at increasing speed through the newspaper quotations. The farmer

> has now by the intersection of railroads and telegraph lines, been placed in apposition with the busy world. He dares not sell a bushel of potatoes or a stack of hay, without consulting first his newspaper, and then the telegraphic wires, to learn whether some event has occurred which may enhance the price of his products. Instead of cultivating his land, he is busy in the forest getting railroad ties.

It was a life of "external forms," but it was modern life withal.[33] Connecting the country with railroads was, wrote the *New York Daily Times* in 1853, "unquestionably the task for the present generation to accomplish; and the best mode of doing it, one of the greatest problems of the time." It invited the wealth and labor of the nation to transform two simple tracks into an agent of civilization and Christianity.[34] To listen overmuch to the precursors of a movement to freight railroad corporations with "social responsibility" seemed at the time not only unnecessary but also counterproductive. Thus American society allowed itself to be influenced to its core by the "creature" it supposedly had created to serve it.

In 1890 Horatio Allen, who had first run *Stourbridge Lion* in Pennsylvania, died at his home in South Orange, New Jersey. What a transformation, what an evolution in the railroad and the railroad's America he had lived to see! His confidence about railroads had led to his appointment in 1827 as assistant to John Jervis, the chief engineer of the Delaware & Hudson

Canal. He arranged for the building of a 15-mile strap-iron line and for the importation from England of three steam locomotives. Robert Stephenson refused the commission, so busy was he already building locomotives for the British lines. But Allen, who stayed in England the better part of a year, was able to make a deal with Foster, Roswick & Company of Stourbridge, England. It shipped the first engine, named *Stourbridge Lion* because of the red lion's head painted on its boiler, in April 1829. Arriving by ship at New York Harbor, the marvel went on view mounted on blocks at the West Point Foundry for the directors of the canal company and others to examine. There it stayed, with its spokes and felloes of wood, iron tires, upright boiler, and side-mounted "grasshopper"-type walking beams, until the spring of 1829, when the weather allowed it to be shipped by canal to its intended destination and Allen's first heart-stopping trip down the line.[35]

Every year since that day the railroad has become more ubiquitous and more axiomatic. The United States' railroad length in 1890 was 163,562.12 miles.[36] It meant, wrote a reporter in 1890, "a tremendous change in the conditions of living and in business habits. Men whose ideas were formed . . . years ago are forced to adapt themselves to the new order or fall to the rear of the procession."[37] Such sentiments had been expressed in the United States since the complaints of the new generation of the 1840s against the "old fogeys" of the 1820s. Progress was a permanent feature. Ringing a bell for it was a regular thing also, lest anyone, in his great hurry, forget and backslide.

NOTES

PREFACE

1. Paul Gates, *The Illinois Central and Its Colonization Work* (Cambridge: Harvard University Press, 1934), 84.
2. John Larson, *Bonds of Empire: John Murray Forbes and Western Development in America's Railway Age* (Cambridge: Harvard University Press, 1984), xviii.
3. Quoted in Edward Kirkland, *Men, Cities, and Transportation: A Study in New England History, 1820–1900* (Cambridge: Harvard University Press, 1948), 1:198.
4. Guillaume Poussin, *The United States: Its Power and Progress* (Philadelphia: Lippincott, Grambo, 1851), 374–375.
5. *United States Magazine and Democratic Review* (Washington, D.C.), vol. 21, 338.
6. John Majewski, *A House Dividing: Economic Development in Pennsylvania and Virginia Before the Civil War* (Cambridge: Cambridge University Press, 2000), 10.
7. Bruce Mazlish, ed., *The Railroad and the Space Program: An Exploration in Historical Analogy* (Cambridge: MIT Press, 1965). Leo Marx, *The Machine in the Garden: Technology and the Pastoral Ideal in America* (New York: Oxford University Press, 1967). James Ward, *Railroads and the Character of America, 1820–1887* (Knoxville: University of Tennessee Press, 1986).
8. Langdon Winner, *Autonomous Technology: Technics-out-of-Control as a Theme in Political Thought* (Cambridge: MIT Press, 1977), 2.
9. L. Ray Gunn, *The Decline of Authority: Public Economic Policy and Political Development in New York, 1800–1860* (Ithaca: Cornell University Press, 1988), 8.
10. Albert Fishlow, *Railroads and the Transformation of the Ante-Bellum Economy* (Cambridge: Harvard University Press, 1965), 4, 125.
11. Robert Fogel, *Railroads and American Economic Growth: Essays in Economic History*. Baltimore: Johns Hopkins University Press, 1964, 11, 249.
12. For development of this point at length, see Gunn, *The Decline of Authority.*
13. Henry Steele Commager, *The American Mind* (New Haven: Yale University Press, 1950), 5–6.
14. *Connecticut Courant* (Hartford), September 4, 1832.
15. *National Era* (Washington, D.C.), January 24, 1850, 13.
16. New York: Harcourt, Brace, 1922.
17. *Western Journal of Agriculture, Manufactures, Mechanic Arts, Internal Improvements, Commerce and General Literature* (St. Louis), vol. 3, no. 2 (November 1849), 71.

18. *Christian Observer* (Louisville), vol. 33, no. 29 (July 22, 1854), 116.

19. Frederick Marryat, *A Diary in America: With Remarks on Its Institutions* (Philadelphia: Carey & Hart, 1839), 72.

20. Cheap Edition (London: Chapman and Hall, 1850), 44–45. The first edition was in two volumes (1842).

21. Daniel Drake, *Discourse on the History, Character, and Prospects of the West: Delivered to the Union Literary Society of Miami University, Oxford, Ohio, at Their Ninth Anniversary, September 23, 1834* (Cincinnati: Truman and Smith, 1834), 30.

22. Joseph Story, *The Miscellaneous Writings: Literary, Critical, Juridical, and Political* (Boston: James Munroe, 1835), 141.

23. *Scientific American* (New York), vol. 2, no. 29 (May 26, 1860), 345.

24. *The Spirit of the Age* (New York), vol. 1, 201.

25. Winner, *Autonomous Technology*, 295.

26. Ibid., 10–11.

27. *The Charleston Mercury*, February 12, 1856.

INTRODUCTION: TREADING ON ENCHANTED GROUND

1. "A Traveller's Notes" to *Bucks County Patriot,* in *Connecticut Mirror* (Hartford), July 9, 1827. *Daily National Intelligencer* (Washington, D.C.), September 27, 1826, and September 18, 1827.

2. *Niles Register*, quoted in *Republican Star and General Advertiser* (Easton, Md.), June 30, 1829.

3. *Daily National Journal* (Washington, D.C.), October 16, 1826.

4. Quoted in *Berkshire Star* (Pittsfield, Mass.), December 28, 1826.

5. *Raleigh Register and North-Carolina Gazette*, June 1, 1827.

6. *Salem Gazette* (Mass.), June 5, 1827. *Essex Register* (Salem, Mass.), June 11, 1827.

7. *Daily National Intelligencer* (Washington, D.C.), June 20, 1827.

8. *New York Spectator*, September 14, 1827.

9. *Daily National Intelligencer* (Washington, D.C.), September 18, 1827.

10. Anne N. Royall, *Mrs. Royall's Pennsylvania, or, Travels Continued in the United States* (Washington, D.C.: Printed for the Author, 1829), 1:133–134, 137.

11. *New-Hampshire Sentinel* (Keene), July 6, 1827. *Daily National Intelligencer*, October 5, 1827. *Berkshire Star* (Pittsfield, Mass.), December 28, 1826.

12. *Daily National Intelligencer* (Washington, D.C.), October 15, 1827.

13. For an account of a serious accident, see *Niles' Weekly Register*, August 18, 1827.

14. *New York Spectator*, September 14, 1827.

15. *Daily National Intelligencer* (Washington, D.C.), October 5, 1827.

16. Quoted in *Delaware Advertiser and Farmer's Journal* (Wilmington), October 9, 1828.

17. Brooke Hindle and Steven Lubar, *Engines of Change: The American Industrial Revolution, 1790–1860* (Washington, D.C.: Smithsonian Institution Press, 1986), 84. *Boston Patriot and Morning Advertiser*, May 22, 1816.

18. Peter Bernstein, *Wedding of the Waters: The Erie Canal and the Making of a Great Nation* (New York: W.W. Norton, 2005), 344.

19. For an overview of early railroads and canals, see George Rogers Taylor, *The Transportation Revolution, 1815–1860* (New York: Harper & Row, 1951).

20. *Louisville Public Advertiser* (Ky.), April 9, 1825.

21. *Daily National Intelligencer* (Washington, D.C.), November 12, 1825.

22. Ibid., January 17, 1826.

23. *Washington Expositor* (Washington, D.C.), July 30, 1808.

24. *Richmond Enquirer*, December 20, 1817.

25. John Majewski, *A House Dividing: Economic Development in Pennsylvania and Virginia Before the Civil War* (Cambridge: Cambridge University Press, 2000), 124.

26. *Richmond Enquirer*, June 25, 1819.

27. Quoted in *Hartford Daily Courant*, October 14, 1851.

28. *Kline's Carlisle* (Pa.) *Gazette*, June 19, 1812.

29. *New York Mercantile Advertiser*, quoted in *American Watchman* (Wilmington, Del.), February 23, 1814. For Evans's career see Siegfried Giedion, *Mechanization Takes Command: A Contribution to Anonymous History* (New York: W.W. Norton, 1969), 79–86. First published by Oxford University Press in 1948.

30. *State Gazette* (Trenton, N.J.), June 12, 1850. *American Watchman* (Wilmington, Del.), February 23, 1814.

31. London paper, quoted in *North Star* (Danville, Vt.), November 9, 1824.

32. *New York Spectator*, March 7, 1826.

33. *Norwich Courier* (Conn.), April 5, 1826.

34. *Berkshire Star* (Pittsfield, Mass.), June 7, 1827.

35. *Western Carolinian* in *Carolina Observer* (Fayetteville, N.C.), March 8, 1826.

36. *Augusta Chronicle* (Ga.), November 25, 1826.

37. *Raleigh Register and North Carolina Gazette*, January 29, 1828.

38. *Louisville Public Advertiser*, August 16, 1826.

39. *Camden Gazette* (S.C.), January 17, 1822.

40. Letter from Columbia in *Louisiana Advertiser* (New Orleans), December 24, 1827.

41. *Charleston Courier*, quoted in *Louisville Public Advertiser*, January 23, 1828. *Augusta Chronicle* (Ga.), March 21, 1828.

42. *Georgia Journal*, quoted in *Augusta Chronicle* (Georgia), February 29, 1828.

43. Letter from Charleston, December 25, 1827, quoted in *Saturday Pennsylvania Gazette* (Philadelphia), January 12, 1828.

44. *Augusta Chronicle and Georgia Advertiser*, January 11, 1828.

45. *U.S. Telegraph and Commercial Herald* (Washington, D.C.), March 1, 1827.

46. *Daily National Intelligencer* (Washington, D.C.), March 8, 1827.

47. *United States Telegraph* (Washington, D.C.), March 15, 1827.

48. *Daily National Intelligencer* (Washington, D.C.), April 27, 1827. *Louisiana Advertiser* (New Orleans), April 28, 1827.

49. *United States Telegraph* (Washington, D.C.), March 22, 1827.

50. *Baltimore American*, quoted in *United States Telegraph* (Washington, D.C.), March 15, 1827.

51. *Proceedings of Sundry Citizens of Baltimore* (Baltimore: Printed by W. Wooddy, 1827), 3, 5, 17, 20, 21, 28.

52. F. Harrison Jr., U.S. Assistant Engineer, *Report of the Engineers, or the Reconnaissance and Surveys; Made in Reference to the Baltimore and Ohio Rail Road* (Baltimore: Printed by W. Wooddy, 1828).

53. *Niles' Weekly Register*, vol. 33 (June 23, 1827), 282–283. An outstanding recent history of the early B&O is James D. Dilts, *The Great Road: The Building of the Baltimore and Ohio, the Nation's First Railroad, 1828–1853* (Palo Alto: Stanford University Press, 1993).

54. *Baltimore in the New Nation, 1789–1861* (Chapel Hill: University of North Carolina Press, 1980), 92, 114.
55. *Niles' Weekly Register*, vol. 33 (March 17, 1827), 33.
56. *Essex Register* (Salem, Mass.), April 9, 1827.
57. *Maryland Gazette* (Annapolis), February 14, 1828.
58. *Frederick Examiner*, quoted in *Baltimore Patriot*, February 14, 1828.
59. *Pittsfield Sun* (Mass.), June 14, 1827.
60. *Baltimore Patriot*, January 12, 1828.
61. Quoted in *New York Spectator*, May 1, 1827.
62. *Louisville Public Advertiser*, May 26, 1827.
63. *Delaware Patriot & American Watchman* (Wilmington), February 12, 1828.
64. *The Scioto Gazette* (Chillicothe, Ohio), May 3 and June 14, 1827.
65. *Louisiana Advertiser* (New Orleans), June 8, 1827.
66. *Niles Weekly Register*, vol. 5 (February 5, 1814), 374.
67. Taylor, *Transportation Revolution*, 43–44.
68. *Hazard's Register of Pennsylvania*, vol. 8, no. 1 (July 2, 1831), 6; vol. 8, no. 24 (December 10, 1831), 418.
69. *Louisville Public Advertiser*, March 20, 1830.
70. *York Recorder*, quoted in *Baltimore Patriot*, January 29, 1829.
71. *Newburyport Herald* (Mass.), June 17, 1823.
72. *Pittsburgh Mercury*, quoted in *Columbia Telescope and South Carolina Journal* (Raleigh), March 4, 1825.
73. *Saturday Pennsylvania Gazette* (Philadelphia), May 31, 1828.
74. Quoted in *Berkshire Star* (Pittsfield, Mass.), March 30, 1826.
75. Ibid., December 28, 1826.
76. Ibid.
77. Russell Jervis et al. in *Boston Courier*, January 18, 1827.
78. *Essex Register* (Salem, Mass.), June 11, 1827.
79. *Star*, quoted in *Saturday Pennsylvania Gazette* (Philadelphia), December 29, 1827.
80. *Berkshire Star* (Pittsfield, Mass.), August 2, 1827.
81. *Village Register and Norfolk County Advertiser* (Dedham, Mass.), March 28, 1828.
82. Oscar Handlin and Mary Handlin, *Commonwealth: A Study of the Role of Government in the American Economy: Massachusetts, 1774–1861*, rev. ed. (Cambridge: Harvard University Press, 1969), 182, 188, 190, 193.
83. *New York Spectator*, February 15, 1828.
84. Columbus, Ohio, paper, quoted in *Louisville Public Advertiser*, October 29, 1825. *Indiana Journal* (Indianapolis), March 20, 1827.
85. *Baltimore Patriot*, January 3, 1828.
86. *Carolina Observer* (Fayetteville, N.C.), January 31, 1828.
87. *Louisville Daily Journal*, March 27, 1855.
88. *North American and United States Gazette* (Philadelphia), February 22, 1853.
89. Letter from Edmund Gaines to Governor of Georgia, *Daily National Intelligencer*, September 24, 1834.
90. *Daily National Intelligencer* (Washington, D.C.), March 28, 1840.
91. *Commercial Advertiser* (New York), quoted in *New York Spectator*, June 21, 1831.
92. Quoted in John Larson, *Bonds of Empire: John Murray Forbs and Western Development in America's Railway Age* (Cambridge: Harvard University Press, 1984), 42.

93. *New Hampshire Patriot and State Gazette* (Concord), October 7, 1841.
94. *Boston Herald*, December 16, 1853.
95. *Knickerbocker*, quoted in *Newport Mercury* (R.I.), May 23, 1835.
96. James Brooks in *Cleveland Herald*, June 18, 1835.
97. *Herald* (New York), May 3, 1837.
98. Quoted in *Daily National Intelligencer* (Washington, D.C.), October 17, 1835.
99. Poussin, *The United States*, 374–375.
100. *New Hampshire Statesman and State Journal* (Concord), June 29, 1939.
101. Correspondence in *Portland Daily Advertiser,* quoted in *Daily National Intelligencer* (Washington, D.C.), January 9, 1837.
102. *New Hampshire Sentinel* (Keene), April 1, 1840.
103. Robert McFarlane in *Scientific American*, quoted in *American Phrenological Journal* (New York), vol. 13, no. 2 (February 1851), 37.
104. *Rhode Island American and Gazette* (Providence), September 18, 1832.
105. *New Hampshire Sentinel* (Keene), January 15, 1835.
106. *Ohio Observer* (Hudson), July 9, 1840. *New England Weekly Review* (Hartford), August 15, 1840.
107. *Salem Gazette* (Mass.), March 12, 1830.
108. *Littel's Living Age* (New York), vol. 16 (January 8, 1848), 66.
109. Lecture on the "Spirit of the Age," quoted in *New York Herald*, April 3, 1850.
110. *United States Magazine and Democratic Review* (Washington, D.C.), vol. 20 (May 1847), 392.
111. *Sun* (Baltimore), April 23, 1850.
112. John R. Godley, *Letters from America* (London: Murray, 1844), 1:139.
113. Elizabeth Bishop to Robert Lowell, April 29, 1973, in Thomas Travisano, ed., *Words in Air: The Complete Correspondence Between Elizabeth Bishop and Robert Lowell* (New York: Farrar, Straus and Giroux, 2008), 744.
114. *Baltimore Patriot*, June 10, 1831.

CHAPTER 1: BALTIMORE LOOKS WEST

1. Charles Carroll, *Travels in North America in the Years 1827 and 1828* (Philadelphia: Carey, Lea & Carey, 1829), 101.
2. *Baltimore Patriot*, June 21, 1828.
3. Ibid., June 30, 1828.
4. Ibid., July 2, 1828.
5. Ibid., July 5, 7, 1828.
6. James D. Dilts, *The Great Road: The Building of the Baltimore and Ohio, the Nation's First Railroad, 1828–1853* (Palo Alto: Stanford University Press, 1993), 1.
7. *Baltimore Patriot,* July 8, 1828.
8. *Boston Gazette,* quoted in *Salem Gazette* (Mass.), July 11, 1828.
9. *Baltimore American*, quoted in *Niles' Weekly Register*, vol. 35 (July 12, 1828), 316.
10. *Baltimore Patriot*, January 8, 1829.
11. *United States Telegraph* (Washington, D.C.), February 15, 1830.
12. *United States Telegraph* (Washington, D.C.), quoted in *Delaware Patriot and American Watchman* (Wilmington), July 18, 1828.
13. *Baltimore Patriot*, July 12, 1818.
14. *Aurora & Pennsylvania Gazette* (Philadelphia), August 11, 1828.

15. Quoted in *Connecticut Courant* (Hartford), January 6, 1829.

16. *Baltimore Patriot*, January 14, 1829.

17. *National Intelligencer*, quoted in *Virginia Free Press and Farmers' Repository* (Charleston, W.V.), February 10, 1830.

18. Letter to editor, *Daily National Intelligencer* (Washington, D.C.), February 20, 1830.

19. Letter to editor, "Plain Facts and Plain Thoughts on Railways!," ibid., March 3, 1830.

20. *Baltimore Patriot*, January 14, 1829.

21. Ibid., February 2, 1830.

22. *Watch Tower* (Cooperstown, N.Y.), March 7, 1831.

23. Quoted in *Richmond Enquirer*, March 29, 1831.

24. *Baltimore Patriot*, February 27, 1830.

25. Dilts, *The Great Road*, 114–116. *Daily National Journal* (Washington, D.C.), October 13, 1831. *Maryland Gazette* (Annapolis), January 5, 1832. *Virginia Free Press & Farmers' Repository* (Charlestown, W.V.), May 17, 1832. *Daily National Intelligencer*, June 15 and July 23, 1832.

26. *United States Telegraph* (Washington, D.C.), June 4, 1832.

27. *Daily National Intelligencer*, July 23, 1832.

28. Ibid., August 8, 1832.

29. *Baltimore Republican*, quoted in ibid., August 8, 1832.

30. *Daily National Intelligencer*, August 8, 1832.

31. *Daily National Intelligencer*, June 10, 1829.

32. *Baltimore Patriot*, June 16, 1829.

33. Dilts, *The Great Road*, 151–152, 184.

34. Robert Benson of Liverpool to Thomas Ellicott, February 1, 1830, quoted in *Baltimore Patriot*, March 22, 1830.

35. *Daily National Intelligencer*, August 3, 1831.

36. Edward Hungerford, *The Story of the Baltimore & Ohio Railroad, 1827–1927* (New York: G.P. Putnam's Sons, 1928), 137–140.

37. *Chambersburg Repository*, quoted in *Daily National Intelligencer*, April 27, 1827.

38. *Baltimore Patriot*, January 28, 1829.

39. Letter of December 13, 1827, quoted in *Saturday Pennsylvania Gazette* (Philadelphia), December 29, 1827.

40. *Saturday Pennsylvania Gazette* (Philadelphia), February 16, 1828.

41. Letter from Pittsburgh, quoted in *Baltimore Patriot*, February 19, 1828.

42. *Baltimore Patriot*, January 5, 1828.

43. *Baltimore Patriot*, September 14, 1831.

44. *Hartford Times* (Conn.), June 29, 1829.

45. *New York Herald*, July 22, 1837.

46. Quoted in *Baltimore Patriot*, January 26, 1829.

47. *Delaware Patriot and American Watchman* (Wilmington), February 12, 1828.

48. *Philadelphia National Gazette*, quoted in *Louisiana Advertiser* (New Orleans), May 7, 1827.

49. *Philadelphia National Gazette*, quoted in *Baltimore Patriot*, February 14, 1828.

50. *Saturday Pennsylvania Gazette* (Philadelphia), February 16, 1828.

51. *Aurora and Pennsylvania Gazette* (Philadelphia), January 3, 1829.

52. Ibid., July 27, 1829.

53. Ibid., February 20, 1829.

54. Ibid., June 10, 1829.
55. *National Gazette*, quoted in *Providence Patriot and Columbian Phenix* (Providence, R.I.), June 13, 1829.
56. *United States Telegraph* (Washington, D.C.), June 20, 1829.
57. *Daily National Journal* (Washington, D.C.), May 21, 1831.
58. Hungerford, *Story of the Baltimore & Ohio Railroad*, 242.
59. *Norwich Courier* (Conn.), December 9, 1829.
60. *Liverpool Times*, quoted in *Eastern Argus* (Portland, Me.), December 15, 1829.
61. *New Bedford Mercury* (Mass.), January 1, 1830.
62. *Baltimore Patriot*, June 16, 1829.
63. *New York Spectator*, December 29, 1829.
64. *Baltimore Patriot*, January 2, 1830.
65. Ibid., January 4, 6, 1830.
66. *United States Telegraph* (Washington, D.C.), January 11, 1830. *Baltimore Patriot*, January 11, 1830.
67. *Augusta Chronicle* (Ga.), June 2, 1830.
68. *Baltimore Patriot*, May 24, 1830.
69. Ibid., May 28, 1830.
70. Ibid., June 9, 1830.
71. *Baltimore American*, quoted in *Ithaca Journal* (N.Y.), June 9, 1830.
72. *Baltimore Patriot*, June 14, 1830.
73. DeWitt Clinton, quoted in *New York Herald*, June 21, 1830. *Baltimore Chronicle*, quoted in *Raleigh Register and North Carolina Gazette*, June 10, 1830.
74. *Daily National Journal* (Washington, D.C.), June 28, 1830. *Baltimore Patriot*, June 28, 1830.
75. *New York Herald*, July 31, 1830.
76. *Baltimore Patriot*, August 17, 1830. *Baltimore Gazette*, quoted in *Daily Louisville Public Advertiser*, August 24, 1830.
77. *Baltimore Patriot*, August 25, 26, 1830. *Daily National Intelligencer*, September 2, 1830.
78. *Connecticut Mirror* (Hartford), October 2, 1830.
79. *Baltimore Patriot*, October 13, 1830.
80. Ibid., September 22, 1831. *New York Spectator*, October 7, 1831.
81. *New York Courier and Enquirer*, quoted in ibid., October 19, 1830.
82. *Baltimore Patriot*, November 3, 1830.
83. *Wheeling Gazette,* quoted in Hazard's *Register of Pennsylvania*, vol. 16 (October 10, 1835), 232.
84. *Salem Gazette* (Mass.), July 17, 1829.
85. *Daily Dispatch* (Richmond), February 1, 1856.
86. *New Hampshire Sentinel* (Keene), June 12, 1829.
87. *Daily Dispatch* (Richmond), February 1, 1856.

CHAPTER 2: THE VAST MACHINERY

1. *Salem Gazette* (Mass.), June 22, 1830.
2. *New Hampshire Post*, quoted in *Boston Courier*, March 1, 1830.
3. Stephen Salsbury, *The State, the Investor, and the Railroad: The Boston & Albany, 1825–1867* (Cambridge: Harvard University Press, 1967), 1, 35, 53.

4. *Boston Courier*, January 1, 1835.

5. Salsbury, *The State, the Investor, and the Railroad*, 296. *Salem Gazette* (Mass.), July 4, 1835.

6. *Essex Gazette* (Haverhill, Mass.), August 22, 1829.

7. *Salem Observer*, quoted in ibid., September 5, 1829.

8. *Salem Observer*, quoted in ibid., September 12, 1829.

9. *Salem Observer*, quoted in ibid., September 26, 1829.

10. *Farmers' Cabinet* (Amherst, N.H.), January 23, 1830.

11. *Virginia Free Press and Farmers' Repository* (Charlestown, W.V.), January 27, 1830.

12. *Aurora and Pennsylvania Gazette*, June 4, 1829.

13. Message of Governor, quoted in *Daily National Intelligencer* (Washington, D.C.), June 8, 1829.

14. *Baltimore Patriot*, January 23, 1830.

15. *New York Herald*, March 5, 1830. *Raleigh Register and North Carolina Gazette*, June 19, 1829.

16. Oscar Handlin and Mary Handlin, *Commonwealth: A Study of the Role of Government in the American Economy: Massachusetts, 1774–1861*, rev. ed. (Cambridge: Harvard University Press, 1969), 173–174.

17. Theodore Sedgwick Jr., quoted in *Berkshire Journal* (Lennox, Mass.), December 3, 1829.

18. Quoted in *Daily National Intelligencer* (Washington, D.C.), February 18, 1830.

19. *Connecticut Mirror* (Hartford), January 16, 1830.

20. Salsbury, *The State, the Investor, and the Railroad*, 31.

21. Ibid., 80, 93.

22. *Eastern Argus* (Portland, Me.), January 15, 1830.

23. *Boston Courier*, February 11, 1830.

24. *Boston Patriot*, quoted in *Baltimore Patriot*, February 8, 1830. *Providence Patriot and Columbian Phenix* (R.I.), July 7, 1830. *Boston Commercial Advertiser*, quoted in *Louisville Public Advertiser*, February 19, 1830.

25. Report of Lemuel Shaw, *Boston Courier*, July 15, 1830.

26. *Boston Courier*, July 15, 1830.

27. Letter to editor from "Mentor," in *Boston Courier*, July 19, 1830.

28. "Juris Consultus" in *Boston Courier*, July 22, 1830.

29. "Mentor" in ibid., August 2, 1830.

30. Salsbury, *The State, the Investor, and the Railroad*, 108, 110.

31. *New Hampshire Statesman and State Journal* (Concord), November 17, 1830.

32. *Farmers' Gazette* (Barre, Mass.), May 15, 1835. *New Hampshire Statesman and State Journal* (Concord), May 23, 1835. *Portsmouth Journal of Literature & Politics* (N.H.), May 30, 1835.

33. *Boston Evening Gazette*, quoted in *The Globe* (Washington, D.C.), April 28, 1835. *New York Spectator*, June 4, 1835.

34. *New York Journal of Commerce*, quoted in *Portsmouth Journal of Literature & Politics* (N.H.), May 2, 1835.

35. *New York Spectator*, June 4, 1835.

36. Elkanah Watson, quoted in *New York Spectator*, October 1, 1830.

37. *Portsmouth Journal of Literature & Politics* (N.H.), January 3, 1835.

38. *New York Spectator*, June 4, 1835.

39. *Boston Courier*, June 25, 1835.

40. *New Hampshire Sentinel* (Keene), May 28, 1835. *Boston Evening Gazette*, quoted in *The Globe* (Washington, D.C.), April 28, 1835.
41. *Boston Daily Advertiser*, quoted in *Daily National Intelligencer*, April 28, 1835.
42. William D. Howells, *Suburban Sketches* (New York: Hurd & Houghton, 1871). Sam Warner, *Streetcar Suburbs: The Process of Growth in Boston, 1870–1890* (Cambridge: Harvard University Press, 1962).
43. *New York Spectator*, December 29, 1841.
44. *North American and Daily Advertiser* (Philadelphia), December 30, 1841.
45. *Louisiana Advertiser* (New Orleans), December 24, 1827.
46. *New Hampshire Patriot and State Gazette* (Concord), January 7, 1828.
47. *Augusta Chronicle and Georgia Advertiser*, January 11, 1828.
48. *Charleston Courier*, quoted in *Louisville Public Advertiser*, January 23, 1828.
49. Letter from Charleston in *Saturday Pennsylvania Gazette*, January 12, 1828.
50. *Charleston Mercury*, quoted in *Vermont Watchman and State Gazette* (Montpelier), April 29, 1828.
51. *Augusta Chronicle and Georgia Advertiser*, January 7, 1829.
52. *Baltimore Patriot*, January 13, 1829.
53. *Augusta Chronicle and Georgia Advertiser*, February 7, 1829.
54. *Charleston Mercury*, quoted in *Columbia Telescope* (S.C.), February 13, 1829.
55. *Baltimore Patriot*, January 7, 1830.
56. *Louisville Public Advertiser*, January 8, 1830. *Raleigh Register and North Carolina Gazette*, January 7, 1830.
57. See letter from R.V. Hayne to *Charleston Gazette*, quoted in *United States Telegraph* (Washington, D.C.), February 9, 1830.
58. *Greenville Mountaineer* (S.C.), January 23, 1830. Letter to President of South Carolina Canal and Rail Road Co., quoted in *Raleigh Register and North Carolina Gazette*, January 25, 1830.
59. *Augusta Chronicle*, January 13, 1830.
60. *The Southern Times* (Columbia, S.C.), February 4, 1830.
61. *Baltimore Patriot*, January 7, 1830.
62. A recent well-crafted version of this thesis is Susan Dunn, *Dominion of Memories: Jefferson, Madison, and the Decline of Virginia* (New York: Basic Books, 2007).
63. Ulrich Phillips, *A History of Transportation in the Eastern Cotton Belt to 1869* (New York: Octagon Books, 1958), 20, 145. First published by Columbia University Press in 1908.
64. Aaron Marrs, *Railroads in the Old South: Pursuing Progress in a Slave Society* (Baltimore: Johns Hopkins University Press, 2009), 3–6, 198.
65. See *New York Enquirer*, quoted in *New Hampshire Patriot* (Concord), June 14, 1830. Marrs, *Railroads in the Old South*, 25.
66. *Vermont Gazette* (Bennington), July 27, 1830.
67. This thesis is advanced in Edward Ayers, *What Caused the Civil War? Reflections on the South and Southern History* (New York: W.W. Norton, 2005).
68. Letter from Fayetteville dated May 13, 1830, quoted in *Raleigh Register and North Carolina Gazette*, May 20, 1830.
69. *The Southern Review*, quoted in *Greenville Mountaineer* (S.C.), May 28, 1831.
70. *Richmond Enquirer*, June 24, 1831.
71. Ibid., August 9, 1831.
72. Ibid., November 15, 1831.

73. *Virginia Free Press and Farmers' Repository* (Charlestown, W.V.), December 15, 1831.
74. *Richmond Enquirer*, January 12, 1832.
75. *Huntsville Advocate*, quoted in *Greenville Mountaineer* (S.C.), July 2, 1831.
76. *Carolina Observer* (Raleigh, N.C.), January 11, 1832.
77. Ibid., March 20, 1832.
78. *Milledgeville Recorder*, quoted in *Berkshire Journal* (Lennox, Mass.), June 28, 1831.
79. *Baltimore Patriot,* June 24, 1829.
80. Ibid., January 21, 1830.
81. *The Southern Review*, quoted in *Greenville Mountaineer* (S.C.), May 28, 1831. *Newport Mercury* (R.I.), June 25, 1831, reported a boiler explosion on *Best Friend.* The definitive source on early locomotives is John H. White, *American Locomotives: An Engineering History, 1830–1880* (Baltimore: Johns Hopkins University Press, 1968).
82. *United States Telegraph* (Washington, D.C.), July 2, 1831.
83. *Albany Argus*, quoted in *Sun* (Pittsfield, Mass.), August 18, 1831. *New York Spectator,* September 2, 13, 1831.
84. *Charleston City Gazette*, quoted in *Baltimore Patriot*, October 4, 1831. *Fredericktown Herald*, quoted in *Baltimore Patriot*, December 5, 1831.
85. *Daily National Intelligencer*, quoted in *Baltimore Patriot*, October 3, 1831.
86. *New York Evening Post*, quoted in *Daily National Intelligencer* (Washington, D.C.), June 29, 1831.
87. *Charleston City Gazette*, quoted in *Baltimore Patriot*, October 4, 1831.
88. *The Southern Patriot* (Charleston), August 10, 1833.
89. *The Southern Patriot* (Charleston), May 16, 1832.
90. *Augusta Courier*, quoted in *The Floridian* (Tallahassee), June 12, 1832.
91. *The Southern Patriot* (Charleston), June 7, 1838.
92. *Greenville Mountaineer* (S.C.), October 13, 1832.
93. *Georgia Telegraph* (Macon), November 7, 1832.
94. *Charleston Mercury*, quoted in *Fayetteville Observer* (N.C.), May 14, 1833.
95. Phillips, *A History of Transportation*, 155–156.
96. *Charleston Courier*, quoted in *Richmond Enquirer*, May 31, 1833.
97. Phillips, *History of Transportation*, 145.
98. *New York Spectator*, August 15, 1833.
99. Smeaton, quoted in *Richmond Enquirer*, July 15, 1833.
100. *Baltimore American*, quoted in *Fayetteville Observer*, September 10, 1833.
101. *Fayetteville Observer* (N.C.), September 10, 1833.
102. *Richmond Enquirer*, May 30, 1834.
103. *The Southern Patriot* (Charleston), May 24, 1834.
104. *New London Gazette and General Advertiser* (Conn.), August 27, 1834.
105. *The Southern Patriot* (Charleston), April 9, 1835.
106. Ibid., May 23, 1834.
107. *The Globe* (Washington, D.C.), September 26, 1833.
108. *Georgia Telegraph* (Macon), August 18, 1836.
109. *Baltimore American*, quoted in *Fayetteville Observer* (N.C.), September 10, 1833.
110. Quoted in *Raleigh Register and North Carolina Gazette*, June 24, 1834.
111. *New York Times*, quoted in *Daily National Intelligencer*, October 5, 1835.
112. *Columbia Telescope* (S.C.), September 20, 1834.
113. *The Mississippian* (Jackson), October 31, 1834.

114. *Virginia Free Press* (Charlestown, W.V.), November 13, 1834.

115. *Virginia Free Press and Farmers' Repository* (Charlestown, W.V.), August 22, 1833.

116. Richmond, quoted in *Virginia Free Press and Farmers' Repository* (Charlestown, W.V.), November 14, 1833.

117. *The Mississippian* (Jackson), January 30, 1835.

118. Quoted in *Raleigh Register and North Carolina Gazette*, November 12, 1833.

CHAPTER 3: NETWORK

1. *Albany Argus*, quoted in *New Hampshire Statesman and State Journal* (Concord), June 2, 1832.

2. *New York Spectator*, January 6, 1834.

3. *Boston Courier*, December 2, 1833.

4. Ibid., December 19, 1833. *Poulson's Philadelphia Advertiser*, quoted in *Salem Gazette* (Mass.), July 31, 1835.

5. Philip Nicklin, *A Pleasant Peregrination Through the Prettiest Parts of Pennsylvania* (Philadelphia: Grigg and Elliott, 1836), 120.

6. Solomon W. Roberts, "Reminiscences of the First Railroad over the Allegheny Mountain," *The Pennsylvania Magazine of History and Biography*, vol. 2, no. 4 (1878), 370–373.

7. Letter from Pittsburgh, quoted in *Daily National Intelligencer* (Washington, D.C.), November 3, 1834.

8. *Poulson's Philadelphia Advertiser*, quoted in *Salem Gazette* (Mass.), July 31, 1835.

9. "JBW" in *Daily Cleveland Herald*, September 2, 1835.

10. *Philadelphia Commercial Herald*, quoted in *Farmers' Gazette* (Amherst, N.H.), November 21, 1834.

11. *Wheeling Gazette*, quoted in *The Globe* (Washington, D.C.), October 8, 1835.

12. A.D. Jones, *Illinois and the West: With a Township Map, Containing the Latest Surveys and Improvements* (Boston: Weeks, Jordan, 1838), 17.

13. Solomon Roberts, *An Account of the Portage Rail Road: Over the Allegheny Mountain, in Pennsylvania* (Philadelphia: N. Kite, 1836), 11.

14. John Majewski, *A House Dividing: Economic Development in Pennsylvania and Virginia Before the Civil War* (Cambridge: Cambridge University Press, 2000), 118.

15. Lorett Treese, *Railroads of Pennsylvania: Fragments of the Past in the Keystone Landscape* (Mechanicsburg, Pa.: Stackpole Books, 2003), 12–13.

16. *Saturday Evening Post* (Philadelphia), quoted in *Arkansas Gazette* (Little Rock), May 8, 1833.

17. *Niles' Weekly Register*, quoted in *The Southern Patriot* (Charleston), June 26, 1833.

18. *U.S. Gazette*, quoted in *Boston Courier*, June 14, 1832.

19. *Daily National Intelligencer* (Washington, D.C.), January 2, 1832. *Philadelphia Sentinel*, quoted in *Richmond Enquirer*, January 5, 1832.

20. *Philadelphia Gazette*, quoted in *Rhode Island American and Gazette* (Providence), March 2, 1832.

21. *Baltimore Patriot*, November 8, 1831. John Thomas Sharf, *History of Delaware, 1609–1888* (Philadelphia: L.J. Richards, 1880), 1:428–429. *Daily National Intelligencer* (Washington, D.C.), August 27, 1833.

22. "An Eye Witness" in *National Gazette*, quoted in *Boston Courier*, April 16, 1832.

23. *Boston Courier*, July 4, 1832.

24. *Daily National Intelligencer* (Washington, D.C.), August 27, 1833.
25. *New Hampshire Sentinel*, January 15, 1830.
26. *New York Spectator*, January 29, 1830. *Baltimore Patriot*, January 29, 1830. *Buffalo Journal*, quoted in *Scioto Gazette* (Chillicothe, Ohio), February 10, 1830.
27. Franklin, quoted in *Mechanics' Free Press* (Philadelphia), April 10, 1830.
28. B.F. Wells, quoted in *Providence Patriot and Columbia Phenix* (Providence, R.I.), December 21, 1833.
29. *New York Spectator*, May 31, 1831.
30. Ibid., June 3, 1831. *Rhode Island American and Gazette* (Providence), June 7, 1831.
31. *New London Gazette and General Advertiser* (Conn.), March 7, 1832.
32. *Baltimore Patriot*, January 20, 1830.
33. Ibid.
34. *New York Enquirer*, quoted in *Baltimore Patriot*, February 5, 1830.
35. "T" in *New York Herald*, February 5, 1830.
36. *Baltimore Patriot*, April 5, 1830.
37. Ibid., August 6, 26, 1830. *New York Herald*, July 31, 1830. *Eastern Argus* (Portland, Me.), August 23, 1831.
38. *Albany Argus*, quoted in *New York Spectator*, July 29, 1831.
39. *Albany Daily Advertiser*, quoted in *New York Spectator*, September 13, 1831.
40. *Albany Daily Advertiser*, quoted in *Watch-Tower* (Cooperstown, N.Y.), October 3, 1831.
41. *Salem Gazette* (Mass.), September 13, 1831.
42. *Troy Sentinel*, quoted in *New York Spectator*, August 2, 1831. *Baltimore Patriot*, July 18, 1831. *New York Spectator*, November 1, 1831.
43. "A Merchant," quoted in *New York Mercury*, November 16, 1831.
44. Edward Hungerford, *Men of Erie: A Story of Human Effort* (New York: Random House, 1946), 19, 109.
45. *New York Herald*, September 15, 1836.
46. Ibid., November 7, 1837.
47. Dilts, *The Great Road*, 380.
48. Eleazar Lord, *A Historical Review of the New York and Erie Railroad* (New York: Mason Bros., 1855), 16. Biographical background on Lord is in Hungerford, *Men of Erie*, 17–19.
49. *New York Spectator*, January 31, 1832.
50. *Salem Gazette* (Mass.), February 24, 1832.
51. Quoted in *Vermont Patriot and State Gazette* (Montpelier), August 6, 1832.
52. Hungerford, *Men of Erie*, 20.
53. Lord, *Historical Review*, 16–36.
54. *New York American*, quoted in *Vermont State Paper* (St. Albans), December 1, 1835.
55. *New York Times*, quoted in *Vermont Patriot and State Gazette* (Montpelier), June 6, 1836.
56. *New York Spectator*, November 12, 1835.
57. *Newport Mercury* (R.I.), November 14, 1835.
58. *New York Spectator*, November 26, 1835.
59. *Boston Commercial Gazette*, quoted in *Commercial Bulletin and Missouri Literary Register* (St. Louis), November 20, 1835.

60. *Buffalo Journal*, quoted in *New York Spectator*, November 26, 1835.
61. *New York Herald*, December 1, 1835.
62. Ibid., December 23, 1835.
63. *New York Spectator*, November 12, 1835.
64. *National Banner and Nashville Whig* (Nashville, Tenn.), March 23, 1836.
65. L. Ray Gunn, *The Decline of Authority: Public Economic Policy and Political Development in New York, 1800–1860* (Ithaca: Cornell University Press, 1988), 1, 9, 10, 23.
66. *Poughkeepsie Journal*, quoted in *New York Spectator*, October 20, 1836.
67. Lord, *Historical Review*, 37.
68. *New York Spectator*, March 15, 1838. *Sun* (Baltimore), April 24, 1838.
69. *Richmond Enquirer*, April 5, 1838.
70. Lord, *Historical Review*, 40–42, 60–64.
71. Henry Flint, *The Railroads of the United States: Their History and Statistics . . .* (Philadelphia: John E. Potter, 1868), 175–176.
72. Lord, *Historical Review*, 107, 128.
73. *Pittsfield Sun*, October 1, 1835.
74. *New York Journal of Commerce*, quoted in *Richmond Enquirer*, October 20, 1835.
75. *New Hampshire Gazette*, (Portsmouth), October 6, 1835.
76. *Boston Atlas*, February 12, 1838.
77. *Pennsylvania Inquirer and Daily Courier*, December 21, 1838.
78. *Pittsfield Sun* (Mass.), May 24, 1838.
79. *Georgia Journal*, quoted in *Richmond Enquirer*, August 7, 1829.
80. *Georgia Telegraph* (Macon), November 6, 1834.
81. Milton Heath, *Constructive Liberalism: The Role of the State in Economic Development in Georgia to 1860* (Cambridge: Harvard University Press, 1954), 1, 14.
82. J.B. Davis, quoted in *Augusta Chronicle* (Ga.), December 31, 1825.
83. *Georgia Telegraph* (Macon), May 7, 1838.
84. Phillips, *Transportation in the Eastern Cotton Belt*, 258–272, 303, 307, 309.
85. Heath, *Constructive Liberalism*, 233–239, 258, 290.
86. Quoted in *Greenville Mountaineer* (S.C.), November 15, 1834.
87. *Savannah Republican*, quoted in *Georgia Telegraph* (Macon), April 16, 1835.
88. *Daily National Intelligencer*, October 5, 1836.
89. *Georgia Telegraph* (Macon), September 17, 1835.
90. *Georgia Telegraph* (Macon), June 30, 1836.
91. Phillips, *History of Transportation in the Eastern Cotton Belt*, 189, 230.
92. *Fayetteville Observer* (N.C.), January 19, 1837.
93. *Daily Cleveland Herald*, January 20, 1837.
94. *Virginia Free Press* (Charlestown, W.V.), April 20, 1837. *Telegraph and Texas Register* (Houston), September 16, 1837.
95. *Georgia Telegraph* (Macon), April 23, 1838.
96. Ibid., May 7, 1838.
97. *Boston Courier*, December 31, 1838.
98. *U.S. Gazette*, quoted in *Daily National Intelligencer*, February 19, 1839.
99. Majewski, *A House Dividing*, 128.
100. *United States Telegraph* (Washington, D.C.), August 19, 1833.
101. *Richmond Whig*, quoted in *Richmond Enquirer*, April 18, 1837.
102. *New York Spectator*, April 16, 1838.
103. *Petersburg Times*, quoted in *Carolina Observer* (Fayetteville, N.C.), October 30, 1832.

104. *Daily National Intelligencer* (Washington, D.C.), quoted in *Connecticut Mirror* (Hartford), November 24, 1832.

105. *Petersburg Intelligencer*, quoted in *Richmond Enquirer*, December 4, 1832.

106. "Z" in *Petersburg Intelligencer*, quoted in *Richmond Enquirer*, February 16, 1833.

107. *Lynchburg Virginian*, May 13, 1833.

108. *Scottsville Farmer*, quoted in *Richmond Enquirer*, December 4, 1832.

109. "Henry" in *Richmond Enquirer*, May 17, 1833.

110. *Raleigh Register and North Carolina Gazette*, July 2, 1833.

111. *Richmond Whig*, quoted in *Ohio Statesman* (Columbus), October 9, 1838.

112. *Richmond Enquirer*, August 9, 1833.

113. *Connecticut Courant* (Hartford), October 28, 1833.

114. *Daily National Intelligencer* (Washington, D.C.), January 20, 1834.

115. *Boston Investigator*, January 31, 1834.

116. *The Mississippian* (Jackson), October 3 and November 1, 1834.

117. *The Floridian* (Tallahassee), May 31, 1834. There is mention of a Pacific railroad in *Salem Gazette*, October 13, 1835.

118. *New York Spectator*, October 7 1833. D.A. Smith in *Fayetteville Observer* (N.C.), September 16, 1834.

CHAPTER 4: DEFAULT

1. *Cleveland Daily Herald*, March 31, 1843.

2. "J.T.C.," quoted in *New York Herald*, December 3, 1843.

3. L. Ray Gunn, *The Decline of Authority: Public Economic Policy and Political Development in New York, 1800–1860* (Ithaca: Cornell University Press, 1988), 146–153, 159.

4. Quoted in *Wisconsin Enquirer* (Madison), May 6, 1840.

5. *Knickerbocker*, quoted in *Wisconsin Enquirer* (Madison), May 6, 1840.

6. *An Article on the Debts of States* (Cambridge: Metcalf, Keith and Nichols, Printers, 1844), 7.

7. *New Hampshire Sentinel* (Keene), April 6, 1837.

8. *Farmers' Cabinet* (Amherst, N.H.), April 14, 1837.

9. *Richmond Enquirer*, June 27, 1837.

10. *Portsmouth Journal of Literature and Politics* (N.H.), October 20, 1838. *Arkansas State Gazette* (Little Rock), June 19, 1839.

11. *Madisonian* (Washington, D.C.), August 19, 1837.

12. *New York Herald*, May 3, 1837.

13. Ibid., January 1, 1842.

14. "B," quoted in *Daily National Intelligencer*, January 9, 1837.

15. *Daily Cleveland Herald* (Ohio), January 20, 1837.

16. *Salem Gazette* (Mass.), March 17, 1837.

17. Quoted in *Richmond Enquirer*, April 18, 1837.

18. *Arkansas State Gazette* (Little Rock), June 6, 1837.

19. *Richmond Enquirer*, June 27, 1837.

20. Quoted in *Virginia Free Press* (Charleston, W.V.), August 3, 1837.

21. Gunn, *Decline of Authority*, 26–28.

22. *Madisonian* (Washington, D.C.), August 19, 1837.

23. *Baltimore American*, quoted in *Daily National Intelligencer* (Washington, D.C.), September 8, 1837.

24. *Ohio Statesman* (Columbus), October 11, 1839.

25. Ibid., October 30, 1839.

26. *New Yorker*, quoted in *Ohio State Journal* (Columbus), November 6, 1839.

27. "C," quoted in *Boston Courier*, March 11, 1841.

28. *Merchant's Magazine*, quoted in *Barre Gazette* (Mass.), May 15, 1840.

29. *North American and Daily Advertiser* (Philadelphia), June 10, 1840.

30. *The Mississippian* (Jackson), October 9, 1840.

31. *Ohio Statesman* (Columbus), November 20, 1839.

32. *Portsmouth Journal of Literature and Politics* (N.H.), October 20, 1838.

33. *New Hampshire Patriot and State Gazette* (Concord), January 8, 1840.

34. *Sun* (Pittsfield, Mass.), May 7, 1840.

35. *Hunt's Merchant's Magazine*, quoted in *Barre Gazette* (Mass.), May 15, 1840.

36. *Morning Herald* (New York), May 25, 1840.

37. *New York Spectator*, August 1, 1839.

38. *Morning Herald* (New York), May 4, 1839.

39. *Ohio Statesman* (Columbus), October 11, 1839.

40. Ibid., October 30, 1839.

41. *Virginia Free Press* (Charlestown, W.V.), January 31, 1839.

42. *Boston Daily Atlas*, quoted in *Portsmouth Journal of Literature and Politics* (N.H.), April 13, 1839.

43. Quoted in *Wisconsin Enquirer* (Madison), October 26, 1839.

44. "Aristides," letter from Alton Illinois, February 4, 1840, quoted in *Boston Courier*, February 27, 1840.

45. *Wisconsin Enquirer* (Madison), November 7, 1840.

46. *Louisville Public Advertiser*, January 14, 1841.

47. *Daily National Intelligencer* (Washington, D.C.), January 7, 1840.

48. Letter from Frederick County, Maryland, March 20, 1843, quoted in *The Southern Patriot* (Charleston), March 29, 1843.

49. *Charleston Mercury*, February 13, 1840.

50. *Virginia Free Press* (Charleston, W.V.), March 26, 1840.

51. *North American and Daily Advertiser* (Philadelphia), April 18, 1840.

52. *The Charleston Mercury*, June 1, 1843. *The Southern Patriot* (Charleston), May 30, 1843.

53. Sidney Smith, quoted in *Hartford Daily Courant*, November 30, 1843.

54. *Harrisburg Intelligencer*, quoted in *Boston Daily Atlas*, August 17, 1841.

55. *Daily National Intelligencer*, March 27, 1840.

56. *North American and Daily Advertiser* (Philadelphia), June 8, 1840.

57. *Boston Daily Atlas*, April 1, 1843.

58. *St. Augustine Herald*, quoted in *Louisville Public Advertiser*, January 5, 1841.

59. *Raleigh Register*, quoted in *Southern Patriot* (Charleston, S.C.), January 20, 1843.

60. *The Mississippian* (Jackson), October 9, 1840.

61. *Correspondence to Richmond Whig*, quoted in *Emancipator and Free American* (New York), February 23, 1843.

62. *Raleigh Register and North-Carolina Gazette*, November 13, 1840.

63. *Georgia Telegraph* (Macon), December 1, 1840.

64. *Boston Daily Atlas*, January 11, 1842.

65. *Sun* (Pittsfield, Mass.), May 19, 1842. *Daily National Intelligencer*, May 20, 1842.

66. *Daily National Intelligencer*, May 20, 1842.

67. *Emancipator and Republican* (Boston), March 8, 1849.
68. *New Hampshire Patriot and State Gazette* (Concord), October 19, 1840.
69. *Cleveland Daily Herald*, November 13, 1840.
70. *New York Herald*, September 26, 1844.
71. *Daily National Intelligencer* (Washington, D.C.), December 7, 1843. *Boston Herald*, March 8, 1849.
72. *Hudson River Chronicle* (Sing Sing, N.Y.), May 24, 1842.
73. Howard Bloom, *The Genius of the Beast: A Radical Re-vision of Capitalism* (Amherst, N.Y.: Prometheus, 2010), 113–114.
74. *Cleveland Daily Herald*, March 31, 1843.
75. *Sun* (Baltimore), April 20, 1843.

CHAPTER 5: RIDING THE RAILS

1. *European Delineation of American Character, as Contained in a Letter from a Foreign Traveller in New York, to His Friend in London. . . .* (New York: Printed for the Booksellers, J. Gray, 1820), 522.
2. *Daily National Intelligencer*, quoted in *Baltimore Patriot*, October 3, 1831.
3. *Poulson's American Daily Advertiser*, quoted in *Hazard's Register of Pennsylvania*, vol. 10, no. 6 (October 20, 1832), 247–248.
4. *Philadelphian*, quoted in *Hazard's Register of Pennsylvania*, vol. 10, no. 19 (November 10, 1832), 304.
5. Extensive reports on coal prospects and mining railroads are quoted in *Hazard's Register of Pennsylvania*, vol. 11, no. 8 (February 23, 1833), 122, and vol. 11, no. 16 (April 20, 1833), 247. Ibid., vol. 11, no. 19, 206–297, contains a list of all fourteen Pennsylvania railroads operating in the spring of 1833.
6. *New York Constellation*, quoted in *Hazard's Register of Pennsylvania*, vol. 10, no. 20 (November 17, 1832), 319.
7. *Hazard's Register of Pennsylvania*, vol. 13, no. 15 (April 12, 1834), 230.
8. Ibid., vol. 14, no. 9 (August 30, 1834), 136.
9. *Germantown Telegraph*, quoted in ibid., vol. 16, no. 9 (August 29, 1835), 134.
10. *Boston Daily Mail*, quoted in *New Hampshire Sentinel* (Keene), January 7, 1846.
11. *Frank Leslie's Illustrated Newspaper*, January 14, 1860, 104.
12. *Chicago Daily Tribune*, June 2, 1854, and July 13, 1855.
13. John Dagget, *Remarks and Documents Concerning the Location of the Boston and Providence Rail-road Through the Burying Ground in East Attleborough . . .* (Boston: Printed by Light & Horton, 1834), 17, 26, 28.
14. Michel Chevalier, *Society, Manners, and Politics in the United States, Being a Series of Letters on North America* (Boston: Weeks, Jordan, 1839), 286–287.
15. Eliza Steele, *A Summer Journey in the West* (New York: J.S. Taylor, 1841), 25–26.
16. Alexander Mackay, *The Western World, or, Travels in the United States in 1846–1847 Exhibiting Them in Their Latest Development, Social, Political and Industrial: Including a Chapter on California* (London: R. Bentley, 1849), 1:34.
17. *Salem Gazette*, October 23, 1835.
18. "J.H.," quoted in *Boston Courier*, July 18, 1839.
19. *Boston Courier*, quoted in *Newport Mercury*, April 25, 1835.
20. *Portsmouth Journal of Literature and Politics* (N.H.), July 2, 1836.

21. Mary Duncan, *America as I Found It* (New York: R. Carter & Bros., 1852), 379.

22. *New Haven Palladium*, quoted in *Constitution* (Middletown, Conn.), August 17, 1859.

23. *Boston Herald*, September 17, 1855.

24. *New York Herald*, September 22, 1841.

25. Mackay, *The Western World*, 1:122.

26. "Viator," quoted in *Hazard's Register of Pennsylvania*, vol. 14, no. 18 (November 1, 1834), 277–278.

27. Dickens, *American Notes*, 107.

28. Frederika Bremer, *The Homes of the New World: Impressions of America . . .* (New York: Harper & Brothers, 1853), 1:48, 539.

29. Freeman Hunt, *Letters About the Hudson River: And Its Vicinity: Written in 1835 & 1836* (New York: F. Hunt, 1835), 79–81.

30. *Emancipator and Weekly Chronicle* (New York), June 11, 1845.

31. *Georgia Telegraph* (Macon), May 6, 1856.

32. Mackay, *The Western World*, 1:56. Segregation of the railroads will await full discussion in Chapter 12.

33. Mrs. [Matilda Charlotte] Houston, *Hesperos, or, Travels in the West* (London: J.W. Parker, 1850), 1:33.

34. Charles Lyell, *A Second Visit to the United States of North America* (London: J. Murray, 1849), 2:339. Lyell quoted Edward Everett to the effect that a literature could not be called cheap when it started by "costing a man his eyes, and ends by perverting his taste and morals."

35. Duncan, *America as I Found It*, 380.

36. Hugo Reid, *Sketches in North America; with Some Account of Congress and of the Slavery Question* (London: Longman, Green, Longman & Roberts, 1861), 13, 23–24, 28–29.

37. *New York Journal of Commerce*, quoted in *Hartford Daily Courant* (Conn.), July 19, 1850.

38. *New York Daily Times*, January 1, 1852.

39. *New York Daily Times*, August 28, 1852.

40. *Baltimore American*, quoted in *Daily National Intelligencer* (Washington, D.C.), June 24, 1857.

41. *Boston Herald*, April 27, 1853.

42. *New York Times*, March 25, 1859.

43. Houston, *Hesperos*, 1:34.

44. *Delaware Journal*, quoted in *Milwaukee Daily Sentinel and Gazette*, July 20, 1850.

45. *Sun* (Baltimore), July 21, 1842.

46. William Ferguson, *America by River and Rail, or Notes by the Way on the New World and Its People* (London: J. Nisbet, 1856), 223.

47. William Chambers, *Things as They Are in America* (Philadelphia: Lippincott, Grambo, 1854), 49, 51.

48. Chevalier, *Society, Manners, and Politics in the United States*, 286.

49. Maxwell, Archibald, *A Run Through the United States: During the Autumn of 1840* (London: H. Coborn, 1841), 1:200.

50. *New York Daily Times*, June 10, 1857.

51. Quoted in *Daily Picayune* (New Orleans), December 26, 1844.

52. "JEC," quoted in *Charleston Mercury*, August 3, 1849.

53. Mackay, *The Western World*, 1:192.

54. Granley Berkeley, *The English Sportsman in the Western Prairies* (London: Hurst & Blackett, 1861), 94.

55. Mackay, *The Western World,* 1:150–151.

56. Berkeley, *The English Sportsman,* 59.

57. Mackay, *The Western World*, 1:146.

58. Marryat, *A Diary in America*, 2:72.

59. Harriet Martineau, *Society in America* (New York: Saunders and Otley, 1837), 2:8.

60. Mackay, *The Western World*, 1:34, 57.

61. Lyell, *A Second Visit to the United States,* 1:234.

62. Mackay, *The Western World,* 2:201. For cholera, see *Journal of Commerce*, quoted in *Hartford Daily Courant*, July 21, 1849.

63. The classic call for reform in railroad health practices was Samuel Crumbine, *Frontier Doctor* (Philadelphia: Dorrance, 1948), 164 ff.

64. *Daily True Delta* (New Orleans), May 5, 1861.

65. Bremer, *The Homes of the New World* (New York: Harper & Brother, 1853), 2:598.

66. Steele, *A Summer Journey,* 26.

67. Francis Lieber, *The Stranger in America, or Letters to a Gentleman in Germany: Comprising Sketches of the Manners, Society, and National Peculiarities of the United States* (Philadelphia: Carey, Lea & Blanchard, 1835), 181.

68. Martineau, *Society in America,* 2:9.

69. Letter from Bluff Glen, quoted in *Daily Dispatch* (Richmond), August 27, 1852.

70. Alexander Majoribanks, *Travels in South and North America* (London: Simpkin, Marshall, and Company, 1853), 295.

71. John Godley, *Letters from America* (London: Murray, 1844), 1:50.

72. J.G. Kohl, *Travels in Canada: And Through the States of New York and Pennsylvania* (London: G. Manwaring, 1861), 1:239.

73. George Combe, *Notes on the United States of North America During a Phrenological Visit in 1839–1840* (Philadelphia: Carey & Hart, 1841), 2:71.

74. *U.S. Gazette*, quoted in *United States Telegraph* (Washington, D.C.), December 6, 1836.

75. *New York Journal of Commerce*, quoted in *Daily National Intelligencer* (Washington, D.C.), January 28, 1835.

76. *Wisconsin Patriot* (Madison), May 26, 1855.

77. *New York Times,* July 9, 1859.

78. *New Hampshire Statesman and State Journal* (Concord), November 14, 1840.

79. *New York Times,* July 9, 1859.

80. *Hartford Daily Courant* (Conn.), May 4, 1853.

CHAPTER 6: THE SOULLESS CORPORATION

1. *U.S. Gazette*, quoted in *Fayetteville Observer* (N.C.), May 26, 1835.

2. *Evening Journal*, quoted in *Daily National Intelligencer* (Washington, D.C.), June 29, 1833.

3. *Connecticut Courant* (Hartford), July 25, 1836.

4. Nathaniel Hawthorne, *House of Seven Gables* (Boston: Ticknor, Reed, and Fields, 1851), 173–174.

5. Quoted in *Salem Gazette*, June 5, 1835.

6. *Salem Gazette*, June 9, 1835.
7. For the argument that people would move to Salem for cheaper rents, see *Portsmouth Journal of Literature and Politics* (N.H.), January 3, 1835.
8. Quoted in *Salem Gazette*, June 12, 1835.
9. *Salem Gazette*, June 16, 1835.
10. Ibid., June 23, 1835.
11. Ibid., July 10, 1835.
12. Quoted in *Portsmouth Journal*, July 11, 1835.
13. *Daily National Intelligencer* (Washington, D.C.), March 28, 1836.
14. "Subscriber," quoted in *Salem Gazette*, July 17, 1835.
15. *Connecticut Courant* (Hartford), July 25, 1836.
16. *Salem Gazette*, February 23, 1836.
17. Ibid., March 4, 1836.
18. *Salem Register*, quoted in Boston *Courier*, July 10, 1837. *Salem Gazette*, October 17, 1837.
19. *New York American*, quoted in *Daily National Intelligencer*, March 21, 1838. *Portsmouth Journal* (N.H.), April 28, 1838. *Salem Gazette*, June 12, 1838. The opening of the Eastern Railroad to Salem is described in *Farmers' Cabinet* (Amherst, N.H.), August 31, 1838.
20. *Salem Gazette*, August 31, 1838.
21. *Essex Gazette* (Haverhill, Mass.), June 21, 1839.
22. *New-Bedford Mercury* (Mass.), September 7, 1838.
23. Speech of George Peabody, quoted in *Salem Gazette*, September 7, 1838.
24. *Boston Post*, quoted in *Salem Gazette*, September 7, 1838.
25. Hawthorne, *House of Seven Gables*, 278–279.
26. *New Hampshire Statesman and Concord Register*, January 9, 1830.
27. *Farmers' Cabinet* (Amherst, N.H.), January 23, 1830.
28. *New Hampshire and Concord Register*, March 26, 1831.
29. *Farmers' Gazette* (Amherst, N.H.), September 19, 1834.
30. *Portsmouth Journal of Literature and Politics* (N.H.), January 3, 1835.
31. *New Hampshire Statesman and State Journal* (Concord), May 23, 1835.
32. Quoted in *New Hampshire Sentinel* (Keene), May 28, 1835.
33. *New Hampshire Gazette*, quoted in *Salem Gazette*, August 11, 1835.
34. *Salem Gazette*, February 23, 1836.
35. *Virginia Free Press* (Charlestown, W.V.), April 14, 1836.
36. *Portsmouth Journal of Literature and Politics* (N.H.), May 25, 1839.
37. Ibid., June 1, 1839.
38. *New Hampshire Gazette* (Portsmouth), June 11, 1839.
39. *Portsmouth Journal of Literature and Politics*, June 15, 1839.
40. *New Hampshire Gazette* (Portsmouth), January 14, 1840.
41. *New Hampshire Statesman and State Journal* (Concord), July 13, 1839.
42. "A Spectator," quoted in *New Hampshire Gazette* (Portsmouth), February 25, 1840.
43. *New Hampshire Gazette*, March 3, 7, 1840.
44. Quoted in *Boston Daily Atlas*, June 28, 1843.
45. The phrase is from *New Hampshire Sentinel* (Keene), June 3, 1840.
46. "W," quoted in *New Hampshire Patriot and State Gazette* (Concord), June 8, 1840.
47. *New Hampshire Patriot and State Gazette*, October 19, 1840.
48. *Portsmouth Journal of Literature and Politics*, November 14, 1840.

49. Ibid., December 12, 1840.

50. *New Hampshire Patriot and State Gazette*, October 7, 1841.

51. "AK," in *Essex Banner*, quoted in ibid., November 25, 1841.

52. *New Hampshire Patriot and State Gazette* (Concord), May 23, 1844.

53. Ibid., May 30, 1844.

54. "Hillaborough," quoted in *Farmers' Cabinet* (Amherst, N.H.), August 15, 1844.

55. See, for example, the relatively positive reaction to the building of the Concord Railroad in *New Hampshire Statesman and State Journal* (Concord), January 2, 1841.

56. *Portsmouth Journal of Literature and Politics,* October 20, 1838.

57. *New Hampshire Patriot and State Gazette* (Concord), April 24 and May 22, 1845.

58. *Albany Argus*, quoted in *New Hampshire Patriot and State Gazette*, February 12, 1841.

59. *New Hampshire Patriot and State Gazette*, May 27, 1841.

60. Ibid., January 16, 1845.

61. *Boston Daily Atlas*, April 14, 1845.

62. *Boston Journal*, quoted in *The Semi-Weekly Eagle* (Brattleboro, Vt.), September 2, 1852.

63. *New Hampshire Patriot and State Gazette*, April 24, 1845.

64. Ibid., January 8, 1847.

65. *Hartford Daily Courant*, July 3, 1845.

66. *New Hampshire Sentinel* (Keene), June 20, 1850.

67. *New York Daily Times*, January 8, 1857.

68. Henry Carey, *Beauties of the Monopoly System of New Jersey* (Philadelphia: C. Sherman, Printer, 1848), 2–3.

69. *Boston Herald,* August 9, 1850.

CHAPTER 7: SCALDED BY THE STEAM

1. *Boston Pearl*, quoted in *Boston Courier*, August 1, 1836.

2. *New Hampshire Gazette*, quoted in *Salem Gazette*, August 11, 1835.

3. *Salem Gazette*, February 19, 1836.

4. *Connecticut Courant* (Hartford), January 30, 1841.

5. *Baltimore American*, quoted in *New York Herald*, November 2, 1841.

6. *Boston Courier*, September 8, 1836.

7. *Daily Cleveland Herald*, November 2, 1855.

8. *News* (St. Louis), quoted in ibid., November 10, 1855.

9. *Daily National Intelligencer*, January 12, 1860.

10. *Philadelphia Commercial Herald*, quoted in *The Globe* (Washington, D.C.), November 12, 1833.

11. J.H. Sloan, quoted in *Daily National Intelligencer* (Washington, D.C.), November 15, 1833.

12. *Westfield Spectator* (Mass.), quoted in *Cleveland Daily Herald*, October 11, 1841.

13. *Farmers' Cabinet* (Amherst, N.H.), October 15, 1841.

14. *Boston Herald*, January 7, 1853. *Cleveland Herald*, January 8, 1853. *Boston Atlas*, quoted in *Hartford Daily Courant*, January 8, 1852.

15. *Boston Herald*, January 8, 1853.

16. *Louisville Daily Journal*, May 12, 1853. *Daily Cleveland Herald*, May 12, 1853.

17. *Boston Daily Atlas*, May 9, 1853.
18. *Daily National Intelligencer* (Washington, D.C.), May 9, 1853.
19. *Daily Cleveland Herald*, May 12, 1853.
20. *Fayetteville Observer* (N.C.), May 12, 1853.
21. *Boston Herald*, May 20, 1853.
22. *Fayetteville Observer* (N.C.), September 3, 1855.
23. "Mr. Ray," a passenger, quoted in *New York Tribune*, quoted in *Louisville Daily Journal*, September 3, 1855.
24. *Daily Picayune* (New Orleans), September 12, 1855.
25. *Charleston Mercury*, September 3, 1855.
26. *New York Herald*, September 3, 1855.
27. Ibid., September 8, 1855.
28. *Wisconsin Patriot* (Madison), May 26, 1855.
29. *New York Daily Times*, November 7, 1855.
30. *Louisville Daily Journal*, November 29, 1855.
31. *Milwaukee Daily Sentinel*, June 30, 1859.
32. Letter to editor, quoted in *Virginia Free Press* (Charleston, W.V.), July 7, 1859.
33. *Daily National Intelligencer* (Washington, D.C.)., April 10, 1840.
34. *Boston Courier*, April 8, 1841.
35. *Daily National Intelligencer*, August 8, 1843.
36. *Philadelphia Gazette*, quoted in *New London Gazette*, August 26, 1835.
37. *New York Spectator*, March 21, 1836.
38. *Sun* (Baltimore), June 2, 1838.
39. Ibid., December 2, 1842.
40. *Concord Daily Patriot*, quoted in *The Southern Patriot* (Charleston), November 21, 1842.
41. *New York Daily Times*, May 26, 1852.
42. *Newark Daily Advertiser*, quoted in *New York Spectator*, January 27, 1837.
43. *Boston Courier,* October 21, 1841.
44. *Hartford Daily Courant*, September 12, 1850.
45. *New York Daily Times*, March 20, 1852.
46. Ibid., March 26 and April 5, 1852.
47. *New York Times*, May 17, 1858.
48. *Chicago Daily Tribune*, May 18, 1858.
49. August 20, 1843.
50. *New York Herald*, August 3, 1843.
51. *Hartford Daily Courant*, August 7, 1843.
52. *New York Herald*, November 29, 1843.
53. Samuel Hammond, *Country Margins and Rambles of a Journalist* (New York: J.C. Derby, 1855), 54.
54. *New York Daily Times*, August 28, 1852.
55. *Daily Dispatch* (Richmond), August 30, 1852.
56. *Daily Picayune* (New Orleans), May 15, 1853. *New York Daily Times,* May 19, 1853.
57. *New York Herald*, May 19, 1853.
58. *Boston Herald*, May 19, 1853.
59. *North American and United States Gazette* (Philadelphia), August 19, 1853.
60. *Boston Herald*, June 3, 1853.
61. *New York Daily Times*, June 21, 1853.

62. *New York Herald*, August 13, 1853.
63. *Sun* (Baltimore), July 22, 1853.
64. *Boston Daily Atlas*, August 16, 1853.
65. Vol. 9, no. 220 (February 18, 1860), 178.
66. *Frank Leslie's Illustrated Newspaper,* January 28, 1860.
67. *Daily Evening Bulletin* (San Francisco), September 8, 1858.
68. Quoted in *Boston Courier*, April 16, 1838.
69. Quoted in *New Hampshire Statesman and State Journal* (Concord), January 4, 1840.

CHAPTER 8: THE NEAR WEST

1. Quoted in *Emancipator* (New York), June 10, 1841.
2. *Commercial Bulletin and Missouri Literary Register* (St. Louis), October 7, 1835.
3. Citizens of Cincinnati, *Rail-road from the Banks of the Ohio River to the Tide Waters of the Carolinas and Georgia* (Cincinnati: Printed by James and Gazley, 1835), 8.
4. *Daily National Intelligencer*, November 5, 1833.
5. Address by Governor, quoted in *Boston Courier*, January 1, 1835.
6. *North and West*, quoted in *The Globe* (Washington, D.C.), June 30, 1836.
7. *Indiana Journal* (Indianapolis), May 15, 1835. "Jack," quoted in ibid., July 17, 1835.
8. *Virginia Free Press* (Charlestown, W.V.), January 8, 1835. *National Banner and Nashville Whig*, February 18, 1835. *The Mississippian* (Jackson), July 1, 1836.
9. *The Globe* (Washington, D.C.), July 2, 1835.
10. *New Hampshire Gazette* (Portsmouth), October 13, 1835.
11. *The Southern Patriot* (Charleston), October 21, 1835.
12. *North American and Daily Advertiser* (Philadelphia), May 18 and September 2, 1842. *Cleveland Daily Herald*, June 2, 1842. *Daily National Intelligencer*, August 12, 1842. *North American and Daily Advertiser* (Philadelphia), August 28, 1840. The American superintendent was G.W. Whistler, father of the famous artist. The main locomotive supplier to Russia was William Norris of Philadelphia.
13. *Virginia Free Press* (Charlestown, W.V.), January 8, 1835.
14. *Cincinnati Whig*, quoted in *Salem Gazette*, December 3, 1835.
15. *New Orleans Bee*, quoted in *United States Telegraph* (Washington, D.C.), September 19, 1835.
16. *Virginia Free Press* (Charlestown, W.V.), March 9, 1835.
17. *New Orleans Commercial Bulletin*, quoted in *Nashville Banner and Nashville Whig*, July 13, 1835.
18. *Richmond Enquirer*, October 23, 1835.
19. C. Woodruff, quoted in *The Mississippian* (Jackson), February 12, 1836.
20. A railroad engineer, "Dubuque," to editors of *Iowa News*, quoted in *Milwaukee Sentinel*, January 8, 1839.
21. *New York Herald*, November 30, 1839.
22. *Richmond Whig*, quoted in *Richmond Enquirer*, April 18, 1837.
23. *Memphis Eagle*, quoted in *Charleston Mercury*, July 27, 1853.
24. *New York Journal of Commerce*, quoted in *Richmond Enquirer*, October 20, 1835.

25. "X.Y.," quoted in *Atlas* (Boston), February 12, 1838.
26. *New York Spectator*, September 23, 1840. This issue contains a complete description of the routes, purposes, and current earnings of the entire list.
27. "X.Y.," quoted in *Atlas* (Boston), February 12, 1838.
28. *New York Express*, quoted in *North American* (Philadelphia), September 20, 1839.
29. *Boston Daily Atlas*, October 5, 1839.
30. J.G. Bennett, letter from Boston, September 5, 1840, quoted in *New York Herald*, September 7, 1840.
31. *Boston Daily Atlas*, October 5, 1839.
32. Address of Everett from *Boston Morning Post,* quoted in *Boston Courier*, October 10, 1839.
33. H.A.S. Dearborn, quoted in *Boston Courier*, November 16, 1840.
34. *New Hampshire Sentinel* (Keene), November 18, 1840.
35. A stockholder, quoted in *Boston Courier*, February 10, 1840.
36. *Daily National Intelligencer*, February 13, 1840.
37. Ibid., March 27, 1840.
38. *New Hampshire Statesman and State Journal* (Concord), April 24, 1841.
39. *The North American and Daily Advertiser* (Philadelphia), May 20, 1841.
40. *Boston Daily Atlas*, June 23, 1841.
41. Ibid., February 1, 1843.
42. Ibid., October 4, 1841.
43. *New York Standard,* quoted in ibid., July 24, 1841.
44. *New York Herald,* quoted in *Barre Gazette* (Mass.), January 14, 1842.
45. *New York Spectator*, April 2, 1842.
46. *Cleveland Daily Herald*, June 7, 1842.
47. *Milwaukee Daily Sentinel*, December 10, 1845.
48. *New York Journal of Commerce,* quoted in *Boston Daily Atlas*, October 23, 1846.
49. *North American and Daily Advertiser,* (Philadelphia), August 14, 1841.
50. *New York Morning News,* quoted in *Charleston Mercury,* October 17, 1845.
51. *Farmer's Cabinet* (Amherst, N.H.), July 7, 1843.
52. *Transcript,* quoted in *Boston Daily Atlas*, October 31, 1842.
53. *Newburyport Herald,* quoted in *Emancipator and Weekly Chronicle* (Boston), April 15, 1845.
54. *New York Morning News,* quoted in *Charleston Mercury*, August 21, 1845.
55. *New York Morning News,* quoted in *Charleston Mercury*, October 17, 1845.
56. *New York Journal of Commerce,* quoted in *Boston Daily Atlas*, October 23, 1846.
57. *Boston Herald*, April 15, 1851.
58. *Daily Picayune* (New Orleans), September 27, 1851.
59. *New York Herald*, May 11, 1839.
60. *Daily Ohio State Journal* (Columbus), November 9, 1841.
61. *New York Spectator*, September 25, 1841.
62. *Daily National Intelligencer*, November 19, 1841.
63. *New York Herald*, January 1, 1842.
64. *Albany Journal,* quoted in *Cleveland Daily Herald*, January 6, 1842.
65. *New York Herald*, December 13, 1841.
66. Moses Leonard and others, quoted in *New York Spectator*, January 15, 1842.
67. "An Old Merchant," quoted in ibid., January 19, 1842.

68. "Ros," quoted in *Vermont Chronicle* (Bellows Falls), January 19, 1842.
69. New York newspaper, quoted in *Milwaukee Sentinel*, November 25, 1843. *Boston Daily Atlas,* January 18, 1844.
70. William Seward, quoted in *New York Spectator*, January 22, 1842.
71. *New York Herald*, April 25, 1842.
72. *Pittsfield Sun* (Mass.), June 2, 1842.
73. Hungerford, *Men of Erie*, 65.
74. *New York Herald*, June 4, 1842.
75. Hungerford, *Men of Erie*, 67.
76. *New York Herald*, March 8, 1844.
77. Ibid., April 21, 1844.
78. Ibid., April 26 and July 8, 1844.
79. *Cleveland Daily Herald* (Ohio), January 8, 1849.
80. *Milwaukee Sentinel and Gazette,* January 30, 1849.
81. Letter to *New Orleans Bulletin,* quoted in *Daily National Intelligencer*, May 7, 1849.
82. *New York Tribune*, quoted in *Hartford Daily Courant*, June 14, 1850.
83. *Cleveland Daily Herald* (Ohio), February 4, 1841.
84. *Buffalo Courier*, quoted in *Cleveland Daily Herald* (Ohio), February 7, 1851.
85. *Cleveland Daily Herald,* quoted in *The Ohio Observer* (Hudson), March 5, 1851.
86. *New York Tribune*, quoted in *Hartford Daily Courant*, April 3, 1851. *The Ohio Observer* (Hudson), April 23, 1851.
87. *Milwaukee Sentinel*, April 8, 1851.
88. *Cleveland Daily Herald* (Ohio), April 28, 1851.
89. *Milwaukee Sentinel*, May 12, 1851.
90. *Hartford Daily Courant*, May 27, 1851.
91. "Citizen of Virginia," quoted in *Virginia Free Press* (Charlestown, W.V.), January 31, 1839.
92. Message of Maryland governor, quoted in *Daily National Intelligencer* (Washington, D.C.), January 7, 1840.
93. *Boston Daily Atlas*, November 1, 1842.
94. *Sun* (Baltimore), November 4, 1842. *Scioto Gazette* (Chillicothe, Ohio), November 10, 1842.
95. *Louisville Daily Journal*, November 24, 1842.
96. Letter from Cumberland of April 9, 1843, quoted in *Ohio Statesman* (Columbus), April 19, 1843.
97. Quoted in *Daily National Intelligencer* (Washington, D.C.), October 12, 1843.
98. *Buffalo Commercial Advertiser*, quoted in ibid., October 13, 1843.
99. *Scioto Gazette* (Chillicothe, Ohio), July 10, 1845.
100. Pittsburgh newspaper, quoted in *New York Herald*, August 22, 1845. *The North American* (Philadelphia), January 11, 1847. *The Ohio Observer* (Hudson), January 13, 1847. *Scioto Gazette* (Chillicothe, Ohio), September 19, 1844.
101. Quoted in *Louisville Daily Journal*, August 24, 1850. For a list of Georgia railroads, see *Savannah Daily Republican*, January 25, 1851.
102. *Missouri Courier* (Hannibal), April 24, 1851.
103. A good account of one of Swann's speeches is in *Sun* (Baltimore), June 30, 1852.
104. *Daily Ohio Statesman* (Columbus), August 30, 1852. *Cleveland Daily Herald*, December 24, 1852.

105. *Baltimore American,* quoted in *Daily Ohio State Journal* (Columbus), December 28, 1852.
106. *Louisville Daily Journal,* January 26, 1853.
107. *Cincinnati Gazette,* quoted in *Memphis Daily Appeal,* January 26, 1853.
108. *Boston Herald,* February 19, 1853.

CHAPTER 9: SOUTHERN STRATEGY

1. Phillips, *History of Transportation,* 168–190. *Greenville Mountaineer* (N.C.), January 5, 1838.
2. *The Mississippian,* quoted in *National Banner and Nashville Whig,* February 18, 1835.
3. *New Orleans Bee,* quoted in *The Globe* (Washington, D.C.), April 24, 1835.
4. *The Southern Patriot* (Charleston), May 12, 1835.
5. "R," quoted in *Richmond Enquirer,* May 15, 1835. *The Globe* (Washington, D.C.), April 24, 1835.
6. *New Orleans Bee,* quoted in *United States Telegraph,* September 19, 1835.
7. *New Hampshire Gazette* (Portsmouth), October 20, 1835.
8. *The Mississippian* (Jackson), January 30, 1835.
9. *Richmond Enquirer,* May 22, 1835.
10. *The Mississippian* (Jackson), quoted in *The Floridian* (Tallahassee), October 17, 1835.
11. Letter from "Botetourt," Salem, Va., August 1, 1835, quoted in *National Banner and Nashville Whig,* October 23, 1835.
12. "Fiat Justitia," quoted in *The Mississippi Free Trader and Natchez Gazette,* October 27, 1835.
13. *The Mississippian* (Jackson), January 29, 1836.
14. *Vicksburg Register,* quoted in *The Mississippian* (Jackson), January 29, 1836.
15. C. Woodruff, *Circular to the Citizens of the State of Mississippi,* quoted in *The Mississippian* (Jackson), February 12, 1836.
16. *Vicksburg Register,* quoted in *The Mississippian* (Jackson), February 12, 1836.
17. *The Mississippian* (Jackson), February 19, 1836.
18. William Darby, quoted in *Daily National Intelligencer,* February 25 and May 16, 1836.
19. *New Orleans Bee,* quoted in *National Banner and Nashville Whig,* October 28, 1836.
20. *New Orleans Standard,* quoted in *Arkansas State Gazette* (Little Rock), December 6, 1836.
21. *The Mississippian* (Jackson), July 1, 1836.
22. *The Southern Patriot* (Charleston), October 20, 1835.
23. Ibid., October 21, 1835.
24. *Daily National Intelligencer* (Washington, D.C.), October 5, 1836.
25. *The Southern Patriot* (Charleston), October 21, 1835. *New York Spectator,* October 19, 1835.
26. *Cincinnati Evening Post,* quoted in *The Mississippi Free Trader and Natchez Gazette,* February 12, 1836.
27. *Salem Gazette* (Mass.), January 29, 1836.
28. *The Mississippian* (Jackson), quoted in *The Floridian* (Tallahassee), October 17, 1835.
29. *Kanawha Banner,* quoted in *Daily National Intelligencer,* April 7, 1836.

30. William Darby, quoted in *Daily National Intelligencer* (Washington, D.C.), May 16, 1836.
31. *Daily National Intelligencer* (Washington, D.C.), October 5, 1836.
32. *Greenville Mountaineer* (N.C.), January 5, 1838.
33. *Columbia Telescope* (S.C.), March 17, 1838.
34. Letter from Hayne to editor of *Cincinnati Post*, July 21, 1838, quoted in *Daily Commercial Bulletin* (St. Louis), August 13, 1838.
35. *New Bedford Mercury* (Mass.), August 17, 1838.
36. *Columbia Telescope* (S.C.), March 17, 1838.
37. Letter from "Wetumka Alabama," quoted in *Richmond Enquirer*, March 20, 1838.
38. *Emancipator* (Boston), September 20, 1838.
39. "Old South," quoted in *Richmond Enquirer*, October 23, 1838.
40. *Fayetteville Observer*, October 2, 1839.
41. *Boston Courier*, October 10, 1839.
42. Phillips, *A History of Transportation*, 218–219.
43. J. Crawford, President, Annual Report, quoted in *Georgia Telegraph* (Macon), December 1, 1840. *United States Telegraph,* January 7, 1837.
44. Phillips, *A History of Transportation*, 303, 318. Milton Heath, *Constructive Liberalism: The Role of the State in Economic Development in Georgia to 1860* (Cambridge: Harvard University Press, 1954), 271.
45. Heath, *Constructive Liberalism*, 277, 292.
46. "A Subscriber," quoted in *Savannah Georgian*, quoted in *Georgia Telegraph* (Macon), December 10, 1839.
47. *Georgia Telegraph* (Macon), April 23, 1838.
48. *Southern Recorder*, quoted in ibid., May 25, 1841.
49. Clinton, quoted in *Charleston Mercury,* October 18, 1843.
50. *Georgia Telegraph* (Macon), September 10, 1844.
51. *Marietta Hellicon*, quoted in *Weekly Nashville Union*, April 1, 1846.
52. *The Whig* (Jonesborough, Tenn.), June 2, 1841.
53. *Mississippi Free Trader and Natchez Daily Gazette*, July 31, 1843.
54. *Memphis Daily Appeal*, January 26, 1855.
55. *Louisville Daily Journal*, January 14, 17, 19, 1856.
56. *Philadelphia North American*, quoted in *Georgia Telegraph* (Macon), May 23, 1848.
57. "Anti-Debt," quoted in *Charleston Mercury*, October 21, 1847.
58. Ibid., October 23, 1847.
59. Ibid., October 25, 1847.
60. Ibid., October 27, 1847.
61. Ibid., October 30, 1847.
62. "No Alarmist," quoted in ibid., November 18, 1847.
63. Beaufort, quoted in *Charleston Mercury,* July 11, 1855. *Charleston Mercury,* February 25, 1858.
64. "Anti-Debt," quoted in *Charleston Mercury,* November 26 and December 4, 1847.
65. *Charleston Mercury*, February 2, 19, 1848.
66. *Daily Picayune* (New Orleans), June 3, 1855.
67. Ibid., October 12, 1851.
68. *Daily Dispatch* (Richmond), January 28, 1853.
69. *Louisville Daily Journal*, July 19, 1849.

70. "Ocmulgee," quoted in *Savannah Daily Republican*, May 24, 1851.

71. *Georgia Telegraph* (Macon), March 1, 1853.

72. *Daily Picayune* (New Orleans), November 17, 1855.

73. *Louisville Daily Journal*, November 26, 1855.

74. *Georgia Telegraph* (Macon), June 3, 1856. *Raleigh Register* (N.C.), February 15, 1860. *Charleston Courier*, March 29, 1860.

75. *Daily Cleveland Herald*, October 18, 1856. *New York Daily Times*, November 4, 1845.

76. *Richmond Examiner*, quoted in *New York Herald*, August 30, 1847.

77. *Texas State Gazette* (Austin), June 9, 1855.

78. *Daily Columbus Enquirer* (Ga.), May 5, 1860.

79. *The Constitution* (Washington, D.C.), May 16, 1860.

CHAPTER 10: THE PRAIRIE AND THE RIVER

1. *Milwaukee Sentinel*, February 12, 1842.

2. *Milwaukee Daily Sentinel*, January 23, 1845.

3. *Milwaukee Daily Sentinel and Gazette*, March 6, 1848.

4. *Ohio Statesman* (Columbus), August 27, 1845.

5. *Indiana Journal* (Indianapolis), October 23, 1835.

6. For the career of Cairo, see Herman Lantz, *A Community in Search of Itself: A Case History of Cairo, Illinois* (Carbondale: Southern Illinois University Press, 1972).

7. *Boston Courier*, March 7, 1836.

8. *Baltimore Chronicle,* quoted in *Commercial Bulletin and Literary Register* (St. Louis), March 30, 1836.

9. *Scioto Gazette* (Chillicothe, Ohio), June 24, 1835.

10. *Daily National Intelligencer*, October 8, 1835. Letter, John Jones to General Assembly of Ohio, February 27, 1843, quoted in *Ohio State Journal* (Columbus), June 7, 1843.

11. *Southern Times and State Gazette* (Columbia, S.C.), October 23, 1835.

12. "A Citizen," quoted in *Daily Cleveland Herald*, November 4, 1835.

13. *Urbana Citizen*, quoted in *Daily National Intelligencer* (Washington, D.C.), October 4, 1843. *Ohio Statesman* (Columbus), June 26, 1844.

14. *Buffalo Commercial Advertiser*, quoted in *Daily National Intelligencer* (Washington, D.C.), October 13, 1843.

15. Letter, John Jones to General Assembly of Ohio, February 27, 1843, quoted in *Ohio State Journal* (Columbus), June 7, 1843.

16. Letter from "MS" from Buffalo, August 5, 1845, quoted in *Cleveland Daily Herald*, August 8, 1845.

17. *Ohio Statesman* (Columbus), August 27, 1845.

18. *Ohio Observer* (Hudson), July 29, 1846.

19. Letter from "Indiana," quoted in *Louisville Daily Journal*, August 29, 1845.

20. *Sandusky Clarion*, quoted in *Cleveland Daily Herald*, May 27, 1847.

21. *Cleveland Daily Herald*, January 6, 1848.

22. *New York Herald*, January 21, 1850.

23. "Quevedo," quoted in *Daily Ohio State Journal* (Columbus), January 6, 1852.

24. *St. Louis Republican*, February 8, 1852.

25. *Missouri Courier* (Hannibal), November 25, 1852.

26. *Boston Herald*, June 20, 1857.

27. *Pittsburgh Gazette*, quoted in *Cleveland Daily Herald*, February 9, 1852.

28. *New York Daily Times*, June 9, 1852.

29. *Ohio State Journal* (Columbus), December 27, 1852.

30. Speech of Thomas Swan at Parkersburg, quoted in *Sun* (Baltimore), June 30, 1852.

31. "W.C.B.," quoted in *Boston Daily Atlas*, July 23, 1852.

32. Ibid.

33. *Cleveland Daily Herald*, July 19, 1860.

34. Ibid., December 28, 1852.

35. *Toledo Blade*, quoted in *New York Daily Times*, January 14, 1853.

36. *Cleveland Daily Herald*, March 1, 1853.

37. Carter Goodrich, *Government Promotion of American Canals and Railroads, 1800–1890* (New York: Columbia University Press, 1960), 144.

38. *Detroit Journal*, quoted in *Georgia Telegraph* (Macon), March 3, 1836.

39. *Milwaukee Sentinel*, June 8, 1838.

40. Goodrich, *Government Promotion,* 144–145. *Cleveland Daily Herald*, March 9, 1846.

41. Letter from Detroit, August 30, 1838, quoted in *New Bedford Mercury* (Mass.), October 5, 1838.

42. *Detroit Free Press*, quoted in *New Hampshire Gazette* (Portsmouth), June 18, 1839.

43. *Boston Post*, quoted in *Ohio Statesman* (Columbus), December 22, 1843.

44. Larson, *Bonds of Empire*, 23–24.

45. *Cleveland Herald*, September 7, 1846.

46. *Journal of Commerce*, quoted in *Daily National Intelligencer* (Washington, D.C.), September 16, 1846.

47. *Boston Daily Atlas,* March 9, 1847. *Daily Ohio Statesman* (Columbus), August 19, 1848.

48. *North American and United States Gazette* (Philadelphia), March 1, 1848.

49. *Chicago Democrat*, quoted in *New York Herald*, November 13, 1844.

50. *Cleveland Daily Herald*, December 20, 1851.

51. *Milwaukee Daily Sentinel*, February 17, 21, 1852. *New York Daily Times*, May 25, 1852.

52. *Milwaukee Daily Sentinel and Gazette*, April 9, 1851.

53. *Milwaukee Daily Sentinel*, May 3, 1852.

54. *Detroit Free Press*, quoted in *Daily Ohio Statesman* (Columbus), August 4, 1852.

55. *Boston Daily Advertiser*, August 13, 1855.

56. Ibid., September 3, 1855.

57. *Daily Dispatch* (Richmond), July 9, 1856.

58. *Chicago Daily Tribune*, March 10, 1858.

59. Ibid., April 28, 1857.

60. "Grand Haven," quoted in *Milwaukee Daily Sentinel*, May 20, 1853.

61. *Detroit Tribune*, quoted in *Chicago Daily Tribune*, April 2, 1857.

62. "J.S.W.," quoted in *Lake Superior Miner* (Ontonagon, Mich.), January 16, 1858.

63. *Chicago Daily Tribune*, April 24, 1858.

64. William Cronan, *Nature's Metropolis: Chicago and the Great West* (New York: W.W. Norton, 1991), 68.

65. Correspondent to *Pittsburgh Conference Journal*, quoted in *New York Spectator*, March 31, 1836.

66. Paul Gates, *The Illinois Central and Its Colonization Work* (Cambridge: Harvard University Press, 1934), 24, 30.
67. *North and West*, quoted in *The Globe* (Washington, D.C.), June 30, 1836.
68. *Daily Missouri Republican* (St. Louis), February 5 and March 9, 1850. Gates, *Illinois Central*, 86. There was a report late in 1852 that the Chicago and Galena Union had a 40 percent return on capital. *Chicago Daily Tribune*, December 13, 1852.
69. Frederick Cleveland and Fred Powell, *Railroad Promotion and Capitalization in the United States* (London: Longmans, Green, 1909), 82. Richard Overton, *Burlington Route: A History of the Burlington Lines* (New York: Alfred A. Knopf, 1965), 11–12. *Milwaukee Daily Sentinel*, February 24, 1854. On the Rock Island, see also the popular account William Hayes, *Iron Road to Empire: The History of 100 Years of the Progress and Achievements of the Rock Island Lines* (Omaha, Neb.: Simmons-Boardman Books, 1953).
70. Overton, *Burlington Route*, xxv–xxvi, 42, 119.
71. Gates, *Illinois Central*, 19, 86.
72. *New York Commercial*, quoted in *Sun* (Pittsfield, Mass.), December 2, 1847.
73. "Hiatt," quoted in *Daily National Intelligencer* (Washington, D.C.), February 2, 1848.
74. Cleveland and Powell, *Railroad Promotion*, 245, 250.
75. Overton, *Burlington Route*, 73.
76. Gates, *Illinois Central*, 120, 174, 256.
77. *Charleston Mercury*, February 4, 1852.
78. *Hartford Daily Courant*, September 25, 1850.
79. *Daily National Intelligencer* (Washington, D.C.), March 13, 1852.
80. *Hartford Daily Courant*, June 3, 1852.
81. *Chicago Tribune*, quoted in *Charleston Mercury*, July 27, 1852.
82. *Hartford Daily Courant*, March 19, 1852.
83. *Congressional Globe*, 31st Cong., 1st session, April 29, 1850, 845–851.
84. "Metropolis," quoted in *Georgia Telegraph* (Macon), January 14, 1851.
85. *Charleston Mercury*, February 4, 1852.
86. *Fayetteville Observer* (N.C.), March 30, 1852.
87. *Milwaukee Daily Sentinel*, November 27, 1852.
88. Ibid., January 14, 1854.
89. *State Gazette* (Trenton, N.J.), March 22, 1854.
90. *Milwaukee Daily Sentinel*, April 25, 1854.
91. *Fayetteville Observer* (N.C.), May 23, 1853.
92. *North American and United States Gazette* (Philadelphia), February 10, 1853. *Milwaukee Daily Sentinel*, April 25, 1854.
93. *Chicago Daily Tribune*, February 21, 1853.
94. Letter from Peru, Illinois, quoted in *New York Daily Times*, April 23, 1853.
95. *Chicago Daily Tribune*, May 4, 1853.
96. Ibid., April 15, 1853.
97. "R.K.," quoted in *Milwaukee Daily Sentinel*, September 5, 1853.
98. *American Railroad Journal*, quoted in *Cleveland Daily Herald*, October 8, 1853.
99. *Cleveland Daily Herald*, January 4, 1854.
100. *Chicago Daily Tribune*, January 25, 1854.
101. *Chicago Democratic Press*, quoted in *Hartford Daily Courant*, February 8, 1854.
102. *Milwaukee Daily Sentinel*, June 21, 1853.

103. Letter from Detroit, quoted in *Chicago Daily Tribune*, January 19, 1854.
104. Letter from correspondent, June 5, 1854, quoted in *New York Daily Times*, June 12, 1854.
105. *New York Herald*, June 5, 1854.
106. Albany exchange, quoted in *Milwaukee Daily Sentinel*, June 16, 1854.
107. *Sun* (Pittsfield, Mass.), May 8, 1856.
108. *Ohio State Journal* (Columbus), May 7, 1856.
109. *St. Louis Republican*, quoted in *Chicago Daily Tribune*, June 12, 1854.
110. *New York Herald*, July 4, 1855.
111. *Ohio Observer* (Hudson), July 25, 1854.
112. *Memphis Daily Appeal*, January 2, 1855.
113. Governor's message, quoted in *Boston Daily Advertiser*, January 9, 1855.
114. *Chicago Daily Tribune*, January 16, 1855.
115. Letter from Chicago, February 4, 1855, quoted in *New York Daily Times*, February 9, 1855.
116. *Chicago Press*, February 7, 1855, quoted in *New York Herald*, February 13, 1855.
117. *New York Herald*, February 13, 1855.
118. *Chicago Tribune*, quoted in *Louisville Daily Journal*, February 9, 1855.
119. Letter, quoted in *Louisville Daily Journal*, February 12, 1855.
120. *St. Louis Intelligencer*, quoted in *New York Herald*, February 11, 1855.
121. *New York Herald*, February 13, 1855.
122. *Baltimore Patriot*, quoted in *Charleston Mercury*, February 19, 1855.

CHAPTER 11: PANIC

1. *New Hampshire Statesman* (Concord), August 31, 1849.
2. *New York Herald*, quoted in *Charleston Mercury*, September 8, 1849.
3. *Georgia Telegraph* (Macon), September 18, 1849.
4. *New York Herald*, January 3, 1857.
5. Ibid., August 8, 1849.
6. *Vermont Chronicle* (Bellows Falls), July 11, 1854. *Boston Transcript*, quoted in *Cleveland Daily Herald*, July 13, 1854.
7. *Daily National Intelligencer*, July 8, 1854.
8. *State Gazette* (Trenton, N.J.), July 18, 1854.
9. *New York Herald*, July 10, 1854.
10. *Boston Traveller*, quoted in *New Hampshire Statesman* (Concord), July 29, 1854.
11. *New York Herald*, July 8, 1854.
12. *Boston Herald*, July 27, 1854.
13. *Frederick Douglass' Paper* (Rochester, N.Y.), January 5, 1855. *Daily National Intelligencer*, December 21, 1855.
14. *New York Herald*, July 10, 11, 1855.
15. *Frank Leslie's Illustrated Newspaper* (New York), December 29, 1855.
16. *New York Herald*, August 2, 1854.
17. *Charleston Mercury*, August 14, 1854.
18. *Louisville Daily Journal*, August 19, 1854.
19. "Honesty," quoted in *Hartford Daily Courant*, October 2, 1854.
20. *Hartford Daily Courant*, November 27, 1854.
21. *New York Evening Post*, quoted in *Milwaukee Sentinel*, May 14, 1842.

22. *New York American*, quoted in *Boston Daily Atlas*, July 11, 1843.
23. "Truth," quoted in *North American and Daily Advertiser*, February 2, 1844.
24. Ibid., February 9, 1844.
25. "E.C.," quoted in ibid., August 24, 1847.
26. *North American and United States Gazette* (Philadelphia), February 2, 1852.
27. Report of J.H. Adams and Wm. Gatewood, quoted in *Charleston Mercury*, May 5, 1848.
28. *Raleigh Register*, January 13, 1849.
29. James Gadsden to stockholders, quoted in *Savannah Daily Republican*, December 20, 1849.
30. *New York Herald*, quoted in *Charleston Mercury*, September 8, 1849. *New York Herald*, quoted in *Georgia Telegraph* (Macon), September 18, 1849.
31. *Daily Picayune* (New Orleans), February 1, 1852.
32. *State Gazette* (Trenton, N.J.), April 20, 1855.
33. *New York Herald*, June 7, 1850.
34. *Boston Herald*, July 17, 1855.
35. *New York Post*, quoted in *Chicago Daily Tribune*, August 4, 1857.
36. *Boston Herald*, August 16, 1856.
37. *Boston Daily Advertiser*, July 20, 1855.
38. *Boston Herald*, July 28, 1855.
39. *New York Herald*, August 4, 1849.
40. *Louisville Daily Journal*, October 5, 1852.
41. *State Gazette* (Trenton, N.J.), March 10, 1856.
42. *New York Herald*, January 23, 1857.
43. Ibid., June 30, 1856.
44. *Louisville Daily Journal*, November 8, 1856.
45. *Daily Cleveland Herald*, October 14, 1853.
46. *New York Herald*, April 22, 1857.
47. *Chicago Daily Tribune*, June 15 and August 4, 1857.
48. *Hartford Daily Courant*, August 25, 1857.
49. Ibid., August 26, 1857. *New York Post*, quoted in *Chicago Daily Tribune*, September 7, 1857.
50. *Chicago Daily Tribune*, August 29, 1857.
51. *Richmond Enquirer*, quoted in *New York Herald*, August 30, 1857.
52. *Chicago Daily Tribune*, September 2, 1857.
53. *Hartford Daily Courant*, September 3, 1857.
54. *New York Herald*, September 3, 1857.
55. Ibid., September 11, 1857.
56. *Hartford Daily Courant*, September 15, 1857.
57. *New York Herald*, August 25, 1857.
58. Ibid., September 28, 1857.
59. *Hartford Daily Courant* (Conn.), September 3, 1857.
60. *New York Post*, quoted in *Chicago Daily Tribune*, September 7, 1857.
61. *Hartford Daily Courant* (Conn.), September 9, 1857.
62. *New York Times*, October 1, 1857.
63. *Columbus Gazette*, October 9, 1857.
64. *New York Times*, September 26, 1857.
65. *Chicago Daily Tribune*, October 12, 1857. *Charleston Mercury*, October 14, 1857.

66. *Chicago Daily Tribune*, October 16, 1857.

67. *Detroit Free Press*, quoted in *Chicago Daily Tribune*, November 13, 1857.

68. *Hartford Daily Courant*, October 14, 1857.

69. Ibid., October 20, 1857.

70. *Boston Herald*, March 30, 1858.

71. *New York Tribune*, quoted in *Charleston Mercury*, October 19, 1857.

72. Quoted in *Press* (Philadelphia), January 11, 1858.

73. *New York Herald*, August 20, 1860.

74. *Hartford Daily Courant* (Conn.), August 17, 1857.

75. *Cleveland Daily Herald* (Ohio), August 20, 1857.

CHAPTER 12: WE FLY BY NIGHT

1. *Boston Commercial Gazette*, quoted in *Dover Gazette and Stafford Advertiser* (Dover, N.H.), December 2, 1834.

2. *Boston Daily Atlas*, December 4, 1834.

3. "T," quoted in *Baltimore Patriot*, December 16, 1834.

4. Lancaster paper, quoted in *Newport Mercury*, February 8, 1834.

5. Letter to *Baltimore Gazette*, quoted in *Daily National Intelligencer* (Washington, D.C.), December 20, 1834.

6. *Rhode Island Republican* (Newport), March 4, 1835.

7. "Spy," quoted in *Farmer's Gazette* (Barre, Mass.), March 6, 1835.

8. *Boston Transcript*, quoted in *Daily National Intelligencer* (Washington, D.C.), March 27, 1835.

9. *Cincinnati Gazette*, quoted in *Boston Courier*, March 12, 1840.

10. *Salem Advertiser*, quoted in *Dover Gazette and Stafford Advertiser* (N.H.), March 5, 1842.

11. *North American and Daily Advertiser* (Philadelphia), September 5, 1842.

12. *Amherst Express*, quoted in *Boston Daily Atlas*, March 10, 1845.

13. *New York Daily Times*, August 29, 1854.

14. Joe Hammer, quoted in *Boston Herald*, January 8, 1855.

15. *Southern Patriot* (Charleston), June 7, 1838. *Daily Picayune* (New Orleans), May 26, 1840.

16. *Daily Picayune* (New Orleans), July 25, 1841.

17. *Natchez Courier* (Miss.), May 21, 1852.

18. *Daily Cleveland Herald*, October 18, 1856.

19. *Sun* (Baltimore), March 14, 1861.

20. *Texas State Gazette* (Austin), August 25, 1854. See also for this argument *Charleston Mercury*, March 2, 1855.

21. *Boston Herald*, February 7, 1856.

22. *Newburyport Herald*, quoted in *New York Spectator*, August 24, 1842.

23. *Louisville Journal*, quoted in *Scioto Gazette* (Chillicothe, Ohio), April 22, 1854.

24. *Madison Visitor*, quoted in *Macon Daily Telegraph* (Ga.), March 20, 1861.

25. *Louisville Daily Journal*, September 23, 1854.

26. *Daily Picayune* (New Orleans), October 22, 1859.

27. *Augusta Dispatch*, quoted in *Charleston Courier*, January 26, 1860.

28. *Emancipator and Free American* (New York), January 26, 1843.

29. *Liberator* (Boston), March 19, 1841.

30. "Solon," quoted in *Richmond Enquirer*, September 17, 1833.
31. *Emancipator* (New York), March 15, 1838.
32. *Charleston Mercury*, July 10, 1850.
33. Letter to editor, quoted in *New Orleans Commercial Bulletin*, June 4, 1833.
34. *New York Spectator*, August 15, 1833.
35. *Liberator* (Boston), March 19, 1841.
36. George Bradburn, quoted in ibid., April 2, 1841.
37. *New York Herald*, July 24, 1841.
38. *Lynn Record*, quoted in *Liberator* (Boston), August 13, 1841.
39. *Colored American*, quoted in *Liberator* (Boston), September 17, 1841.
40. *Quincy Patriot*, quoted in *Liberator* (Boston), October 15, 1841.
41. *Georgia Telegraph* (Macon), April 12, 1842.
42. *Emancipator and Free American* (New York), September 22, 1842.
43. Letter in *Richmond Whig*, quoted in *Emancipator and Free American* (New York), February 23, 1843.
44. *Hartford Daily Courant*, November 3, 1857.
45. *Cincinnati Enquirer*, quoted in *Newark Advocate* (Ohio), March 9, 1860.
46. *Daily Evening Bulletin* (San Francisco), February 25, 1860.
47. *Spirit of the Times* (Philadelphia), quoted in *New York Herald*, August 1, 1840. *New Hampshire Patriot and State Gazette* (Concord), August 3, 1840. *Virginia Free Press* (Charleston, W.V.), August 6, 1840. *New York Star*, quoted in *New England Weekly Review* (Hartford, Conn.), August 8, 1840.
48. *Baltimore Patriot*, April 27, 1829.
49. *Boston Daily Advertiser*, quoted in *Daily National Intelligencer* (Washington, D.C.), April 28, 1835.
50. *Boston Chronicle*, quoted in *The Globe* (Washington, D.C.), May 5, 1835.
51. *New York Herald*, February 4, 1836.
52. *Boston Herald*, June 13, 1851.
53. *Circleville Herald*, quoted in *Daily Scioto Gazette* (Chillicothe, Ohio), July 16, 1851.
54. *Richmond Enquirer*, November 9, 1838.
55. *Hudson River Chronicle* (Sing Sing, N.Y.), December 29, 1840.
56. *Portsmouth Journal* (N.H.), November 10, 1838.
57. *New York Daily Times*, October 4, 1851.
58. "Aliquis," quoted in *New York Herald*, September 21, 1844.
59. *New York Journal of Commerce*, quoted in *Hartford Daily Courant* (Conn.), July 19, 1850.
60. *New York Herald*, November 12, 1852.
61. Ibid., November 25, 1852.
62. *New York Daily Times*, March 14, 1855.
63. *Boston Herald*, December 14, 1855.
64. Ibid., March 31, 1857.
65. *Chicago Daily Tribune*, August 13, 1858.
66. *Louisville Daily Journal*, August 25, 1859.
67. *Frank Leslie's Illustrated Newspaper* (New York), April 7, 1860.
68. *New York Herald*, August 19, 1860. *Daily True Delta* (New Orleans), May 5, 1861.
69. *New York Spectator*, January 18, 1836.
70. *Hartford Daily Courant* (Conn.), July 2, 1840.
71. *New York Herald*, July 7, 1840.

72. *Boston Daily Atlas*, January 26, 1842.

73. *Boston Courier*, January 27, 1842.

74. *Barre Gazette* (Mass.), January 28, 1842.

75. *New York Herald*, September 29, 1843.

76. Ibid., October 3, 1843.

77. *Louisville Daily Journal*, February 12, 1844.

78. *Charleston Mercury*, July 1, 1844.

79. *Constitution* (Middletown, Conn.), July 31, 1844.

80. *Boston Daily Atlas*, August 10, 1844.

81. J.G. Bennett, quoted in *New York Herald*, February 10, 1841. *Southern Patriot* (Charleston), February 10, 1843.

82. Brooke Hindle and Steven Lubar, *Engines of Change: The American Industrial Revolution, 1790–1860* (Washington, D.C.: Smithsonian Institution Press, 1986), 168.

83. *Connecticut Courant* (Hartford), February 20, 1841.

84. *Cleveland Daily Herald*, June 7, 1842. *Berkshire County Whig* (Pittsfield, Mass.), August 8, 1844.

85. *New York Spectator*, April 22, 1839.

86. *Pennsylvania Inquirer and National Gazette* (Philadelphia), September 30, 1843. *Boston Courier*, April 25, 1844. *New York Herald*, May 13, 1844. *Hartford Daily Courant*, August 10, 1844. *The Mississippian* (Jackson), October 30, 1844. *Daily National Intelligencer* (Washington, D.C.), January 22, 1845.

87. "Constitution," quoted in *Tri-Weekly Ohio Statesman* (Columbus), May 23, 1845.

88. *New York Herald*, January 14, 1837. *Pennsylvania Inquirer and Daily Courier* (Philadelphia), June 11, 1838.

89. *Sun* (Baltimore), June 8, 1838.

90. *Delaware Journal*, quoted in *Daily Courant* (Hartford), December 6, 1838.

91. *Daily Herald and Gazette* (Cleveland), May 24, 1838.

92. *Hartford Daily Courant*, November 11, 1858.

93. *New York Times*, March 25, 1859.

94. Ibid., June 13, 1859. *Charleston Mercury*, November 9, 1859.

95. *New York Tribune*, quoted in *Wisconsin Daily Patriot* (Madison), November 16, 1850.

CHAPTER 13: MR. WHITNEY'S DREAM

1. *Sun* (Pittsfield, Mass.), April 24, 1845.

2. *Morning News* (New London, Conn.), January 31, 1845.

3. *New York Herald*, February 3, 1845.

4. Ibid., September 20, 1847.

5. *Sun* (Pittsfield, Mass.), February 13, 1845.

6. *Sun* (Baltimore), May 3, 1845.

7. Asa Whitney, quoted in *Ohio Statesman* (Columbus), February 14, 1845.

8. Cambridge: Harvard University Press, 1950.

9. *New Hampshire Patriot and State Gazette* (Concord), February 20, 1845.

10. Quoted in *Georgia Telegraph* (Macon), March 18, 1845.

11. *Sun* (Pittsfield, Mass.), May 8, 1845.

12. *Daily National Intelligencer*, May 28, 1845. *Southern Patriot* (Charleston), May 31, 1845. *New Hampshire Patriot and State Gazette* (Concord), June 5, 1845.

13. Asa Whitney, quoted in *Daily National Intelligencer* (Washington, D.C.), July 3, 1845.
14. *Milwaukee Daily Sentinel*, June 14, 1845.
15. *New York Herald*, June 27, 1845.
16. Ibid., October 10, 1845.
17. *Louisville Daily Journal*, November 29, 1845.
18. "Brindley," quoted in ibid., January 9, 1847.
19. Ibid., January 15, 1847.
20. *Hartford Daily Courant*, July 3, 1847.
21. Letter from Richard Elliot to Asa Whitney, quoted in *Scioto Gazette* (Chillicothe, Ohio), February 5, 1846.
22. Letter from Whitney in St. Louis, September 20, quoted in *Hartford Daily Courant*, October 8, 1845.
23. *The North American* (Philadelphia), November 13, 1845. *Mississippi Free Trader and Natchez Gazette*, November 22, 1845.
24. *Weekly Ohio State Journal* (Columbus), December 3, 1845.
25. *Pensacola Gazette* (Fla.), February 28, 1846.
26. *Milwaukee Daily Sentinel*, January 13, 1846.
27. *New York Herald*, February 13, 1846. *Barre Gazette* (Mass.), February 27, 1846.
28. *New York Herald*, March 3, 1846.
29. Asa Whitney, quoted in ibid., July 21, 1846.
30. *New York Tribune*, quoted in *Barre Gazette*, September 18, 1846.
31. Quoted in *Scioto Gazette* (Chillicothe, Ohio), November 4, 1846.
32. "B," quoted in *Louisville Daily Journal*, February 6, 1847.
33. *Louisville Daily Journal*, November 25, 1856.
34. *New York Evening Post*, quoted in *Barre Gazette* (Mass.), November 27, 1846.
35. *Ohio Statesman* (Columbus), November 27, 1846.
36. *Hartford Daily Courant*, December 8, 1846.
37. *North American* (Philadelphia), December 24, 1846. *Boston Daily Atlas*, September 17, 1847, and January 1849.
38. Whitney speech, quoted in *Hartford Daily Courant*, June 2, 1847.
39. "B," quoted in *Louisville Daily Journal*, June 11, 1847.
40. Jerome Cotton, quoted in *Cleveland Daily Herald,* January 13, 1851.
41. *The Californian* (Monterey), May 29, 1847.
42. *New York Herald*, January 6, 1848.
43. Ibid., August 6, 1848.
44. *The Texian Advocate* (Victoria, Tex.), May 4, 1848.
45. *New York Herald*, July 17, 1848.
46. *United States Magazine and Democratic Review*, vol. 25 (September 1849), 246.
47. *New York Herald*, November 24, 1848.
48. *Raleigh Register*, January 6, 1849.
49. *Mississippi Free Trader and Natchez Gazette*, February 17, 1849. *Raleigh Register* (N.C.), February 17, 1849.
50. *Louisville Daily Journal*, February 6, 1849.
51. *Daily Picayune* (New Orleans), March 17, 1849.
52. *Louisville Daily Journal*, May 5, 1849. *Missouri Courier* (Hannibal), October 25, 1849. *Charleston Mercury*, November 12, 1849.

53. *Charleston Mercury*, June 14, 1849.

54. "JED," quoted in *Daily Picayune* (New Orleans), September 24, 1849.

55. *Boston Daily Atlas*, October 2, 1849.

56. *Boston Courier*, November 1, 1849.

57. *Charleston Mercury*, November 12, 1849. *Scioto Gazette* (Chillicothe, Ohio), November 14, 1849.

58. *Missouri Courier* (Hannibal), October 25, 1849.

59. *New York Herald*, March 24, 1850.

60. *Boston Daily Atlas*, April 8, 1850.

61. "A," quoted in *Daily National Intelligencer*, April 11, 1850.

62. *Milwaukee Sentinel*, June 22, 1850.

CHAPTER 14: PACIFIC OR BUST

1. *Cleveland Daily Herald*, July 1, 1846.

2. *Boston Courier*, November 1, 1849.

3. *Springfield Republican*, quoted in *Hartford Daily Courant*, January 29, 1850.

4. *Placer Times* (Sacramento, Calif.), May 1, 1850.

5. *Sun* (Baltimore), April 23, 1850.

6. Craig Miner, "Stereotyping and the Pacific Railway Issue, 1845–1865," *Canadian Review of American Studies*, vol. 6, no. 1 (Spring 1975), 59, 70.

7. *Daily Picayune* (New Orleans), January 7, 1851.

8. *New York Daily Times*, September 22, 24, 1852. *Daily Dispatch* (Richmond), September 25, 1852.

9. *Hartford Daily Courant*, December 17, 1852.

10. Ibid., December 20, 1851.

11. Speech of Buckner Payne, quoted in ibid., December 27, 1851.

12. *Daily Picayune* (New Orleans), January 2, 4, 1852.

13. Address by J.T. Trezevant, quoted in *Memphis Daily Appeal*, January 17, 1852. See also speech of James Robb, quoted in ibid., January 18, 1852.

14. *Alta California* (San Francisco), January 1, 1852.

15. Speech of William Gwin, August 30, 1852, *Congressional Globe*, 32nd Congress, 2nd session, 2467.

16. *New York Herald*, December 31, 1852.

17. *Milwaukee Daily Sentinel*, January 22, 1852. *Daily Picayune* (New Orleans), January 20, 1852.

18. *Daily Picayune* (New Orleans), January 7, 1853.

19. Ibid., February 18, 1853.

20. William Goetzmann, *Army Exploration in the American West, 1803–1863* (New Haven: Yale University Press, 1959), 262, 295.

21. For the surveys, see ibid., 262–304, and also Goetzmann, *Exploration and Empire: The Explorer and the Scientist in the Winning of the American West* (New York: Alfred A. Knopf, 1966), 265–302.

22. *Milwaukee Daily Sentinel*, January 22, 1852.

23. *New York Daily Times*, November 23, 1853.

24. "M," quoted in *Daily Register* (Raleigh, N.C.), September 21, 1853.

25. Goetzmann, *Army Exploration*, 270.

26. Gil Blas, quoted in *Daily Picayune* (New Orleans), January 26, 1853.

27. *Charleston Mercury*, October 24, 1853.

28. *New York Herald*, November 9, 1853.

29. *New York Tribune*, quoted in *Milwaukee Daily Sentinel*, November 11, 1853.

30. *New York Daily Times*, November 14, 1853.

31. *American Railroad Journal*, quoted in *Vermont Chronicle* (Bellows Falls), November 22, 1853.

32. *New York Herald*, November 22, 1853.

33. *Daily South Carolinian* (Columbia), June 12, 1854.

34. R.J. Walker, Jeptha Fowlkes, C.S. Woodhull, and T. Butler King, quoted in *New York Herald*, June 21, 1854.

35. *Texas State Gazette* (Austin), July 29, 1854.

36. *New Orleans Delta*, quoted in *Hartford Daily Courant*, August 3, 1854.

37. *Nacogdoches Chronicle*, quoted in *Texas State Gazette* (Austin), April 28, 1855.

38. *Texas State Gazette* (Austin), July 29, 1854. *Hartford Daily Courant*, August 3, 1854.

39. *Missouri Democrat*, quoted in *Milwaukee Daily Sentinel*, January 10, 1855.

40. *Texas State Gazette* (Austin), April 14, 1855.

41. *Memphis Daily Appeal*, May 11, 1859. *Daily Picayune* (New Orleans), June 15, 1859. *Louisville Daily Journal*, July 21, 1859.

42. *Louisville Daily Journal*, May 17, 1859.

43. Ibid., July 21, 1859.

44. *Hartford Daily Courant*, August 3, 1854.

45. *New Orleans Delta*, quoted in *The San Antonio Ledger,* August 17, 1854.

46. *Daily Picayune* (New Orleans), December 15, 1854.

47. *Louisville Daily Journal*, January 1, 1855.

48. Ibid., July 4, 1856.

49. *New York Herald*, October 30, 1855.

50. *Daily Picayune* (New Orleans), December 23, 1855. *Louisville Daily Journal*, January 15, 1856.

51. *Louisville Daily Journal*, December 19, 1856.

52. R.J. Walker, quoted in *Memphis Daily Appeal*, December 28, 1856.

53. *Louisville Daily Journal*, January 11, 1857.

54. *Knoxville Whig*, quoted in *Memphis Daily Appeal*, January 11, 1857.

55. *Daily Picayune* (New Orleans), March 3, 1857.

56. Ibid., May 11, 1859.

57. *Daily Missouri Republican* (St. Louis), December 12, 1858.

58. *Louisville Daily Journal*, July 21, 1859.

59. *Dallas Herald*, August 24, 1859.

60. *Memphis Daily Appeal*, October 22, 1859.

61. *Louisville Daily Journal*, November 26, 1859.

62. "J," quoted in *Memphis Daily Appeal*, December 17, 1859.

63. *Daily Picayune* (New Orleans), February 14, 1860. *Fayetteville Observer* (N.C.), February 20, 1860.

64. *New York Herald*, January 15, 1860.

65. *Houston Telegraph*, quoted in *Charleston Courier Tri-Weekly*, April 3, 1860.

66. *Daily National Intelligencer* (Washington, D.C.), April 21, 1860.

67. *Charleston Mercury*, January 26, 1855.

68. *Baltimore Patriot*, quoted in *Charleston Mercury*, February 19, 1855.

69. *New York Herald*, March 11, 1855.

70. *Chicago Daily Tribune*, January 31, 1856.
71. *Daily Evening Bulletin* (San Francisco), November 26, 1859. *The Constitution* (Washington, D.C.), March 27, 1860.
72. Report of Committee of Fifteen, quoted in *Daily Evening Bulletin* (San Francisco), May 10, 1860.
73. *New York Times*, February 4, 1860.
74. *Daily Picayune* (New Orleans), February 10, 1860.
75. *San Antonio Ledger*, March 10, 1860.
76. *Boston Daily Advertiser*, March 30, 1860.
77. *Omaha Nebraskian*, April 14, 1860.
78. *New York Times*, May 7, 1862.
79. *New York Daily Times*, December 20, 1854.
80. See, for example, *Congressional Globe*, 37th Congress, 2nd session, Senate, May 20, June 18 and June 20, 1862, 2216, 2776–2788, 2832–2840.
81. Stephen Ambrose, *Nothing Like It in the World: The Men Who Built the Transcontinental Railroad, 1863–1869* (New York: Simon and Schuster, 2000), 83.
82. Maury Klein, *Union Pacific: The Birth of a Railroad, 1862–1893* (Garden City, N.Y.: Doubleday, 1987), 13.
83. *Chicago Daily Tribune*, September 4, 1862.
84. *Daily Evening Bulletin* (San Francisco), July 11, 1862.
85. Klein, *Union Pacific*, 16.

CONCLUSION: ADAPTING TO THE MACHINE

1. Lynn White, *Medieval Technology and Social Change* (Oxford: Clarendon, 1962).
2. Siegfried Giedion, *Mechanization Takes Command: A Contribution to Anonymous History* (New York: W.W. Norton, 1969). First published by Oxford University Press in 1948.
3. Langdon Winner, *Autonomous Technology: Technics-out-of-Control as a Theme in Political Thought* (Cambridge: MIT Press, 1977), 3.
4. Ian Kennedy and Julian Treuherz, *The Railway: Art in the Age of Steam* (New Haven: Yale University Press, 2008), 21, 38–39.
5. Winner, *Autonomous Technology*, 7.
6. Quoted in James Young, *Henry Adams: The Historian as Political Theorist* (Lawrence: University Press of Kansas, 2001), 74.
7. Quoted in Winner, *Autonomous Technology*, 195, 197.
8. Quoted in *Pennsylvania Inquirer and Daily Courier* (Philadelphia), January 16, 1840.
9. *Knickerbocker*, quoted in *New Hampshire Sentinel* (Keene), April 1, 1840.
10. *Sun* (Baltimore), April 6, 1840.
11. Peter Gay, *Pleasure Wars: The Bourgeois Experience—Victoria to Freud* (New York: W.W. Norton, 1998), 9–11.
12. Winner, *Autonomous Technology*, 84.
13. Howard Kunstler, *The Geography of Nowhere: The Rise and Decline of America's Man-Made Landscape* (New York: Simon and Schuster, 1993), 108, 121.
14. Mark Helprin, *Digital Barbarism: A Writer's Manifesto* (New York: HarperCollins, 2009), 1, 9, 32, 57.
15. John Senior, *The Restoration of Christian Culture* (Norfolk, Va.: HIS, 2008), 83.

16. Kennedy, *The Railway*, 23, 31, 42.
17. John Stilgoe, *Metropolitan Corridor: Railroads and the American Scene* (New Haven: Yale University Press, 1983), ix, 11–12.
18. Helprin, *Digital Barbarism*, 9, 10, 12.
19. Joseph Corn, *The Winged Gospel: America's Romance with Aviation, 1900–1950* (New York: Oxford University Press, 1983).
20. See, for example, Jill Jonnes, *Empires of Light: Edison, Tesla, Westinghouse, and the Race to Electrify the World* (New York: Random House, 2003).
21. *New York Railroad Journal*, quoted in *Weekly Wisconsin Patriot* (Madison), August 21, 1858.
22. For some illustration of the way the South in the 1850s thought of Northern "enthusiasms," see Craig Miner, *Seeding Civil War: Kansas in the National News, 1854–1858* (Lawrence: University Press of Kansas, 2008), 29–32.
23. Steve Fraser, *Every Man a Speculator: A History of Wall Street in American Life* (New York: HaperCollins, 2005), 43.
24. Ibid., 44.
25. *Savannah Daily Republican*, June 28, 1850.
26. *Daily Missouri Republican* (St. Louis), February 9, 1850.
27. *Sun* (Baltimore), May 19, 1845.
28. *Louisville Daily Journal*, August 24, 1850.
29. *Farmers' Cabinet* (Amherst, N.H.), May 6, 1852.
30. *Kansas Herald of Freedom* (Lawrence), October 8, 1859.
31. *Sun* (Baltimore), May 19, 1845.
32. *Kansas City Star*, August 15, 1887.
33. *Boston Herald*, December 16, 1853.
34. *New York Daily Times*, January 28, 1853.
35. William Hayes, in *New York World*, quoted in *The Atchison Champion*, February 19, 1890.
36. Department of the Interior, Census Office, *Report on Transportation Business in the United States at the Eleventh Census: 1890. Part I—Transportation by Land* (Washington, D.C.: Government Printing Office, 1895), 5.
37. *Milwaukee Sentinel*, March 7, 1890.

BIBLIOGRAPHY

———⟩○⟨○○⟨———

NEWSPAPERS AND MAGAZINES

Alta California (San Francisco, California)
American Phrenological Journal (New York, New York)
American Watchman (Wilmington, Delaware)
Arkansas Gazette (Little Rock, Arkansas)
Arkansas State Gazette (Little Rock, Arkansas)
Atlas (Boston, Massachusetts)
Augusta Chronicle (Augusta, Georgia)
Augusta Chronicle and Georgia Advertiser (Augusta, Georgia)
Aurora and Pennsylvania Gazette (Philadelphia, Pennsylvania)
Baltimore Patriot (Baltimore, Maryland)
Barre Gazette (Barre, Massachusetts)
Berkshire County Whig (Pittsfield, Massachusetts)
Berkshire Journal (Lennox, Massachusetts)
Berkshire Star (Pittsfield, Massachusetts)
Boston Atlas (Boston, Massachusetts)
Boston Courier (Boston, Massachusetts)
Boston Daily Advertiser (Boston, Massachusetts)
Boston Daily Atlas (Boston, Massachusetts)
Boston Herald (Boston, Massachusetts)
Boston Investigator (Boston, Massachusetts)
Boston Patriot and Morning Advertiser (Boston, Massachusetts)
The Californian (Monterey, California)
Camden Gazette (Camden, South Carolina)
Carolina Observer (Fayetteville, North Carolina)
Charleston Courier (Charleston, South Carolina)
Charleston Courier Tri-Weekly (Charleston, South Carolina)
Charleston Mercury (Charleston, South Carolina)
Chicago Daily Tribune (Chicago, Illinois)
Christian Observer (Louisville, Kentucky)
Cleveland Daily Herald (Cleveland, Ohio)
Cline's Carlisle Gazette (Carlisle, Pennsylvania)
Columbia Phenix (Providence, Rhode Island)
Columbia Telescope (Columbia, South Carolina)
Columbia Telescope and South Carolina Journal (Raleigh, South Carolina)
Columbus Gazette (Columbus, Ohio)

Commercial Bulletin and Missouri Literary Register (St. Louis, Missouri)
Connecticut Courant (Hartford, Connecticut)
Connecticut Mirror (Hartford, Connecticut)
Constitution (Middletown, Connecticut)
Constitution (Washington, D.C.)
Daily Columbus Inquirer (Columbus, Georgia)
Daily Delta (New Orleans, Louisiana)
Daily Dispatch (Richmond, Virginia)
Daily Evening Bulletin (San Francisco, California)
Daily Herald and Gazette (Cleveland, Ohio)
Daily Missouri Republican (St. Louis, Missouri)
Daily National Intelligencer (Washington, D.C.)
Daily National Journal (Washington, D.C.)
Daily Ohio State Journal (Columbus, Ohio)
Daily Ohio Statesman (Columbus, Ohio)
Daily Picayune (New Orleans, Louisiana)
Daily Register (Raleigh, North Carolina)
Daily Scioto Gazette (Chillicothe, Ohio)
Daily South Carolinian (Columbia, South Carolina)
Daily True Delta (New Orleans, Louisiana)
Delaware Advertiser and Farmer's Journal (Wilmington, Delaware)
Delaware Patriot and American Watchman, (Wilmington, Delaware)
Dover Gazette and Stafford Advertiser (Dover, New Hampshire)
Eastern Argus (Portland, Maine)
Emancipator (New York, New York)
Emancipator and Free American (New York, New York)
Emancipator and Republican (Boston, Massachusetts)
Emancipator and Weekly Chronicle (Boston, Massachusetts)
Essex Gazette (Haverhill, Massachusetts)
Essex Register (Salem, Massachusetts)
Farmers' Cabinet (Amherst, New Hampshire)
Farmers' Gazette (Barre, Massachusetts)
Fayetteville Observer (Fayetteville, North Carolina)
The Floridian (Tallahassee, Florida)
Frederick Douglass' Paper (Rochester, New York)
Georgia Telegraph (Macon, Georgia)
The Globe (Washington, D.C.)
Greenville Mountaineer (Greenville, South Carolina)
Hartford Daily Courant (Hartford, Connecticut)
Hartford Times (Hartford, Connecticut)
Hazard's Register of Pennsylvania (Philadelphia, Pennsylvania)
Herald (New York, New York)
Hudson River Chronicle (Sing Sing, New York)
Indiana Journal (Indianapolis, Indiana)
Ithaca Journal (Ithaca, New York)
Lake Superior Miner (Ontanagon, Michigan)
Liberator (Boston, Massachusetts)
Littell's Living Age (New York, New York)

Louisiana Advertiser (New Orleans, Louisiana)
Louisville Daily Journal (Louisville, Kentucky)
Louisville Public Advertiser (Louisville, Kentucky)
Macon Daily Telegraph (Macon, Georgia)
Madisonian (Washington, D.C.)
Maryland Gazette (Annapolis, Maryland)
Mechanics' Free Press (Philadelphia, Pennsylvania)
Memphis Daily Appeal (Memphis, Tennessee)
Milwaukee Daily Sentinel (Milwaukee, Wisconsin)
Milwaukee Daily Sentinel and Gazette (Milwaukee, Wisconsin)
Milwaukee Sentinel (Milwaukee, Wisconsin)
The Mississippian (Jackson, Mississippi)
The Mississippi Free Trader and Natchez Gazette (Natchez, Mississippi)
Missouri Courier (Hannibal, Missouri)
Missouri Literary Register (St. Louis, Missouri)
Morning News (New London, Connecticut)
Nashville Banner and Nashville Whig (Nashville, Tennessee)
The Natchez Courier (Natchez, Mississippi)
National Era (Washington, D.C.)
New Bedford Mercury (New Bedford, Massachusetts)
New England Weekly Review (Hartford, Connecticut)
New Hampshire Gazette (Portsmouth, New Hampshire)
New Hampshire Patriot and State Gazette (Concord, New Hampshire)
New Hampshire Sentinel (Keene, New Hampshire)
New Hampshire Statesman (Concord, New Hampshire)
New Hampshire Statesman and Concord Register (Concord, New Hampshire)
New Hampshire Statesman and State Journal (Concord, New Hampshire)
New London Gazette (New London, Connecticut)
New London Gazette and General Advertiser (New London, Connecticut)
New Orleans Commercial Bulletin (New Orleans, Louisiana)
New York Daily Times (New York, New York)
New York Herald (New York, New York)
New York Mercury (New York, New York)
New York Spectator (New York, New York)
New York Times (New York, New York)
Newark Advocate (Newark, Ohio)
Newburyport Herald (Newburyport, Massachusetts)
Newport Mercury (Newport, Rhode Island)
Niles' Weekly Register (Baltimore, Maryland)
North American (Philadelphia, Pennsylvania)
North American and Daily Advertiser (Philadelphia, Pennsylvania)
North American and United States Gazette (Philadelphia, Pennsylvania)
North Star (Danville, Vermont)
Norwich Courier (Norwich, Connecticut)
The Ohio Observer (Hudson, Ohio)
Ohio State Journal (Columbus, Ohio)
Ohio Statesman (Columbus, Ohio)
Omaha Nebraskian (Omaha, Nebraska)

Pennsylvania Gazette (Philadelphia, Pennsylvania)
Pennsylvania Inquirer and Daily Courier (Philadelphia, Pennsylvania)
Pensacola Gazette (Pensacola, Florida)
Pittsfield Sun (Pittsfield, Massachusetts)
Placer Times (Sacramento, California)
Portsmouth Journal (Portsmouth, New Hampshire)
Portsmouth Journal of Literature & Politics (Portsmouth, New Hampshire)
Press (Philadelphia, Pennsylvania)
Providence Patriot and Columbian Phenix (Providence, Rhode Island)
Raleigh Register (Raleigh, North Carolina)
Raleigh Register and North Carolina Gazette (Raleigh, North Carolina)
Republican Star and General Advertiser (Easton, Maryland)
Rhode Island American and Gazette (Providence, Rhode Island)
Rhode Island Republican (Newport, Rhode Island)
Richmond Enquirer (Richmond, Virginia)
Salem Gazette (Salem, Massachusetts)
Salem Observer (Salem, Massachusetts)
San Antonio Ledger (San Antonio, Texas)
Saturday Pennsylvania Gazette (Philadelphia, Pennsylvania)
Savannah Daily Republican (Savannah, Georgia)
Scientific American (New York, New York)
Scioto Gazette (Chillicothe, Ohio)
The Semi-Weekly Eagle (Brattleboro, Vermont)
The Southern Patriot (Charleston, South Carolina)
The Southern Times (Columbia, South Carolina)
The Spirit of the Age (New York, New York)
Spirit of the Times (Philadelphia, Pennsylvania)
St. Louis Republican (St. Louis, Missouri)
State Gazette (Trenton, New Jersey)
Sun (Baltimore, Maryland)
Sun (Pittsfield, Massachusetts)
Telegraph and Texas Register (Houston, Texas)
Texas State Gazette (Austin, Texas)
The Texian Advocate (Victoria, Texas)
Tri-Weekly Ohio Statesman (Columbus, Ohio)
United States Magazine and Democratic Review (Washington, D.C.)
United States Telegraph (Washington, D.C.)
U.S. Telegraph and Commercial Herald (Washington, D.C.)
Vermont Chronicle (Bellows Falls, Vermont)
Vermont Gazette (Bennington, Vermont)
Vermont State Paper (St. Albans, Vermont)
Vermont Watchman and State Gazette (Montpelier, Vermont)
Village Register and Norfolk County Advertiser (Dedham, Massachusetts)
Virginia Free Press (Charleston, West Virginia)
Virginia Free Press and Farmers' Repository (Charleston, West Virginia)
Washington Expositor (Washington, D.C.)
Watch Tower (Cooperstown, New York)
Weekly Ohio State Journal (Columbus, Ohio)

Weekly Wisconsin Patriot (Madison, Wisconsin)
Western Journal of Agriculture, Manufactures, Mechanic Arts, Internal Improvements, Commerce and General Literature (St. Louis, Missouri)
The Whig (Jonesborough, Tennessee)
Wisconsin Daily Patriot (Madison, Wisconsin)
Wisconsin Enquirer (Madison, Wisconsin)
Wisconsin Patriot (Madison, Wisconsin)

PRINTED PRIMARY MATERIAL

Archibald, Maxwell. *A Run Through the United States: During the Autumn of 1840.* 2 vols. London: H. Coborn, 1841.
Berkeley, Granley. *The English Sportsman in the Western Prairies.* London: Hurst & Blackett, 1861.
Bremer, Frederika. *The Homes of the New World: Impressions of America.* 2 vols. New York: Harper & Brother, 1853.
Carey, Henry. *Beauties of the Monopoly System of New Jersey.* Philadelphia: C. Sherman, Printer, 1848.
Chambers, William. *Things as They Are in America.* Philadelphia: Lippincott, Grambo, 1854.
Chevalier, Michel. *Society, Manners, and Politics in the United States, Being a Series of Letters on North America.* Boston: Weeks, Jordan, 1839.
Citizens of Cincinnati. *Rail-road from the Banks of the Ohio River to the Tide Waters of the Carolinas and Georgia.* Cincinnati: Printed by James and Gazley, 1835.
Congressional Globe (Washington, D.C.)
Crumbine, Samuel. *Frontier Doctor.* Philadelphia: Dorrance, 1948.
Curtis, Benjamin. *An Article on the Debts of States.* Cambridge, Mass.: Metcalf, Keith and Nichols, 1844.
Dagget, John. *Remarks and Documents Concerning the Location of the Boston and Providence Rail-road Through the Burying Ground in East Attleborough. . . .* Boston: Printed by Light & Horton, 1834.
Dickens, Charles. *American Notes.* Cheap Edition. London: Chapman and Hall, 1850.
Drake, Daniel. *Discourse on the History, Character, and Prospects of the West: Delivered to the Union Literary Society of Miami University, Oxford, Ohio, at Their Ninth Anniversary. Sept. 23, 1834.* Cincinnati: Truman and Smith, 1834.
Duncan, Mary. *America as I Found it.* New York: R. Carter & Bros., 1852.
European Delineation of American Character, as Contained in a Letter from a Foreign Traveller in New York, to His Friend in London. . . . New York: Printed for the Booksellers, J. Gray, 1820.
Ferguson, William. *America by River and Rail, or Notes by the Way on the New World and Its People.* London: J. Nisbet, 1856.
Flint, Henry. *The Railroads of the United States: Their History and Statistics. . . .* Philadelphia: John E. Potter, 1868.
Godley, John R. *Letters from America.* 2 vols. London: Murray, 1844.
Hall, Basil. *Travels in North America in the Years 1827 and 1828.* Philadelphia: Carey, Lea & Carey, 1829.
Harrison, F., Jr. *Report of the Engineers, or the Reconnaissance and Surveys; Made in Reference to the Baltimore and Ohio Rail Road.* Baltimore: Printed by W. Wooddy, 1828.

Hawthorne, Nathaniel. *House of Seven Gables.* Boston: Ticknor, Reed, and Fields, 1851.

Howells, William Dean. *Suburban Sketches.* New York: Hurd & Houghton, 1871.

Houston, Mrs. [Matilda Charlotte]. *Hesperos, or, Travels in the West.* 2 vols. London: J.W. Parker, 1850.

Hunt, Freeman. *Letters About the Hudson River: And Its Vicinity: Written in 1835 & 1836.* New York: F. Hunt, 1835.

Jones, A.D. *Illinois and the West: With a Township Map, Containing the Latest Surveys and Improvements.* Boston: Weeks, Jordan, 1838.

Kohl, J.G. *Travels in Canada: And Through the States of New York and Pennsylvania.* 2 vols. London: G. Manwaring, 1861.

Lieber, Francis. *The Stranger in America, or Letters to a Gentleman in Germany: Comprising Sketches of the Manners, Society, and National Peculiarities of the United States.* Philadelphia: Carey, Lea & Blanchard, 1835.

Lord, Eleazar. *A Historical Review of the New York and Erie Railroad.* New York: Mason Bros., 1855.

Lyell, Charles. *A Second Visit to the United States of North America.* 2 vols. London: J. Murray, 1849.

Mackay, Alexander. *The Western World, or, Travels in the United States in 1846–1847: Exhibiting Them in Their Latest Development, Social, Political, and Industrial: Including a Chapter on California.* 3 vols. London: R. Bentley, 1849.

Majoribanks, Alexander. *Travels in South and North America.* London: Simpkin, Marshall, 1853.

Marryat, Frederick. *A Diary in America: With Remarks on Its Institutions.* Philadelphia: Carey & Hart, 1839.

Martineau, Harriet. *Society in America.* 2 vols. New York: Saunders and Otley, 1837.

Nicklin, Phillip. *A Pleasant Peregrination Through the Prettiest Parts of Pennsylvania.* Philadelphia: Grigg and Elliott, 1836.

Poussin, Guillaume. *The United States; Its Power and Progress.* Philadelphia: Lippincott, Grambo, 1851.

Proceeedings of Sundry Citizens of Baltimore; Convened for the Purpose of Devising the Most Efficient Means of Improving the Intercourse Between the City and the Western States. Baltimore: Printed by W. Wooddy, 1827.

Reid, Hugo. *Sketches in North America; With Some Account of Congress and of the Slavery Question.* London: Longman, Green, Longman, & Roberts, 1861.

Roberts, Solomon. *An Account of the Portage Rail Road: Over the Allegheny Mountain, in Pennsylvania.* Philadelphia: N. Kite, 1836.

Royall, Anne N. *Mrs. Royall's Pennsylvania, or, Travels Continued in the United States.* 2 vols. Washington, D.C.: Printed for the Author, 1829.

Sharf, John Thomas. *History of Delaware, 1609–1888.* 2 vols. Philadelphia: L.J. Richards, 1880.

Steele, Eliza. *A Summer Journey in the West.* New York: J.S. Taylor, 1841.

Story, Joseph. *The Miscellaneous Writings: Literary, Critical, Judicial, and Political.* Boston: James Munroe, 1835.

BOOKS AND ARTICLES

Ambrose, Stephen. *Nothing Like It in the World: The Men Who Built the Transcontinental Railroad, 1863–1869.* New York: Simon & Schuster, 2000.

Ayers, Edward. *What Caused the Civil War? Reflections on the South and Southern History*. New York: W.W. Norton, 2005.

Bernstein, Peter. *Wedding of the Waters: The Erie Canal and the Making of a Great Nation*. New York: W.W. Norton, 2005.

Bloom, Harold. *The Genius of the Beast: A Radical Re-vision of Capitalism*. Amherst, N.Y.: Prometheus Books, 2010.

Browne, Gary. *Baltimore in the New Nation, 1789–1861*. Chapel Hill: University of North Carolina Press, 1980.

Cleveland, Frederick, and Fred Powell. *Railroad Promotion and Capitalization in the United States*. London: Longmans, Green, 1909.

Commager, Henry S. *The American Mind*. New Haven: Yale University Press, 1950.

Cronan, William. *Nature's Metropolis: Chicago and the Great West*. New York: W.W. Norton, 1991.

Dilts, James D. *The Great Road: The Building of the Baltimore and Ohio, the Nation's First Railroad, 1828–1853*. Palo Alto: Stanford University Press, 1993.

Fishlow, Albert. *Railroads and the Transformation of the Ante-Bellum Economy*. Cambridge: Harvard University Press, 1965.

Fogel, Robert. *Railroads and American Economic Growth: Essays in Econometric History*. Baltimore: Johns Hopkins University Press, 1965.

Gates, Paul. *The Illinois Central and Its Colonization Work*. Cambridge: Harvard University Press, 1934.

Giedion, Siegfried. *Mechanization Takes Command: A Contribution to Anonymous History*. New York: W.W. Norton, 1969. First published by Oxford University Press in 1948.

Goeztmann, William. *Army Exploration in the American West, 1803–1863*. New Haven: Yale University Press, 1959.

———. *Exploration and Empire: The Explorer and the Scientist in the Winning of the American West*. New York: Alfred A. Knopf, 1966.

Goodrich, Carter. *Government Promotion of American Canals and Railroads 1800–1890*. New York: Columbia University Press, 1960.

Gunn, L. Ray. *The Decline of Authority: Public Economic Policy and Political Development in New York, 1800–1860*. Ithaca: Cornell University Press, 1988.

Handlin, Oscar, and Mary Handlin. *Commonwealth: A Study of the Role of Government in the American Economy: Massachusetts, 1774–1861*. Rev. ed. Cambridge: Harvard University Press, 1969.

Hayes, William. *Iron Road to Empire: The History of 100 Years of the Progress and Achievements of the Rock Island Lines*. Omaha, Neb.: Simmons-Boardman Books, 1953.

Heath, Milton. *Constructive Liberalism: The Role of the State in Economic Development in Georgia to 1860*. Cambridge: Harvard University Press, 1954.

Hindle, Brooke, and Steven Lubar. *Engines of Change: The American Industrial Revolution, 1790–1860*. Washington, D.C.: Smithsonian Institution Press, 1986.

Hungerford, Edward. *Men of Erie: A Story of Human Effort*. New York: Random House, 1946.

———. *The Story of the Baltimore & Ohio Railroad, 1827–1927*. New York: G.P. Putnam's Sons, 1928.

Kirkland, Edward. *Men, Cities, and Transportation: A Study in New England History, 1820–1900*. 2 vols. Cambridge: Harvard University Press, 1948.

Klein, Maury. *Union Pacific: The Birth of a Railroad, 1962–1893*. Garden City, N.Y.: Doubleday, 1987.

Lantz, Herman. *A Community in Search of Itself: A Case History of Cairo, Illinois.* Carbondale: Southern Illinois University Press, 1972.

Larson, John. *Bonds of Empire: John Murray Forbs and Western Development in America's Railway Age.* Cambridge: Harvard University Press, 1984.

Lippmann, Walter. *Public Opinion.* New York: Harcourt Brace, 1922.

Majewski, John. *A House Dividing: Economic Development in Pennsylvania and Virginia Before the Civil War.* Cambridge: Cambridge University Press, 2000.

Marrs, Aaron. *Railroads in the Old South: Pursuing Progress in a Slave Society.* Baltimore: Johns Hopkins University Press, 2009.

Marx, Leo. *The Machine in the Garden: Technology and the Pastoral Ideal in America.* New York: Oxford University Press, 1967.

Mazlish, Bruce. *The Railroad and the Space Program: An Exploration in Historical Analogy.* Cambridge: MIT Press, 1965.

Miner, Craig. "Stereotyping and the Pacific Railway Issue, 1845–1865." *Canadian Review of American Studies* 6:1 (Spring 1975): 59–73.

Overton, Richard. *Burlington Route: A History of the Burlington Lines.* New York: Alfred A. Knopf, 1965.

Phillips, Ulrich. *A History of Transportation in the Eastern Cotton Belt to 1869.* New York: Octagon Books, 1958. First published by Columbia University Press in 1908.

Roberts, Solomon W. "Reminiscences of the First Railroad over the Allegheny Mountain." *Pennsylvania Magazine of History and Biography* 2:4 (1878): 370–393.

Salsbury, Stephen. *The State, the Investor, and the Railroad: The Boston & Albany, 1825–1867.* Cambridge: Harvard University Press, 1967.

Scheiber, Harry. *Ohio Canal Era: A Case Study of Government and the Economy, 1820–1861.* Athens: Ohio University Press, 1969.

Smith, Henry Nash. *Virgin Land: The American West as Symbol and Myth.* Cambridge: Harvard University Press, 1950.

Taylor, George Rogers. *The Transportation Revolution, 1815–1860.* New York: Harper & Row, 1951.

Travisano, Thomas, ed. *Words in Air: The Complete Correspondence Between Elizabeth Bishop and Robert Lowell.* New York: Farrar, Straus and Giroux, 2008.

Treese, Lorett. *Railroads of Pennsylvania: Fragments of the Past in the Keystone Landscape.* Mechanicsburg, Pa.: Stackpole Books, 2003.

Ward, James. *Railroads and the Character of America, 1820–1887.* Knoxville: University of Tennessee Press, 1986.

Warner, Sam. *Streetcar Suburbs: The Process of Growth in Boston, 1870–1890.* Cambridge: Harvard University Press, 1962.

White, John H. *American Locomotives: An Engineering History, 1830–1880.* Baltimore: Johns Hopkins University Press, 1968.

Winner, Langdon. *Autonomous Technology: Technics-out-of-Control as a Theme in Political Thought.* Cambridge: MIT Press, 1977.

Wright, Gavin. *Old South, New South: Revolutions in the Southern Economy Since the Civil War.* New York: Basic Books, 1986.

Young, James. *Henry Adams: The Historian as Political Theorist.* Lawrence: University Press of Kansas, 2001.

INDEX

Jones, John, 176
Joy, James F., 179
Jupiter (locomotive), 24

Kankakee *Gazette*, 190
Kendall, Amos, 220
Keystone State (steamboat), 151
Kimball, David, 133
King, Mayor, 126
King, Thomas Butler, 244–245, 246–247
Klein, Maury, 250
Knickerbocker Magazine, 233
Knoxville, railroad convention in, 65
Kohl, John, 105
Kunstler, James Howard, 256

Labor, 207, 208, 209, 210
  management and, 215, 263
Lady Franklin (steamboat), 188
Lafayette, Marquis de, 20
Lake Champlain & Ogdensburg Railroad, 53
Lake Erie, 175
  boats on, 151, 180
  connecting, 58, 60, 61, 62, 64, 148, 150,
    173–174, 178, 180
Lake Erie & Mad River Railroad, 72
Lake Huron, connecting, 173–174
Lake Michigan, 187
  connecting, 140, 141, 142, 174, 179, 181,
    189, 227
Lake Superior, connecting, 181
Land grants, 185, 186, 227, 243, 245, 248
Language, railroads and, 16, 17
Larson, Paul, vii, ix
Latrobe, Benjamin, 154
Le Constitutionel, 205
"Lecture on Civilization" (Young), 74
Lexington & Ohio Railroad, 28
Liberator, 214
Lieber, Francis, 103
Lincoln, Abraham, 108
Lippmann, Walter, xii
Little Miami Railroad, 175, 176, 177, 215
Liverpool & Manchester Railroad, 9, 31, 35
Liverpool Times, 26–27
Livingston, Robert, 5
Locofocos, 84, 88, 145, 186, 233
Locomotives, xvi, 6, 13, 17, 27, 30, 77, 92–93,
  94, 133, 150, 154, 187, 190, 197, 240, 248,
  252
  admiration for, 95–96
  building, 140, 177, 210, 222–223
  bull charging, 108

coal and, 90
cultural modification by, 206
design of, 207
first, 32
illustration of, 104
importing, 265
photo of, 55, 224
trials for, 26, 58
Long, Stephen H., 30, 49, 57, 164
Long Island Railroad, 73, 143
Lord, Eleazar, 61, 63, 64
Louis Phillippe, 106, 223
Louisville, 212
  changes for, 166
  railroads and, 175
  subscription by, 167
Louisville & Memphis Railroad, 247
Louisville & Nashville Railroad, 167
Louisville, Cincinnati & Charleston Railroad,
  67, 155, 160, 161, 162, 163, 164
Louisville Daily Journal, 195
Louisville Journal, 212
Lowell, Robert, 18
Lowell Courier, 110
Lumber River & Cape Fear Railroad, 71
Lumpkin, Governor, 67
Lyell, Sir Charles, 102
Lynchburg, railroads and, 69, 158
Lynchburg & New River Railroad, 45

M&H. *See* Mohawk & Hudson Railroad
Machine in the Garden, The (Marx), ix
Mackay, Alexander, 94, 97, 101, 102
Macon, railroad convention in, 54
Macon & Western Railroad, 66
Mad River & Lake Erie Railroad, 175, 176, 177
Mad River Company, 176
Mail service, 220, 221, 261
  illustration of, 221
Main Line Canal, 24, 142
Main Line system, 10, 56
Majewski, John, viii, 5
Majoribanks, Alexander, 104
Marrs, Aaron, 43
Marryat, Frederick, xii, 101–102
Martineau, Harriet, 102, 103–104
Marx, Leo, ix
Mauch Chunk Railway, 1–2, 3, 5, 6, 8, 24, 33,
  54, 90
Mayflower (steamer), 180
Maysville Road, 43
Mazlish, Bruce, viii
Mechanization Takes Command (Giedion), 253